# Law and the City

Edited by
Andreas Philippopoulos-
Mihalopoulos

Routledge·Cavendish
Taylor & Francis Group
a GlassHouse book

First published 2007
by Routledge-Cavendish
2 Park Square, Milton Park, Abingdon, Oxon OX14 4RN

Simultaneously published in the USA and Canada
by Routledge-Cavendish
270 Madison Ave, New York, NY 10016

a GlassHouse book

*Routledge-Cavendish is an imprint of the Taylor & Francis Group,
an informa business*

© 2007 Andreas Philippopoulos-Mihalopoulos

Typeset in Times New Roman by
Newgen Imaging Systems (P) Ltd, Chennai, India
Printed and bound in Great Britain by
MPG Books Ltd, Bodmin, Cornwall

*British Library Cataloguing in Publication Data*
A catalogue record for this book is available
from the British Library

*Library of Congress Cataloging in Publication Data*
Philippopoulos-Mihalopoulos, Andreas.
        Law and the city / Andreas Philippopoulos-Mihalopoulos.
        p. cm.
        1. Municipal corporations. 2. Local government – Law
and legislation. I. Title.

K3431.P55 2007
342' .09–dc22                                            2006026696

ISBN10: 1–904385–54–0 (hbk)
ISBN10: 0–415–42034–3 (pbk)

ISBN13: 978–1–904385–54–7 (hbk)
ISBN13: 978–0–415–42034–1 (pbk)

# Law and the City

*Law and the City* offers a lateral, critical and often unexpected description of some of the most important cities in the world, each one from a distinct legal perspective.

An invaluable 'guide' to adopting a different approach to the city and its history, culture and everyday experience, *Law and the City* is not simply an exploration of the relationship between these two spheres. Rather, it details a flourishing of law's spatiality and urban legal locality; an unfolding of both the juridical urban body and the city's legal dreams, of both the 'urban law' and the 'juridical polis'. Enlightening, and at the same time problematising the reader, *Law and the City* is an innovative collection of truly global dimensions that will provide compelling reading both for specialists and for critical travellers.

**Andreas Philippopoulos-Mihalopoulos** is a Reader in Law at the University of Westminster, London. His research interests include critical legal theory, European and International legal theory, human rights, autopoiesis, phenomenology, urban theory, psychoanalysis, theology, geography, art theory, and thier moments of mutual collapsing.

To Venice
('ogni volta che descrivo una città dico
qualcosa di Venezia')

# Contents

# Contributors

**Antonio Azuela** (Mexico City, 1951) holds a law degree from the Universidad Iberoamericana (Mexico) an LlM from Warwick University, and a PhD in sociology from Mexico's National University (UNAM). Since the mid-seventies he has been engaged in research and teaching on urban and environmental law from a socio-legal perspective. His most recent book (*Visionarios y Pragmáticos ante la Juridificación de la Cuestión Ambiental*, Mexico: Ediciones Fontamara, 2007) is a sociological reconstruction of his experience as General Attorney for the Environment in the Mexican Federal Government, from 1994 to 2000. He is a supporter of Club America, the most ancient and hated football team in Mexico City.

**Bill Bowring** is a barrister and Professor of Law at Birkbeck, University of London. He has many publications on topics of international law, human rights and Russian law, in which he is an expert. He founded and is Chair of the European Human Rights Advocacy Centre (EHRAC), which is assisting with over 1000 cases against Russia, Georgia and Latvia at the European Court of Human Rights. He speaks fluent Russian, has travelled to Russia for international organisations on a regular basis and considers himself to be a Muscovite. He was deported from Russia on 15 November 2005, but that had nothing to do with his contribution to this book.

**Chris Butler** teaches public law and social theory in the Law School at Griffith University. His recent research has focused on the importance of the work of Henri Lefebvre for critical legal studies. He has a passionate interest in the historical relationship between modernism and everyday life in Australian suburbia and an enduring curiosity for the urban spaces of Central and Eastern Europe. Currently he is writing on the relationships between law, landscape and social rhythms.

**Bela Chatterjee** is a Lecturer in law at Lancaster University. Her research examines aspects of sexuality, gender and law, particularly in relation to cyberspace and new technologies. Although she has spent time in several of the world's cities, including Tokyo, London, Stockholm, Gothenburg, Sydney, Brisbane, Beijing and Singapore, she considers herself a country girl at heart.

**Julia H Chryssostalis** trained in law and political philosophy and is a Principal Lecturer at the School of Law, University of Westminster. She writes on law and literature, law and psychoanalysis, critical theories of subjectivity and sovereignty, the European post-national polity, constitutional relics and other remainders. She has translated works by amongst others Toni Negri and Giorgio Agamben. In an otherwise nomadic existence, Athens is the place to which she constantly returns.

**Jason Keith Fernandes** received his law degree from the National Law School of India, Bangalore. Dissatisfied, he wandered the earth till he found the Master's program at the International Institute for the Sociology of Law, Oñati. A passionate consumer of the urban experience and confused subject of the postcolonial moment, his interests lie in State-citizen relations, the devolution of power, comparative colonial and postcolonial studies, and identity politics. He has currently returned to teach at the National Law School of India, Bangalore.

**Peter Goodrich** now lives and works in Manhattan, an island off the East Coast of America. He feels marginally safe, locally anonymous and an expatriate for love, as all Englishmen should be. He writes on the debris of law and of law schools and is currently Professor of Law and Director of the Programme in Law and Humanities at Cardozo School of Law, New York. His most recent book, *The Laws of Love. A Brief Historical and Practical Manual* was published by Palgrave Macmillan in 2006.

**Penny Green** is Professor of Law and Criminology at the University of Westminster. She has written widely on the subject of state crime, Turkish criminal justice, 'natural' disasters, European asylum policy and drug trafficking. Her publications include *State Crime: Governments, Violence and Corruption*; *Criminal Policy in Transition*; *Drugs, Trafficking and Criminal Policy and The Enemy Without*. She is currently researching the role of civil society in controlling state crime, particularly that of illegal logging and criminalising the market in looted antiquities.

**Patrick McAuslan** is Professor of Law in the School of Law at Birkbeck, University of London. He was previously Professor of Public Law at LSE, Professor of Urban Management with special reference to land at UCL and Professor of Law at Warwick University. His speciality is law and development, and land law. He has been active in these areas as a teacher, author and consultant for over 40 years from the time he was a founder member of the Faculty of Law at the University of Dar es Salaam in Tanzania in 1961. He subsequently worked in many countries in Africa, Asia, the Caribbean and Europe as a consultant for the UN, the DFID and donor agencies, advising on land policy, land management and natural resource management, and assisting on the drafting of new legislation. His latest book *Bringing the Law Back In: Essays in Land, Law and Development* was published in 2003.

**Leslie J Moran** is Professor of Law, Birkbeck, University of London. He has published extensively on space identity and law. His most recent monograph in this area is 'Sexuality and the Politics of Violence and Safety' (2004, Routledge) written with Professor Beverley Skeggs. He is currently undertaking research on law and the city in South Africa with particular reference to homophobic violence and spatial justice.

**Andreas Philippopoulos-Mihalopoulos**, LLB, LLM, PhD, is a Reader at the School of Law, University of Westminster. He has published journal articles and book chapters in the areas of critical theory, phenomenology, environmental law, autopoiesis, comparative law, law and literature, gender, human rights, art and law and so on. His monograph *Absent Environments: Theorising Environmental Law and the City* is published by Routledge. He is content only between places: the one he leaves behind and the one he is about to arrive.

**Thilo Tetzlaff** is an associate at BIRD & BIRD. He has published in the areas of EU Law, Public and Comparative Law. After completing his PhD in 2000, he taught in some cities in Asia and met his secret lover, Singapore. He has been a Lecturer at the Institute of Global Law, UCL 2002–2005. He was also one of the men watching Arsenal versus Tottenham in a beach bar at Robertson Quay. He claims to know 80 per cent of Singapore's cocktail bars and accepts invitations to the other 20 per cent.

**Chris Thornhill** is Professor of European Political thought at the University of Glasgow. He is the author of several books on Critical Theory and on German legal and political philosophy. He has a particular interest in the application of the paradigms of Niklas Luhmann's social theory to questions of political, historical and constitutional analysis.

Trained in political philosophy, **Mariana Valverde** now works mainly in the sociology of law. Her interests range from the philosophical (e.g. a co-edited anthology on Nietzsche and legal theory published by Routledge in 2006) to the micro-empirical. The chapter in this volume is the first 'product' of a three-year research project that covers recent shifts in black-letter local law but also documents the workings of urban law 'in action' in the city of Toronto, mainly in the areas of bylaw enforcement and municipal licensing.

**Johan van der Walt** lectured in private law and jurisprudence at the University of Johannesburg from 1996 to 2006, and he is presently teaching at The University of Glasgow. His main research interest lies in the field of legal philosophy with a special emphasis on the implications of the phenomenological tradition (especially the work of Husserl, Heidegger, Derrida and Nancy) for legal theory. He has been working for some years now on the theme of 'law and sacrifice' and his book *Law and Sacrifice: Towards a Post-Apartheid Theory of Law* appeared with Birkbeck Law Press in 2005.

# Introduction

## In the lawscape*

*Andreas Philippopoulos-Mihalopoulos*

## 'Law and . . . ': anything new?

What is the point of yet another '*Law and...*' text? Are not geography, literature, medicine, religion, psychoanalysis, history, science, the senses, or even fashion,[1] adequate law's conjunctives? What new can '*...and the City*' offer to the critical front of attack against law and its perceived boundaries? The short answer is 'nothing'. The long answer is this very book. And the more agreeable answer can come from a stroll in the cities of the book,[2] but with the book in hand, a sort of city-break guide for the critical traveller. It is only then that the novelty becomes apparent: the present book reveals something that existed all along but never quite managed to attract the epistemological stare. The interrelation between law and the city, the *lawscape* as it will be defined later in this introduction, is revealed here in its singular multiplicity. By bringing together law and the city, this collection looks into the recesses of both spheres and allows one to flow through the other exposing their often incestuous intimacy. This is not simply an exploration of the relation between law and the city, but the flourishing of law's spatiality and urban legal locality, the unfolding of the juridical urban body and the city's legal dreams, the 'urban law' and the 'juridical polis' in one encompassing gesture.

The city is seen here in its plurality, as the multiple locality that appropriates the law in its genesis and embodiment. At the same time, the city is revealed as the ecumenical phenomenon that escapes the dimensionality of geography and extends to cover a utopian no-place where *nomos* and *polis* meet as coevals and reveal a prior engagement so inextricable that in effect has managed hitherto to remain invisible. Each chapter of the collection focuses on the interstices between a specific city and its *nomos* proper, both as a generalisable example and

---

* I am indebted to Beverley Brown for our lunches at Pellici, Les Moran for the Japanese dinner, Mariana Valverde for pointing out obscurities, Peter Goodrich, Professor-out-of-Law, Julian Webb for his complex meticulousness, Steven Truxal Jr for his patience and Julia Chryssostalis for everything else.

1 Goodrich, 1995, 1998; Bentley and Flynn, 1996; Reece and Freeman, 1998; Freeman, 1999; Aristodemou, 2000; and Grantmore, 2003, for linking law with fashion and thus making a much better use of what was originally planned to be the title of the present volume – namely, *Lex and the City*.

2 A conscious approximation of 'disciplinary city' and 'practice of everyday life' (de Certeau, 1984).

a distinct case study, and thus fleshes out the specificities of the lawscape as felt, adumbrated, remembered and communicated. The cities included in this volume are major metropoles with their distinct problems, cultural heritages and future pretences. The law focuses either on the individual dimension of the urban experience (e.g. safety, sexuality, identity), or the transindividual (e.g. immigrants, asylum seekers, prostitution, globalisation, cosmopolitanism, colonisation), or the structural (e.g. the sacred, the aesthetic, the temporal, the political), or indeed on the instances of their mutual collapse. But even at their deepest point of specificity or the highest point of abstraction, the lawscapes included here never sever their links with their other side – be this the concrete locality or the vanishing totality.

In escaping the confinements of the strictly geographical, political, social (or indeed the exclusively global or local) and so on reference, the chapters go beyond the usual planning or regulatory approaches to the city as a legal space – although these too are covered contextually. Of course, 'context is everything'.[3] Geography is a context for law, just as history, economics, politics, religion, society, non-society and so on. However, this introduction – and this anthology for that matter – is well beyond trying to make a point about the importance of the context. The context is the text, and the text is the body of the law, the body on which the law is inscribed, the body is the law, the law is its context. Nothing can be considered eccentric in this proposition anymore. If, however, the term 'context' must be employed, then this urban context textures the legal fibres and interdigitates with the law in its inception and perception. The description of the lawscape – any lawscape – initiates a complex discussion on the itinerant manner in which the city appropriates the law and the law the city: a line of passage that transverses both the text and its syntax, aiming for a utopia whose *topos* has returned but whose emplacement remains perpetually postponed.

## Why now?

There is no doubt that the law-and-city thematic bears a relation to the existing 'law and geography', 'law and space', 'law and architecture' and so on. But *Law and the City* brings forth a self-standing transdisciplinary event not adequately covered in any of the above. Thus, the question 'anything new?' can be rephrased as follows: why is it that this epistemological and ontological co-extensiveness between law and the city merits and needs to be brought forth *now*?

Several grounds can be offered, some more banal than others. Thus, on a general level, an urban crisis is observed, especially in the less developed parts of the world, and on the levels of ecology, housing, health, population, economy and climate, all of them variously interlaced with legal pre-existences, impositions, misapplications and inabilities.[4] Regardless of whether the crisis is

---

3  The first phrase of the introduction to *Law and Geography* by Holden and Harrison, 2003.
4  McAuslan, 1985, 2003; Gilbert and Gugler, 1992; Harvey, 1996; Potter and Lloyd-Evans, 1998; Nivola, 1999; Hardoy *et al.*, 2001 .

indeed urban or simply better observed on urban surfaces, a phenomenology of the contemporary city demands an understanding of its legal edifices, just as an understanding of law demands a thorough observation of its urban traces. Linked to that, there is a torrential tendency towards urbanisation which eschews the hitherto observable divisions between metropoles and outlets, and extends to a massive colonisation of anything geographically and symbolically in-between. While the world has not yet been converted into an ccumenopolis[5] or a megalopolis,[6] the tendency towards understanding political and legal localities in urban terms marginalises any legal signification of the non-urban, except of course if the countryside reaches the symbolic through protest – but even that will have to take place in the city. Thus, sheer urban population statistics, coupled with passionate debates on monumentalism – an urban phenomenon par excellence and something that could arguably constitute the last of the great symbolic acts, if it were not for the actual debate on monumentalism claiming that position[7] – remind the world where its perceptions of power stem from and turn to. Such power lines have now turned to the connection with their spatiolegal production processes, both as units of communicational seclusion, and as a common *nomotop* appearing invariably in every human island one cares to observe,[8] upsetting standard delineations between centre and margin.

The futility of the argument is, of course, painfully obvious, and the ecological repercussions of the urban expansion attest to that. Law's attempt to limit the urban effects on the natural environment is a potent indication of the imbalance between the economic and the legal, revealing once again the urban as the playing field of such power restructurings.[9] The urban-focused discussion on sustainability through international and national legislative initiatives in particular, has made apparent the commonalities and differences between the developed and less-developed world cities, as well as the structures sustaining such (im)balances, thereby initiating a discussion which is complex, multifaceted and, above all, pressing.[10]

On a broader spectrum, globalisation and its self-legitimising mythology have affected the legal innards of the urban in that cities are now seen, at worst as a relic of state law rituals, and at best as a terminal in a networked pluriverse of global conceptions of il/legality.[11] The suspicion that globalisation theory is probably more tangible than globalisation itself has some interesting consequences,[12] one of them being the paradoxicality of its all-encompassing grand pretences claiming

---

5 Doxiadis and Papaioannou, 1974.
6 Gottman, 1961.
7 Jencks and Sudjic, 2005.
8 Sloterdijk, 2006.
9 OECD, 1990; Fernandes and Varley, 1998.
10 For a theoretical discussion on aspects of urban environmental law, see Philippopoulos-Mihalopoulos, 2004a,b, 2007.
11 Sassen, 1994; Castells, 1996; Mitchell, 1997.
12 Luhmann, 1982; Knox and Taylor, 1995; Hirst and Thompson, 1996; Scholte, 1996.

justification on anything *occurring*. Hence, 'localisation' – a simple occurrence that has been successfully enveloped in the globalisation discourse – is paired up with urban mobilisations, thus generously awarding the urban with an antipodian place to the global. Be it a reaction to threats of invisibilisation or to new-fangled names for always-already events, it is time that urban legalities joined the battle for vocabulary.[13]

Finally, another factor contributing to the present relevance of the interweaving is the urban-specific legal reactions to terrorism. Cities have always been the stage of the terrorist spectacle, variably in their role of victim, hero, defender or begetter. But the host has now become the hostage.[14] The difference resides in the symbolic understanding of urban terrorist attacks (or threats thereof) as events that destabilise, not only global geopolitics, military movements and national votes,[15] but also identity construction and dignity boundaries.[16] City-specific legal barbicans are erected to fend off identity structures, and differentiate legal from non-legal bodies (i.e. outside the il/legality discourse), and accepted tourists from suspected terrorists.[17]

It is obvious that the city finds itself within the law and lends itself to juridical architectonics, just as the law finds itself inhabiting buildings and getting lost behind street corners. These are not just coarse metaphors: they may be coarse (and of course metaphors), because the vocabulary to describe the intercourse between law and the city is woefully lacking; but, being metaphors, they patiently educate their text until it is fully fledged to flee the nest and stand elegantly without their help. This book is part of such an education: through the descriptions, the book builds a vocabulary.

## Vantage points and blind spots

A vantage point does not guarantee overview of the interweaving between the law and the city. It is a theoretical position from which awareness of one's emplacement, along with a certain attentiveness towards the existence of blind spots, can begin. Blind spots are spaces *au-delà*, beyond the frame of a topical description, but at the same time, the companion of every description, the space left outside the description by virtue of being the space from which the description is performed.[18] They are always there, just invisible to the one describing, since they are to be found, as it were, behind one's back. A blind spot can be revealed if one positions oneself at a different angle; but the revelation of one always produces another, like a dog chasing its tail.

---

13  Valdes, 2003.
14  Derrida's interview in Borradori, 2003.
15  'Residents and elected representatives have an impossible task...of finding local solutions to global contradictions.' Bauman, 2003: 101.
16  Strawson, 2002.
17  Massumi, 1993; see also generally Virilio, 2005.
18  See Philippopoulos-Mihalopoulos, 2004c.

It is perhaps not inappropriate to say that the relation between law and the city is a blind spot that has so far escaped direct observation. This collection puts several vantage points together, attempting in this way to target the elusive blind spot from multiple angles. At the same time, the collection respects this elusiveness, by encouraging the production of further blind spots, all of them equally potent in their shady state of exposure, each one of them worthy of further repositionings that would enable closer observation, and so on *ad infinitum*. But even though the project cannot posit an end to such a horizon (or tail-) chasing, it certainly has an adequate starting basis. It is greatly facilitated by some existing 'vantage points', namely bodies of work which have already dealt with some aspects of law and the city, and have constructed a potentially relevant vocabulary. An analysis, or even a comprehensive list of these, is obviously well beyond the limits of this epigrammatic introduction; it is, however, possible to offer some snapshots of these positions, while gradually proceeding to a clearer delineation of a theoretical proposition with regard to *Law and the City*.

Arguably, the most relevant vantage point for the observation of the lawscape would be the feminist understanding and use of urban space as an instance of critique of a specifically gendered sexual reality.[19] The relation between space, place, bodies and the law has been explored by feminism as part of a greater identity project that reverses the usual prioritisations of the male, the mind, the public domain, time and reality, in favour of new semiologisations of their relation with the female, the body, the private, space and the imaginary. A spatialised biopolitical understanding of identity is another readily available route of understanding the urban-legal interweaving, either through a phenomenology of urban (limitation and facilitation of) movement,[20] a sensualisation of the quotidianity of law,[21] a legal mapping of sexuality, a criminological analysis of space,[22] or an exploration of the 'cognitive unconscious'[23] both in legal and ethical terms as urban *conatus*. Such routes are particularly relevant to the present project, because they have the potential to distract the quest from its usual identity focus, safely couched in its well-rehearsed sameness/difference discourse, and refocus instead on utopianism and other monadological conceptualisations of identity that open up to a temporal and spatial *emplacement* of operationality (the 'how' rather than the 'what').[24]

Another relevant position for the exploration of the lawscape is the aesthetisation of the legal in its urban apparitions. While intimately connected to the biopolitical, this theoretical exploration diverts slightly from the emplaced body, and focuses more on the sensual adumbration of the legal-urban in its

19 Indicatively, Butler, 1993; Rose, 1993; Greed, 1994; Little, 1994; Grosz, 1995; Cooper, 1998.
20 Sennett, 1970; Butler and Parr, 1999; Finnegan, 2002; Moran, 2002.
21 Lash, 2001; and to some extent, Valverde, 2003.
22 Moran *et al.*, 2003.
23 Lakoff and Johnson, 1999.
24 Nancy, 1999; see also Philippopoulos-Mihalopoulos, 2006.

excretal, carnal, aural and other interconnection with the individual.[25] Aesthetic engagement[26] and types of organised social participation *à la Situationiste*,[27] are ways of mobilising the political potential of the city, thereby recalling basic notions of the triangulation between the urban, the legal and the political, such as the city as *polis* and the ideal conversion from *urbs* to *civitas*. Politics here stands also as a symbol for the engagement of the urban with society at large, especially as an actor above and beyond nation-state, such as the example of the Refugee Cities project,[28] or theoretical instantiations of the legal autonomy of *polis*.[29] It is indeed the case that the political is regularly used as a mediator between the legal and the spatial. While this reveals the political character of both law and space, there is a difficulty when it comes to circumventing the political in order to focus on the legality of the *polis*.[30]

The aforementioned can also be grouped together, to some extent, under the generic title of 'Law and Space'. Slightly more specialised positions, at least in terms of their legal angle, include theoretical and applied approaches to urban environmental and planning law. These areas have been significantly revamped by the 'sustainable cities' movement, which, apart from mobilising the political, introduces ethical and scientific/technological considerations in the legal discussion, and offers ways of reconceptualising the direct connection between the urban and the legal through psychological perception of environmental and living conditions, social participation, issues of environmental risk, community-based decision-making and of course the materiality of planning and environmental urban inequalities.[31]

The aforementioned list of vantage points, and the ensuing awareness of blind spots, reveals an interesting combination: once the awareness of a blind spot is adumbrated, the conditions that trigger such awareness (such as the gendered, the aesthetic, the political, the environmental and other enablers that spark off the suspicion that there exists a blind spot) must paradoxically be removed in order for law and the city to be revealed and observed *as such*, rather than as a cross-section of other more 'established' theoretical positions. Sticking with the enabling but ultimately 'safe' impetus may restrain one from throwing oneself in

25  Hyde, 1997; Longhurst, 2000.
26  Blomley, 1998.
27  The 'unitary city', as Debord, Baudrillard, Lefebvre and others were advocating. See McDonough, 2004, for the original Situationist texts.
28  Derrida, 2001.
29  Thus, Nancy's (2005) pronouncement: 'The *polis* rests firstly on the fact that it gives itself its own law [*loi*]. It can invoke a prescription or a divine guarantee for this law; but it is to the *polis* itself that the determined establishment, formulation, observation and improvement of law belongs.' See also Bonomi and Abruzzese, 2004.
30  Hence Blomley's linguistic game of *splice* (2003: 29), which embodies a literal attempt to create a new vocabulary directly connecting the spatial and the legal.
31  Haughton and Hunter, 1994; Burges *et al.*, 1997; Girard *et al.*, 2004; Philippopoulos-Mihalopoulos, 2007.

the obscurity of the 'revealed' blind spot. In other words, while the aforementioned vantage points constitute valuable beginnings, they cannot be considered adequate conclusions with regard to law and the city. To that effect, the blind spot, once delineated, must be construed free from epistemological buttresses, and in sole reference to the lacerated crossings of the distinction between law and the city. In the generalised endeavour, therefore, to construct an adequate vocabulary for the present purposes, I suggest the neologism *lawscape*: for it seems to me that the term is simultaneously implicit of the friction between law and the city; an appropriate linguistic structure limited by self-imposed internal strictures; and a necessarily abstract start to the project of decontextualising the interweaving between law and the city (the *conditio sine qua non* for further contextualisations and concreticisations of the kind the reader can find in this volume). With this, the text can proceed to its final theoretical positioning.

## Lawscape

When trying to define the lawscape, one is inevitably faced with a fundamental question: is law and city just a transdisciplinary coincidence, or a crucial ontological continuum? In other words, are they just two things brought together arbitrarily, or one latent thing waiting impatiently to be brought forth in a single linguistic gesture? While the question is obviously leading, it also leads to a necessary preliminary remark: the lawscape is not just the law and the city. Still, one has to start from somewhere. Arguably, the most suitable start is neither the law nor the city, but the 'and' between them. One, however, has to proceed with caution: the 'and' here does not have the usual function of 'opening up' law's closure, as most 'Law and ...' constructions seem to imply.[32] Legal closure is hardly a problem, if indeed conceptualised on the basis of its fundamental paradox, which requires 'closed' to be ontologically constructed as simultaneously 'open'.[33] Thus, the 'and' of the title does not break the law open, but institutes a *continuum* between law and city, showing how the two have always-already been co-extensive and indeed *tautological*.

Interestingly, it is the latter that proves to be a far greater problem than any impression of closure: the possibility of tautology between law and the city points to the imperialistic 'openness' of law's operations, which tend to describe themselves in totalising terms. Thus, 'law is everywhere'[34] is not just a comment

---

32  See indicatively, Blomley, 1994; Holden and Harrison, 2003; Norrie, 1993; Freeman, 1999.

33  The law is convincingly open to the horizon of cognitive probabilities, and it is through this observation of the horizon that the law 'brings forth' whatever there is to be brought forth in terms of its constituent elements. Cf. Edgar Morin's (1986: 203) oft-cited adage 'the open rests on the closed' as the elegant version of Niklas Luhmann's (1992: 1423) 'normative closure, cognitive openness'. For an extended discussion, see Philippopoulos-Mihalopoulos, 2007.

34  Sarat, 1990: 343.

on the current state of societal juridification, but also a veritable expression of law's self-description as a discourse within whose cognitive boundaries the whole horizon can potentially fit. This totalising view has as a consequence some anticipated self-misdescriptions: first, that law is a reliable panacea for society's conflicts; and second, that law's monopoly on normativity allows and calls for blanket-applicability. A way to avoid such totalisation is by counterposing law to other disciplines. Thus, the 'and' of the title has the added responsibility to contain *difference*, which complements and conditions the *continuum*. The difference operates as a limiting factor of the tautology between the law and the city, and is manifested, on the side of law, in three interlinked ways: as boundaries of law's colonising presence; as limitations of law's perceived societal relevance; and as internal ruptures to a perceived ability and need for a uniform, homogeneous and universalising normativity. At the same time, law operates as a limitation for the increasing urban colonisation, both actually and in terms of discourse, since a tautology between law and the city would also entail an urban monopoly on legal production and consumption. The attempted confluence of law and the city is an exercise in anxiety, where the two potentially 'infinite' values perform acrobatics of control and excess, constantly checking on each other's limits and limitations.[35] These acrobatics between law and the city, or to put it more pictorially, the palpitating boundary between continuum (and the subsequent fear of tautology) and difference, reveals the probability of a perilously fluctuating viewpoint, from which the link between law and the city can be observed in its differentiated unity.

In view of the above, the fundamental question (epistemological arbitrariness) the connection between law and the city in a way that avoids both ontological tautology and epistemological arbitrariness, can be more relevantly resemiologised as the distinction between continuum and difference of the law and the city within the definitional ambits of the lawscape proper. This internalisation opens up a number of observational levels. On the epistemological level, the link is fairly tangible: the one operates as a means of better understanding the other, or at least certain aspects of it. Thus, law's obsession with naming, categorising, organising and 'tidying up' is revealed in the city's working order (semblance or reality, depending on the city) both socially and spatially. Conversely, the city's multipolarity and social differentiation (again, to a city-dependent degree) helps visualise the 'material' side of the law, namely its relation to violence in the sense of its force of perception/application,[36] its attempt to control power struggles, and of course its role in the process of capital production and consumption.[37]

---

35 In Bonomi and Abruzzese, *La Città Infinita* ('The Infinite City'), Abruzzese (2004: 38) writes: 'The word "city" is thus as powerful as the word "infinite." Put together, they implode in one another (forcing themselves in the impossible coexistence between control and excess).'
36 Delaney, 2003: 79.
37 Lefebvre, 1991.

Still somewhat in epistemology but looking sideways towards ontology, the interweaving is best presented, at least initially, as a metaphor: thus, one would dare say that the city operates as law's 'megaphone'. In the city, law's presence is magnified to a deafening extent – so much so that one no longer feels its presence: planning restrictions, environmental regulations, zoning, social control, borders between private, public and restricted access areas, pavements, roads, traffic lights, metro barriers, flow of people, headscarves at schools, hoods in shopping malls, power architecture and landscaping, are just a few of the urban legal moments. In the city, law's presence is concentrated and overt, in close contact with the production, consumption and disposal processes, intensified due to the physical proximity.[38] The city remains the great testing ground for law, its loudspeaker and its gaming table. And, in turn, the law is the city's measure, the (in)flexible, (un)reliable metallic ruler that makes its presence felt through inches and centimetres of propinquity and distance, determining identity and difference. Law is the regulator of spaces between places, connecting and severing urban beings, urban objects, urban desires and fears, amongst themselves and with whatever is imagined to be outside the urban.

The facetious question, therefore, whether the law dictates the city or the city dictates the law is to be answered with a stentorious circularity.[39] It is indeed the case that normativity is put at the service of spatial order with a view to producing a better urban society (and one only needs to think of Plato's normative *polis*, Descartes's 'enlightened' city, or More's *Utopia*), just as spatial conditions beget different legal responses (such as Rousseau's envisaged role for the law and the police against what he thought of as inherently 'scheming' and 'depraved' urban nature).[40] However, this is somewhat misleading: the point is not so much that different spatial needs (even differently perceived) create different legal reactions and vice versa. The latter is only to be expected, and has already been somewhat captured by what the editors of the *Legal Geographies Reader* call the 'irreducible interpenetration' between law and geography.[41] What is important here, and has until now remained largely a blind spot, is the a priori interweaving of need (condition) and response (in the form of decision for law, and spatialisation for the city), the perpetual circularity between law and the city in the form of always-already protended invitation to condition: the invitation to 'intervention' of the one to the other is *always* offered and *already* imbricated in the body of the other.[42] In that sense, the reciprocal invitation comes even before the need to invite, with the result that the always-already interpenetration of the two bodies is so obvious that it becomes invisibilised. This is the reason for

38 Bauman, 2003: 106. See also Philippopoulos-Mihalopoulos, 2004b.
39 For the same question but formulated between space and society, see Harvey, 2000.
40 Rousseau, 1960: 58.
41 Blomley, Delaney and Ford, 2001: xvi. However, they subsequently equate the connection to 'an identity', which is markedly different to what is suggested here.
42 An obvious influence: Derrida, 1999.

which it appears impossible to be aware of the frequency of the legal presence in the city, and conceptually strenuous to think of law's materiality as formed in its urban grounding. The a priori nature of the interweaving means that there is no easily identified origin, cause or indeed discernible direction of influence in the connection.[43]

This is the *lawscape*: neither a tautology nor a simple disciplinary coincidence, lawscape is the ever-receding horizon of prior invitation by the one (the law/the city) to be conditioned by the other (the city/the law). It is the topos where *logos* and *polis* are fused in an embrace of escaping distance. In lawscape, the city and the law are found to operate in a double state of co-presence and absence, as expressed by the conjunction 'and'. Thus, co-presence in the sense of *continuum*; and absence in the sense of spatial and temporal *difference*. This difference explains what appears as (delayed or timely) urban and legal 'reactions' to legal interventions and urban change of conditions (when these 'reactions' could be more correctly construed as 'pro-actions'). It is also through this 'conditioning' effect of the invitation for conditioning, that difference fulfils its role of limiting law's imperialistic tendencies without interrupting the continuum of the lawscape.

In the receding circularity of the lawscape, one can talk about the performativity of the legal meaning of space and the spatial meaning of law. In performing the act of naming (by categorising, instituting boundaries, excluding, etc.), the law simultaneously names, performs and imbues the urban with a universe of legal mythology. Similarly, when the lived urban space relies on legal mythologies in order to regulate itself, it simultaneously names (itself, according to the law), performs and imbues the law with a universe of urban narrative. This is a process of receding collaborative performativity:[44] although performativity still depends on the hearer's acceptance, the acceptance (the invitation to the performative act) is always-already given. Indeed, levels of performativity are evident at any point in the urban legal landscape: managing to appear as a coherent, emplaced and (more or less) functional whole, thereby without interrupting the continuum, the lawscape, in its absolute materiality of a stroll around the city, reveals palimpsestically (i.e. by burying the old under new layers) its fractured, conflictual and piecemeal nature.[45] The practical question, ultimately, is how to see through these layers and acquire a sense of spatialised history of the urban manifestations of the law; in other words, how can further blind spots be revealed?

For this, another paradox is required: the observer is to be positioned on the blind spot of urban-legal reality, in other words, firmly on the clouds of utopia.

---

43  This difficulty obviously does not limit itself to epistemological observation but permeates the ontology of the lawscape. For a further analysis of this, see Philippopoulos-Mihalopoulos, 2007.

44  Thomas, 1997.

45  For 'The city is the historical site of creative destruction.' Harvey, 2004: 236.

Utopian projects are vociferous lawscapes, enabling the legal body to extend on a phantasmic articulation of the urban, which, in turn, is dreamt by the law in a state of justice-induced excitement. Utopias are temporal leaps out of the present (on the trapeze of the past) and into a future vocabulary of possibility, where both law and the city, in their identity, delve into the horizon and construct ideality in the form of *absence*: absence of law for law (since justice is in place, law is superfluous), and absence of city for city (since *ou-topos* is the place of no place). Possibly because of theory's reluctance to deal with, not what is *not* there, but the fact that there *is* something there where only nothing could be (solution to *aporia*, limits of ignorance, populated *néant*, the exception to the exception, anxiety that opens up to nothingness and so on), utopias are generally *déclassées* from contemporary theory's echelons.[46] Describing the impossible as possible is claustrophobic, horizon-limiting, an asphyxiating boundary of becoming a gift of death. If utopias are seen as a *possibility*, then the world is better off without this form of totality. If, however, utopias are retained as the *improbable* tautology between law and the city, contingently hidden away in the folds of the horizon and only relevant when absent, a Deleuzean *entre-moment* of empty time,[47] a foamy *nomotop* that makes itself invisible through its very articulation,[48] then utopias can indeed be retained as meaningful theoretical constructions.[49] In other words, it is the very contingency of utopia that renders any such contingency utopian. In that sense, the identity between law and the city can only be explored as a utopian contingency, which, however, informs their co-extensiveness both as destination and critique.

It is in utopia that the observer of the lawscape is positioned. As the blind spot of urban reality, utopia offers an interesting vantage point, paradoxically both in (as destination) and out (as critique) of the lawscape, rendering the emplaced observer both aware of the utopian probability and unaware of the utopian impossibility. In that sense, all the contributors to this collection are valiant utopists (despite the objections most of them would have to such an epithet), oscillating between desire and disgust, nostalgia and *ennui*, affection and criticism of their chosen lawscape. They expose existing blind spots and produce new ones because they constantly reposition themselves and shift between two antipodian positions: the Baudelairian *flâneur* and the Lefebvrian *observer*. Thus, the utopists contained in *Law and the City* manage to remain behind the window in which Lefebvre positioned them,[50] while moving up and

46  Philippopoulos-Mihalopoulos, 2001, 2005.
47  Deleuze, 1997.
48  Sloterdijk, 2005.
49  The times this has been the case, utopias are revealed to be 'exceptionally' relevant, immune to reality, unscathed from application, and powerful as critique. Indicatively: Mumford, 1923; Deleuze, 1989; Benhabib, 1990; Paquot, 1996; Cornell, 1998; Douzinas, 2000; Harvey, 2000.
50  Lefebvre, 1996.

down the verticality of the lawscaped layers, observing both the translucency of the 'minor jurisprudences'[51] of flow and everydayness,[52] and the opacity of the grand lawscaped horizon, offering words of description that hope to appear as self-description to the utopias ahead.

For the difficulty of the project (and ultimately, its utopian novelty) is precisely this: the conversion of descriptions into self-descriptions; namely, the construction of lexical tools with which each side of the lawscape (either law or city) will internalise the other side (respectively, city and law) and convert it from a horizontal potentiality to an internal verticality, thereby utilising it in the (vertical and palimpsestic) perpetuation of its own delineation within the lawscaped unity.[53]

We hope that the present anthology offers at least a glimpse of that.

## The lawscapes

The collection consists of a series of snapshots of legal urban entanglements, private moments revealed to privileged observers. Each chapter is an 'illicit', furtive glance at the urban body of the law in its constructed contortions. What is remarkable about every single one of the contributions is that they are all unashamedly personal, involved, corporeal. Each chapter has a little bit of its author in its text, just as each author has a little bit of their chosen city of law in their body. These lawscapes appear in various guises: historical spectres, architectural wanderings, textual whispers, 'urbane' soliloquies,[54] mnemonic mappings and sexual acrobatics, always filtered through the emplaced subjectivity of their author. The reader is guided through legal streets and urban labyrinths, constantly stirred by the author's tagging at their sleeve, pointing at well-hidden sights, confused texts, criminal spaces, rightful buildings, sacred bodies, ostracised names, self-searching panoramas.

The book is nominally split into five sections, with three chapters each. This symmetry is greatly arbitrary. Putting into categories a voyage of truly global

---

51 Goodrich, 1996.

52 'Flow' and 'everydayness' are, according to Amin and Thrift, 2004: 232, the main elements of potential urban emancipation. See also Massey, 1994 and Shields, 1997.

53 But what is self-description, if not the text of the chapters that follow? Surely, the case must be that, when a distinguished scholar describes the interweaving of law and city in this book, it is the closest one gets to a self-description. Well, almost. It is an auspicious start, and an integral part of the process of 'bringing forth'. However, self-description amounts to a perceived absence of the need for description. If the self-description vocabulary is adequate, then description is perceived as superfluous, for the simple reason that description amounts nearly always to critique, since there is always a 'mismatch' between the two due to their different blind spots. In that sense, schematically, description is the tool through which self-description is triggered to an awareness of its blind spot, and is enabled to bring forth the necessary vocabulary for such an awareness (only to be proven inadequate through further descriptions). See Philippopoulos-Mihalopoulos, 2007.

54 Goodrich, 2005, reminds us that 'urbane' connotes both ethics and civility, embodying a humanistic concern with learning and communication.

dimensions is a futile exercise in simplification; not only because the chapters are very different to each other, but, paradoxically, because they remain thoroughly connected. The city in its abstract ecumenicity appears in every one of the cities in the volume, without, however, affecting the fact that each city is particular. Whatever their focus or methodology, the lawscapes of the volume implode under the weight of the urban and legal materiality contained in their text. The confluence appears invariably in every chapter as a latent discovery which, having found its outlet at last, pushes its authors to the limits of a generally tidy, but often (deliciously often) fiery and intravenous soliloquy on their chosen city. Thus, any impression of containment within a symmetrical structure is quickly evaporated when faced with what this book is really about: namely a singular explosion of multiplicity, characterised by epistemological enthusiasm and a sense of overdue novelty.

The first section, *Architectonics of Power*, focuses on the ways in which the law resists and is in turn seduced by spatial politics of power in historically or religiously (or both) burdened urban geographies. This is less about architecture and power, and more about the processes of such power structuring within a metropolitan setting. Thus, Chris Thornhill's **Berlin** goes before and beyond the Berlin wall, constructing the city's passage from the paradox of a territorial legitimation of politics, to the paradox of constitutionalisation as an act of mutual legitimation between law and politics. Through a historiography of constitutional power from 1866 to the present, Thornhill shows how this passage happened on the basis of a spatial paradox: that of Berlin's intentional exclusion from the topography of constitutional genealogy, despite its gradual enthronement as the country's legal capital and constitutional centre. It is because of its absence that Berlin returns to haunt German politics to the extent that it does now. The same absence of spatial exclusivity is taken up in Bill Bowring's **Moscow**, as the phantom of a city always on the other side of its apocalyptic descriptions: neither simply an echo of St Petersburg, nor entirely liberated from the imperial city's legacy; neither the model communist city, nor the encapsulation of modernity; neither a product of its cosmopolitan past, nor a messianic saviour of the world; neither the city of the Devil, nor the city of God: Bowring's Moscow remains constantly absent from the corrupt theatre of its roles, like a powerless pantocrator who still struggles with the shadows of its own edifices, letting the various spatial manifestations of legal and political power battle in a landscape of incestuous nepotism. More of the latter, together with a strong dosage of religious politics is one of the aspects of the 'paradox of modernity' described in Penny Green's buzzing **Istanbul**. The paradox, tellingly encountered in the urban span across two continents, floods in the political and legal bays of the city, and makes itself present in a greatly blurred distinction between secularism and political Islam. Istanbul's lawscape is, once again, to be found on the other side of habitual expectations about democracy, modernity, headscarf symbolism, illegal settlements and football players, and challenges the usual understanding of liberalism, secularism, private/public divisions, gender roles and identity.

From the streets of Istanbul, the anthology proceeds to the *Streets of the Real*, where the law attempts to name the streets of a city brimful with projections of ludic desires, fears of strangers, libidinous consumerism, and postcolonial antics of ethnic and political unity. Leslie Moran's **London** is a violent playfield where assumptions about stranger violence and violence in public spaces are being reassessed. Through a thorough analysis of community survey results rather than official police data on homophobic and transphobic violence in London, Moran constructs a lyrical phenomenology of the 'stranger' as the third figure of the friend-enemy binarism, on which opposites conflate in the form of desire and fear. The ambivalence characterising the social figure of the stranger radiates in the surrounding spatiality, rendering the city an unreadable place ridden with uncertainty and a profound loss of direction, where the usual perceptions of home safety and public danger undermine each other and belie standard expectations on the locus of violence. In another register, but still perambulating in streets of urban desire, Thilo Tetzlaff's (or should one say Samantha Jones's?) **Singapore** ventures a 'stranger's' view of what typically augurs to be the strictest and most law-ridden city in the world. Faithful to her passions, Samantha explores Singapore in pursuit of sex and the city, but miraculously discovers that things are not as asphyxiating as she had been led to believe. Singapore's lawscape is an (un)expected postmodern *mêlée* of postcolonial emancipation, western consumerism and hybridal architecture, regularly tickled by cosmopolitan 'comfort', obscure regulations and law-escaping citizens. Tetzlaff draws a camp and insidiously tight lawscape where law and the city – in a city which is also a country – would often seem to be the same thing; however, the dreaded tautology is rapidly escaped by the sheer explosion of lightness and life coming from the streets. The same street élan emerges in Jason Fernandes's **Panjim**, where different imageries on what the Goan capital should be blend with each other and create a fractured and permeable lawscape, where nothing is excluded and all is accepted as an imaginary possibility of cross-projection: thus, the Portuguese and the British spectres interdigitate and are further superimposed on the consciousness and physicality of the citizens of Panjim, leaving the local law battling between its various roles as the European fantasy destination, the Indian heritage revival site, the postcolonial identity source and the regulator of the all-important street-name politics.

*Spatial Legality, Illegality and Legitimacy* begins with Julia Chryssostalis's **Athens** as the space in which legality and illegality act in equal measure, and where legitimacy finds refuge in the historical heritage of the city as the absolute ideal of civic and urban form. In Chryssostalis's Athens, the law witnesses its spatialised body becoming re-membered (through various conservation and renovation projects), re-modelled (through major infrastructure works), re-built (through a series of building booms) and eventually lost in a hallucinatory façade of order, policing and regulation. The lawscape is brought face to face with its crisis in an elegant paean to the polis of poleis, begotten and simultaneously devoured by its very own desire. The desire for order is also evident in Antonio Azuela's **Mexico City**, whose planning law and policy attempts to legalise the already legal, de-legalise the illegal and legitimise its own extraordinary absurdity. In an 'action-packed' performativity-flirting jumpcut technique, Azuela presents eight vignettes of Mexico City in the last 60 years, capturing those rare moments where the law looks at its reflection on the mirror and turns the other way. A deluge of spatiolegal misrecognitions, fictitious retroactive validations, comedies of political errors, thundering earthquakes and whispers of rumours flood the lawscape and produces, not only a ridicule of the idea of legal coherence, but importantly a dislocation, where the edifices that would guarantee a logical continuity are nowhere to be found. Still on dislocated ground, but this time in a specific attempt to expose the continuity of law's inadequacy from a postcolonial point of view, Patrick McAuslan's **Dar es Salaam** is an astutely personal testament and testimony of land law's self-complexification in the context of a less developed country. The lawscape, in many respects characteristic of postcolonial Africa and defaced by its overexposure to a still colonising international community, is itself a jumpcut essay in the permeability between legality and illegality with regard to housing, urban sustainability, informal economy, planning and mortgage law. Its spasmodic movement is explained in the light of fear of the masses, and its exodus can be seen as a desperate attempt to find legitimacy 'outside', in the International community's too little or too much involvement.

Mariana Valverde's **Toronto** is the ideal place to begin the search for *The Other Intramuros*. A trio sonata of (mis)apprehension, Valverde's 'multicultural' Toronto is immured in the administrative corridors of the city's Licensing Tribunal, where the subtly ironic author observes cab drivers of different ethnic backgrounds balancing on shaky grounds of confession, repentance and forgiveness, thus enabling (Christian) ethics to be converted into legal pronouncements on the basis of 'factual' statements. The Torontonian lawscape makes for compulsive reading, complete with the kind of identification which only canonical soap-operas can offer these days, but with the bonus feeling that one is reading something rather 'large'. The latter is confirmed by the uncomfortable understanding that one (including the eavesdropping author) has to take a stance on the court drama happenings in hand. Equal levels of discomfort are experienced in Chris Butler's **Sydney**, where asylum seekers claim a slice of the big urban spectacle. Butler's lawscape is one of contrast between the 'aspirational' bourgeoisie of the affluent suburbs and the asylum seeker of the segregated, unserviced and isolated urban hinterlands. With intellectual rigour, Butler employs Lefebvre's 'right to the city' as a way out of an increasing political and emotive capitalisation of the refugee, and ventures a spatiolegal substitution of the existing national parochialism with a 'grounded' adequacy of contextualised urban emplacement that will confer to a 'temporal visa' (the equivalent to a 'bare' right to the city) the ability to pull the other away from the isolation of administrative and legal claustrophobia and into the materiality of a 'spatial citizenship'. Similar issues of isolation and alterification are dealt with in Johan van der Walt's **Johannesburg**, the segregated and zoned city par excellence, whose conceptual and material barriers between racial enclaves are presently reinforced by the spatial expansion of private corporatism and the generalised lack of an operable vision for urban civility, racial unity and functioning public space. Instead of the exclusive focus by current politics on economic growth, van der Walt describes an evocative Johannesburg along the lines of Nancy and Frug's conceptions of identity and community, where the act of 'brushing shoulders' would bridge the gap between the liberal individual and the nation-state, and would institute the city as a locus of bringing forth the trapped alterity within.

The final section traces imaginary *Lines in the Lawscape* that separate while conflating, not only what they separate, but mainly their own longilinear bodies in transitory, always postponed embraces. 'My' **Brasília** is precisely that: a demise of my personal distinctions and my fight with past visits and visitations. Brasília is the oscillation before the *topos* of the utopia, the cake and its eating, the hysteria of perfection, which even the law gladly abandons; utopia here is described as the place of perpetual justice, a wet dream in a nice floral package, where law sits back and admires its oeuvre. In the utopian lawscape, the law is absent and the city carries on its clockwork, a beaming babel of bare brilliance. But the route to utopia is smudged with environmental disasters, illegal labour, segregation, isolation and dysfunctionality. Brasília relates the story of why this should be the last utopia to be constructed but not the last utopia to be sought. And one seeks elsewhere, in the aether of the matrix: Bela Chatterjee's **Cyber City** ploughs lines of information grids where sex workers protect themselves both from physical street dangers, and from the law itself. Instead of the moralising legal judgement that controls the movements of sex traders in 'material' cities, Chatterjee makes a feminist-informed juridical use of the digital concept of 'code' as the self-executing constraint, which operates as a line of postponement and relative security around the sex worker. While this could be relevant in a context where 'real' cities reach beyond their mere analogue and are replicated in forms of anchorless hyperarchitecture, it soon proves to be an expected extension of the materiality of law: in a final coup, the self-executing code executes itself, anchors its fate with that of spatial law, and discovers that utopia can turn dystopia at the click of the mouse. Peter Goodrich's **Manhattan** is also a folded, transitory space, but this time of jammed fitting, where the triangular island is forced to match the juridical regularity of the grid, and everything not matching the 'vision' (trombones, jazz, Jews, Harlem) is snipped out. But even in such a squeeze, Germans, Jews (again), artists, homosexuals, sub-yuppies, lawyers, musicians – especially those – trace the city's rectilinear public sphere and insert in it 'microtopias' of explosion, ruptures of the quotidian, folds where the inside laps onto the outside and in their discordant event smudge the grid. The ruptures open up and in/out come *caritas*, non-law, naked breakfast takers, the *au-delà* of Manhattan and a trombone, all thrown on the island of deconstruction, the archetypal city as event and as lawscape, whose priority is compromised by its origin in Goodrich's supreme onomatology. For if Berlin is the root of Manhattan, Berlin is also always to come, and the reader can now go back to the beginning – a little circular game, not because there is *no*where else to go, but because this *now*-here is where utopia lies.

## Bibliography

Amin, A and Thrift, N (2002) *Cities: Reimagining the Urban*, Cambridge: Polity

Amin, A and Thrift, N (2004) 'The "Emancipatory" City?', in Lees, L (ed.), *The Emancipatory City: Paradoxes and Possibilities*, London: Sage

Aristodemou, M (2000) *Law & Literature: Journeys from Her to Eternity*, Oxford: Oxford University Press

Baudrillard, J (1992) *L'Illusion de la Fin*, Paris: Galilée

Bauman, Z (2003) *Liquid Love*, Cambridge: Polity

Benhabib, S (1990) 'Postmodernism and Critical Theory: On the Interplay of Ethics, Aesthetics and Utopia in Critical Theory', 11(2) *Cardozo Law Review* 1435–1449

Benjamin, W (2002) *The Arcades Project*, trans. H Eiland and K McLaughlin, Cambridge, MA: Harvard University Press

Bentley, L and Flynn, L (eds) (1996) *Law and the Senses: Sensational Jurisprudence*, London: Pluto Press

Blomley, N (1994) *Law, Space and the Geographies of Power*, New York and London: Guilford Press

Blomley, N (1998) 'Landscapes of Property', 32(3) *Law and Society Review* 567–612

Blomley, N (2003) 'From "What" to "So What?": Law and Geography in Retrospect', in Holder, J and Harrison, C (eds), Current Legal Issues 5, *Law and Geography*, Oxford: Oxford University Press

Blomley, N, Delaney, D and Ford, R (eds) (2001) *The Legal Geographies Reader*, Oxford: Blackwell

Bonomi, A and Albruzzese, A (eds) (2004) *La Città Infinita*, Milano: Bruno Mondadori

Borradori, G (2003) *Philosophy in a Time of Terror: Dialogues with Jürgen Habermas and Jacques Derrida*, Chicago, IL: University of Chicago Press

Burges, R, Carmona, M and Kolstee, T (eds) (1997) *The Challenge of Sustainable Cities: Neoliberalism and Urban Strategies in Developing Countries*, London: Zed Books

Butler, J (1993) *Bodies That Matter: On the Discursive Limits of 'Sex'*, London: Routledge

Butler, R and Parr, H (eds) (1999) *Mind and Body Spaces: Geographies of Illness, Impairment and Disability*, Routledge: London

Castells, M (1996) *The Rise of the Network Society*, Oxford: Blackwell

de Certeau, M (1984) *The Practice of Everyday Life*, trans. S Rendall, Berkeley, CA: University of California Press

Cooper, D (1998) *Governing out of Order: Space, Law and the Politics of Belonging*, London: Rivers Oram Press

Cornell, D (1998) *At the Heart of Freedom: Feminism, Sex, and Equality*, Princeton, NJ: Princeton University Press

Delaney, D (2003) 'Beyond the World: Law as a Thing of this World', in Holder, J and Harrison, C (eds), *Law and Geography*, Oxford: Oxford University Press

Deleuze, G (1989) *Cinema 2: The Time Image*, trans. H Tomlinson and R Galeta, London: Athlone Press

Deleuze, G (1997) *Essays Critical and Clinical*, Minneapolis, MN: University of Minnesota Press

Derrida, J (1999) *Adieu to Emmanuel Levinas*, Stanford, CA: Stanford University Press

Derrida, J (2001) 'On Cosmopolitanism', in *On Cosmopolitanism and Forgiveness*, London: Routledge

Descartes, R (1992) *A Discourse on Method*, trans. J Veitch, London: Everyman Library

Douzinas, C (2000) 'Human Rights and the Postmodern Utopia', 11(2) *Law and Critique* 212–240

Doxiadis, C and Papaioannou, J (1974) *Ecumenopolis: The Inevitable City of the Future*, Athens: Athens Centre of Ekistics

Fernandes, E and Varley, A (eds) (1998) *Illegal Cities: Law and Urban Change in Developing Countries*, London: Zed Books

Finnegan, R (2002) *Communicating: The Multiple Modes of Human Interconnection*, London: Routledge

Freeman, M (1999) *Law and Literature*, Oxford: Oxford University Press

Gilbert, A and Gugler, J (1992) *Cities, Poverty and Development: Urbanization in the Third World*, Oxford: Oxford University Press

Girard, L, Forte, B, Cerreta, M, de Toro, P and Forte, F (eds) (2004) *The Human Sustainable City: Challenges and Perspectives from the Habitat Agenda*, Aldershot: Ashgate

Goodrich, P (1995) *Oedipus Lex: Psychoanalysis, History, Law (Philosophy, Social Theory, and the Rule of Law)*, Berkeley, CA: University of California Press

Goodrich, P (1996) *Law in the Courts of Love*, London: Routledge

Goodrich, P (2005) 'The Importance of Being Earnest: Satire and the Criticism of Law', 15(1) *Social Semiotics* 43–58

Goodrich, P and Carlson, D G (eds) (1998), *Law and the Postmodern Mind: Essays on Psychoanalysis and Jurisprudence*, Ann Arbor, MI: University of Michigan Press

Gottman, J (1961) *Megalopolis*, New York: Free Press

Grantmore, G (2003) 'Lex and the City', 91 *The Georgetown Law Journal* 913–926

Greed, C (1994) *Women and Planning*, London: Routledge

Grosz, E (1995) *Space, Time and Perversion*, London: Routledge

Hardoy, J, Mitlin, D and Satterthwaite, D (2001) Environmental Problems in an Urbanizing World: Finding Solutions in Africa, Asia and Latin America, London: Earthscan

Harvey, D (1996) *Justice, Nature and the Geography of Difference*, Oxford: Blackwell

Harvey, D (2000) *Spaces of Hope*, Edinburgh: Edinburgh University Press

Harvey, D (2004) 'The Right to the City', in Lees, L (ed.), *The Emancipatory City: Paradoxes and Possibilities*, London: Sage

Haughton, G and Hunter, C (1994) *Sustainable Cities*, London: Regional Studies Association

Hayward, K (2004) *City Limits: Crime, Consumer Culture and the Urban Experience*, London: Glasshouse Press

Hirst, P and Thompson, G (1996) *Globalisation in Question*, Cambridge: Polity Press

Holder, J and Harrison, C (eds) (2003) *Law and Geography*, Oxford: Oxford University Press

Hyde, A (1997) *Bodies of Law*, Princeton, NJ: Princeton University Press

Jencks, C and Sudjic, D (2005) 'Prospect Debate: Can We Still Believe in Iconic Buildings?', 111 (June) *Prospect* 22–26

Koffman, E and Youngs, G (eds) (1996) *Globalization: Theory and Practice*, London: Pinter

Knox, P and Taylor, P (eds) (1995) *World Cities in a World-System*, Cambridge: Cambridge University Press

Lakoff, G and Johnson, M (1999) *Philosophy in the Flesh*, London: HarperCollins

Lash, S (2001) *Critique of Information*, London: Sage

Lefebvre, H (1991) *The Production of Space*, Oxford: Blackwell

Lefebvre, H (1996) *Writings on Cities*, Kofman, E and Lebas, E (trans. and ed.), Oxford: Blackwell

LeGates, R and Stout, F (eds) (2000) *The City Reader*, London: Routledge

Little, J (1994) *Gender, Planning and the Policy Process*, Oxford: Pergamon

Longhurst, R (2000) *Exploring Fluid Boundaries*, London: Routledge

Luhmann, N (1982) 'World Society as a Social System', in Geyer, F and van der Zouwen, J (eds), *Dependence and Equality: A Systems Approach to the Problems of Mexico and Other Developing Countries*, Oxford: Oxford University Press

Luhmann, N (1992) 'Closure and Structural Coupling', 13 *Cardozo Law Review* 1419–1442

Massey, D (1994) *Space, Place and Gender*, Cambridge: Polity

Massumi, B (ed.) (1993) *The Politics of Everyday Fear*, Minneapolis, MN: University of Minnesota Press

McAuslan, P (1985) *Urban Land and Shelter for the Poor*, Nottingham: Earthscan

McAuslan, P (2003) *Bringing the Law Back In: Essays in Land, Law and Development*, Ashgate: Aldershot

McDonough, T (ed.) (2004) *Guy Debord and the Situationist International: Texts and Documents (October Books)*, Cambridge, MA: MIT Press

Mitchell, D (1997) 'The Annihilation of Space by Law: The Roots and Implications of Anti-Homeless Laws in the US', 29(3) *Antipode* 303–335

Moran, L (2002) 'The Queen's Peace: Reflections on the Spatial Politics of Sexuality in Law', in Holder, J and Harrison, C (eds), Current Legal Issues 5, *Law and Geography*, Oxford: Oxford University Press

Moran, L, Skeggs, B, Tyrer, C and Corteen, K (2003) *Sexuality and the Politics of Violence*, London: Routledge

Morin, E (1986) *La Méthode II: La Connaissance de la Connaissance*, Paris: Seuil

Mumford, L (1923) *The Story of Utopias*, London: Harrap

Nancy, J L (1999) *La Communauté Désoeuvrée*, Paris: Christian Bourgois

Nancy, J L (2005) *Church, State, Resistance*, Keynote Address, trans. V Voruz and C Perrin, *Critical Legal Conference* 2005, University of Canterbury, Kent

Nivola, P (1999) *Laws of the Landscape: How Policies Shape Cities in Europe and America*, Washington, DC: Brookings Institution Press

Norrie, A (1993) *Closure or Critique: New Directions in Legal Theory*, Edinburgh: Edinburgh University Press

OECD (1990) *Environmental Policies for Cities in the 1990s*, Paris: OECD

Paquot, T (1996) *L'Utopie: l'Idéal Piégé*, Paris: Hatier

Philippopoulos-Mihalopoulos, A (2001) 'Mapping Utopias: A Voyage to Placelessness', 12(2) *Law and Critique* 135–157

Philippopoulos-Mihalopoulos, A (2004a) 'Caspian Catachreses: Environmental Transplanting in a Space of Flows', in Paterson, J, Bantekas, I and Suleimenov, S (eds), *Kazakhstan Oil and Gas Law: National and International Perspectives*, The Hague: Kluwer

Philippopoulos-Mihalopoulos, A (2004b) 'Boundaries of Exclusions Past: the Memory of Waste', in Lippens, R (ed.), *Imaginary Boundaries of Justice*, Oxford: Hart

Philippopoulos-Mihalopoulos, A (2004c) 'Between Law and Justice: A Connection of No Connection between Luhmann and Derrida', in Himma, K E (ed.), *Law, Morality, and Legal Positivism*, Stuttgart: Franz Steiner Verlag

Philippopoulos-Mihalopoulos, A (2005) 'Between Light and Darkness: *Earthsea* and the Name of Utopia', 8(1) *Contemporary Justice Review* 45–57

Philippopoulos-Mihalopoulos, A (2006) 'Before: Identity, Gender, Human Rights', 14(3) *Feminist Legal Studies*

Philippopoulos-Mihalopoulos, A (2007) *Absent Environments: Theorising Environmental Law and the City*, London: Routledge-Cavendish

Plato (2000) *The Republic*, Ferrari, G (ed.), trans. T Griffith, Cambridge: Cambridge University Press

Potter, R and Lloyd-Evans, S (1998) *The City in the Developing World*, Harlow: Longman

Reece, H and Freeman, M (eds) (1998) *Law and Science*, Oxford: Oxford University Press

Rose, G (1993) *Feminism and Geography*, Minneapolis, MN: University of Minnesota Press

Rousseau, J J (1960) *Politics and the Arts*, A Bloom (ed. and trans.), Glencoe, IL: Free Press

Sandercock, L (ed.) (1997) *Towards Cosmopolis: Planning for Multicultural Cities*, Chichester: Wiley

Sarat, A (1990) '" .... The Law is All Over": Power, Resistance and the Legal Consciousness of the Welfare Poor', 2(2) *Yale Journal of Law and Humanities* 343–380

Sassen, S (1994) *Cities in a World Economy*, London: Pine Forge

Scholte, J A (1996) 'Beyond the Buzzword: Towards a Critical Theory of Globalization', in Koffman, E and Youngs, G (eds), *Globalization: Theory and Practice*, London: Pinter

Sennett, R (1970) *Flesh and Stone*, New York: Norton

Shields, R (1997) 'Flow as a New Paradigm', 1(1) *Space and Culture* 1–7

Sloterdijk, P (2006) 'The Nomotop: On the Emergence of Law on the Island of Humanity', 18 (1) *Law and Literature* 1–14

Soja, E (1998) *Postmodern Geographies: The Reassertion of Space in Critical Social Theory*, New York and London: Verso

Strawson, J (ed) (2002) *Law after Ground Zero*, London: Glasshouse Press

Thomas, J (1997) *Meaning in Interaction*, London: Longman

Valdes, F (2003) 'City and Citizen', foreword to special issue on City and the Citizen: Operations of Power, Strategies of Resistance, 52(1) *Cleveland State Law Review* 1–41

Valverde, M (2003) *Law's Dream of a Common Knowledge*, Princeton, NJ: Princeton University Press

Virilio, P (2005) *City of Panic*, trans. J Rose, Oxford: Berg Publishers

# Part I

# Architectonics of power

# Chapter 1

# Berlin

## The untrusted centre of the law

*Chris Thornhill*

In 1849, Prussian troops suppressed the short-lived liberal-revolutionary parliament in Frankfurt am Main, thus putting an end both to the immediate political ambitions of the German Liberal movement and to the immediate prospects of German national statehood. The Liberals of this time had formed a parliament in 1848 because they wished to obtain, at the same time and through the same process, both a unified nation-state, centred in the traditionally liberal city of Frankfurt, and an early-democratic constitutional legal state. They thus viewed national unity as undesirable without a constitutional order, and they viewed the consolidation of a nation-state as a key element in the creation of a democratic polity. The post-Kantian demands of these Liberals, urging the institution of a nation-state guaranteeing a separation of powers, freedom of economic interaction and private rights based in universal natural law,[1] stood in sharp contrast to the legal-political ideas which were dominant in Berlin and throughout Prussia in that era. In Prussia, Hegel's conservative-reformist pluralism and Savigny's conservative-reformist gradualism, rivals for ideological dominance in the 1820s, had, by the 1840s, yielded ground to the doctrines of Friedrich Julius Stahl, which pleaded for the formation of a Christian legal state, with little concrete procedural check on royal prerogative and still less concession to the national *demos* as the origin of constitutional authority.[2] These principles were concretely reflected in the first constitutions written for Prussia – the counter-revolutionary documents, imposed in 1848–1850 and in force until 1918 – which, after 1849, instituted an anti-democratic weighted franchise and left legislative power in Prussia in the hands of a monarchical executive.

After the dissolution of the revolutionary parliament in 1849, in consequence, the prospect that a united Germany would ultimately take the form, not of a unified *Rechtsstaat* in Frankfurt, but of a highly reactionary and coercively centralised state, anchored in the Prussian capital of Berlin, weighed heavily on

1  Rotteck and Welcker, 1843: VI, 733.
2  Stahl, 1856: 413.

the minds of Liberal politicians and political thinkers. The failure of the Liberal movement in 1848 had been caused mainly by the weakness and the compliance of the Liberals themselves.[3] However, the crisis of Liberalism was associated in the popular Liberal mind with the conservative constitutional traditions of Prussia, exemplified by the reluctance of the Prussian King Friedrich Wilhelm IV to accept the crown of a constitutionally united and representative German state. The violent dispersal of pro-constitutional factions by the Prussian army in 1849 symbolically reinforced the conviction that the united German state would not evolve as a legal state as long as the military and aristocratic elite in Berlin continued to exert undiminished influence over all of Germany, and as long as the means of violence remained concentrated in a narrow bloc around Berlin.

Niklas Luhmann has argued that the institutionalisation of power in modern European societies has tended to evolve through two distinct stages, and that these two stages have been marked by the use of different means for generating legitimacy in the political system. First, Luhmann explains, the modern state has its origins in the dissolution of stratificatory or late-feudal political order, in which the political system was strongly personalised, territorially fluid and amorphously coupled with law, religion, the arts, education and the economy. The modern political order first emerged as the functions that are constitutive of politics differentiated themselves as a reality of meaning distinct from those of other social systems (especially religion and economy), and as politics began to generate communications through *power* without any structural or overarching foundation for such communications. What is now construed as politics, therefore, initially arose through a primary yet paradoxical marking of *power* against *not-power*, of those themes and those people which are *subject to power* against those which are *not subject to power*, and this marking made cohesive sense of politics only through its *difference* against other – perhaps religious, legal or aesthetic – systems of social exchange. In this process, the 'state' evolved as an apparatic structure, which enabled politics to explain its power to its addressees through reference to a territorial and administrative focus of *sovereignty*, and even to reflect and legitimise itself, as a sovereign, as the fulcrum of all authority and as the guarantor of the common good.[4] The state, asserting the sovereignty of power as concentrated in one place and no other, thus proposed itself as a form which obscured the originary paradox or contingency of power, and so legitimised power as a resource which could be used and communicated through all society.[5] The central sovereign state, in other words, emerged to cover power's paradox, such that power, though self-generating,

---

3 For a more sympathetic consideration of the position of the Liberals in 1848–1849, see Nipperdey, 1983: 661–670.
4 Luhmann, 2000: 126.
5 Luhmann, 1991: 126.

could refer to this state, and to the state's sovereignty or legitimacy, as its own originating source and content. Second, Luhmann then continues, the ongoing differentiation of the system of politics ultimately led, beyond mere sovereignty, to the institution of the state as a *legal state* or a *constitutional state*. The legal state first enabled power to transmit or generalise itself through society in the easily universalised medium of law, and to produce greater flexibility in its operations by moving away from mandatory or vertical patterns of coercion, which might provoke unmanageable levels of social resistance, or restrict politics to binding or excessively simplified programmes. In the legal state, consequently, both power and law valorised their contingent origins as residing in a legal – or even moral–consensual – formalisation of power;[6] to this end, the legal state surrounded itself with symbolic signifiers of consensus, procedural compliance and formal self-circumscription (with constitutions, parliaments, elections, separated powers, corporate lobbies, protest groups etc.). The legal state, however, is also nothing more than a semantic moment in the reflection and plausibilisation of power's paradox, in which the coupling of law and power – as democratic legitimacy or constitutional order – underwrites and obscures the self-referring contingency of both power and law.

Following the heuristic paradigms which Luhmann's social theory contains, it is not difficult to view the aftermath of 1849 in Germany as a time in which an abnormal protraction of the first self-paradoxification of the political system as a sovereign territorial state obstructed the unfolding of the second self-paradoxification of the political system as a legal state, and in which the intense attachment of power to *place* or to *persons* impeded the ultimate democratic coding and universalisation of power in the medium of law. Indeed, it is not difficult to view the unhappy German Liberals after 1849 as experiencing a devastating delay in the second, or legal-democratic, wave of political paradoxification, leading to a slowing-down of democratic formation in Germany and to an unusual persistence, well into the condition of high modernity, of vertical or extra-legal mechanisms for power-transmission. Certainly, the eventual unification of Germany under Bismarck in 1870–1871 appeared, in certain respects, to corroborate the anxieties of the Liberals of 1849, and to bind all German states into a highly territorialised regime, with its origins in the Prussian tradition of neo-mercantilist economic intervention and neo-absolutist or Caesaristic doctrines of the strong central executive.[7] The initial period of unification, to be sure, was widely experienced as an era of legal and ideological purification. At this time, all elements of German society which professed adherence to legal codes and principles running counter to the ideals of national unity – first Roman Catholics and Jews, then Socialists – were subject to humiliating ostracisation and surveillance, and heady rhetorics of Prussian-led

---

6  Luhmann, 2004: 371.
7  See on this, Fehrenbach, 1969: 53.

nationhood formed the order of the day.[8] Subsequently, the central ambitions of the Wilhelmine era, reflected in the colonial policies of the 1890s, also added to the impassioned mood of national celebration, and reinforced the impression that Germany was now a greater Prussia, and that the German nation-state had grown, not from an act of democratic foundation, but from a preliminary ritual of territorial appropriation – or *Landnahme*.

The perception of Imperial Germany (the *Kaiserreich*) as an extension of the absolutist territorial state in Prussia still shapes recent historiographical writing. Indeed, it is still quite commonplace to see a thick continuous line drawn between the (apparent) Prussianist politics of the strong state in the Imperial period, the evolution and collapse of the Weimar Republic, and the emergence of totalitarian populism under Hitler in the early 1930s.[9] At the heart of these perceptions, naturally, stands the city of Berlin itself. Berlin is widely localised, between 1871 and 1945, as the central point in three political systems – Imperial Germany, the Weimar Republic and Nazi Germany – which were pervasively influenced by extreme political centralisation and authoritarian nationalism.

Contemporary political anxieties, nationalist rhetorics and historiographical impressionism have served, however, rather to distort the political character of Berlin during its formation and consolidation as the capital of a high-modern German state. In fact, Berlin is unusual amongst European capital cities precisely for the fact that its status as the capital has only been reluctantly and ambivalently recognised in the legal-constitutional fabric of the political systems over which it has governed, and it has only played a marginal and paradoxical role in the constitutional foundation of these systems. In this light, Berlin can surely not be defined as the site of strong statehood, of anti-modern recalcitrance, or of stubborn resistance to the gradual imposition of legal-democratic procedures on territorial power. Instead, the city emerges as an exceptional place, marked by a complex struggle to sustain even the most rudimentary paradoxes of political order, whose self-formation both as a geo-political and as a legal-democratic centre has been deeply fitful and unstable. Far from acting as an over-powerful check on the legal-democratic telos of modern politics, therefore, Berlin is a city which recedes from the paradox of its own centration and physical sovereignty. In fact, if Berlin has truly obstructed the evolution of power as democratic power in modern Germany, this is not because of its overbearing authority, but because of its paradoxical powerlessness: because of its inability to found a primary political order, on whose platform, secondarily, a legally or democratically organised political system might evolve. From 1866 to the present, Berlin has been the seat of government of six German states – the North German Confederation (1866–1870), Imperial Germany (1871–1918), the Weimar Republic (1919–1933), the National Socialist era (1933–1945) and the reunited

---

8  See, for instance, Treitschke, 1898: I, 103.
9  See Mommsen, 1990: 12–13; Canis, 1997: 10; Wehler, 1969: 499.

Federal Republic of Germany (1999–). In each of these systems, however, the legal and constitutional framework of the state has been instituted outside Berlin and it has, in certain respects, been either indifferent or hostile to Berlin. Berlin's assumption of legal power in the political regimes which it has controlled has in each case been a *post factum* occurrence, and the city itself has suffered repeated effacement and evacuation as power has been drawn and redrawn through the different experiences of statehood which have formed modern Germany.

The foundation of the *Kaiserreich*, for example, had its origins in the aftermath of the Austro-Prussian war in 1866, and Berlin played little role in this highly improvised process. After he had presided over the defeat of Austria and subsequently organised the North German states in the North German Confederation (*Norddeutscher Bund*), Bismarck retreated on holiday to the island of Rügen in the Baltic in late 1866. Once on holiday, however, Bismarck put himself to the task of planning the first draft of a constitution for the political order which he had created and so of marking Berlin as the physical focus of coercion. It was thus only through Bismarck's *vacation* from Berlin that the city became the terrain of governance, and the conditions under which Berlin assumed entitlement to apply governmental power were traced merely through an external constitutional act, not generated by potent internal interests in territorial authority. Bismarck's constitutional ideas of 1866 was, with certain amendments, accepted and ratified as the basis for the Confederation. Just over four years later, in fact, after the Franco-Prussian war in 1870–71, Bismarck's constitution was ultimately transferred, more or less integrally, onto the united German Empire or *Kaiserreich*, and it remained the foundation of the political structure of Germany until the collapse of the Prussian monarchy in 1918.

As well as resulting from the hurried character of Bismarck's policies, however, the constitution of the *Kaiserreich* was also, in part, determined by abiding regional apprehensions and anti-Prussian resentment in the wake of 1849. For this reason, the 1871 Constitution was marked by an attitude of great caution towards the question of political centralisation, and its approach to the vesting of central authority in Berlin was extremely circumspect. On one level, the constitution does not fail – still today – to satisfy the expectations and suspicions of Prussian authoritarianism which have always surrounded it. The democratic institutions founded by the Imperial constitution were notoriously fragile and limited in competence, and, although after 1894 the Imperial Parliament (*Reichstag*) was a symbolic emblem of democratic rule, constitutional provisions for parliamentary-democratic procedure and representation could easily be circumvented – either by prerogative methods sanctioned by the constitution itself, or through the strategic manufacturing of coalitions in parliament by the *Reichskanzler* (who, from 1871 until 1890, was Bismarck himself). Under the Imperial constitution, therefore, the *Reichstag* possessed few of the legislative features which are now commonly associated with parliaments in modern-style democracies: it could not form governments or cabinets, its delegates could not obtain executive power, and – most significantly – it did not hold full legislative initiative, as it was merely entitled to approve, to reject, or, exceptionally, to propose laws. All delegates in the *Reichstag* knew therefore, as Max Weber observed, that their power did not exceed the limits of 'negative politics': that is, that they could aspire to little beyond the pursuit of blocking manoeuvres against the Imperial executive and other non-elected bodies.[10]

On a manifest level, therefore, the *Kaiserreich* was characterised by a weak parliament and, it scarcely made plausible sense of itself as a legally circumscribed system of authority. In fact, it still contained residues of pre-modern stratificatory order, as it allowed supreme executive power to remain – in part – with the unregulated remnants of a dynastic regime, and it sanctioned *de facto* the monopolisation of power by a personal or territorial junta around the *Kaiser* and the Prussian political-economic elite, based in and around Berlin. However, it is important to note that this constitution also included important counterweights to arbitrary Prussian rule. These counterweights reflect the structural peculiarities of the Imperial system, and throw complex light on the role of Berlin in Imperial politics. Notably, Art 5 of the Constitution placed the Federal Council (*Bundesrath*) alongside the *Reichstag* and the *Kaiser* as a third focus of legislative authority and influence. The *Bundesrath* was clearly susceptible to Prussian influence; Prussia had almost a third of the votes in the council and the *Kaiser* possessed presidial authority over it. Nonetheless, the Federal Council comprised delegates from all constituent states of the Empire, and all participated in legislation. Whilst it restricted *popular-democratic* balance and participation, the Imperial Constitution acknowledged the importance of countervailing *regional* power. Even adherents to Bismarck's conservative and minimal-democratic policies, who thought little of the *Reichstag* as an organ of legislation, insisted on the integrity of the *Bundesrath* as a dynamic element of representative governance.[11]

On these grounds, the position of Berlin under the Imperial Constitution appears both rhetorically misrepresented and fundamentally precarious. At one level, evidently, power was consolidated to a high degree around the Prussian royal family, the Hohenzollerns. However, because of the regional and Liberal anxieties surrounding the dominance of Prussia, Berlin's role in the united Germany was also fractured and counterbalanced. Indeed, at both executive and sub-executive level the new Imperial state clearly failed to order itself as an effectively centralised apparatus, and it was plainly not equipped to accomplish many of the basic tasks which constitute and define statehood. For instance, although Art 35 of the Imperial Constitution nominally brought most areas of taxation under central jurisdiction, fiscal organisation and administration were not co-ordinated by Berlin but were left, largely, to the regional states. This was an extremely destabilising factor in the overall political system of the Empire;

---

10  Weber, 1922a: 221.
11  Laband, 1901: II, 27.

it was one major cause of the chronic fiscal problems experienced by the Empire up to the First World War,[12] and it was one of the main longer-term causes of the hyperinflation of the early 1920s. Similarly, the Imperial state initially possessed only a rather tenuous control of the judicial system, and jurisdictional competence was devolved to regional courts until the establishment of a central court (*Reichsgericht*) in 1879 – which was in fact based, not in Berlin, but in Leipzig. Even after this point, boundaries between Imperial and regional jurisdiction were not always clearly defined and regional courts retained a high degree of autonomy against rulings of the Central Court. In addition to this, although Prussian civil law was increasingly implemented throughout Germany after 1866, the regional states preserved independent systems of civil law and independent civil-law courts until the introduction of the Civil Code (*Bürgerliches Gesetzbuch*) in 1900.[13]

As a consequence of these processes, Berlin played a highly ambivalent role in Imperial Germany. Indeed, if the symbolic condensation of power in one place or one state is the first constitutive factor in the paradox of power, this paradox, in the case of Berlin, remained, well into the modern political era, *doubly* or *internally* paradoxical: Berlin's position as capital of a united Germany was very weak, and crucial functions of state-law and state-power – especially those pertaining to civil law and fiscal revenue – were only inconclusively integrated into a central jurisdictive apparatus. In fact, although the Imperial state explained its legitimacy by referring to the personalised networks around the Prussian executive, it did not finally succeed in establishing itself as a political order physically and functionally consolidated around Berlin. In double paradox, therefore, for all the personal authoritarianism of the Imperial executive in Berlin, Berlin itself remained a fragile bearer of legal and political force, and only very gradually and sporadically did it begin to fulfil the legal functions usually associated with the capital city of a modern state.

This imbalanced relation between the power exercised by the Prussian monarchy and the precariousness of Berlin as a location of legal-constitutional order came most clearly into view after the fall of the Hohenzollerns in late 1918, and in the ensuing debates on the foundation of the first German democracy. Although the Weimar Constitution of 1919 is chiefly remembered as a radical-democratic, or at least post-traditional constitution,[14] for contemporaries the most salient aspect of the constitution was not its (ultimately vain) claim to provide mechanisms for collective control of property or for the organic administration of the economy. Rather, its main feature was that this was a constitution which bore the primary imprint of the ideals and the concerns, not of revolutionaries, but of the German Liberal class, whose democratic-reformist

---

12  Generally on this point, see Witt's, 1970, classic study.
13  On the processes driving legal convergence between 1866 and 1900, see John, 1989: 42–72.
14  Scheuerman, 1996: 5.

ambitions had so often been thwarted by the dragging force of Prussian conservatism. From the outset, consequently, the Weimar Constitution contained a powerful bias against Prussia and against Berlin. The most influential constitutional fathers in 1918–1919, most notably Hugo Preuß, Friedrich Naumann and Max Weber, were left-liberal intellectuals and lawyers, and all of these, to a greater or lesser degree, identified the excessive influence of Prussia and of the conservative establishment in and around Berlin as the main obstacle preventing the emergence of a unified German democracy.[15] Indeed, Preuß, whose influence on the constitution was greatest,[16] came from the Germanist school of legal theory around Otto von Gierke. The main intention of this school was to show that excessive political centralisation contradicts the corporate spirit of German legal principles.[17] For this reason, Preuß resolved to create a state which, in his view, was a truly a state: that is, one which was not overburdened by regional interference and which legally integrated all citizens of Germany into a cohesively and equally unified juridico-political order.

In this respect, the Weimar Constitution marked the belated revenge on Berlin of the generations of liberals whose bid for power in 1848 had failed so traumatically, and who had then been systematically marginalised for most of the Imperial era. At the heart of the liberal programme expressed in the constitution were two key points. First, the constitutionalists of 1919 insisted on the institution of a strong unitary sovereign state, in which Imperial law prevailed over regional law (especially in Arts 6–13) and in which all states assumed comparable importance: this was intended to weaken the political dominance of Berlin and to ensure that decisions at Imperial level could not be undermined by Prussian influence. Second, the constitutional fathers were also plainly committed to parliamentary sovereignty, and they sought to secure increased legislative competence for the democratic *Reichstag* in Berlin so that democratic law had primacy over all regional interests.

In their desperation to break with Prussian tradition, however, the authors of the Weimar Constitution unwittingly and ironically replicated one important aspect of the Imperial Constitution. Although recognising Berlin as the institutional capital, the Weimar Constitution was not written in Berlin; in fact, in

---

15 See Naumann, 1910: 76. Naumann saw Liberal ambitions thwarted by an unholy alliance of Roman Catholic politicians and Prussian Conservatism. Weber, 1922b: 407, denounced 'Prussian plutocracy' as a major obstacle in the path of democratic reform. During the *Kaiserreich*, Hugo Preuß ascribed the political weaknesses of the reformist-democratic movement to the fact that the 'leading state' in the Empire still retained an 'incomplete and deeply fractured constitutional life' (Preuß, 1897: 96). After 1919, Preuß continued to demand a diminution of Prussian authority. He argued at this juncture that the removal of power from Prussia under the 1919 constitution had not gone nearly far enough, and that Prussia should in fact be weakened still further through the granting of 'extended autonomy' and powers of 'self-administration' to the particular Prussian provinces (Preuß, 1926: 438–439).

16 See Schulz, 1963: 123–124.

17 See Preuß, 1889: 110–111; Gierke, 1873: 30.

symbolic detachment from Berlin, it was written in Weimar. The constitutional fathers made a train journey from Berlin to Weimar to draft the constitution: this, they hoped, would distance their work from Prussia and associate it with the humanist literary tradition, embodied in Weimar by Goethe and Schiller. Central to the 1919 Constitution, therefore, were an erasure of the forms and tokens of power vested in Berlin by Bismarck, and, once again, a radically external re-marking of Berlin as the site and terrain of power.

The Republic of 1919, which should properly have been called the Berlin Republic, thus became known as the Weimar Republic, and the constitution of 1919, which should have been termed the Berlin Constitution, became known as the Weimar Constitution. Paradoxical in the denunciation of Berlin implicit in the reference to Weimar in these titles, however, was the fact that the Weimar Constitution, pledged to a fully unitary state, did not lead to a diminution of the political authority exercised in Berlin; in fact, it strongly reinforced Berlin in its function as capital of all Germany. The constitution certainly divorced power in Berlin from its traditional setting in the Prussian dynastic milieu, and it greatly reduced the authority exercised by the state of Prussia over other federal states. However, the 1919 Constitution gave a far more consistently centralised structure to the Imperial state, and it significantly increased the stability of its parliamentary organs, its fiscal apparatus, and its executive institutions, all of which were in Berlin. The state of the *Kaiserreich* might therefore be viewed as a weak state which was forced to dramatise the paradox of power so vividly in order to generate obedience and perform its regulatory tasks that it was (and still is) widely viewed as a strong state. The state of the Weimar Republic, in contrast, was a state which could apply power through relatively consistent channels and required little paradoxical self-reference to fulfil its political functions – yet it was (and still is) perceived as a very weak state. Unlike its predecessor, in any case, the Weimar state was a state which enjoyed full fiscal and judicial sovereignty and was relatively free of personal and dynastic intervention. The weakening of Prussian control envisioned and effected by the liberals thus actually resulted in a rapid consolidation of Berlin's capacities, at Imperial level, for legislative and administrative control.

If the constitutional fathers of 1918–1919 saw Prussia and Berlin as the greatest problem for them to solve, however, it is a fateful irony that their endeavours to diminish Prussian power in the name of national-democratic foundation ultimately misfired in quite a catastrophic style. By the early 1920s it had already become clear that the political direction of Prussia had changed fundamentally from before 1914. Once its constituents had been fully politically enfranchised, and once the Prussian parliament had been severed from monarchical influences, Prussia became by far the most pro-Republican of the major German states. Prussia infact remained the most potent symbol of loyalty to the German Republic throughout the entire Weimar era and, extraordinarily, its parliament (*Landtag*) was run by a coalition containing the Social Democratic Party from the beginning to the end of democratic rule. Moreover, Prussia was the only state which sought to ensure that its major institutions were administered by politicians, judges and civil servants who had reliable democratic credentials and affiliations.[18] After the Wall Street Crash in late 1929 and the subsequent inception of presidential rule in early 1930, the German state was rapidly invaded by factions who had little or no democratic mandate and who used the economic weakness of the state to limit the competence of the *Reichstag* and the parliamentary apparatus. At this time, the Prussian parliament in Berlin remained the only major institution in the Empire still committed to democratic governance, and it provided the only organised bulwark against the rapidly rising tide of anti-republican political extremism.[19]

Owing to the unitarist, federally egalitarian, and parliamentary-democratic impulses cemented in the 1919 Constitution, however, Prussia now barely possessed a shadow of the power which it had which it had assumed in the Imperial period. Moreover, the notorious Art 48 of the Constitution gave to the President of the Republic the power to overrule, and even use military power against any regional state not prepared to accept Imperial legislation. This meant that when, after 1930, the anti-democratic factions in the *Reichstag* (located in Berlin) turned against the pro-democratic factions of the Prussian *Landtag* (also located in Berlin), the *Reichstag* was able to supplant the *Landtag* and arrogate responsibility for all internal governance in Prussia. This eventually occurred in the infamous *Preußenschlag* of 1932, when Chancellor Franz von Papen, with theoretical assistance from Carl Schmitt, employed exceptional powers established under Art 48 to annex the by-now deadlocked Prussian parliament to the *Reich* and thus eliminate the Prussian democratic assembly as a force equipped to defend the republican system. In retrospect, Papen's annexation of the Prussian *Landtag* can be seen to have marked the first notable step in the early stages of the emerging policy of *Gleichschaltung*. The usurpation of Prussian power by the Imperial government (both of which were represented in Berlin) led to the elimination of Berlin as an independent political factor, and this was the foundation for the ultimate erosion of the key institutions of the Weimar democracy, and for the colonisation of these by groups determined to overthrow the Republic.

Two particularly striking points emerge from this. First, the anxiety about Berlin, which had led to the foundation of a unitary democratic Imperial state in 1919, ultimately contributed (albeit unexpectedly) to the vulnerability of Weimar democracy. The hatred for Berlin amongst the post-1848 Liberals thus ultimately produced a bitter and disastrous legacy for Liberal interests and institutions in Germany. Second, if we take the *Preußenschlag* as the effective inception of the process of *Gleichschaltung*, it can also be seen that the party-regime of the NSDAP, although seeking to break both with Prussian statism and Weimar democratic republicanism, shared one important common feature with Imperial

---

18  See Müller, 1983: 149–180.
19  Dietrich Orlow, 1986: 9, makes a strong case for Prussia in the 1920s as a model 'not of authoritarianism, but of the viability of parliamentary democracy in Germany'.

Germany and the Weimar Republic. This regime, namely, was also a political order whose centre of govenment was Berlin, but whose constitutional foundations were defined through a strategic diminution and incapacitation of Berlin. It is notable in this light that Papen's *Preußenschlag* involved the imposition of a state of exception (*Ausnahmezustand*) over Berlin and Prussia. As Schmitt knew and Luhmann later intuited, the state of exception is the most violent and paradoxical moment of political re-marking. The state of exception is the place where power, as revelation,[20] is allowed – exceptionally and *decisively* – to found itself *ex nihilo*, against all other options of power-application and legal transmission stored in the existing communications of law and power. In 1932, this state of exception entailed the dramatic eradication of all traces of independent legal order in Berlin and the violent constitutional recasting of Berlin as the capital city of a rapidly evolving, and very distinct, regime. The first policies after the *Preußenschlag* then concentrated on replacing the republican and Social Democratic elements of the Prussian civil service, judiciary and parliamentary bureaucracy. These policies were ultimately pursued, in a still more comprehensive manner, by the National Socialists.

After the end of the Nazi regime in 1945, the legal and constitutional ambivalence surrounding Berlin articulated itself once again, albeit in slightly new terms. For obvious reasons, the processes of refoundation and reconstitutionalisation in Germany after 1945 were, in key respects, shaped by the interests of the different occupying forces in the eastern and western regions of Germany, and the scope for autonomous constitutional foundation was limited. In the West, for instance, German lawyers had drafted various regional constitutions during the interim period 1945–1949, all showing clear continuities with the principles of economic democracy which had influenced early-Weimar constitutional thought. These constitutions, however, were never used, as they were overruled by the occupying forces.[21] In consequence, the 1949 Constitutions of the Federal Republic of Germany (FRG) and of the German Democratic Republic (GDR) were marked by a sprit of ungainly compromise between discernibly German constitutional ideas and ideas derived either from Anglo-American or Soviet constitutional thinking. The ultimate form of the *Grundgesetz* of the FRG, for example, was marked by American principles of anti-trust and anti-corporate legislation. It consequently moved close to a pure-parliamentary constitutional model, renouncing the direct-democratic and economic-democratic conceptions which had appeared in earlier constitutions – although it did, under Arts 20 and 28, still include some rudimentary provision for some degree of social participation and economic redistribution.[22] In this, the *Grundgesetz* also finally abandoned the politics of the strong executive which had formed a constant

---

20  Schmitt, 1985: 5–11.
21  See Bernecker, 1979: 277.
22  For debates on this, see Niclauß, 1974: 33–52.

element in the German political system since the Prussian Constitutions of 1848–1850; the desire to efface the last residues of the Prussian legal structures was thus, again, a palpable reference for the constitutional designers in the Parliamentary Council before 1949.

The GDR Constitution of 1949, by way of contrast, retained greater similarities with earlier – unmistakably German – constitutional models and principles. This Constitution sought significantly to expand, under Art 17, the rights of economic co-determination already enshrined in the Weimar Constitution, and under Art 3 it made (albeit highly hypothetical) provision for elements of direct democracy and immediate political petition (*Eingaben*), which built on and extended the popular-democratic ambitions of previous documents. After 1949, moreover, the GDR was the German state which had its governmental and constitutional centre in Berlin and which placed itself on a continuum with political traditions associated with Berlin. The government of the GDR in fact quite selectively marked or constructed a memory of Berlin, from which it could continuously derive a sense of legitimacy and German power. The GDR government, for instance, oversaw – exceptionally – the demolition by explosives of the palace of the Prussian royal family in 1950, yet also publicly linked itself with socialist and anti-fascist traditions in the Weimar Republic, and it reclaimed the buildings of the democratic Prussian *Landtag* for representative functions. In contrast to this, the hallmark policies of the Adenauer era in the West duplicated the vengeful hostility to Berlin which had shaped earlier political systems. Adenauer's own political education, as a Rhineland Catholic, had been shaped by the memory of Prussian anti-Catholicism in the 1870s, and his commitment to Western integration, to military alliance with the United States, and to close economic collaboration with France, all hinged on a geo-political denigration of Berlin and Prussia. The new Republic in the West also originated, like its precursors, from an attitude of fierce anti-Prussianism, which implicitly saw the state created by Bismarck in Berlin as responsible for the disasters of National Socialism and the war. Indeed, Adenauer's early stabilisation of the FRG around a centrist-democratic constitutional consensus was underscored, to no small degree, by a concerted marginalisation of Berlin and the Berlin *Hinterland* from the political and legislative process. The anxiety of the nineteenth-century German liberals – namely, that the foundation of a democratic state would not be possible with Berlin as capital – proved, therefore, to be correct. It was only when Berlin was dismembered and its western districts finally severed from Prussia that it was effectively integrated into a constitutionally balanced political order.

After the collapse of the GDR in 1989 and the reunification of Germany in 1990, the GDR Constitution was abandoned and the *Grundgesetz* of the FRG was taken as the foundation for all laws and policies in the reunited Germany. Not surprisingly, those with long political memories began at this time uncomfortably to ruminate on the question of whether Berlin would or should once again become the capital city. In 1991, however, it was voted in the *Bundestag* in Bonn that the organs of government, with competences defined under the *Grundgesetz*, would be physically relocated to Berlin, and this decision was ratified in 1994.

In 1999, then, Berlin once again became the material ground of political authority in all Germany. Through this process, the *Reichstag*, originally designated for government over a *Reich*, was rebuilt, reinvented, and allowed to assume governmental power over a Republic of federal states. Berlin and its institutional embodiment thus experienced a common fate, in that they now finally gained power over a state and a territory very distinct from those for which they had been conceived and constructed. Opponents of a transfer of government from the *Bundestag* in Bonn to the *Reichstag* in Berlin accentuated their claim that democratic stability in the FRG had been obtained precisely because it was not centred in Berlin, and had disconnected itself from the Prussian tradition. Advocates of the transfer emphasised, variously, both the continuities and the discontinuities in this process of relocation, and they envisioned symbolic advantages resulting from the transfer. The idea of continuity – the image of a Germany with its political institutions once again placed in its major city – clearly appealed to a resurgent liberal-nationalist outlook, seeking to normalise Germany's relation to its history, and hoping to revive the distant national-liberal vision of a powerful Germany comfortable in its borders. The idea of discontinuity – the image of a Germany whose organs of political representation and legal formation now had, apart from their external shell and physical location, little in common with their previous Prussian incarnations – attracted distinct, but still analogous arguments and perspectives, seeking to demonstrate that Germany could now finally assume the role of a harmlessly centralised nation-state.

The most striking continuity in the recent history of Berlin, however, is the one which is scarcely mentioned. Since 1999 Berlin has once again been the seat of government of Germany under a constitutional order which it did not create and which was, perhaps to a greater extent even than its predecessors, originally imposed as a restriction of its influence and importance. Now, however, the preconditions for democratic governance are greatly altered. The earlier Prussian traditions of strong-state constitutional politics and nationalistically inflected public law have evidently lost their practical purchase, and Berlin is now free to propose its centrality without enraging or intimidating the democratically minded Liberals in other parts of the country. The suspicion remains, nonetheless, that Berlin has finally succeeded in becoming the living centre of democratic law only because now the paradox of national sovereignty no longer finds its most plausible expression in closed states, strong states or even in nationally limited legal states, and because the physical concentration of legal power has been supplanted by the more complex and decentred paradoxes and interdependencies of power in the world-society.[23] In other words, it is only now, that Berlin is not called upon to sustain the first political paradox of territorial sovereignty, that it is able to uphold the second political paradox of democratic governance and universal law.

23 Luhmann, 1971: 1–35.

## Bibliography

Bernecker, W L (1979) 'Die Neugründung der Gewerkschaften in den Westzonen 1945–1949', in Becker, J, Stammen, T and Waldmann, P (eds), *Vorgeschichte der Bundesrepublik Deutschland. Zwischen Kapitulation und Grundgesetz*, Munich: Fink

Canis, K (1997) *Von Bismarck zur Weltpolitik. Deutsche Außenpolitik 1890 bis 1902*, Berlin: Akademie Verlag

Fehrenbach, E (1969) *Wandlungen des deutschen Kaisergedankens 1871–1918*, Vienna/Munich: Oldenbourg

Gierke, O (1873) *Das deutsche Genossenschaftsrecht*, vol II: *Geschichte des deutschen Körperschaftsbegriffs*, Berlin: Weidmann

John, M (1989) *Politics and the Law in late Nineteenth-century Germany. The Origins of the Civil Code*, Oxford: Oxford University Press

Laband, P (1901) *Das Staatsrecht des deutschen Reiches*, in 4 vols, 4th ed., Tübingen: J.C.B. Mohr

Luhmann, N (1971) 'Die Weltgesellschaft', 57(1) *Archiv für Rechts- und Sozialphilosophie* 1–35

Luhmann, N (1991) *Political Theory in the Welfare State*, Bernarz Jr, J (trans.), Berlin/New York: de Gruyter

Luhmann, N (2000) *Die Politik der Gesellschaft*, Frankfurt am Main: Suhrkamp

Luhmann, N (2004) *Law as a Social System*, Ziegert, K (trans.), Kastner, F, Nobles, R, Schiff, D and Zieger, R (eds), Oxford: Oxford University Press

Mommsen, W J (1990) *Der autoritäre Nationalstaat. Verfassung, Gesellschaft und Kultur im deutschen Kaiserreich*, Frankfurt am Main: Fischer

Müller, H (1983) 'Verwaltungsstaat und parlamentarische Demokratie: Preußen 1919–1932', in Ritter, G A (ed.), *Regierung, Bürokratie und Parlament in Preußen und Deutschland von 1848 bis zur Gegenwart*, Düsseldorf: Droste

Naumann, F (1910) *Die politischen Parteien*, Berlin: Buchverlag der Hilfe

Niclauß, K (1974) 'Der Parlamentarische Rat und das Sozialstaatspostulat', in 15 *Politische Vierteljahresschrift* 33–52

Nipperdey, T (1983) *Deutsche Geschichte. Bürgerwelt und starker Staat*, Munich: Beck

Orlow, D (1986) *Weimar Prussia 1918–1925. The Unlikely Rock of Democracy*, Pittsburgh: University of Pittsburgh Press

Preuß, H (1889) *Gemeinde, Staat, Reich als Gebietskörperschaften. Versuch einer deutschen Staatskonstruktion auf Grundlage der Genossenschaftstheorie*, Berlin: Julius Springer

Preuß, H (1897) *Die Junkerfrage*, Berlin: Rosenbaum & Hart

Preuß, H (1926) 'Ist Preußen ein Land?' in *Staat, Recht und Freiheit*, Tübingen: J.C.B. Mohr

Rotteck, K and Welcker, K (1843) *Das Staats-Lexikon* (15 vols), Leipzig: Brockhaus

Scheuerman, W E (1969) 'Introduction', in *The Rule of Law under Siege. Selected Essays of Franz L. Neumann and Otto Kirchheimer*, Berkeley, CA/London: University of California Press

Schmitt, C (1985) *Political Theology. Four Chapters on the Concept of Sovereignty*, Schwab, G (trans.), Cambridge, MA/London: MIT Press

Schulz, G (1963) *Zwischen Demokratie und Diktatur. Verfassungspolitik und Reichsreform in der Weimarer Republik*, vol. I: *Die Periode der Konsolidierung und der Revision des Bismarckschen Reichsaufbaus 1919–1930*, Berlin: de Gruyter

Stahl, F J (1856) *Die Philosophie des Rechts*, vol. II: *Rechts- und Staatslehre auf der Grundlage christlicher Weltanschauung*, 3rd ed, 2nd div, *Die Staatslehre und die Principien des Staatsrechts*, Heidelberg: J.C.B. Mohr

Treitschke, H (1898) *Politik* (2 vols), Leipzig: Hirzel

Weber, M (1922a) 'Die Lehren der deutschen Kanzlerkrisis', in *Gesammelte politische Schriften*, Tübingen: J.C.B. Mohr

Weber, M (1922b) 'Parlament und Regierung im neugeordneten Deutschland', in *Gesammelte Politische Schriften*, Tübingen: J.C.B. Mohr

Wehler, H-U (1969) *Bismarck und der Imperialismus*, Cologne: Kiepenheuer & Witsch

Witt, P-C (1970) *Die Finanzpolitik des deutschen Reiches von 1903 bis 1913. Eine Studie zur Innenpolitik des Wilhelminischen Deutschlands*, Düsseldorf: Droste

# Chapter 2

# Moscow

## Third Rome, model communist city, Eurasian antagonist – and power as no-power?

*Bill Bowring*

## Introduction

Moscow looms large in the political, religious and legal imagination as capital and symbol of the former Soviet Union, and now as the centre of power of the largest state in the world by territory, if sadly diminished in population.[1] It is by far the largest city in Europe, and contains 15 per cent of Russia's total population. Its inhabitants number 11,200,000,[2] compared with London's 7,360,000[3] – and London is much larger than Rome, Paris or Berlin. A further 6,618,538 people live in Moscow Oblast (District), the ring of dormitory and industrial towns surrounding Moscow. At least 2 million people a day travel into Moscow, for work or shopping.[4] The area of the city itself is 1,080.83 sq. km, as against London's 1,500.00 sq. km, meaning that its territory is much more densely settled than London's. Moscow's Metro, its pride and joy, has 170 stations, as against London's 275,[5] but it carries 3,200,600,000 passengers a year, as against London's 1,000,000,000. The energy of Moscow is such that every day spent in the city is extraordinarily tiring. Every person of any ambition in Russia has found their way to Moscow, and is armed with sharp elbows and a quick temper. This behaviour is described in Russian as '*khamstvo*' – 'boorishness' in the dictionaries.

For the first-time visitor to Moscow, the greatest shock, however, is its sheer size and scale. Eight- to ten-lane radial highways intersect with the newly built eight-lane Circular Road and the multi-lane Garden Ring, as well as a new, third, circular motorway. The Moscow air has become unbearably toxic with traffic fumes from the gridlocked streets.[6] These highways are surrounded by enormous

---

1 Russia's population is now around 146 million, from about 150 million in 1995.
2 Official statistics 2003–2004, at www.mos.ru/cgi-bin/pbl_web?vid=2&osn_id=0&id_rub=1716&news_unom=31003, and 2002 census.
3 Official statistics at http://www.go-london.gov.uk/london_statistics/key_stats_2004.pdf
4 http://en.wikipedia.org/wiki/Moscow_Oblast
5 See http://tube.tfl.gov.uk/content/faq/facts.asp
6 Alden and Crow, 1998: 374.

buildings. The seven Stalin Gothic skyscrapers, the 'seven sisters',[7] are the true embodiment of Gotham City, and the many buildings of the post-Communist period tower over the human inhabitants of the city with similar panache. Mayor Luzhkov has ordered that building projects embody the 'Moscow style'. Even the frequent visitor is confronted each time by gigantic new buildings – mostly luxury apartments and offices – every time she enters the city.

This Moscow is a startling transformation of the city Walter Benjamin found in 1926–1927. The narrow sidewalks he wandered gave Moscow 'a provincial air, or rather the character of an improvised metropolis that has fallen into place overnight'.[8] '[N]owhere does Moscow really look like the city it is, rather it more resembles the outskirts of itself',[9] and he referred to Moscow's 'village character'.[10] At the same time, he remarked: 'Above all the juridical uncertainties in domestic affairs. On the one hand, NEP[11] has been authorised, but on the other it is only tolerated in the interest of the state. Any NEP man can, from one day to the next, fall victim to a turnabout in economic policy or a passing whim of propaganda.'[12] These observations resonate in the present day, as I show later.

One of the latest newly constructed buildings could serve as a monumental centrepiece for this chapter. On 20 December 2003, the 'Triumph Palace' apartment building was topped out, making it the tallest building in Europe and second tallest residential building in the world, at 264 m, that is, 866 ft.[13] It now has 61 storeys, with over 1,000 luxury apartments: it is reserved for the very rich. It dominates the highway from the centre of Moscow to the main international airport. Most surprisingly, it is built, deliberately, in the 'Stalin Gothic' style, like the 'seven sisters' – Moscow State University and the Ministry of Foreign Affairs for example. Its marketing material refers to the 'good old days', when the Soviet Union, and Moscow as its capital, were truly respected, and standards were maintained.

At the same time, the building symbolises the absence of law in Moscow. A Moscow journalist commented:

> According to eyewitness accounts, the presentation of the Triumph Palace project to the city main architect's office Urban Development Council (a mandatory procedure for all large-scale construction projects) sparked off a hitherto unseen outrage. What was the problem? Maybe the fact that the

---

7  See www.washingtonpost.com/wp-srv/inatl/exussr/july/29/cakes2907.htm
8  Benjamin, 1986: 31.
9  Ibid. 67.
10  Ibid. 112.
11  Lenin's New Economic Policy, allowing a certain amount of capitalism, and was still in place in 1926–1927 when Benjamin was in Moscow. Stalin rejected the policy in 1927–1928. See Davies, 1997 at www.users.globalnet.co.uk/~semp/nep.htm
12  Benjamin, 1986: 70.
13  See www.emporis.com/en/wm/bu/?id=102052

Triumph Palace had by the time of discussion reached the fifth storey level? Or that it managed to skirt the ECPC (approval by the Expert Consultative Public Council of any significant project in the central part of the city is also a mandatory procedure)? But this has long been common practice in the city. What was really shocking was the construction company's intention (according to construction firm Donstroi's ad) to build an 'eighth Stalin-era high rise'. Donstroi designed its 43-storey 'prestige symbol of a new era' – 'a grand palace for well-to-do people', a sample of 'neoclassicist architecture' – in the image of the seven Stalin-era skyscrapers built in Moscow half a century ago.[14]

This chapter explores the relationship between Moscow and law. The law in question is not simply state law. Moscow is a city which exists on a number of interwoven dimensions. On one dimension, it is the legal capital of the civic entity named Russia, or the Russian Federation – it has two official names. But to this day, it harbours its past as the 'model communist city' as it was intended to be in the time of Leonid Brezhnev, General Secretary of the Soviet Communist Party from 1964 to 1982. Another dimension is its status at the centre of a messianic vision of Russia as saviour of the world, and the historical heart of the Russian Orthodox Church. It also bears in its place-names and the family names of its illustrious citizens, the traces of its Turkic past; and it is home to an ever-growing Muslim population, giving it the largest Muslim population of any non-Muslim city in the world. And it has been immortalised as the City of the Devil.

## The rise of Moscow's power

Moscow was not significant when Russia was born. Russia emerged in the ninth century AD, in a mix of Vikings (Varangians) and Slavs, protected by a Turkic semi-nomadic aristocracy, living on the river Dnieper, and centred on Kiev.[15] In AD 980, Prince Vladimir (later Saint Vladimir) inherited the crown of Rus, thanks to the help of an army recruited in Sweden. Vladimir embraced Christianity and allied himself with Byzantium, marrying the sister of the Byzantine emperor, Anna, in AD 988. He expanded Kievan Rus with successful campaigns against the Poles, Bulgars and Pechenegs, and decreed the conversion of Novgorod and Kiev to orthodox Christianity ('The Baptism of Russia'). According to the chronicles:

> Vladimir sent emissaries to inquire into the teaching and rituals of Islam, Judaism, Catholicism and Orthodoxy. They reported that the Catholic ritual was without beauty and that Islam did not permit the consumption of alcohol ... Judaism they passed over in silence, but the Orthodox divine service

14 Davidova, 2002.
15 Hosking, 2001: 29–33.

they described as being so beautiful that 'we knew not whether we were in heaven or on earth'.[16]

On 31 May 1223 (in the reign of Henry III, the Plantagenet king of England), the army of Kievan Rus was defeated by the Mongol armies of Chingiz Khan at the battle of the Kalka river, in present-day eastern Ukraine. In 1240 the Mongols sacked Kiev, and established control over the whole of Russia for more than 200 years, not so much occupying the territory, as receiving tribute and relying on divisions between the Russian principalities. This permitted the hitherto insignificant settlement of Moscow to grow in power. It became a separate principality in 1263.

Most importantly, Moscow became the spiritual centre of Russian Orthodoxy. In 1299 Metropolitan Petr chose Moscow as the location of the see of all Rus.[17] Petr was canonised a year after 1326, the year of his death, '...in a ceremony designed to make Moscow the lasting centre of the Orthodox Church in Rus. His tomb became a shrine for all Orthodox believers and greatly enhanced the standing of the city'.[18] From this symbolically significant moment, the principality of Moscow began to expand in all directions.

Soon Moscow could challenge the Mongols. On 8 September 1380 an army commanded by the Prince of Moscow, Dmitrii I (1359–1389), defeated the Golden Horde at the battle of Kulikovo (near Tula, south of Moscow). However, Mongol rule in Russia did not end until 1480, at the 'Great Standing on the Ugra River', a standoff between Akhmat Khan of the Golden Horde and Grand Duke Ivan III of Russia.

## Moscow as the 'Third Rome'

Ivan III (1440–1505 – the reign of Henry VI in England) was the first ruler of Moscow to proclaim himself first 'grand duke of all the Russias' and, increasingly, Tsar of Russia. With the fall of Constantinople in 1453, there was a growing tendency to refer to Moscow as the 'Third Rome'. In 1510 (the reign of Henry VIII of England) the Russian Orthodox monk Filofei composed a panegyric letter to Tsar Vasilii III (1505–1533) in which he warned: 'And now I say unto Thee, take care and take heed, pious Tsar: all the empires of Christendom are united in thine. For two Romes have fallen, and the Third exists and there will not be a fourth. Thy Christian Empire, according to the great theologian, will not pass away... '[19]

Hosking writes: 'Moscow thus became symbolically both the "Third Rome" and the "Second Jerusalem," inheritor of both the Roman Empire and the Christian Church.'[20]

---

16  Hosking, 2001: 38.
17  Ibid. 72.
18  Ostrowski, 1993; Fennell, 1995: 134–136.
19  Andreyev, 1959.
20  Hosking, 2001: 107.

## Loss of status, destruction and resurrection as communist model

Moscow did not enjoy its political and legal pre-eminence for long. In 1712, Peter the Great made his city, St Petersburg (which had been founded on 16 May 1703 as a fortress)[21] the imperial capital, thus demoting Moscow to the 'second capital'. While St Petersburg represented modernity, Germanic discipline and Europe, Moscow was the home of Russia's mysticism and messianism, and of those aristocrats who declined a life of service to the Tsar.

For centuries, numerous invaders tried to take possession of the city and destroy it. In 1812 Napoleon's army captured Moscow. When the city was abandoned and set on fire in order to rob the French of supplies and force them to retreat, Napoleon is said to have exclaimed: 'What a people! They are Scythians! What resoluteness! The barbarians!' By 20 September 1812 more than four fifths of the city had been destroyed.[22]

After 1812, the city was rebuilt, with stone mansions, boulevards and parks. Industrial manufacture, and the population, started growing. In 1811, the population of Moscow had been about 275,000 people; by 1862 the population was 378,000, while in 1897 there were more than 1 million inhabitants. On 1 November 1851, the first railway linked Moscow and St Petersburg. In 1867 most of the streets were gas lit. The telegraph was opened in 1872 and the first telephone station in 1882. The first tram appeared in Moscow streets in 1889. At the beginning of the twentieth century, Moscow became one of the largest industrial and cultural centres of Russia.

The Bolshevik Revolution of October 1917 restored Moscow to its former greatness. On 12 March 1918, Moscow was declared the capital of Russian Socialist Federation of Soviet Republics (RSFSR), and remained the capital, this time of the USSR, from 1922 to 1991.

Viktor Tupitsyn evokes the nature of the new relationship of Moscow to the former capital in terms of cultural production:

> Compared with other urban centres, Moscow cultural life has always been characterised by a higher level of 'transparency' owing to the closeness of the state leadership's watchful eye. This partially explains why manifestations of what Walter Benjamin called 'optical unconscious' are generally more opaque, corporeal and sensual on the Banks of Neva than they are in Moscow, where the initiative – until fairly recently – belonged to conceptual art (read: transparent, sterile, intellectualised).[23]

At the same time, the Revolution of 1917 and Moscow's reinstatement as the capital of the RSFSR and then the USSR, transformed Moscow from the city of obscurantism and mysticism to a city of modernity. For a decade, Moscow

---

21 www.saint-petersburg.com/history/foundation.asp
22 Figes, 2003: 150.
23 Tupitsyn, 2002: 37.

became the great city of the avant-garde in art, architecture, literature, music and theatre. As Figes points out:

> It was a city of unprecedented freedom and experimentation in life as in art, and the avant-garde believed, if only for a few years in the 1920s, that they saw their ideal city taking shape in it. Tatlin's 'tower' – his unrealised design for a monument to the Third International in Red Square – expressed those revolutionary hopes.

His design symbolised the city's messianic role; 'From the idea of Moscow as the Third Rome to the Soviet one of it as leader of the Third International, it was but a short step in the city's mission to save humanity.'[24]

The Soviet period was also one of considerable improvement for ordinary families. By 1980, Carol Nechemias was able to write

> While Soviet dwelling units remain small and crowded, the problem of privacy – in terms of private versus communal apartments – is being solved. In 1960, 60 per cent of Soviet urban dwellers lived in communal flats in which they shared kitchen and toilet facilities with more than one family; this figure dropped to roughly 50 per cent by 1965, to 25 per cent by 1975, and, according to Soviet estimates, will stand at about 20 per cent in 1980. For the bulk of Soviet families, a private apartment is becoming the norm.[25]

## Moscow as the City of the Devil

This is the point at which I turn to Moscow as the City of the Devil, a source of diabolical paradox, something that the 'Triumph Palace', in its overbearing pomposity, triumphantly exemplifies. This is the law and the no-law of the devil. As Daniel Vyleta puts it,[26] a key difference between Stalin's system and liberal democracies lies

> ...in the paradox that Stalinist totalitarianism actively produces the self it demonizes, while the discourses of liberal democracies typically celebrate the values of individualism and privacy...A state in which life remains nasty, brutish and short, thus, becomes the ultimate perversion of its own *raison d'être*. In which case, the USSR under Stalin truly did have need for its satanic visitor, for – and this is the novel's final irony and triumph – it is the devil who becomes Bulgakov's great symbol of hope, mercy and humanity.

Vyleta is, of course, referring to Mikhail Bulgakov's masterpiece *The Master and Margarita*, which was written in the 1930s, but not published until 1996–1997.[27]

24  Figes, 2003: 215.
25  Nechemias, 1981: 5.
26  Vyleta, 2000: 49.
27  Bulgakov, 1996.

Orlando Figes reminds us that in this novel '...the Devil visits Moscow and brings its cultural temples crashing down; Satan descends on the city...with a band of sorcerers and a supernatural cat called Behemoth. They cause havoc in the capital, exposing it as morally corrupt, before flying off to the Sparrow Hills, where Napoleon (that other devil) had first set his sights on the city.'[28] As Vyleta points out, this novel does not portray heroes and heroines of socialist labour, but 'agitated theatre managers and gluttonous housing officials, second-rate politicians and retired, lottery-winning historians...Bulgakov offers us Moscow without the lipstick, naked and unplugged'.[29]

The novel's central question is put by the Devil to his assistant while on the stage of Moscow's huge Variety Theatre (you must read the novel to find out what he is doing there): '[H]ave the Muscovites changed inwardly?'[30] Vyleta continues: 'Not only does the Devil reiterate the binary opposition of inside-outside, the reader might sense here the author's rather Stalinist hope that the people have actually improved, and that the project of engendering new, socialist subjects may have worked after all.' The Devil's answer, however, is a negative one: 'They're people like any others. They're over-fond of money, but then they always were...They're thoughtless, of course...but then they sometimes feel compassion too...they're ordinary people, in fact they remind me very much of their predecessors, except the housing shortage has soured them....'[31]

Thus, Bulgakov's picture of Moscow's Soviet society is one in which every person accepts the discrepancy between public game and private self. 'Everyone is, by definition, a crook, because he/she holds on to a private self, and everyone needs and cherishes a private self in order to survive.'[32] Drawing on Žižek's view of the 'cynical subject' – 'they do not know it, but they do it'[33] – Vyleta suggests that the charade continues because the Muscovite is '...the cynical, liberal subject – that is the kind of subject most prevalent in Bulgakov's Moscow, and, for all the official doctrine, it may be the kind of subject most conducive to political stability: a game-player who cannot see beyond the monopoly board'.[34]

## Moscow as the City of God

This chapter now makes an abrupt transition from the City of the Devil to the City of God. God's law plays a crucial role in Moscow's self-understanding. It has been the capital of the Russian Orthodox Church since 1448.[35] In 1589,

---

28  Figes, 2003: 215.
29  Vyleta, 2000: 40.
30  Bulgakov, 1996: 143.
31  Ibid. 147.
32  Vyleta, 2000: 45.
33  Žižek, 1989: 28.
34  Vyleta, 2000: 46.
35  See the official history at www.mospat.ru/text/e_history/id/176.html

Metropolitan Job of Moscow became the first Russian patriarch. Hosking writes: ' "Moscow the Third Rome," then, was not originally a political theory, but rather a moral and religious one, and it should be understood as part of a complex of symbols and narratives which emphasised the sacred and exclusive heritage of Rus.'

Indeed, the Church seems to have somewhat revanchist geopolitical ambitions. Art 3 of the Charter of the Russian Orthodox Church, of August 2000,[36] provides:

> The jurisdiction of the Russian Orthodox Church shall include persons of Orthodox confession living on the canonical territory of the Russian Orthodox Church in Russia, Ukraine, Byelorussia, Moldavia, Azerbaijan, Kazakhstan, Kyrgyzia, Latvia, Lithuania, Tajikistan, Turkmenistan, Uzbekistan and Estonia and also Orthodox Christians living in other countries and voluntarily joining this jurisdiction.

This sounds remarkably similar to the territory of the former Soviet Union.

The Russian Orthodox Church has always been closely tied to political power. The research carried out by Zoe Knox shows that ' . . . in fact, the Church is not independent. It is granted a privileged position by virtue of its strong links to the government'.[37]

Furthermore, the messianism to which I have already referred is central to Russian self-perception. In words often cited in contemporary Russia, the former Bolshevik and religious philosopher Nikolai Berdyaev (1874–1948) wrote in 1911:

> The Russian national self-consciousness was begotten in the positing of the problem of East and West . . . Even the fact alone, of the struggle of Slavophilism and Westernism, . . . testifies to the centrality of this problem. Slavophilism was the first experience of national self-consciousness and of our national ideology . . . Russia – is the Third Rome. This proud awareness courses through almost all of Russian history.[38]

## From 'Third Rome' to centre of 'Eurasianism'

Moscow is also home to about 2 million Muslims (Russia as a whole has at least 23 million Muslims, about 15 per cent of its total population), giving it the largest population of Muslims of any non-Muslim city in the world. It also has a Muslim history embedded in its place and family names. The Arbat, Moscow's central pedestrian street, is a Turkic word, as is Baltschug, location of one of the most luxurious hotels.

---

36  In English, www.russian-orthodox-church.org.ru/s2000e39.htm
37  Knox, 2003: 591.
38  Berdyaev, 1911.

Many eminent Russians were descendants of Turkic noble families: Leo Tolstoy, direct descendant of Idris dynasty; Fedor Dostoevskiy of the Cheleby dynasty; Alexander Kuprin, Tugan-Baranovski and Anna Akhmatova of the Chagoday dynasty. Equally, many Russian family names are Turkic in origin: the writer Aksakov (meaning 'limping' in Turkic); the Napoleonic general Kutuzov (from khuduz, or qutuz, meaning 'furious'); and the White commander Kolchak (from kholchakh, meaning 'glove').[39] Other examples are: Turgenev (from the Mongol word for 'swift'); Bulgakov; Chaadaev; Rimsky-Korsakov; Berdyaev; Bukharin; Sheremetev and Rakhmaninov.

The most recent recognition of this fact is called 'Eurasianism'. Daniel Rancour-Laferriere points out: 'Among Russian nationalists it has been the Eurasianists who have been the most willing to recognize the mixed genetic roots and the assimilationist background of Russians.'[40] 'Eurasianism' is now influential in Moscow political circles. Bonnett notes that it is based on 'Slavophile' traditions:

> To a degree unique among 'other major European' nations, the assumption that 'European civilisation' was inherently superior to all others, or even a meaningful category, was actively contested. Russia's defeat by Britain, France and Turkey during the Crimean War (1853–6), combined with a persistent unease at the prospect of Russia ever really being accepted as fully European, encouraged those voices that condemned Westernisation as the spirit of alienation, materialism and superficiality. Throughout the mid and late 19th century, Slavophile and pan-Slavic critics poured scorn on the empty and instrumental world of the Occident.[41]

This was the fertile ground upon which the notion of 'Eurasianism' emerged in the post-1917 context of the White emigration. The philologist and ethnographer Count Nikolai Trubetskoi (1890–1938) wrote his key work *Yevropa i chelovechestvo* (Europe and humanity)[42] in 1920 (it was published in Sofia), and inspired a group of authors to publish *Iskhod k Vostoku* (Exodus to the East) in 1921.[43] He argued that no European state could be compared with Russia, since Russia is not a nation in the ordinary sense of the word, but a whole continent – Eurasia. 'Turkic blood mingles in Russian veins with that of the Ugro-Finns and the Slavs' he wrote, and referred to Russia's 'non-European, half-Asiatic face'. As Mark Bassin points out, Trubetsoi insisted that Russia's 'existence as an empire was a thing of the past; Russians now represented just

39 Polyakov, 1999.
40 www.panorama.ru/works/patr/ir/13.html
41 Bonnett, 2002: 444.
42 Trubetskoi, 1995: 55–104.
43 Luks, 1996: 58–59.

another of the constituent "ethnographic" groups which collectively comprised Eurasia's multi-cultural complexion'.[44]

Ilan Berman identifies a change of course by President Putin, in the direction of Eurasianism. He argues that '... indeed, by all indications, the growing emphasis on geopolitics from all corners of the Russian political spectrum is rapidly elevating Eurasianism to the level of a mainstream ideology.'[45] Berman catalogues the growing influence of the doctrine and its controversial guru, Aleksandr Dugin,[46] on Russian official and policy-makers, and points out that on 10 November 2000, Putin himself affirmed that 'Russia has always seen itself as a Euro-Asian nation'.[47]

## Moscow as a centre of law – and of no-law

Earlier I cited Benjamin's reference to the 'juridical uncertainties' of early Soviet Moscow. What of law in the new, 'capitalist' Moscow? As a centre of law, under the controversial but remarkably resilient Constitution of 1993, Moscow is the capital[48] and one of the 89 subjects[49] of the Russian Federation. It is constitutionally the 'permanent seat' of the Constitutional Court of the Russian Federation,[50] of the Supreme Arbitrazh (Commercial) Court of the Russian Federation,[51] and the Supreme Court of the Russian Federation, which stands at the head of the system of courts of general jurisdiction. The Moscow City Court, which is the city's court of appeal, has 174 judges; there are 33 district courts, with 560 judges as well as the Moscow Arbitrazh (Commercial) Court with 180 judges; and 384 districts of justices of the peace. It also houses the highest proportion of practising lawyers in Russia, as well as the leading law schools. The innocent novice might expect Moscow to be a centre of respect for the rule of law.

As a centre of lawlessness, however, the city is not simply the place where the fallen oligarch and former owner of the Yukos oil colossus, Mikhail Khodorkovsky has, along with colleagues, been tried and sentenced to imprisonment in a labor camp bringing to mind the words of Walter Benjamin cited earlier. This trial was of doubtful legality, closely tied to the forced (re)nationalisation of the greater part of the assets of the YUKOS oil producer.[52]

---

44  Bassin, 2001: 3.
45  Berman, 2001; see also Berman, 2002.
46  Dugin is a former member of the radical anti-Semitic *Pamyat* movement, and later of the racist Conservative Revolution, and has close links with the 'national-Bolshevik' Eduard Limonov. See also Kullberg, 2001 and Yasmann, 2001.
47  Putin, 2000.
48  Art 70, www.constitution.ru/en/10003000-04.htm
49  As a 'city of federal importance' according to Art 65 of the Constitution.
50  Art 115, Federal Constitutional Law on the Constitutional Court of the Russian Federation of 21 July 1994, at http://ks.rfnet.ru/english/ksangl.htm
51  Art 52, Federal Constitutional Law on the Supreme Arbitrazh Court of the Russian Federation of 28 April 1995, at www.arbitr.ru/as/doc/10064323/10064323-001.htm
52  See www.khodorkovskytrial.com

It is also the city where, on two occasions, the Mayor of the city, Yurii Luzhkov, had defied a clear decision of the Constitutional Court of the Russian Federation: once in 1996,[53] and then again in 1998.[54] The issue was racist discrimination – the system of registration in Moscow, which is a direct descendant of the system of internal passports that tied the agricultural population to the land in the USSR. Luzhkov had a different motivation. According to Human Rights Watch,[55] under this system '...police routinely check passports on the basis of skin color, invade the privacy of homes, illegally detain and fine refugees, and beat detainees with impunity'. The HRW report documents a well-established pattern of police 'visits' to private apartments – frequently with the threat of use of force – to carry out passport and registration checks. After threats of violence or arrest, they require refugees to pay a monthly bribe to shield them from further harassment. The Constitutional Court held that the system is discriminatory and violates the human rights provisions of the Constitution. Weiler comments that Mayor Luzhkov '...rules in a corrupt and personalistic manner and has made Moscow his private fiefdom in important respects. The abusive practices of Moscow law enforcement are largely attributable to the impunity that he grants his police officers.'[56]

There is another question with regard to Mayor Luzhkov. As reported on 19 October 2004, there was an outcry when his wife, Yelena Baturina, who heads one of the largest construction firms with many contracts from the city of Moscow, was listed as Russia's first woman dollar billionaire by Forbes magazine.[57]

The Moscow judicial system itself is not immune. In the first place, – and in violation of the Constitution's provisions for judicial independence – the courts are heavily dependent on the city for funding. Furthermore, the Chairman of the Moscow City Court, Olga Yegorova, has become notorious for her control of her own and the lower courts in Moscow, and for a large number of judicial dismissals. The Moscow City Court is the court which hears all appeals in cases such as that against Khodorkovsky. Judge Yegorova, who was appointed on 29 December 2000, is a judge with close relations to the Kremlin. A leading journalist has reported[58] that Olga Yegorova's candidacy for the post of Chairman was refused by the President's own personnel commission. Judicial appointments are made by the President. Under normal circumstances Yegorova should only have been able to apply for the post again after a year. But this was overruled in her case, after, it is said, interventions by former FSB officers who are now in

---

53 Case on registration (*propiska*); Decision of 4 April 1996, No 1996 9P at http://ks.rfnet.ru/pos/ p9_96.html

54 Decision of 2 February 1998, http://ks.rfnet.ru/pos/p4_98.html

55 Human Rights Watch, 1997.

56 Weiler, 2004: 91.

57 See www.telegraph.co.uk/news/main.jhtml?xml=/news/2004/10/19/wmosc19.xml&sSheet=/news/ 2004/10/19/ixworld.html

58 Korolkov, 2004.

leading positions around President Putin. The fact that her husband is General Yegorov of the FSB may have helped.

Judge Yegorova is able to pressurise or dismiss any judge in Moscow. In 2001, eight judges resigned from Moscow City Court, while four were sacked; and in 2002 a further ten judges resigned.[59] The case of a judicial whistle-blower, former Judge Olga Kudeshkina, has become a national *cause celebre*. Another four former judges had complained by December 2003 about the fact that Moscow City Court 'acts under instructions', and that Judge Yegorova interferes in the court with the objective of inhibiting the exercise of justice.[60]

## Conclusion – power and no power?

Moscow's status as capital is, it seems, once more under threat. President Vladimir Putin is a St Petersburg man. He was born and educated in Leningrad. After service in the KGB in the former German Democratic Republic, he returned to government service in the city until 1996. When he became Director of the FSB (formerly KGB) in July 1998, acting Prime Minister in August 1999, and President in March 2000, he took care to surround himself not only with KGB/FSB, but, in particular, with St Petersburg cronies. Thus, the current Director of the FSB, Nikolai Patrushev, who was appointed by Putin, spent most of his career in St Petersburg. Putin's Chief Secretary and Deputy Chief of the Kremlin administration, Igor Sechin, is also a veteran of the KGB/FSB, and closely connected with Putin in St Petersburg since 1991.[61] Aleksei Kudrin, the Minister of Finance, is another 'St Petersburg crony'.

Even more importantly, the key figure in Putin's legal reforms – until he was sent in September 2004 to be Putin's Plenipotentiary in the Southern Federal District, which includes Chechnya – was Dmitry Kozak, also born in Ukraine, but educated in St Petersburg. He made his career in the city. He was the driving force behind Putin's legal reforms: the three new procedural codes enacted from 2001 to 2003, Criminal,[62] Arbitrazh (Commercial)[63] and Civil.[64] At the time, it seemed that Putin was seeking to emulate the great legal reforms carried out – in St Petersburg – by Tsar Aleksandr II in 1864: creation of a system of justices of the peace, installation of jury trial throughout Russia with the exception of Chechnya; enhanced judicial status; and a much reduced role for the prosecutor in criminal and civil trials.

The nature of the threat to Moscow was spelled out by one of Putin's closest confidantes, former Deputy Prime Minister of Russia Valentina Matvienko. On 6 October 2003, she was elected the new Governor of St Petersburg. Although born

59  Korolkov, 2004.
60  See www.newsru.com/Russia/03Dec2003/4more_print.html
61  www.future-of-russia.org/issues/fsb_boys.cfm
62  Into force on 1 July 2002.
63  Into force in September 2002.
64  Into force in January 2003.

in Ukraine, she was educated and became a Communist Party functionary in Leningrad.[65] On the day of her election, she held a press conference and announced that she had no doubt that part of the functions of the capital of Russia would be moved to St Petersburg. She added that she had in mind the Supreme Court, the Supreme Arbitrazh (Commercial) Court, and the Constitutional Court.[66] Indeed, she had mentioned this plan in her campaign. In her view, the move would add clout to the former Imperial capital and help its economy. Although her proposal was immediately denounced by Moscow Mayor Luzhkov and by many judges, on 24 January 2004 the then Prime Minister Mikhail Kasyanov, ordered the Presidential Administration, the Cabinet of Ministers, and the St Petersburg City Hall to present their conclusions on relocating the three courts to St Petersburg. Buildings were identified in Senate Square where the highest courts of the Russian Empire had been located. He withdrew the order, following a political storm, on 3 February 2004. Nevertheless, on 20 December 2006, the State Duma (the lower house of the Russian Parliament) adopted a law on transfer of the Constitutional Court to St Petersburg. Russian TV showed the judges admiring their magnificent new home – no longer in the captial.[67]

It is not clear whether Moscow's status remains under threat; it is, however, obvious that Moscow is under Putin's rule re-acquiring more and more of the attributes of its Soviet past.

I close with the words of Margarita Tupitsyn who provides us with a wonderful metaphor for contemporary Moscow[68] worth reproducing in full:

> As Tsereteli neared the inauguration of his new museum, the magazine *KhZh* (Khudozhestvennyi zhurnal, Art Journal) published Slavoj Zizek's book *The Sublime Object of Ideology*. The English edition printed in 1989 featured on its cover Max Ernst's illustration for *Une Semaine de Bonté*. A voluptuous woman, with uncovered breasts, is sleeping on a royal bed whose canopy is opened to provide a space for the male gaze. A dreamy woman... is claimed to be susceptible to a melting pot of postmodern ideologies, among which a gendered one continues to stand out. The Russian edition replaced this image with Vitaly Komar and Aleksandr Melamid's canvas *The Origin of Socialist Realism*, a substitute, I presume, which the publisher selected as an operational equivalent to convey the conditions of the Russian context. Here, the voluptuous woman is alert and at work outlining a cast shadow of Stalin's profile. The role of aesthetics is played neither by a female (the Western paradigm) nor by a dictator (the former Soviet one). Instead, it dwells within a shadow cast by the old regime, a shadow that warns us that the object, *the sublime object of ideology* that has cast it, is alive and well.

65  http://petersburgcity.com/city/personalities/matvienko/

66  www.sptimes.ru/archive/times/910/news/n_10619.htm

67  See http://www.newsru.com/Russia/26dec2006/court.html, last accessed on 26th of December 2006.

68  Tupitsyn, 2003: 388.

Moscow's destiny, it seems, is in the balance. There are at least two possibilities. The city may be on its way to a restoration of Stalin's dreams, or to an apotheosis as capital of a new Eurasian antagonist for the West. The 'Triumph Palace' might be a harbinger. Or perhaps St Petersburg will once again displace Moscow. Moscow could become, not only the city of no-law, in danger of sinking under the weight of its corruption, but also the city of no-power.

## Bibliography

Agadjanian, A (2001) 'Public Religion and the Quest for National Ideology: Russia's Media Discourse', 40(3) *Journal for the Scientific Study of Religion* 351–365

Alden, J and Crow, S (1998) 'Moscow: Planning for a World Capital City Towards 2000', 15(5) *Cities* 361–374

Andreyev, N (1959) 'Filofei and His Epistle to Ivan Vasilievich', 38(90) *Slavonic and East European Review* 1–31

Bassin, M (2001) 'Classical Eurasianism and the Geopolitics of Russian Identity', at www.dartmouth.edu/~crn/crn_papers/Bassin.pdf

Benjamin, W (1986) *Moscow Diary*, Smith, G (ed.), Cambridge, MA: Harvard University Press

Berdyaev, N (1911) 'The Problem of East and West in the Religious Consciousness of Vl. Solovyev', reprinted in (1989) *Berdiaev Collection: 'Tipy religioznoi mysli v Rossii'*, (Tom III), Paris: YMCA Press, ctr. 214–241, translation at www.berdyaev.com/berdiaev/berd_lib/1911_053.html (accessed on 24 November 2006)

Berman, I (2001) 'Slouching Toward Eurasia?', *Perspective*, XII/1, at www.bu.edu/iscip/vol12/berman.html (accessed on 24 November 2006)

Berman, I (2002) 'Putin's Problem: The War on Terrorism Gets in the Way of the Eurasian Dream', *National Review Online* at www.nationalreview.com/comment/comment-berman010802.html (accessed on 24 November 2006)

Blockmans, W (2003) 'Reshaping Cities: The Staging of Political Transformation', 30(1) *Journal of Urban History* 7–20

Bonnett, A (2002) 'Communists Like Us: Ethnicised Modernity and the Idea of "the West" in the Soviet Union', 2(4) *Ethnicities* 435–467

Bulgakov, M (1996) *The Master and Margarita*, Glenny, M (trans.), London: The Harvill Press

Caldwell, M (2004) 'Domesticating the French Fry: McDonald's and Consumerism in Moscow', 4(1) *Journal of Consumer Culture* 5–26

Colton, T (1996) *Moscow: Governing the Socialist Metropolis*, Harvard: Belknap Press

Davidova, N (2002) 'Sprouting High Rises Blemish Moscow Skyline', *Moscow News*, 15 August 2002, at http://english.mn.ru/english/issue.php?2002-15-8 (accessed on 24 November 2006)

Davies, N (1997) *Europe: A History*, London: Pimlico

Dolnik, A and Pilch, R (2003) 'The Moscow Theater Hostage Crisis: The Perpetrators, their Tactics and the Russian Response', 8(3) *International Negotiation* 577–611

Fennell, J (1995) *A History of the Russian Church to 1448*, London: Longman

Figes, O (2003) *Natasha's Dance: A Cultural History of Russia*, London: Penguin Books

Gritsai, O and van der Wusten, H (2000) 'Moscow and St Petersburg, a Sequence of Capitals, a Tale of Two Cities', 51(1–2) *Geojournal* 33–45

Hahn, G (2002) 'The Rebirth of Eurasianism', *The Russia Journal* 14, 12–18 July, at www.cdi.org/russia/215-14-pr.cfm (accessed on 24 November 2006)

Holmes, K (2001) 'Understanding Putin's Foreign Policy', *The Heritage Foundation WebMemo* No. 22, at www.heritage.org/Research/RussiaandEurasia/WM22.cfm (accessed on 24 November 2006)

Hosking, G (2001) *Russia and the Russians: A History from Rus to the Russian Federation*, London: Allen Lane, The Penguin Press

Hughes, L (2002) *Moscow and Petersburg: The City in Russian Culture*, Nottingham: Astra Press

Hughes, M (2000) 'State and Society in the Political Thought of the Moscow Slavophiles', 52(3) *Studies in East European Thought* 159–183

Human Rights Watch (1997) 'Moscow: Open Season, Closed City', 1 December 1997, HRW Index No. D910

Knox, Zoe (2003) 'The Symphonic Ideal: The Moscow Patriarchate's Post-Soviet Leadership', 55(4) *Europe-Asia Studies* 575–596

Kolossov, V and O'Loughlin, J (2004) 'How Moscow is Becoming a Capitalist Mega-city', 56(181) *International Social Science Journal* 413–427

Korolkov, I (2004) 'Boss of Justice: Scandals, Which More and More Affect the Colleagues of Judge Yegorova, are Engulfing the Present Chairman of the Capital's Justice System', 16 *Moscow News*, 30 April 2004, at www.mn.ru/issue.php?2004-16-29 (accessed on 24 November 2006)

Kullberg, A (2001) 'From Neo-Eurasianism to National Paranoia: Renaissance of Geopolitics in Russia', *The Eurasian Politician* 4, at www.cc.jyu.fi/~aphamala/pe/issue4/duginism.htm (accessed on 24 November 2006)

Lilly, I (ed.) (2002) *Moscow and Petersburg: The City in Russian Culture*, Nottingham: Astra Press

Luks, L (1996) '*Yevraziistvo i konservativnaya revolutsiya: Soblazn antizapadnichestva v Rossii i Germanii* (Eurasianism and the Conservative Revolution: The Temptation of Anti-Westernism in Russia and Germany)', 3 *Voprosi Philosophii* (Questions of Philosophy) 57–69

Nechemias, C (1981) 'The Impact of Soviet Housing Policy on Housing Conditions in Soviet Cities: The Uneven Push from Moscow', 18(1) *Urban Studies* 1–8

Ostrowski, D (1993) 'Why Did the Metropolitan Move from Kiev to Vladimir in the Thirteenth Century?', in Gasparov, B and Raevsky-Hughes, O (eds) Christianity and the Eastern Slavs: Vol. I: Slavic Cultures in the Middle Ages, 16 *California Slavic Studies*, Berkeley: University of California Press 83–101

Polyakov, V (1999) 'Crimean Tatars', at www.iccrimea.org/polyakov.html (accessed on 24 November 2006)

Putin, V (2000) 'Rossiya: noviye vostochniye perspektivy (Russia: new eastern perpectives)' article of 10 November 2000, at http://president.kremlin.ru/appears/2000/11/10/0000_type_63382_28426.shtml (accessed on 24 November 2006)

Rancour-Laferriere, D (2001) *Russian Nationalism from an Interdisciplinary Perspective: Imagining Russia*, Slavic Studies vol 5, New York: Edwin Mellen Press and at www.panorama.ru/works/pdatr/ir/ (accessed on 24 November 2006)

Service, R (2003) *A History of Modern Russia from Nicholas II to Putin* (Revised Edition), London: Penguin Books

Shevryev, A (2003) 'The Axis Petersburg–Moscow: Outward and Inward Russian Capitals', 30(1) *Journal of Urban History* 70–84

Stephenson, S (2001) 'Street Children in Moscow: Using and Creating Social Capital', 49(4) *The Sociological Review* 530–547

Therborn, G (2002) 'Monumental Europe: The National Years. On the Iconography of European Capital Cities', 19(1) *Housing, Theory and Society* 26–47

Trubetskoi, N (1995) *Istoriya. Kultura. Yazyk (History. Culture. Language)*, Moscow: Publishing Group 'Progress' 'Universe', under the auspices of the Austrian Academy of Science

Tupitsyn, V (2002) 'Pushmi-Pullyu: St Petersburg and Moscow', 16(1) *Third Text* 31–39

Tupitsyn, M (2003) 'Moscow: On the Ruins of the *Third* Museum', 17(4) *Third Text* 379–388

Vyleta, D (2000) 'City of the Devil: Bulgakovian Moscow and the Search for the Stalinist Subject', 4(1) *Rethinking History* 37–53

Weiler, J (2004) *Human Rights in Russia: A Darker Side of Reform*, Boulder, CO/London: Lynne Rienner Publishers

Yasmann, V (2001) 'The Rise of the Eurasians', *Radio Free Europe – Radio Liberty* at www.cc.jyu.fi/~aphamala/pe/issue4/vasmann.htm (accessed on 24 November 2006)

Žižek, S (1989) *The Sublime Object of Ideology*, London: Verso

# Chapter 3

# Istanbul, political Islam and the law

## The paradox of modernity

*Penny Green*

## Introduction

> Flaubert, who visited Istanbul a hundred and two years before my birth, was struck by the variety of life in its teeming streets. In one of his letters he predicted that in a century's time it would be the capital of the world. The reverse came true: after the Ottoman empire collapsed, the world almost forgot that Istanbul existed. The city into which I was born was poorer, shabbier and more isolated, than it had ever been in its two-thousand-year history. For me it has always been a city of ruins and end-of-empire melancholy.[1]

> In many ways Istanbul is emblematic of the multi-faceted and multi-layered post-modern city growing from the ashes and embers of modernist experiments; the mechanization of agriculture, which led to a mass rural exodus that glutted the cities with migrants; city planning, with its triumphs of engineering and failure to predict and ameliorate human needs; the belief in rational progress and technology challenging human desires for eternal values and local belonging. In the 1980s the remaining embers of modernist hopes flared anew, fanned by the winds of capitalism that swept through Turkey's newly opened economic doors ... Since [then] Istanbul has become the Turkish gateway to the world, not only in 'terms of global wealth creation' but also as an entry point for modernization and the global culture it drags in its wake ...[2]

In December 2004, the European Council agreed to open membership negotiations with Turkey on 3 October 2005. In an unprecedented fashion, the EU attached conditions to its European invitation and Turkey's Islamic Prime Minister Recep Tayyıp Erdoğan declared 'we'll do all that is needed'. That Turkey's entry to the European Union should be orchestrated by an explicitly Islamic government is in itself astonishing – more astonishing still is the generally reformist nature of this government. As White suggests above,

1 Pamuk, 2005: 6.
2 White, 1999: 79.

Istanbul-emblematic city of Western, secular modernity – is the 'gateway' to this process. Turkey's consideration as potentially European in a political sense is fundamentally contingent on the capacity of Istanbul's political, cultural and economic capital to deliver modernity. Here I use the term modernity explicitly, because in contrast to White (who seems to use post-modern and modern interchangeably) I would argue that Istanbul is not a post-modern city (whatever that is) but is still firmly in the grips of the modernist project. Marshall Berman, following Marx, artfully defines this modernist project as the 'world- historical processes [which] have nourished an amazing variety of visions and ideas that aim to make men and women the subjects as well as objects of modernisation, to give them the power to change the world that is changing them, to make their way through the maelstrom and make it their own'.[3]

This chapter explores the intersection of political Islam, law and modernity in Istanbul, and in so doing it attempts to throw light on the reformist capacity of a modern Islamic democracy. The chapter proceeds by focusing on a number of themes which illuminate in different ways the relationship between Islam, law and Istanbul – themes which have shaped important aspects of the city's political, social, legal and religious modern history: the paradoxical relationship between secularism and Islam in Turkey; the *gecekondu* squatter housing settlements which characterise life for many in the city; the rise of Recep Tayyıp Erdoğan, symbol of Islamic political and populist success in Turkey; the contentious headscarf debate and the state of crime and criminal justice in this populous city. Throughout the discussion, law emerges as a vehicle of pedagogy, repression or reform.

## Islam, the Republic and law

Understanding modern Istanbul in the context in which this chapter is framed requires some understanding of the complexities which have defined the relationship between secularism and religion in Turkey. The literature[4] suggests that a competitive relationship between secularism and Islamism in Turkey has a history extending at least 75 years before the creation of the Republic. It also suggests that law has played an integral and normative role in defining the dialectical nature of that relationship and the balance of power between the two ideologies at any one historical moment. According to David Shankland, state control over religious affairs has had the effect of reinforcing both republican and Islamic ideologies. He writes ' . . . there has emerged a fascinating arrangement at the heart of the Republican state: a tacit recognition among secularists and believers alike that the state will be used to serve both their respective aims'.[5]

---

3   Berman, 1982: 16.
4   With some exceptions see, for example, Gilsenan, 1982: 261.
5   Shankland, 1999: 2.

Turkish law, like so much else in Turkey, is a patchwork of imported codes and ideas. Long before the establishment of the Republic (following the proclamation of the *Tanziman Fermanı* or Edict of Reorganisation in 1839), Ottoman authorities had begun to introduce some European legal codes which would sit alongside existing Islamic laws and institutions.[6] In the 1850s, Turkey introduced secular courts to deal with conflicts between non-Islamic merchants who traded in Constantinople. As June Starr points out, these courts and attempts to establish institutions for secular education 'were the first challenges by reforming Ottoman bureaucrats to the hegemony of the Ottoman Islamic elites'.[7] Later, with the establishment of the Republic in 1923, the legal system was radically reformed. The Caliphate was abolished in 1924 and, alongside it, Islamic or Shari'a law. To fill the gap, the leaders of the new republic embarked on the wholesale importation of European codes including the Swiss Civil Code and Code of Obligations, the Italian Criminal Code and the French Administrative Code.

At the same time, law played both a normative and pedagogical role in building the republic. From the inception of secularisation, judicial decisions have been imbued with a strong 'public interest' component – that of educating Turkish citizens around the structural values of Turkish republicanism: secularism, nationalism, individualism, populism and gender equality. When the republic was younger, it was the values of the new political elite, in effect an urban elite, which were to imbue the 'periphery'. In Istanbul today this ideological process has been partly reversed, as the religious conservatism of the 'periphery' confronts more publicly the tenets of Kemalist modernism. The enormous pressures attendant upon living in Istanbul – with its inadequate housing, infrastructural weaknesses and so on – has encouraged thousands of recent immigrants who have found integration difficult, to retain stronger ties with the villages they left behind. Many return to their villages for parts of the year, send children to be schooled there, and have local produce sent regularly from village to city.

The establishment of the Turkish Republic in 1923 was a radical break with the centuries-held Islamic power of the Ottoman Empire. Mustafa Kemal Atatürk, founder of the new republic, inspired by the separation of church and state in post-revolutionary France, imposed his own form of *laïcisme* in Turkey.[8] As much as possible, religion was to be confined to the private sphere, but religious practice was to be under continual state surveillance.[9] The architects of the new republic feared that a total separation of church and state would encourage religious interference in the affairs of government, given that Islam embodies not only faith but systems of legal, political and social ideology. Thus, despite secularism,

---

6  Ansay and Wallace, 1987.
7  Starr, 1992: 176.
8  Mango, 1999.
9  Mardin, 1989.

religion played a bifurcated role in building the Republic: 'for the rulers, that of linkage with the lower classes, for the ruled, that of an alternative to the polity and a buffer against officialdom.'[10] Kemalism (the ideology of secular, modern, rational and individualised Turkey) was not so much about the separation between religion and state, as about the absolute control of religious matters and practice.

During the 1980s, as Turkey came out of military rule, 'Istanbul emerged as the showcase and gateway for Turkey's new era of integration into the world scene.'[11] In this period, a campaign began to transform Istanbul into a modern international city capitalising on its Western – Byzantine and Eastern – Ottoman/Islamic heritage. Having lost its status as the country's capital to Ankara with the demise of the Ottoman Empire and the rise of Turkish republicanism, Istanbul had in some quarters come to represent the antithesis of modernity, enlightenment and secularism. For modernisers, Istanbul 'symbolized the decadent capital of the corrupt Ottoman Empire and its entrenchment in Islam'.[12] An ambitious programme of urban renewal led by neo-liberal Mayor Bedrettin Dalan, who saw Istanbul as a 'beautiful diamond in need of polishing', was put in place. But the project was met with resistance by conservationists, particularly Istanbul's Chamber of Architects who objected to what have now famously been called the 'Tarlabasi demolitions' – the destruction of dilapidated, but once elegant, nineteenth-century Ottoman and Levantine architecture – to make way for a pedestrianised Istiklal Boulevard, new roads to assist traffic flow, and a major renovation of the city's infrastructure. With the accomplishment of Dalan's programme, Istanbul, once a centre of the Islamic world, was now increasingly associated with secular modernity.

Özal's liberalisation was not confined to the economic sphere, but significantly extended to Islamic practice too. The world city was also in the process of becoming an Islamic capitalist democracy. Özal encouraged the foundation of Islamic banks, and permitted the *tarikats* to flourish unhindered. The Directorate of Religious Affairs received huge budget increases and as a result the number of *imam hatip* schools also rose dramatically during the 1980s. The generals on the National Security Council consciously exploited this Islamic revival, recognising its power as an alternative ideology to both communism and Kurdish separatism. It was also seen as a 'panacea' for healing the bitter rifts still evident in Turkish political society. Having destroyed the Left in the coup and the politically repressive years following it, the military effectively legitimised the revived voice of Islam as a tolerable, albeit conservative, alternative. In this climate of Islamic co-option into economic and political life, the Welfare Party's political fortunes were able to flourish. Ironically, as White demonstrates, the decimation of the Left created a vacuum in which the critique of social injustice could be filled by populist Islam.[13]

10  Ş. Mardin 1971: 199.
11  Keyder, 1999: 17.
12  Bartu, 1999: 33.
13  White, 1999.

What the rise of political Islam meant for the heterogeneous Istanbul elite was captured well by political scientist Şerif Mardin:

> ...*laic* intellectuals see it as the victory of obscurantism over science, higher bureaucrats as the disintegration of the fabric of the state and the rise of anarchy, fundamentalist *Sunnis* as means of establishing social control over the community, clerical personnel in the higher reaches of the General Directorate of Religious Affairs as a golden opportunity to establish solid foundations for *Sunni* Islam on a national scale...[14]

The ground for the rise of Islamism was now well established. The Refah Party, created in 1983, grew quietly under the hidden leadership of the ultra-conservative, charismatic Necmettin Erbakan until 1987, when he, along with other banned politicians, were permitted to return to political life. Younger members, many of them women, took up social work in the shanty areas of Istanbul and won over many to the 'welfare' intentions of the Islamic Party.

To the shock and astonishment of the secularist political establishment and their supporters, especially in Istanbul, in the March 1994 municipal elections the Refah party succeeded in winning 327 mayoralties, 28 in major cities. Most shocking of all to the nationalists was Refah's success in Ankara and Istanbul. Then, in the December 1995 general elections, Refah moved closer to national government with its 21 per cent victory at the polls. Eventually, in June 1996, Erbakan was to form a coalition with Tansu Çiller's True Path Party (which had mounted a virulent anti-Islamic election campaign but saw the opportunity of a coalition as a way to distract popular attention from corruption charges levelled at Çiller). By 1997 the Military's National Security Council (NSC) – custodians of the secular state – intervened in a civilian coup, or what is now known as the 'February 28 process', and declared the necessity of protecting the laicist principle of Turkish republicanism. Three months later Public Prosecutor Vural Savaş initiated proceedings in the Constitutional Court against the *Refah* Party. In January of the following year, the Constitutional Court found *Refah* guilty of acting 'against the laicist principle of the nation-state'[15] and dissolved the party as unconstitutional. As Koğacioğlu argues, '...the record of the Turkish Constitutional Court in the matter of party dissolutions is consistent with the hegemonic positions reproduced under the influence of the NSC'.[16] Erbakan was once more forced out into the political wilderness.

From the remnants of Refah and its later less successful incarnations, Recep Tayıp Erdoğan now formed and led the hugely successful Justice and Development Party (Adalet ve Kalkınma Partisi, AKP). Like Refah the AKP demonstrated a high commitment to securing full European membership for

14 Mardin, 1973: 180.
15 Koğacioğlu, 2004: 5.
16 Ibid. 4.

Turkey and a commitment to the human rights and democratisation programme entailed in that process. In November 2002, the AKP won the national elections and formed a majority government – the first majority government since 1991.

The rise of political Islam and its mobilising power have been widely attributed to the new patterns of rural immigration to urban centres, particularly Istanbul. Immigrants confronted by distinctly urban problems find solace and support in participatory local (Islamic) politics. Through a series of diverse activities, including 'neighbourly visits', marriage counselling, voluntary work or protests at the local mosque defending religious freedoms, these new urban citizens experience integration through Islamism. And as White illustrates in her anthropological study of Ümraniye, while the power of Islam to mobilise politically is new, the cultural values of this integration process are very familiar.[17] Certainly religious radicalism does not adequately explain the electoral rise of Islamism. According to a study cited by White,[18] 41 per cent of *Refah* voters in the mid-1990s identified themselves as secularists. What these voters complained about was 'the corruption of government, inflation, unemployment, the lack of sufficient public buses, water shortages and scanty garbage pickup'.[19] It was only after *Refah* had acquired political prominence and respectability that the local voters of Istanbul's Ümraniye district began to justify their support for *Refah* in terms of Islamic belief.

### *Gecekondu:* Istanbul's squatter communities

For 15 centuries, Istanbul was a locus of culture,[20] politics, commerce and religion – a fusion of Byzantine, Ottoman and Republican worlds, an axis where East and West converged. The splendours of Istanbul, its Byzantine walls and rich mosaics, its Ottoman mosques and Bosphorus palaces, its ultra-modern shopping malls and office blocks, however, belie another Istanbul. While the wealthy of the city live in gated communities on the city's seven hills, affording glorious views of the Bosphorus, Golden Horn and Marmara Sea, Istanbul's many poor live inland in deprived squatter communities.

In 1935, Istanbul's population stood at around 740,000; today it is estimated to be in the region of 12 million. Growth began in the 1950s, with poorer immigrants from the country's east seeking employment in the golden city. They built shacks on state or privately owned land. Through a legal loophole, these shacks were protected from immediate demolition by the state if they had been built within 24 hours, and thus became widely known as *gecekondu*: quite

---

17  White, 2002a.
18  Ibid. 120.
19  White, 2002b: 79.
20  Evidenced in The Royal Academy of the Arts exhibition 'Turks: Journey of a Thousand Years, 600–1600', 22 January–12 April 2005, London.

literally houses 'built overnight' in response to a lack of affordable social housing.[21]

Around 65 per cent of Istanbul's residential housing is illegal, namely, not subjected to legal regulation. Many of the illegal dwellings are *gecekondu*.[22] Çağlar Keyder describes the wide range of illegality afflicting Turkey's housing industry:

> In some cases the dwellings have been constructed on public land or on land belonging to private owners, and de facto squatting is the result; in others construction has violated zoning regulation, building on farmland or what has been reserved as park space (green area); or construction has been carried out without regard to municipal ordinances, without the proper inspection and permits, and disregarding the engineering, sanitary, aesthetic or habitation norms set by the authorities.[23]

Politicians were happy to issue title deeds and provide services to *gecekondu* developments in return for electoral support; and a land mafia grew rich selling unprotected state land to poor immigrants while the same politicians turned a blind eye.

Around 70–80 per cent of Turkey's land mass is under state ownership (in the cities, however, private ownership exceeds state ownership),[24] a legacy of both the Ottoman empire and the republican nationalist conception of modern Turkey. In the Ottoman empire, all land, unless explicitly recognised as private or belonging to a foundation, was considered to belong to the state. In 1956, large portions of land, were left uninhabited and unclaimed, following the genocide of the Armenians[25] and the exodus of the minority group landowners, namely the Jews, Armenians and Greeks. Ottoman titles were converted to the modern Turkish titles, but large swathes of land, as a result of absentee landholders or individuals who did not visit the registry on a certain day, were put into the name of the Turkish Treasury. The commodification of land was seen as ideological anathema to the principle of authoritarian statism, particularly as private appropriation of state land was popularly understood as a right of citizens.

Thus, state ownership of land, coupled with the customary practice of the unregulated informal appropriation, has suited Turkish politicians operating within a context of populist clientelism. For their own electoral purposes, these

---

21  Kocasoy, 1995.
22  *Gecekondu* are dwellings built on land that the builder does not own, without the owner's permission and constructed without regard to building codes and regulations. They are built in non-residential zones or in violation of city development plans. The *gecekondu* was a post-war response to increasing land prices and the lack of affordable housing in the cities (Kocasoy, 1995).
23  Keyder, 1999: 144.
24  Minister for Housing and Public Works, Ankara, personal communication, December 2001.
25  Between 1915 and 1925 over two million Armenians and Greeks were killed, expelled, exchanged or departed of their own free will (Keyder, 1999: 145).

politicians, through the arbitrary allocation of services, licences, permissions, the regular turning of a blind eye and the granting of other privileges to those building illegally, have been able to secure popular support. At the same time, however, the life safety of those forced to live in the dangerous housing emanating from those decisions has been reduced, as evidenced by the devastating Marmara earthquake in 1999.[26]

> Following the 1980s military coup, when prime minister Turgut Özal's opened the door to the liberalisation and globalisation of the Turkish economy, protectionist trade practices were lifted and public lands were privatised. According to Keyder, Liberalization in the economy and the grudging and incomplete repudiation of populist intervention by the state elite were necessary preconditions for the imposition of a self-regulating market. ... this condition translated to land being made available for legal development, which, in turn, made possible the increasing impact of capitalist enterprise in housing and, interdependently, the emergence of large construction firms.[27]

Hundreds of restrictive rules and regulations were repealed during the 1980s to encourage Turkish entrepreneurs. One of the consequences of Turkish liberalisation, however, was the burgeoning of corruption in the form of political bribery, privileged loans and unfair advantage in the dispensation of public tenders and procurement.[28]

In addition to public lands being made available for privatisation, various enterprising firms and individuals relying on populist government practice, built on undeveloped public land before it became available for sale. Developers learnt to rely on the fact that these illegal housing developments would be pardoned on the eve of elections when government would pass building amnesties which allowed either more storeys to be built on existing developments, or allowed public lands, already home to vast unlicensed housing developments, to be legitimately sold to individuals or companies.

This culture of *laissez-faire* in which it was possible to build wherever and whatever one liked with no adequate regulatory control, was to grow more prevalent over the next 15 years. A notable finding of the post-earthquake engineering teams was that a disproportionate number of newly built structures collapsed in the 1999 disasters.[29] This finding suggests a direct link between the liberalisation and deregulation strategies employed by the Özel regime in the 1980s, and the poor quality housing stock which flourished from that period.

---

26  Green, 2005.
27  Keyder, 1999: 153.
28  Aybar and Lapavitsas, 2001: 302.
29  Green and Ward, 2004.

Istanbul continues to attract the vast majority of the migrating rural poor, despite the often appalling conditions in which they are forced to live in the outlying suburbs of Istanbul's hinterland. In Istanbul's *Umraniye* district, for example, two-thirds of its 620,000 inhabitants were born outside the city.[30] In *Bağcılar*, another impoverished district, around 80 per cent of the population has emigrated from the South East and Black Sea regions. In the city's fast-growing and sprawling hinterland, rural poverty extends into urban poverty. In a 2002 study, *Bağcılar* scored high on all poverty indices. Eighteen per cent of children did not attend school, 20 per cent suffered physical disability and two-thirds of primary breadwinners had only a primary education.[31] Despite the conditions that rural migrants endure, Istanbul continues to be envisioned as a city with streets paved in gold for the rural Anatolian poor. As Shankland observes

> village houses in Anatolia, however remote, often have on their walls a reproduction of an image of Mecca on the one and on the other a picture of Istanbul, featuring often a Sinan mosque, or the Bosphorus bridge with its neo-baroque mosque at one end, graceful spans and a ferry boat passing underneath.[32]

In the villages and towns of Anatolia,

> the image of the ideal urban life has remained steadfastly Istanbul. Nowhere, indeed, is the combination of a modern infrastructure and the presence of Islam more noticeable than in Istanbul, where the centre of the city, untouched by war, with its banks of minarets leaning over the Golden Horn and the hundreds of mosques of different styles waiting to surprise the walker around the city, often seems curiously remote from the ideals of the Republic.[33]

Istanbul was relatively insulated from the dreadful realities of the 15 years of civil war between Kurdish insurgents and the Turkish state, partly due to the geographical remoteness of the conflict. Yet, as MacDowall has observed, many of Istanbul's *gecekondu* settlements have become 'permanent strongholds of Kurdish identity across the republic', making the Kurdish problem 'a visible reality for the citizens of Istanbul 800 miles away from Kurdistan'.[34] Given that Istanbul is, in effect, a 'city of migrants' with over 60 per cent[35] of the city's inhabitants born outside, and given the majority of Istanbul's immigrants are from the Southeast, this is unsurprising.

30  White, 2002a.
31  *Millyet*, 29 August 2002.
32  Shankland, 1999: 17.
33  Ibid. 16.
34  MacDowall, 2000: 402.
35  Sonmez, 1996.

*Gecekondu* has, in recent years, been superseded by the more heavily value-laden term for shanty housing: *varoş*. For middle-class Istanbul, *varoş* encapsulates *oteki Istanbul* (the 'other Istanbul') denoting urban poverty, a Muslim lifestyle, Anatolian roots, the headscarf and traditionalism.[36] But more than this, Erman argues, the *Varoşlu* (the inhabitants of the *varoş*) embody a sense of threat, of political radicalism and potential violence which undermines the secular integrity of the Turkish state.[37] But it is the impoverished urban reality of the *varoş* or *gecekondu* which presents the material threat to the inhabitants of Istanbul. The case of *Öneryıldız v. Turkey* which went before the European Court of Human Rights in June 2002 demonstrates the dangers inherent in Istanbul's shanty town accommodation and the criminal role of state actors in creating and prolonging those dangers. Maşallah Öneryıldız and the twelve members of his family lived in the *gecekondu mahallesi* of Hekimbaşı, built on land adjacent to a major rubbish dump in the working class district of Ümraniye. Despite an expert report (commissioned at the behest of Ümraniye District Council) in May 1991, which highlighted the dangers of the tip for those living in the *gecekondu mahallesi*, conflict between local authorities and in particular between two mayors (Istanbul and Beykoz) prevented action being taken which would have made the dump safe. When on 28 April 1993, a methane gas build-up caused a massive explosion at the dump, the land-slide which followed destroyed 10 homes and killed 39 people – including 9 members of the applicant's family.[38]

## Recep Tayyıp Erdoğan

> I'm a true lover of Istanbul. I was born and grew up here. It is here that I caught sight of the wider horizon . . . It is an act of worship to serve a city that won the praise of our beloved prophet.[39]

Recep Tayyıp Erdoğan, the local football star and devout Muslim, Mayor of Istanbul between 1994 and 1998, imprisoned in 1999 for 'inciting religious hatred', and elected as Turkey's Prime Minister in 2002, in many ways captures the contradictory experience of Istanbul as a world city in the early twenty-first century.

The life story of Turkey's current Prime Minister embodies much that is at the heart of modern paradoxical Istanbul. Born in 1954 in the poor Istanbul neighbourhood of Kasımpaşa on the northern banks of the Golden Horn, Erdoğan is the son of Laz immigrant parents from the eastern part of the Black Sea coast, close to the border with Georgia. Erdoğan's father earned a scant income captaining Bosphorus and Marmara Sea ferries, and family life was reportedly difficult. Erdoğan's piety led him to study at one of the religious

---

36   By contrast, modern, western-oriented secularist elites in Istanbul define themselves as *kent kültürü* or the city cultured (White, 2002b).
37   Erman, 2001.
38   *Öneryıldız v. Turkey* (48939/99) [2002] ECHR 491 (18 June 2002).
39   Recep Tayyıp Erdoğan, cited in Mango, 2004: 189.

*imam hatips* fostered by the republic. While still a teenager, Erdoğan, attracted by Islamic fundamentalism, joined the youth Branch of Necmettin Erbakan's Islamic National Salvation Party. The politically turbulent years of the 1960s and 1970s saw Erdoğan committed to the struggle for Islamic recognition and, by the time Erbakan had re-branded his *Refah Partisi* (Welfare Party) in 1983, Erdoğan was elected Chair of the Party's Istanbul provincial branch.

He came to national prominence, however, in 1994 when he won the local government elections – ahead of an Istanbul icon Zülfü Livanelli, a left wing and hugely popular musician who represented the Kemalists (Republican People's Party). Aged only 40 years, he was now Mayor of the largest and most European of Turkey's cities.

Fear of Islam was now a palpable force within the mainstream media and amongst the middle and ruling classes of Istanbul, particularly around questions of civil rights, the wearing of the headscarf and other social freedoms, as well as the politically fraught notion of Turkish national identity. Nowhere was this fear articulated more viscerally than in Istanbul. It felt as if Istanbul might be entering a dark era of personal restrictions and attacks on civil liberties. Algeria was in the air and Iran darkened the imaginings of middle class, educated Istanbulites. But the fears of the Istanbul secular elite were not, it seems, to be realised.

Erdoğan immediately cast off some of the more visible vestiges of his Islamism (shaving his beard and donning modern suits) but remained, nonetheless, the self-styled 'Imam of Istanbul'. He proved to be a competent administrator and his Istanbul Municipality renovated not only mosques but also churches and synagogues. Istanbul benefited in other ways under the Islamic Mayor. There was visibly less corruption, though Islamists were favoured with municipal contracts and employment opportunities,[40] the streets were cleaner, rubbish was collected and public transport improved. Erdoğan also ordered the planting of hundreds of trees in an effort to improve Istanbul's air quality.

While still Mayor, Erdoğan was charged with the Art 312 offence of 'inciting religious hatred'[41] at a pro-Islamic rally for reciting a poem by Mehmet Ziya Gökalp. The poem, published in an official Turkish school textbook, contained the lines: 'The mosques are our barracks, the domes our helmets, the minarets our bayonets and the faithful our soldiers'. For this he was found guilty and served four months of a ten-month sentence in Pinarhisar Prison 120 miles north-west of Istanbul. He was to emerge from Pinarhisar as a national political figure.

## The headscarf

In the early 1990s, when women in full black chador appeared in the streets of Istanbul, I was assured by Turkish friends that these were tourists from

---

40  Mango, 2004.
41  Art 312 of the Penal Code also prohibits the incitement of class, racial, ethnic, sect or regional hatred in the interest of 'protecting' the integrity of the Turkish republic.

Saudi Arabia: no Turkish woman covered herself in this way apart from immigrant women from the East who wore the traditional village scarf, and older women who wore the headscarf and long coat. Certainly no students at Bosphorus, Marmara or Istanbul university campuses, which I visited on a regular basis, were covered. These colleges were bastions of secularism, that is, at least until the revival of political Islam attracted young radical Muslim women for whom the wearing of the headscarf became a militant form of Islamic and political protest.

A survey reported in 2003 suggests that more than two-thirds of Turkish women now wear the headscarf, but only between 6 per cent and 16 per cent wear the 'Islamic-style' veil.[42] Deniz Kandiyoti describes the wearing of the headscarf as part of a 'patriarchal bargain', wherein the wearer demonstrates submission and propriety in return for protection and support.[43]

One of the many secular reforms introduced in the new republic was a prohibition on certain forms of Islamic dress. The fez was outlawed, to be replaced by the more western flat cap. The headscarf was also banned for public sector workers (who could be fined up to one-quarter of their salaries for a breach) and students. One of the most visible signs of the rise of political Islam since the early 1990s, has been the public defiance by young Islamic women of the headscarf ban.

In January 2002, a new civil code – meeting Turkey's obligations under the United Nations Convention on the Elimination of all forms of Discrimination against Women (CEDAW) – came into force. The new code eliminates the terms 'head of the family', 'husband' and 'wife', and replaces them with 'spouse'; 'illegitimate' disappears and children born outside marriage have equal rights; provisions which ameliorated the sentences delivered to those convicted of 'honour crimes' or harming sex workers have also been abolished.[44] It is still the case, however, that over 50 per cent of women in Istanbul do not work outside the home.[45]

In many respects the issue of the headscarf encapsulates the dilemmas of Turkey's struggle with modernity. The authoritarian imposition of Western dress codes has proven to be one of the most critical sites of Islamic struggle, and the Islamic movement has found a ready pool of young women to defy the headscarf ban in ways which are at once militant and ultimately reactionary. With the revival of political Islam in the 1990s the headscarf became a radicalising symbol for thousands of religiously conservative young women enrolling in the country's universities. These young women, the assertive, educated and to some extent 'liberated' products of Kemalism, became a spearhead of Islamic

42  Buckley and *Understanding Global Issues*, 2003: 16.
43  Kandiyoti, 1988.
44  Women for Women's Human Rights, 2002.
45  Mango, 2004.

fundamentalism. An interview, reported by journalist Steven Kinzer, with a young woman recently expelled from Istanbul University's Medical School for refusing to remove her headscarf before entering an exam (along with several hundred other students) is revealing:

> We love God, we read our Koran, we believe in our religion and we want to apply this religion in our lives. What has happened in the last few weeks makes me very angry. I am protesting as much as possible because I really want to become a doctor. It's bad to become a fanatic but they are pushing us toward fanaticism.[46]

As Feride Acar has argued, 'for the first time in the Turkish Republic's history, the conventional view which equated Islam with women's "imprisonment" at home was being challenged by the appearance of these women demanding an "Islamic way of Life" through open political struggle in which they, very effectively, used the weapons and tactics of modern democracy'.[47] This struggle, nonetheless – whether the genuine product of the women themselves or a cynical manipulation of them by religious leaders – opens 'avenues of experience independent of – and in contradiction to – the dictates of Islam which the same women preach'.[48]

In the much-studied working class Istanbul district of *Ümraniye*, traditional or village forms of patriarchal domination remain prevalent. According to the Turkish Ministry of Women's Affairs, some 44 per cent of women in the district reported that they required the permission of a male member of the family to leave the house alone in daylight hours. In the evenings, this figure rose to 96 per cent. The same report documents female property ownership at only 9 per cent.[49]

But Kemalism is still the most powerful ideology of the elite. At the time of writing, the Turkish President Ahmet Necdet Sezer had just vetoed a bill which had promised an amnesty to 240,000 expelled students, many of whom are young women who have defied the headscarf ban. The bill, proposed by the ruling AKP, was originally blocked by the Kemalist CHP, representatives of the secular elite who sought technical means to prevent the return to education of these Islamic students.[50]

## Crime and the city

For almost five decades, Istanbul has been associated with repressive policing practices and squalid prisons against a landscape of persistent and intransigent

---

46  Cited in Kinzer, 2001: 79.
47  Acar in Tekeli, 1995.
48  Arat in Tekeli, 1995.
49  Turkish Ministry of Women's Affairs, 1994.
50  *Turkish Daily News*, 3–4 March 2006.

human rights violations. Alan Parker's famous portrayal of a foreigner's experience in an Istanbul prison, *Midnight Express*, reinforced an impression of Istanbul as dangerous, brutal and corrupt. But for Istanbul's prison population, violence and corruption has been tempered by a degree of autonomy, free association and community unknown in most Western prison regimes. Prisoners are traditionally housed in large dormitories sleeping up to 60 inmates where security is limited. Paradoxically, life in Istanbul's jails has not been the dehumanising experience of many European prisons. According to one North American former prisoner of Istanbul's *Bayrampaşa* Prison, 'I can tell you stories about that prison that would make your hair stand on end and sound like I survived hell, but to be living it at the time for me was not so bad...there were things, really nice things, that outside could not have happened. There was a sense of belonging together, of camaraderie that you cannot duplicate anywhere.'[51] Those experiences led this former prisoner to choose Istanbul as her permanent home upon release.

That sense of camaraderie and autonomy has, however, been under attack since the early 1990s under combined pressure from the Council of Europe's Committee for the Prevention of Torture (CPT) and the Turkish State to move towards single-cell prison occupation. The Turkish government's desire is to crush political organisation inside the prisons (from Kurdish and Islamic militants), while the CPT argue that dormitory accommodation is a less civilised means of housing prisoners. Paradoxically, the march to an inclusive European modernity is likely to have wide and repressive implications for Turkish penal and criminal justice policy.[52]

Since the late 1960s the left, Kurdish activists and Islamic militants have been the target of the city's repressive apparatus. Pressure from civil society and the impetus of European accession are moving Turkey into a potentially new era of civil rights and liberal democracy. Reforms in the 2000s (nine reform packages in all, six overseen by AKP) have included the abolition of the death penalty in peace-time, the abolition of the ban on minority languages in education, the repeal of the ban on broadcasting in languages other than Turkish and the abolition of the State Security Courts. A new Penal Code in 2004, revised for the first time in 78 years, introduced measures making it easier to convict members of the state security services for human rights violations, provides for tougher penalties for torturers, criminalises genocide, crimes against humanity and the trafficking in people, and removes the statute of limitations for major corruption cases. Rape within marriage has now been recognised as a crime, and the defence of provocation has been removed in cases of 'honour killings'. These are significant and welcomed developments in the sphere of criminal justice; however, democracy may also bring less welcome reforms. As perceptions of

---

51 Personal communication, September 1992, cited in Green, 2000: 204.
52 For a more detailed analysis of Turkish criminal justice, see Green, 2000.

crime risk increase and begin to drive policy (assuming patterns in the West are followed), it is likely that criminal justice reform such as that associated with single-cell prison accommodation will have certain and more widespread regressive effects. Where the citizens of Istanbul have historically treated beggars, touts and petty offenders with a high degree of tolerance, the potential reach of criminal justice into arenas previously ignored will contribute to more of the city's citizens being brought under the control and supervision of the state. Anti-terror strategies are set to hasten this increased penetration of surveillance. When, in November 2003, terrorist explosions destroyed two synagogues, the London based bank HSBC, and the British Consulate killing 60 people, Istanbul experienced a wave of terrorist insecurity previously unknown in the city.

For a city its size, however, Istanbul is still surprisingly free of street crime, although in the last decade there has been a perceptible rise in the fear of such crimes by those who live in the city, and in 2000, Istanbul accounted for over one quarter of all thefts in the country.[53] Media reporting of 'muggings' and street robbery has certainly increased in recent years, yet the government's judicial statistics, suggest that the rate of criminal theft in Turkey is falling.

When I first began researching Turkish criminal justice policy and practice in the early 1990s I was struck by the absence of a generalised 'fear of crime' in both the political and popular discourse, particularly given the defining political role it was playing in the United Kingdom. Much of this absence could, at that time, be attributed to more powerful material and ideological 'public enemies' – Kurdish insurgents, Islamic fundamentalists, the deep state (*derin devlet*)[54] and corrupt politicians.[55] Islamic humanism may also be a significant part of the explanation. Turkish secularism has always recognised the cohesive importance of Islam to moral and social unity. The founders of the Turkish Republic, while regarding religion as backward, superstitious and conservatising, also recognised the inherent value of Islam in contributing to social cohesion, morality and welfare, particularly in periods of rapid social change.[56] As Andrew Mango summarises, 'officially inspired sermons in mosques preach social solidarity and self control. Islam has always made a virtue of getting on with one's neighbours. Charity is a religious duty: a good Muslim does not go to sleep having eaten his fill while his neighbour is hungry.'[57]

The rise and electoral success of political Islam had an important and somewhat paradoxical impact upon criminal justice reform. During Erbakan's period in office, the *Refah* Party consistently rejected the possibility of

---

53  State Institute of Statistics, Judicial Statistics, 2000.
54  The murky relationships which exist between Turkey's political elite, its state functionaries, the intelligence services and organised crime – a relationship feared and condemned by Turkish people as *Derin Devlet*, the 'Deep State'.
55  For a discussion of crime and criminal justice policy in 1990s Turkey, see Green, 2000.
56  Ayata, 1996.
57  Mango, 2004: 127.

a reformed penal code. Rather, Erbakan wished a return to *Shari'a* law. In accordance, the Refah Minister of Justice, Şevkit Kazan, severed links with groups lobbying for reform such as the Bar Association.[58] According to Köksal Bayraktar, this galvanised the politicisation of criminal policy: 'for the first time politicians argued for change – *law became an issue because it organised the secularists... Refah* made people think that the system needs reform, that decisions taken in court shouldn't result in such harsh penalties' (my emphasis).[59] Thus, in order to counter the political impact of *Refah*, secular politicians and academics proposed otherwise unthinkable changes to the existing criminal justice system. Legal politics in the early to mid-1990s came from the perceived political threat the Islamicists presented to the Republic. According to Bayraktar, the reforming politicians were not interested in the finer details of criminal justice or penal reform – these were merely one of vehicles for the wider political changes planned. It was not until September 2004 and under the direction of the AKP, however, that the new Penal Code was finally approved by the Turkish Parliament.

## Conclusion

Istanbul's celebrated novelist and social commentator Orhan Pamuk has captured the dissonance that modernity has fostered in its inhabitants, 'Even as a child, when the city was at its most run-down, Istanbul's own residents felt like outsiders half the time. Depending on how they were looking at it, they felt it was either too Eastern or too Western and the resulting uneasiness made them worry they didn't quite belong.'[60]

Istanbul's 80-year engagement with modernity has been shaped both by law and by an absence of law. The law has played a pedagogical and repressive role in ensuring that Istanbul, and Turkey more widely, has been protected from sectional divisions which might threaten the integrity of the Turkish Republic. In particular, Kurdish and Islamic identities have been viewed as particularly threatening. As Göle has argued, Kemalism has always viewed national or religious identity struggles 'not as natural components of a pluralistic democracy but as sources of instability and as threats to unity and progress'.[61] It is these insecurities and the repressive legal and extra-legal measures which have established human rights violations as endemic, that have made Turkey's entry to the EU so unpalatable for many years. Ironically, it is the Imam of Istanbul, with a moderated version of political Islam and a commitment to full

---

58  Interview with Erlap Özgen, President, Turkish Bar Association, personal communication, Ankara, December 1997.

59  Professor of Criminal Law, Istanbul University, member of the Penal Code Reform Commission, personal communication, Istanbul, December 1997.

60  Pamuk, 2005: 233.

61  Göle, 1997: 84.

democratisation, who stands a greater chance of ultimately securing Turkey's home in Europe.

Istanbul is the embodiment of Turkey's modernisation project – symbolic of Turkey's diversity: it is European, Eastern, Muslim and Turkish. It is also Kurdish, Armenian, Laz, Jewish, Greek, Alevi, Sunni and Shia. For Istanbul, the experience of Islamic governance has not been the illiberal nightmare originally feared. Political Islam has not disrupted the progress towards modernity, rather it may be argued to have augmented and apparently hastened it.

The paradox that underpins Istanbul's troubled encounter with modernity in the 2000s revolves around the delivery of that modernity. It is a modernity undermined by religious traditionalism. A modernity, in significant part to be delivered by representatives of what the secular elite regard as 'the antonym of enlightenment'.[62] It has been Islamist politicians who have shaken hands most encouragingly with Europe. It is the same Islamist politicians who have declared a commitment to the sweeping human rights reforms required of that process,[63] to democratisation and the Copenhagen criteria, and who secured the abolition of the long criticised National Security courts. At the same time, Istanbul has been successfully governed both locally and nationally by religious adherents once greatly feared. While Istanbul adjusts and accommodates to political Islam, real democratic change is likely to be driven by those who have historically been victim to the repressive strictures of Kemalism: *Gecekondu* squatters seeking safer housing, young Muslim women demanding the right to wear what they wish, Kurdish, left-wing and Islamic activists who have been imprisoned and tortured demanding a fair and transparent criminal justice process.

## Bibliography

Acar, F (1995) 'Women and Islam in Turkey', in *Women in Modern Turkish Society*, Tekeli, S (ed.), London: Zed Books, 46–65

Ansay, T and Wallace, D (eds) (1987) *Introduction to Turkish Law*, 3rd ed., Devnter: Kluwer

Arat, Y (1995) 'Feminism and Islam: Considerations on the Journal *Kadin ve Aile*', in Tekeli, S (ed.), *Women in Modern Turkish Society*, London: Zed Books

Ayata, S (1996) 'Patronage, Party, and State: The Politicization of Islam in Turkey', in 50(1), *Middle East Journal*, 40–56

Ayata, S (2002) 'The New Middle Class and the Joys of Suburbia', in Kandiyoti, D and Saktanber, A (eds), *Fragments of Culture: The Everyday of Modern Turkey*, London: IB Tauris

Aybar, S and Lapavitas, C (2001) 'The Recent Turkish Crisis: Another Step Toward Free Market Authoritarianism', in 8, *Historical Materialism*, Summer, 279–308

---

62  Heper, 1997.
63  Albeit marred by recent unsuccessful attempts to criminalise adultery, the continued prosecution of writers and publishers critical of the state and the continuing blight of torture.

Bartu, A (1999) 'Who Owns the Old Quarters? Rewriting Histories in a Global Era', in Keyder, Ç (ed.), *Istanbul: Between the Global and the Local*, Oxford: Rowman and Littlefield, 31–45

Berman, M (1982) *All that is Solid Melts into Air: The Experience of Modernity*, London: Verso

Boland, V (2004) 'Eastern Premise', in *FTmagazine*, 4 December

Bora, T (1999) 'Istanbul of the Conqueror: The "Alternative Global City" Dreams of Political Islam', in Keyder, Ç (ed.), *Istanbul: Between the Global and the Local*, Oxford: Rowman and Littlefield, 47–58

Buckley, R (2003) 'Tension in Turkey: Democracy, Islam and Military Power', in 121, *Understanding Global Issues*, 80 at www.global-issues.co.uk/display.php?title=061761 (accessed 27 November 2006)

Erman, T (2001) 'The Politics of Squatter (Gecekondu) Studies in Turkey: The Changing Representation of Rural Migrants in the Academic Discourse', in 38(7), *Urban Studies*, 983–1002

Fokas, E (2004) 'The Islamist Movement and Turkey – EU Relations', in Uğur, M and Canefe, N (eds), *Turkey and European Integration: Accession Prospects and Issues*, 147–170

Freely, J (1996) *Istanbul, The Imperial City*, London: Penguin

Gilsenan, M 1982 *Recognizing Islam: an Anthropologist's Introduction*, London: Croom Helm

Green, P (2000) 'Criminal Justice and Democratisation in Turkey: the Paradox of Transition', in Green, P and Rutherford, A (eds), *Criminal Justice in Transition: Criminal Policy-Making Toward the New Millennium*, Oxford: Hart, 195–220

Green, P (2005) 'Disaster by Design: Corruption, Construction and Catastrophe', in 45(4), *British Journal of Criminology*, 528–546

Green, P and Ward, T (2004) *State Crime: Governments, Violence and Corruption*, London: Pluto Press

Göle, N (1996) *The Forbidden Modern: Civilization and Veiling*, Ann Arbor, MI: University of Michigan Press

Göle, N (1997) 'The Quest for the Islamic Self within the Context of Modernity', in Bozdogan, S and Kasaba, R (eds), *Rethinking Modernity and National Identity in Turkey*, Seattle, WA: University of Washington Press, 81–94

Gülalp, H (1999) 'Political Islam in Turkey: The and Fall of the Refah Party', in 89(1), *Muslim World*, 22–41

Hale, W (2003) 'Human Rights, the European Union and the Turkish Accession Process', in Çarkoğlu, A and Rubin, B (eds), *Turkey and the European Union: Domestic Politics, Economic Integration and International Dynamics*, London: Frank Cass

Heper, M (1997) 'Islam and Democracy in Turkey: Toward a Reconciliation?' in 51(Winter), *Middle East Journal*, 46–58

Jacoby, T (2004) *Social Power and the Turkish State*, London/New York: Frank Cass

Kandiyoti, D (1988) **'Bargaining with Patriarchy'**, II(3), *Gender and Society*

Keyder, Ç (ed.) (1999) *Istanbul: Between the Global and the Local*, Oxford: Rowman and Littlefield, 31–45

Kinzer, S (2001) *Crescent and Star: Turkey between Two Worlds*, New York: Farrar, Strauss and Giroux

Kocasoy, G (1995) 'Urban Development and the Coastal Zone: Problems in Istanbul and Izmir', in Parker, R, Kremer, A and Munasinghe, M (eds), *Informal Settlements,*

*Environmental Degradation and Disaster Vulnerability: Turkey Case Study*, Washington, DC: The International Decade for Disaster Reduction (IDNDR) and World Bank

Koğacioğlu, D (2004) 'The Tradition Effect: Framing Honor Crimes in Turkey', in 15(2), *Differences*, 118–152

Mango, A (1999) *Atattürk*, London: John Murray

Mango, A (2004) *The Turks Today*, London: John Murray

Mansel, P (1995) *Constantinople: City of the World's Desire*, London: Penguin

Mardin, Ş (1971) 'Ideology and Religion in the Turkish Revolution', in 2(3), (July 1971), *International Journal of Middle East Studies*, 197–211

Mardin, Ş (1973) 'Centre – Periphery Relations: A key to Turkish Politics', in *Daedalus*, 169–190

Mardin, Ş (1989) *Religion and Social Change in Modern Turkey: The Case of Bediiüzzaman Said Nursi*, Albany, NY: SUNY Press

McDowall, D (2000) *A Modern History of the Kurds*, 2nd ed, London: I.B.Tauris

Meeker, M (2002) *A Nation of Empire: The Ottoman Legacy of Turkish Modernity*, Berkeley, CA: University of California Press

Navaro-Yashin, Y (2002) 'The Market for Identities: Secularism, Islamism, Commodities', in Kandiyoti, D and Saktanber, A (eds), *Fragments of Culture: The Everyday of Modern Turkey*, London: IB Tauris, 221–254

*Öneryıldız v Turkey* (48939/99) [2002] ECHR 491 (18 June 2002)

Özdemir, A and Frank, K (2000) *Visible Islam in Modern Turkey*, Basingstoke: Macmillan

Pamuk, O (2005) *Istanbul: Memories of a City*, English edition, London: Faber and Faber

Republic of Turkey, State Institute of Statistics 2000, *Judicial Statistics 2000*

Secor, A J (2001) 'Globalizing Istanbul: Gender and the Local/Global Production of Islamism', Globalization and Democracy Conference, Boulder, Colorado, April 2001, at www.colorado.edu/ibs/PEC/gadconf/papers/secor.pdf, accessed 4 March 2005

Shankland, D (1999) *Islam and Society in Turkey*, Hemingford Grey: Eothen

Shankland, D (2003) *The Alevis in Turkey: The Emergence of a Secular Islamic Tradition*, London: Routledge

Sonmenz, M (1996) 'A Statistical Survey: Istanbul in the 1990's', *Biannual Istanbul*, Spring, 49–50

Starr, J (1992) *Law as Metaphor: From Islamic Courts to the Palace of Justice*, New York: State University of New York Press

Tapper, R (ed.) (1991) *Islam in Modern Turkey*, London: IB Tauris

Tekeli, S (1995) *Women in Modern Turkish Society*, London: Zed Books

Turkish Ministry of Women's Affair (1994), The Status of Women in Turkey, A Report on the Fourth World Conference on Women, May 1994

White, J (1999) 'Islamic Chic', in Keyder, Ç (ed.), *Istanbul: Between the Global and the Local, oxford*: Rowman and Littlefield, 77–91

White, J (2002a) *Islamist Mobilization in Turkey*, Washington, DC: University of Washington Press

White, J (2002b) 'The Islamist Paradox', in Kandiyoti, D and Saktanber, A (eds), *Fragments of Culture: The Everyday of Modern Turkey*, London: IB Tauris, 191–220

Women for Women's Human Rights (2002) *The New Legal Status of Women in Turkey*, Istanbul: New Ways

# Part II

# Streets of the real

# Chapter 4

# Homophobic violence in London

## Challenging assumptions about strangers, dangers and safety in the city

*Leslie J Moran*

Leaving *Heaven*, a gay nightclub located under the commuter hub of Charing Cross Station in central London, David Morely and a friend, headed south over the river Thames. Sitting on a bench on the south bank of the river, in the shadow of various renowned national and international cultural institutions, the *Royal Festival Hall*, *Royal National Theatre* and close by the towering landmark of the *Millennium Wheel*, both were savagely attacked by a group of teenagers. Later that day, as a result of multiple blows, broken ribs and a ruptured spleen, David Morley died in hospital. In reporting the incident, one journalist commented, 'London is generally seen as one of the world's more tolerant cities for homosexuals.'[1] In this violent and shocking incident the image of London as a safe haven for sexual minorities was shattered.

David's death provoked a flurry of reports, in both National and London newspapers, of other incidents of homophobic violence in the capital. These included the stabbing of a gay man on a night bus in north London,[2] and an incident close to two gay bars, just north of Trafalgar Square, on Charing Cross Road.[3] David's death also brought back memories of another awful tragedy: the bombing, in 1999, of *The Admiral Duncan*, a gay bar in the heart of London's Soho in the heart of the capital.[4] The many newspaper accounts of David's death reminded readers that he worked as a barman in *The Admiral Duncan* at the time of the bombing. He had miraculously survived the devastating nail bomb attack on that bar where three people were killed and 70 were injured.

The violence portrayed in these various reports that shatter the image of London as a metropolitan safe haven takes a particular form: stranger violence. What image of violence and space is formed here? It is a violence that takes the form of apparently random acts. Those who perform the violence appear to be unknown to the victim: the perpetrators are anonymous. It is predominantly

---

1  Anon, 2004.
2  Branigan, 2004.
3  Stevens, 2004.
4  Bowley, 2000.

violence between men: its perpetrators are men,[5] and men, more specifically, gay men or those whom the perpetrator assumes to be gay, are the primary targets. The location of the violence is public spaces, in particular the anonymous highways and byways of city centres and areas proximate to gay bars, venues and locales. This is not a type of violence commonly associated with the suburbs or more rural locations, with the more intimate spaces that make up the local neighbourhood, or violence associated with the domestic idyll of home. 'Stranger violence' also has a strong temporal dimension. It is violence associated with a particular time, after dark, more specifically late at night and in the early hours of the morning.

The characterisation of homophobic violence as 'stranger violence' is not limited to media reports. It is prevalent in lesbian and gay representations of homophobic violence. More specifically it is to be found in lesbian and gay victim surveys that have been generated by lesbian and gay community activism.[6] Dedicated to correcting other representations of homophobic violence, these surveys seek to document the violence faced by lesbians and gay men and their ongoing struggle for basic rights as citizens: access to state services relating to safety and security.[7] The violence recorded in these surveys appears to be dominated by 'stranger violence'. For example, most perpetrators are reported as being 'unknown' to the victim.[8] The Pink Shield initiative undertaken in Birmingham, in the heart of Britain, reported that 'around two-thirds of those attacked (68 per cent of men and 83 per cent of women)' were attacked by 'strangers'.[9] A study of gay men in Scotland's capital, Edinburgh, reported that in 61 per cent of incidents of violence, the perpetrator was 'someone never seen before' by the victim.[10] Public space is, these surveys suggest, the primary locus of danger. Stonewall's survey, *Queer Bashing*,[11] to-date the largest UK-wide survey of homophobic violence, reported that 61 per cent of incidents occurred in public places. Areas in and around the gay commercial scene appear as homophobic violence 'hotspots'. In the Birmingham study, the 'Gay Village'

---

5   This is signified in media reports by the perceived need to highlight the presence of female perpetrators in the Morely murder.
6   'Stranger danger' is also a global phenomenon. It is a common dimension of gay-related murders that have played a key role in reform campaigns. See in relation to the United States of America: Loffreda, 2000; Kaufman, 2001. Canada: Janoff, 2005. Australia: Baird, 1997. Campaigns in different cities and countries are inter-connected by the media. For example the death of David Morely was reported on a global basis. Reports appeared on North American Web pages and in news media in South Africa, see 'Teenage Gang Beats Gay Man to Death' in 'Cape Times', http://capetimes.co.za/general
7   Phelan, 2001.
8   Not all surveys ask about perpetrator/victim relations, see for example the UK wide National Advisory Group report in Wake *et al.*, 1999.
9   Pink Shield, 2002: 5.
10  Morrison and Mackay, 2000: 38.
11  Mason and Palmer, 1996.

accounted for nearly 30 per cent of incidents. The anonymous 'city streets' is another prime location. The same survey recorded 12 per cent of incidents on the city's streets.[12] 'Stranger violence', these surveys suggest, is far from being a media distortion of experiences of homophobic violence.

A UK government briefing paper on stranger and acquaintance violence notes the assumptions and understandings found in the 'stranger danger' model of violence have considerable importance. They have an impact upon everyday expectations and perceptions of violence. They also have an impact upon the formulation and development of initiatives to respond to violence, in priority setting and informing the provision of services and their day-to-day operations.[13]

Drawing upon police and community data, this chapter examines evidence that problematises the dominance of the 'stranger danger' model of homophobic violence. This is undertaken by an examination of two dimensions of the data: first, the nature of the interpersonal relationships, between perpetrator and victim, and the spatial dimensions of the violence. The reason for focusing on the interpersonal and spatial aspects of the violence is that both play a key role in generating and sustaining assumptions, expectations and understandings about the nature of homophobic violence. Gail Mason has noted, 'The assertion that [homophobic violence] is random is dependant upon the assumption that the conduct is committed by someone who is not known to the victim...'[14] Likewise, the predominance of the street, gay bars and the like as locations of the violence works to reinforce the attributes of anonymity and randomness at the core of 'stranger violence'. The analysis that follows seeks to problematise the dominance of the 'stranger danger' model, suggesting that it neither represents the most common forms of homophobic violence nor does justice to the diversity of experiences of homophobic violence. The dominance and persistence of the 'stranger danger' model of homophobic violence raises another important issue. What idea of law and order communities and places of safety and danger is being made in and through the 'stranger danger' model of homophobic violence?

## A tale of two studies

My analysis draws upon two studies of homophobic violence in London. The first is a London-wide study, the Understanding and Responding to Hate Crime (URHC) initiative funded by London's Metropolitan Police Service (MPS) and the Home Office.[15] A unique feature of this study is its focus upon routinely collected data, more specifically police data. My analysis is concerned only with

---

12  Pink Shield, 2002: 4.
13  Mattinson, 2001.
14  Mason, 2003: 24.
15  Stanko et al., 2003.

the URHC initiative dealing with homophobic incidents.[16] That part of the project studied homophobic incidents reported to the police between January and June 2001. In the whole of 2001, 1,554 homophobic incidents were reported to the MPS[17] which represents over one-third of all such incidents in the United Kingdom in that year. At the time of the study (and it remains the case) this particular police dataset was the largest body of systematically recorded information about experiences of homophobic violence in any area in the United Kingdom.

The second study has a related but distinct spatial focus and is based upon a very different dataset. The study focuses upon two London boroughs in the south and east of the metropolis; Bexley and Greenwich. The Bexley and Greenwich (BandG) study, undertaken by GALOP, a London-based lesbian and gay anti-violence charity, was commissioned by two south London local government partnerships: Bexley Community Safety Partnership and Greenwich Crime and Disorder Reduction Partnership. Bexley is predominantly a suburban borough on the south-eastern edge of London. At the time of the survey there were no public or commercial lesbian or gay venues or events in the borough. Lesbians and gay men are largely invisible in the public realm in that borough. Greenwich borders the western edge of Bexley. It is spatially more diverse, composed of fashionable historic locales as well as inner city, suburban and dockland/industrial areas. From time to time Greenwich has hosted gay businesses, organisations, events and entertainment venues. It is also the location of the Metro Centre, an HIV resource centre that has a strong gay and lesbian community focus.

Drawing upon a tradition of victim surveys, the BandG survey was designed to generate data that is missing from, or invisible within, police data. Many lesbian and gay community-based victim surveys have drawn attention to the limits of data on violence found in routinely collected police data. A common finding is that less than 1 in 3 homophobic incidents are reported to the police. An awareness of the limitations of police data was the backdrop for the BandG survey.

## Study 1: the understanding and responding to hate crime project

The URHC study of homophobic violence offers an analysis of 754 incidents, identified as homophobic, reported between January and June 2001. In addition, a detailed qualitative re-analysis of one month's reports, January 2001, was undertaken. The objective here was to offer a re-examination of the data captured in police reports. The project produced some startling results.

---

16 Heterosexual domestic violence, racial violence and sexual assaults were also examined as part of the URHC initiative. See Stanko *et al.*, 2003.

17 In 2002, the number of incidents reported dropped to 1385. In 2003, the last year for which figures are available, the numbers rose to 1536.

The URHC *Homophobic Incident Fact Sheet* (undated) offers a snapshot of some key features of the experiences of violence captured in the routinely collected data. For example, a minority of incidents recorded were categorised as incidents of 'violence'. 'Threats' and 'damage to property' make almost a majority of recorded incidents. Most homophobic incidents (3 in 4) involved one victim and one perpetrator. The study reported a disparity between the ages of a majority of the victims, between 21 and 40, and the age of suspects, with a significant number (over 40 per cent) being under 20.

Some findings mirror aspects of the 'stranger violence' model. For example most reported incidents are against men. There were seven male victims of violence for every female victim.[18] An initial analysis of the perpetrator/victim relationship formally recorded on the incident files suggested that in almost 65 per cent of the incidents reported no relationship existed between perpetrator and victim, being described as either 'unknown' or 'no relationship'.

Other findings emerging from the URHC analysis of the police data appeared to challenge some of the assumptions and expectations associated with the 'stranger danger' model. For example, contrary to the expectation that most violence takes place in the late evening/early morning the URHC analysis found, a large proportion of the reported violence occurred in the afternoon and early evening: between 15:00 and 21:00.[19]

I want to examine more closely two findings that relate to some of the key features of the 'stranger danger' pattern of homophobic violence already identified; the perpetrator/victim relationship and the location of violence. The URHC project examined these particular dimensions of homophobic violence by way of a re-examination of police data. A new qualitative analysis was undertaken of 101 incidents, reported in January 2001. This was then compared with the original analysis of the police data captured in the six-month period from January to June. Some interesting and important differences emerged.

Beginning with perpetrator/victim relationship, the dominant category formally recorded in the police data was 'no relationship/unknown' as 65 per cent of the incidents reported were categorised in this way. In the first instance, this would appear to support the 'stranger danger' model of homophobic violence. However, the re-analysis of January 2001's data produced a different picture of the interpersonal dimensions of the reported violence. In part, this change can be accounted for by the poor application of several already used police categories. 'Partner/ex-partner' rose from 2 per cent to 4 per cent. 'Family' increased from 0.3 per cent to 2.0 per cent. 'Business associate' changed from 2.7 per cent to 4 per cent. Another factor is the introduction of two new categories of perpetrators: 'neighbours' and 'locals/local youths'. Almost 21 per cent of perpetrators now

18 This is in sharp contrast to incidents of racial violence for the same period where the ratio of male to female victims was approximately 3:2.
19 URHC Homophobic Violence Factsheet, undated.

fell into the category 'neighbours'. Nearly 28 per cent were 'locals/local youths'. The 'stranger' now appeared to account for just under 15 per cent of perpetrators.

The re-analysis also challenges the spatial assumptions of the 'stranger danger' model of violence: the predominance of 'public space' as the location of sexual violence. Under 40 per cent of incidents now appear to occur in public places: 17.8 per cent in the street, just under 10 per cent in or near bars and clubs and 3 per cent near cruising grounds. Over 50 per cent of incidents are reported as taking place in or near the home (53.5 per cent). The major challenge here is the importance of the home and its immediate environs as a location of homophobic violence. The violence in the relatively anonymous locales of the street and town and city centres now appears to be far from the norm.

What are the conclusions that can be drawn from the re-analysis of the interpersonal dimensions of the reported homophobic violence? The re-analysis of the information recorded in the police data exposes a very different set of interpersonal relations and locations of violence than that captured in the 'official version of those events. The official version appears to be influenced by a set of entrenched and persistent expectations and assumptions associated with the 'stranger danger' model of violence. The re-analysis exposes the operation of these assumptions and expectations that inform the police interpretation and perception of the violence contained within their own data. While the URHC study can tell us little about the gap between the number of homophobic incidents reported to the police and those that are unreported, it points to a new gap: a gap in understanding the nature of the violence being reported. This is a gap between what would appear to be the dominant perceptions, assumptions and understandings about the nature and experiences of homophobic violence and the characteristics of the homophobic incidents actually captured in the incidents reported to the police. The dominant characteristics of the reported incidents are not those associated with 'stranger violence' but more associated with acquaintance violence. It is more likely to take place in or near the home or the person's place of work. Its perpetrators are more likely to be neighbours, local youths and others who may be known to the victim. It might occur at any time of the day or night. The random anonymous acts in public places now appear to be more like an exceptional form of homophobic violence reported to the police rather than its most common form. The effects of this change of understanding, I would suggest, are to be welcomed providing a different, more complicated, diverse and nuanced picture of homophobic incidents. Better quality information may assist in the improvement of police services to those in need.

The new gap exposes and makes problematic some of the key assumptions, understandings and expectations generated by the pattern of 'stranger danger' in previous police representations of their own data. Does it also offer a challenge to many lesbian and gay community victim surveys that also seem to be informed by the 'stranger danger' mode? An immediate response to this new challenge might be that the incidents of 'stranger danger' now revealed to be absent from the official police data, might be found, like the other missing data, in lesbian and gay community victim surveys. The Bexley and Greenwich data and analysis provides an opportunity to explore this matter. It is to the patterns of experience of homophobic violence in this community data that I now want to turn to.

## Study 2: Bexley and Greenwich

The BandG survey used a methodology common to many community-based victim surveys. Data was generated by way of a self-completion questionnaire, which asked a series of questions about homophobic, transphobic[20] and domestic violence experiences of LGBT people in Bexley and Greenwich. The survey questions about violence referred to two time periods: lifetime and the last 12 months.[21] The questionnaire distribution strategy was designed to achieve wide-spread dissemination. The database of 164 completed questionnaires, while small in number, is similar to datasets produced in other community surveys.[22]

In many respects, the lesbian and gay experiences of homophobic violence[23] captured in the BandG data are similar to those captured in other community victims surveys.[24] For example, with regard to lifetime experiences of homophobic violence,[25] 69 per cent of survey respondents reported they had experienced homophobic violence in that period; 3 in 4 male respondents and 2 in 3 female respondents had experiences of homophobic violence. A breakdown of the BandG data into experiences of those identified as living in the two boroughs exposes some differences between experiences in those locations. For example, a smaller number of Bexley respondents (53 per cent) than respondents from Greenwich (73 per cent) had experienced homophobic violence in their lifetime. Variations between different boroughs of London are not unexpected. For example the 2003 survey of LGBT experiences in Newham (Barlow 2003), a London borough to the north and east of Bexley and Greenwich, found that 42 per cent of respondents reported having experienced homophobic incidents during their lifetime.

The similarities between the BandG data and other community victim surveys are not confined to the general findings about lifetime experiences of violence.

---

20  See Moran *et al.*, 2004. For work on transgender experiences of violence, see Moran and Sharpe, 2002 and 2004.
21  In the United Kingdom, victim surveys have asked questions about experiences of violence using a number of different periods of time. Lifetime and 'within the last 5 years' have been most common. The lack of consistency poses problems when comparisons are made. It has been suggested that the period of time used may disproportionately affect the levels of reporting. Green *et al.*, 2001, suggest that, 'respondents are as likely to recall an event occurring during the past year as during the past 5 years, and younger respondents are significantly more likely than older respondents to report having been victimized at some point during their lives' (2001a: 493).
22  For full details of the demographic composition of the respondents, see Moran *et al.*, 2004.
23  The limited data on domestic violence will not be discussed in this chapter.
24  See Wake *et al.*, 1999 and Stormbreak, 2003.
25  Throughout, unless otherwise specified, the phrase 'homophobic violence' includes violence, threats and harassment.

*Table 1* Type of violence: HO ever experienced by gender and borough

| Type of violence/Borough (%) | HO (%) | Bexley (%) | | Greenwich | |
|---|---|---|---|---|---|
| Gender | All | M | F | M | F |
| Physical | 13 | 15 | 0 | 16 | 15 |
| Threat | 34 | 23 | 40 | 39 | 33 |
| Harassmentsolides/Abuse | 40 | 38 | 60 | 39 | 30 |
| Damage to property | 10 | 23 | 0 | 5 | 15 |
| Rape | 2 | 0 | 0 | 0 | 4 |
| Other sexual violence | 1 | 0 | 0 | 0 | 4 |
| Total | 100 | 100 | 100 | 100 | 100 |

Source: Moran *et al.*, 2004.[26]

The types of incidents reported analysed by way of borough and gender (see Table 1) are consistent with other community survey findings.

The results collected in this table suggest that threats and harassment are the dominant forms of violence reported. While there is some variation between the experiences of violence of gay men and lesbians, there are many similarities. Again this is a phenomenon reported in other community surveys. For example the Birmingham's Pink Shield survey reported that 26 per cent male and 14 per cent female respondents experienced incidents of violence while 43 per cent male and 39 per cent female respondents had experienced harassment.[27]

The BandG survey, like other community survey results, points to differences between the violence captured in community surveys and that found in the routinely collected official data. In particular, more experiences of violence and more experiences of violence reported by women are key differences.

The BandG data relating to experiences of violence in the last 12 months provides more details of the violence being experienced. I begin again with some general findings; 38 per cent of all respondents reported experiences of homophobic violence. It is perhaps a trite point to note that respondents report higher levels of violence in their lifetime experience than in the last 12 months. A comparison with other community data is more difficult here as there are fewer community surveys using this time frame. One point of comparison is the Scottish report, *The experiences of violence and harassment of gay men in the city of Edinburgh*.[28] That report found 26 per cent of all respondents had experienced some form of violence in the last 12 months. The BandG data suggests a rather higher rate of experiences of homophobic violence in a 12-month period. Tables 2 and 3 offer a comparison of experiences in the two boroughs.

26  All tables are reproduced with the permission of the authors.
27  Pink Shield, 2002: 5.
28  Morrison and Mackay, 2000.

Table 2  Homophobic incidents in the last
         12 months/Borough

| Borough | Bexley (%) | Greenwich (%) |
|---|---|---|
| Yes | 32 | 45 |
| No | 43 | 40 |
| Not stated | 24 | 15 |

Source: Moran et al., 2004.

Table 3  Homophobic incidents in the last 12 months/
         Borough/Gender

| Borough | Bexley (%) | | Greenwich (%) | |
|---|---|---|---|---|
| Gender | M | F | M | F |
| Yes | 44 | 24 | 54 | 36 |
| No | 38 | 48 | 29 | 52 |
| Not stated | 19 | 24 | 17 | 13 |

Source: Moran et al., 2004.

Again, there is some evidence of differences between the experiences of those in the two boroughs, and between male and female experiences. Residents of Greenwich report more experiences of homophobic violence than Bexley residents. More men than women report experiences of violence. It is by reference to the 12 months' data that I want to explore the significance or otherwise of the 'stranger danger' model of violence, in more detail again by way of a focus on the data relating to the interpersonal and spatial dimensions of the violence reported.

Examining the interpersonal relations in the data we find that in almost two-thirds of all the incidents reported (64 per cent) the victims reported that they knew the perpetrators. This group of persons 'known' to the victims is made up of family and ex-family members (28 per cent), neighbours (15 per cent) colleagues at work and school (14 per cent) and persons 'known by sight' (9 per cent). By contrast, the category 'stranger' accounts for just under 30 per cent of the incidents. This pattern, with a preponderance of perpetrators 'known' to the victim, remains when the data is analysed by reference to respondents who self-identified as living in the two boroughs.

One issue raised by these findings is the importance of 'family members', a category that includes partners and ex-partners, household members and other relatives. While this group of perpetrators was identified by respondents in the context of questions focusing specifically on homophobic incidents (rather than questions of domestic violence), there is some potential for respondents to conflate these different types of violence and thereby the perpetrators of these different modes of violence. When an analysis is conducted without these incidents, 'strangers' account for a rather larger percentage of the total incidents, being 48 per cent of the reported perpetrators.

A slightly higher incidence of stranger violence in the BandG survey may offer some evidence in support of the conclusion that incidents involving strangers are under-reported. However, in considering the relative importance of 'stranger' as a category of perpetrator in community data, a note of caution needs to be raised. The term 'stranger' is problematic. In community victim surveys, at best, it records the victim's knowledge of the perpetrator. As Mason notes, this may not coincide with the perpetrators 'knowledge' of the victim.[29] Unbeknownst to the victim, the perpetrator may, over time, have observed and made judgements about the victim without the victim's knowledge. The perpetrator may 'know' the victim by way of gossip networks operating in a particular location or as a result of regular chance encounters. Furthermore, the perpetrator's 'knowledge' need not be a correct judgement about the victim's sexual orientation. Actual knowledge of the victim's sexuality is not a necessary feature of this judgement. The perpetrator's perception is both necessary and sufficient. Thus, a victim's use of the category 'strangers' may be a partial reading of the nature of the relationship that is played out in the act of violence or harassment.

With these points in mind it remains important to note that 'neighbours' continue to account for a large number of perpetrators (21 per cent), as do colleagues at work and in school and college settings (20 per cent). Perpetrators 'known by sight' accounts for another 11 per cent. In short, perpetrators who are 'known' to the victim remain in the majority.

Turning to the data on locations of violence, Table 4 offers a breakdown of the spatial distribution of violence and a breakdown by way of the different types of violence.

Table 4 Spatial distribution of different types of homophobic violence

| Location/Type of violence | In or near the home | In or near work place school, college | In or near a LGBT venue | Other |
|---|---|---|---|---|
| Physical | 11 | 1 | 3 | — |
| Threat | 20 | 8 | 4 | — |
| Harassment/Abuse | 25 | 13 | 2 | 1 |
| Damage to property | 12 | 1 | — | — |
| Rape | 4 | — | — | — |
| Other sexual violence | 2 | — | — | — |
| Total = 107 | 74 | 23 | 9 | 1 |
| + % | 69 | 21 | 8 | 1 |

Source: Moran et al., 2004.

29  Mason, 2003.

Of particular interest is the dominance of incidents located in or near the home. This location accounts for almost 70 per cent of the incidents reported. Incidents in or near a LGBT venue account for less than 10 per cent of incidents. We should note, however, that it is in this particular location that the balance between different types of violence seems to shift to more serious violence; 33 per cent of incidents in this location were acts of violence rather than threats of harassment. An analysis of the data for the two boroughs produces a similar spatial distribution of violence. A further analysis of the spatial aspects of the reported violence in the borough data by reference to gender, indicates that in Greenwich a larger percentage of women than men report the location of incidents as in or near the home (89 per cent female in contrast to 61 per cent male respondents). In Bexley, men and women report similar spatial distributions; 69 per cent of men and 67 per cent of women experiencing violence in or near the home. In Bexley, no male respondents reported incidents in or near LGBT venues whereas 13 per cent of women had experienced violence in these locations. In contrast to this, 23 per cent of male respondents in Greenwich reported incidents in or near LGBT venues while no women reported this as locations of violence.

What are the conclusions that can be drawn from this reading of the findings of the BandG survey? I would suggest that the findings offer a challenge to the 'stranger danger' model of violence found in other community surveys. This also echoes the challenges to the dominance of the 'stranger danger' model of violence generated by the URHC re-analysis of routine data.

Perhaps the most significant challenge is in the findings that relate to the location of violence in the BandG data. In sharp contrast to other community victim surveys, the BandG data suggests that anonymous public spaces are relatively insignificant as locations of homophobic violence. The home and its immediate environs are the most important. Furthermore, in the BandG findings, violence in or near the home takes on an even greater significance than that indicated in the re-analysis of police data undertaken by the URHC researchers.

How might the different spatial distribution of homophobic violence found in the BandG data be explained? Other researchers, particularly scholars focusing on North America,[30] have indicated that neighbourhoods are a major location of homophobic violence. However, there is a need for caution here. The North American experience may not easily translate into the United Kingdom, or more specifically, the London, context. In good part the spatial concentration of gay men in inner city neighbourhoods in North America cities may provide one explanation for the dominance of the neighbourhood as the locus of homophobic violence in North American studies.[31] These gay neighbourhoods, closely connected to inner

---

30  Green *et al.*, 2001.

31  There is a large body of literature on the spatial concentration of gay men and lesbians in North America, for example, Adler and Brenner, 1992; Bouthillette, 1997; Castells, 1983; Castells and Murphy, 1982; Forest, 1995; Knopp, 1994.

city regeneration and gentrification, produce relatively visible sexual minority communities. While there is some spatial concentration of lesbians and gay men in certain areas of central and east London, as has already been noted, neither Bexley nor Greenwich could be easily characterised in this way. Spatial concentration may not be the primary or only factor giving rise to visibility and thereby knowledge of sexual identity in these particular locations.[32]

At the same time, the dominance of the home and its environs as a key location of homophobic violence may still be intimately connected to knowledge of, and the relative visibility of, lesbians and gay men. An example from the study of lesbian and gay responses to homophobic violence in Manchester and Lancaster illustrates how this proximity might work to produce visibility and knowledge. One of the participants in the Manchester lesbian focus group explained how her children, and their friendships with other children in the neighbourhood, exposed her lesbian relationship to surveillance by neighbours.[33] Here knowledge/visibility is not so much an effect of a concentration of lesbian and gay households in a particular locale but more an effect of an inescapable proximity and intimacy. This arises out of everyday inter-family interactions, neighbourhood encounters and workplace contacts arising out of participation in the multiple networks of interactions that make up the many close relationships that occur as part of the routine of daily life.

Despite the evidence of the under-reporting gap in the BandG findings there are several key points of connection between the types of incidents captured in community based data and the routinely collected police data. More specifically, the BandG survey echoes some of the challenges to the dominance of the 'stranger danger' model of violence made in the URHC study. There appears to be an unexpected concordance between police and community data. At the same time the BandG findings offer a challenge to the dominance of 'stranger violence' reported in community surveys.

Much of the analysis in this chapter has focused upon challenging the dominance of the 'stranger danger' model of homophobic violence. Both the URHC re-analysis of official data and the BandG survey data problematise that dominance. At the same time it is important to recognise that the 'stranger danger' model appears to be a set of assumptions and approaches to violence that is common to what purport to be very different datasets produced in different institutional and social contexts. Their shared resort to the 'stranger danger' model of violence raises an important issue about the social and cultural significance of this model of violence. In the final section of this chapter, I want to address the following questions: What is the social and cultural significance of the 'stranger danger' model of violence? What idea of community, of law and order communities and more specifically of places of safety and danger is being made in and through the 'stranger danger' model of violence in this context?

32  Mason, 2001 and 2002; Corteen, 2002.
33  For a more extended analysis see Moran and Skeggs, 2004: Chapter 8.

## Making strange: homophobic violence and the city

It is through an analysis of the idea of the 'stranger' that I want to offer an insight into the particular social and cultural significance of 'stranger danger'. Zygmunt Bauman offers the following insight into the nature of strangers and strangeness. He begins, 'There are friends and enemies. And there are *strangers*.'[34] Here, Bauman highlights the peculiar position of the stranger and the nature of strangeness. The stranger is a third figure. In the first instance, Bauman suggests, there is the relation of friend to enemy, which he describes as a 'master opposition': between inside and outside. This is a violent hierarchy that

> ...sets apart truth from falsity, good from evil, beauty from ugliness. It also differentiates between proper and improper, right and wrong, tasteful and unbecoming. It makes the world readable and thereby instructive. It dispels doubt... It assures that one goes where one should.[35]

The violent hierarchy has a very specific quality. It produces an effect of certainty and stability. Bauman describes the relation as a 'cosy antagonism' and a 'collusion';[36] here the 'enemy' is always represented as distinct, separate and distant from the friend, geographically, socially and culturally. The third term, 'stranger', is a figure that disrupts this stable and comfortable state of affairs.

The stranger, Bauman tells us, disrupts this cosy state of affairs in the following way. The stranger is '*neither* friend *nor* enemy; because he may be *both*.'[37] The stranger conflates opposites. Thus the stranger is truth *and* falsity; good *and* evil; propriety *and* impropriety. The figure of the stranger, Simmel notes, has also a spatial dimension: the stranger is distant *and* proximate.[38] The stranger is a unity of nearness and remoteness. This characterisation of the stranger is in sharp contrast to the friend/enemy dichotomy in which opposites are managed by way of a clear and relatively stable distribution of the positive (friend) and the negative (enemy).

The figure of the stranger embodies and personifies a troubling and persistent ambivalence, representing the world as an unreadable place, a place of doubt and uncertainty. It is a figure that gives form to an experience of loss, of orientation, of direction and place. In the figure of the stranger the 'distant is actually near'. The stranger also personifies the troubling durability of these concerns as the stranger is the one who comes today *and* stays.[39] As a relation of 'both', 'and', the stranger, Bauman suggests, personifies a special threat and an exceptional danger 'more horrifying than that which one can fear from the enemy.'[40] (1991: 55)

---

34 Bauman, 1991: 53, emphasis in original.
35 Bauman, 1991: 54.
36 Ibid. 55.
37 Ibid. emphasis added.
38 Simmel, 1964.
39 Ibid. 402.
40 Bauman, 1991: 55.

It is the combination of these themes in the figure of the stranger that makes strangeness a powerful and disturbing force.

Simmel (1964) also offers important insights into the social and cultural role of the 'stranger'. 'The stranger' is a figure that embodies particular positive relations and a specific form of interaction, a set of relations through which the dynamics of both the individual and the collective, the group, the community, come into being. Simmel notes, the stranger connects the two, being 'an element of the group itself': *both* a fully-fledged member *and* one who is perceived to be 'outside it and confronting it'.[41]

In her analysis of the pervasive contemporary concern with strangers (which she describes as stranger fetishism), Ahmed offers another important insight.[42] She argues that stranger fetishism is in part a displacement of social relations onto an object (in the traditional Marxist take on fetishism). But it is also more than this: it transforms objects into figures. The figure of the 'friend', 'enemy' and 'stranger', I want to suggest, turns the social relations of good order in general and the legal order in particular, into anthropomorphic categories associated with particular locations. Bhabha suggests that it is the proximity of strangers that forces, figures and enables the production of difference.[43] Shane Phelan argues that, '[u]nderstanding strangeness requires an examination of the regime that creates it.'[44]

How does this translate into the context of 'stranger danger'? How does it help us to understand the particular obsession with 'stranger danger'? First, through the connection with 'strangeness', danger in general and violence in particular are given a distinctive meaning. Making violence 'strange' animates assumptions and expectations that particular types of violence are especially powerful and dangerous, a particularly threatening and disturbing force impacting upon individuals, immediate communities and society at large. Through this association, this violence is figured as a particular terror, experienced as a conflation of opposites: representing disorder at the very heart of order; evil where only good can grow; conflating right and wrong. It ought not to be forgotten that the violence associated with all these characteristics and profoundly disturbing emotions has a particular location: public places. Richard Sennet has documented the now long-standing existential anxieties associated with public places and urban, metropolitan space.[45] Through the dominant assumption of 'stranger danger' violence in public places is understood as an immanent profound threat of loss of place and direction. Through the characterisation of the perpetrator as a 'stranger', namely the outsider who comes *and stays*, that immanent profound threat is given a certain permanence. To mark someone a stranger is to attach these particular

---

41  Simmel, 1964: 402.
42  Ahmed, 2000.
43  Bhabha, 1996.
44  Phelan, 2001: 37.
45  Sennett, 1992; See also Bauman, 2003.

qualities, not only to the act of violence, but also to the body of the person made strange. Strangeness gives form to and incorporates our fears in general and our fears of public places in particular.[46]

If the terror of stranger danger is particularly associated with public places, then perhaps the spatial location of the experience of the 'master opposition' between friend and enemy, the 'cosy antagonism' that makes the social and legal order of the city readable as an achieved good order, is one that is associated with the home and the immediate neighbourhood. The home and the neighbourhood offer a location for a sentimental fantasy of safety and security and of social justice in a city made by way of clear distinctions between order and disorder, of law and lawlessness, of safety and danger. Furthermore, the distinction between home/neighbourhood and public places is a neat division between respectively certainty, clarity and the establishment of proper meanings on the one hand, and uncertainty, confusion and the threat of multiple and divergent meanings on the other. Paraphrasing Bauman, through this opposition, doubt is dispelled. Everything is in its place and as it should be.[47] This master opposition is a violent hierarchy with a very specific quality: it gives rise to an experience of certainty and stability. Confining the destabilising and disorientating violence to the public realm is a comfortable state of affairs, as it preserves the sentimental fantasy of home as a place of good order and safety.

It is in and through this imagined sentimental state of comfort that the 'stranger' is the anthropomorphic term that makes sense of an experience of disruption. Stranger fetishism is a set of assumptions, expectations and emotions to do with reading, interpretation and judgement associated with particular (urban) locations. The stranger signifies difference as disruption. The stranger forces, figures and enables the production of the idea of the group, the community, the city as a place of law and order separated out from the place of lawlessness and disorder. Through these figures associated with the public sphere the idea of the good order of an individual, a particular community, in this instance the city, is imagined, expressed and imposed.

The stranger stands for the perceived blurring of distinctions and the fragility of boundaries conflating order and disorder, safety and danger, security and insecurity, law and lawlessness. Furthermore, through the idea of 'strangeness', the experience of the city as the location of good order is made as an experience of an urban order under threat accompanied by a particular sense of terror, horror, fear,[48] as well as excitement and pleasure.[49] The pervasiveness of 'stranger danger',

---

46  Lesbians and gay men have long experienced the alienating and threatening force of being figured as 'strangers', 'out of place'. See Moran and Skeggs, 2004.

47  Bauman, 1991: 54.

48  Fear, Judith Shklar, 1989, suggests, plays an important role in liberal democracies. On horror and the urban, see Mighall, 1999. For an introduction to the literature on fear of crime, see Hale, 1996.

49  Much less has been written about the excitement cities and the role of strangers in the fabrication of that excitement. For a rare example in the context of fear of crime literature, see Neill, 2001 and Gilloch, 1996.

in both police and community attempts to understand and make sense of homophobic violence, points perhaps to the widespread significance of these existential anxieties in contemporary culture, and the persistence of attempts to preserve the idea of the home and neighbourhood as a haven of good order.[50] As the analysis earlier suggests, they fail to capture the complex reality of homophobic violence, at least in contemporary London.

Following these insights, the task, I want to suggest, then becomes one that requires an exploration of the nature of the social and legal order that is being represented in and through the figure of the stranger in both police and community uses of 'stranger danger'. What social and cultural distinctions of class, gender, race, ethnicity and so on, are being put to work through the figure of the 'stranger', in order to imagine the good order of the city? Sadly, such a task is beyond the confines of this short chapter.

## Conclusions

The murder of David Morely was a devastating event with immediate individual and community impact. The analysis offered here suggests that it is not only exceptional in terms of the extreme nature of the violence but also with regard to the more general portrait of violence that it seems to represent. Most of the homophobic violence taking place in London is routine violence that is occurring in the inner city and suburban homes, in the environs that surround those homes, in the workplace, schools and colleges of the metropolis. It is a violence that is perpetrated by family, friends, neighbours, work-mates and colleagues. Perhaps of more importance is the argument developed here that this diversity of settings and inter-relationships is poorly represented in community surveys that seek to paint a clearer and more accurate picture of experiences of homophobic violence. In part, this might be due to the inadequacies of the surveys themselves. The questions that might expose the complex nature of this violence remain unasked. In part, I have argued, it is due to problematic assumptions, understandings and expectations that inform the generation of these community initiatives.

For a long time these initiatives have been motivated by a belief in a gap between experiences captured in police data and those represented in community-based survey data. While my analysis offers further support for some aspects of this 'gap', it also exposes some key connections and similarities between the picture of homophobic violence represented in these different bodies of data, in particular, police data.

The analysis suggests that the various representations of homophobic violence, be they in the context of police reports or in community surveys, have another dimension in common: a particular investment in a complex of assumptions about the nature and place of violence. The analysis offered here

---

50  See Moran and Skeggs, 2004: Chapter 6.

suggests that the experiences of lesbians and gay men, be they reporting to the police or responding to requests for information from community and activist organisations, are frequently mediated through the 'stranger danger' model of violence. 'Stranger danger' is a fantasy of social order and disorder that appears to be shared by a wide range of institutions, organisations and communities.

In the foregoing analysis, I have suggested that the figure of the stranger plays a key role in the formation of ideas of particular places and communities. The dominance of 'stranger danger' in the context of the datasets on homophobic violence considered here, points to the importance of the fantasy of the stranger in the constitution of London as an imagined sexual community of violence and disorder, and good order. The continued and apparently widespread appearance of the assumptions and expectations associated with 'stranger danger' models of violence raises important challenges for those generating new data about the nature and prevalence of violence. It also raises challenges for those promoting new initiatives that seek to respond to homophobic violence, for those who monitor policing operations, and also for those who carry out the day-to-day operation of existing laws, be they law enforcement agencies or wider support services.

## Bibliography

Adler, S and Brenner, J (1992) 'Gender and Space: Lesbians and Gay Men in the City', 16(1) *International Journal of Urban and Regional Research* 24–34

Ahmed, S (2000) *Strange Encounters: Embodied Others in PostColoniality*, London: Routledge

Anon (2004) 'Teenage Gang Beats Gay Man to Death', 2 November, *Cape Times*, at http://capetimes.co.za (accessed on 5 June 2005)

Baird, B (1997) 'Putting Police on Notice: A South Australian Case Study', in Mason, G and Tomsen, S (eds), *Homophobic Violence*, Sydney: Hawkins Press

Barlow, P (2003) *Speaking Out! Experiences of Lesbians, Gay Men, Bisexuals and Transgender People in Newham*, Newham: London Borough of Newham

Bauman, Z (1991) *Modernity and Ambivalence*, Cambridge: Polity Press

Bauman, Z (2003) *Liquid Love*, Cambridge: Polity Press

Bhabha, H (1996) 'Rethinking Authority: Interview with Homi Bhabha', 2(2) *Angelaki* 59–65

Bouthillette, A M (1997) 'Queer and Gendered Housing: A Tale of Two Neighbourhoods in Vancouver', in Ingram, G B, Bouthillette, A and Retter, Y (eds), *Queers in Space*, Seattle: Bay Press

Bowley, M (2000) 'A Cancer at the Heart of Society', *New Law Journal*, 4 August, 1203

Branigan, T (2004) 'Gay Man Stabbed on Night Bus', *The Guardian*, 6 November, 3

Castells, M (1983) 'Cultural Identity, Sexual Liberation and Urban Structure: The Gay Community in San Fransisco', in Castells, M (ed.), *The City and the Grassroots: A Cross-Cultural Theory of Urban Social Movements*, Berkeley, CA: University of California Press, 169–198

Castells, M and Murphy, K (1982) 'Cultural Identity and Urban Structure: The Spatial Organisation of San Fransisco's Gay Community', in Fainstein, N and Fainstein, S (eds), *Urban Policy under Capitalism*, Beverly Hills, CA: Sage, 223–250

Corteen, K (2002) 'Lesbian Safety Talk: Problematizing Definitions and Experiences of Violence, Sexuality and Space', 5(3) *Sexualities* 259–280

Forest, B (1995) 'West Hollywood as Symbol: The Significance of Place in the Construction of Gay Identity', 13 *Environment and Planning Development: Society and Space* 133–157

Gilloch, G (1996) *Myth and Metropolis: Walter Benjamin and the City*, Cambridge: Polity

Green, D P, McFalls, L H and Smith J K (2001) 'Hate Crime: an Emergent Research Agenda', 27 *Annual Review of Sociology* 479–504

Hale, C (1996) 'Fear of Crime: a Review of the Literature', 14 *International Review of Victimology* 79–150

Janoff, D V (2005) *Homophobic Violence in Canada*, Toronto: University of Toronto Press

Jarman, N and Tennant, A (2003) 'An Acceptable Prejudice? Homophobic Harassment in Northern Ireland', Belfast: Institute for Conflict Research

Kaufman, M (2001) *The Laramie Project*, USA: HBO

Knopp, L (1994) 'Social Justice, Sexuality and the City', 15(7) *Urban Geography* 644–660

Loffreda, B (2000) *Losing Matt Shepard: Life and Politics in the Aftermath of Anti-gay Murder*, New York: Columbia University Press

Mason, A and Palmer, A (1996) *Queer Bashing: A National Survey of Hate Crimes against Lesbians and Gay Men*, London: Stonewall

Mason, G (2001) 'Body Maps: Envisaging Homophobia, Violence and Safety', 10(1) *Social and Legal Studies* 23–44

Mason, G (2002) *The Spectacle of Violence: Homophobia Gender and Knowledge*, London: Routledge

Mason, G (2003) A Study of Allegations of Racial and Homophobic Harassment Recorded by the London Metropolitan Police Service between January and June 2001, Unpublished

Mattinson, J (2001) 'Stranger and Acquaintance Violence: Practice Messages from the British Crime Survey', *Briefing Note* 7/01, Home Office, London

Mighall, R (1999) *A geography of Victorian Gothic Fiction: Mapping History's Nightmares*, Oxford: Oxford University Press

Moran, L J and Sharpe, A (2002) 'Policing the Transgender/Violence Relation', 13(3) *Current Issues in Criminal Justice* 269–286

Moran, L J and Sharpe, A (2004) 'Violence, Identity and Policing: The Case of Violence against Transgender People', 4(4) *Criminal Justice* 395–417

Moran, L J and Skeggs, B (2004) *Sexuality and the Politics of Violence and Safety*, London: Routledge

Moran, L J, Paterson, S and Docherty, T (2004) *'Count me in!' A Report on the Bexley and Greenwich Homophobic Crime Survey*, Bexley and Greenwich, London, at www.galop.org.uk (accessed on 4 December 2006)

Morrison, C and Mackay, A (2000) *The Experience of Violence and Harassment of Gay Men in the City of Edinburgh*, Edinburgh: Scottish Executive Central Research Unit

Neill, W J V (2001) 'Marketing the Urban Experience: Reflections on the Place of Fear in the Promotional Strategies of Belfast, Detroit and Berlin', 38(5–6) *Urban Studies* 815–828

Phelan, S (2001) *Sexual Strangers: Gays, Lesbians and the Dilemmas of Citizenship*, Philadelphia, PA: Temple University Press

Pink Shield Project (2002) *A Matter of Trust: Recommendations from the Pink Shield Project*, Birmingham: Birmingham Police Forum for the Gay Community

Sennet, R (1992) *The Fall of Public Man*, New York: W W Norton

Shklar, J N (1989) 'The Liberalism of Fear', in Rosenblum, N L (ed.), *Liberalism and Moral Life*, Cambridge, MA: Harvard Univesrity Press, 21–38

Simmel, G (1964) 'The Stranger' in Wolff, K H (ed.), *The Sociology of George Simmel*, New York: The Free Press

Stanko, E A, Kielinger, V, Paterson, S and Richards, L (2003) 'Grounded Crime Prevention: Responding to and Understanding Hate Crime', in Kury, H and Obergfell-Fuchs, J (eds), *Crime Prevention, New Approaches*, Mainz: Weisser Ring, 123–152

Stevens, M (2004) 'That blood on the road is mine', 3 November, *The Times*, 2

Stormbreak (2003) *Gay Life and Style: New Millenium Survey*, London: Stormbreak Ltd

URHC (Understanding and Responding to Hate Crime) (undated) *Homophobic Violence Factsheet*, London: Metropolitan Police Service

Wake, I, Wilmot, I, Fairweather, P and Birkett, J (1999) *Breaking the Chain of Hate: A National Survey Examining the Level of Homophobic Crime and Community Confidence Towards the Police Service*, Manchester, National Advisory Group

Chapter 5

# Singapore
## The one-night stand with the law

*Thilo Tetzlaff* *

## Singapore: law and order?

The KrisFlyer armchairs started to feel uncomfortable towards the end of the six-hour flight from Sydney. Yes, they were undeniably the best airline seats available, still, the dry air in the cabin dehydrated the skin and Samantha's legs felt like marble pillars. She had already filled in the immigration card, which contained a bold notice in red: 'death penalty for drug traffickers under Singapore law'. After some googling on Singapore before her trip, Samantha had come to take that warning extremely seriously: the US Department of State also warns travellers about Singapore's 'strict laws and penalties for...jaywalking, littering and spitting, as well as the importation and sale of chewing gum'.[1]

This was not a place of subtle persuasion or lax authority. What a contrast with the cute Mexican policeman who had been satisfied with a closer look at her breast after speeding!

The passport control desks at Changi Airport reflected the various different categories of people entering the country: visitors, temporary workers, permanent residents and citizens. There was no counter, however, for the thousands of illegal immigrants working on construction sites across the city. The cab, an older Chinese driver behind the wheel, left the terminal and followed the coastline. As they reached the end of the coastal highway, Samantha saw a construction worker urinating against the pillar of a bridge – surprisingly he was not shot immediately.

## No slings attached

Before the cab turned into Bras Basah Road, the new attraction of Singapore, the Esplanade – Theatres on the Bay, nicknamed the Durian, appeared at the horizon. The latter building, which looks like a shiny hedgehog, is a key component of the

* For collaboration and contribution I have to acknowledge Laura Edge. The usual claimers and disclaimers apply.

1 http://travel.state.gov/travel/cis_pa_tw/cis/cis_1017.html, accessed 10 January 2005.

Singaporean government's strategic plan to stimulate a creative and innovative atmosphere.[2] Hence, in a true cultural shift, Singapore has adopted the aim of becoming a renaissance city with cultural and artistic vibrancy.[3]

The gentle Singapore Airlines flight attendant, who, unfortunately for Samantha, was gay, had gigglingly revealed to her that next to the Esplanade there was Embassy, the new club scene among the Singaporean gay crowd. Henry explained that in this squeaky-clean city-state, gays had a strong presence, were well-dressed – and with few places to go. Gay life might be narrow and suppressed here, but the overall quality of life in Singapore makes it quite bearable. This is no surprise once one has appreciated the shopping facilities on and around Orchard Road, which combined supreme window displays in the engorged international boutiques with gorgeous staff.

From a legal point of view, s 377 of the Penal Code still sanctions acts of gross indecency between *men* (for a split second Samantha thought about her Brazilian artist friend Maria; and also that during her short stay at the National Museum Samantha saw a sign pointing towards the Board of Censors, where scissors mutilated films such as 'Happy Together' and 'Wedding Banquet'). There have been some winds of change recently, most notably an official statement by Prime Minister Goh Chok Tong to Time magazine that gays may be employed by the civil services.[4] Originally, Singapore followed a rather tough approach on gay rights, but then came the Internet, which opened the gate for every kind of communication. As a result, the strict policy changed from a law and order state of the seventies and eighties, to a more open society.[5] But nothing legally reliable yet. Quite recently, the apparently innocuous movies 'Formula 17' and 'Girlfriend' have been banned for obscure reasons, but that of course is a well-known tactic of censorship at all times. But how can there be censorship at all in a city that wants to be culturally and artistically vibrant, Samantha kept wondering.

The cab finally reached the Raffles, the all-time classic hotel, the tourist trap, the home of the Singapore Sling,[6] the temple of hospitality. As a matter of fact, the design of the hotel has changed considerably since it was built in 1887. In 1990, the owner, DBS Land, closed down the hotel and began to remedy some of the twentieth-century interventions and to restore it to its 1915 grandeur. Now, theatres and a restaurant have been included in precisely the same style as the original. Today's visitor is unable to distinguish between the new parts of the building and those dating from before 1915.[7] This is less a matter of coincidence and more of well-organised planning.

2  www.mnd.gov.sg/newsroom/speeches/speeches_nd2001_280401.htm, accessed 18 January 2005.
3  See Lim, 2002: 13.
4  About the relevance for the democratic structure, see Ramraj, 2003: 469.
5  For the path to an open society, see Kurlantzick, 2000/2001: 562.
6  Recipe at Waller, 2003: 320, Singapore Sling: 1 1/2 oz Gin, 1/2 oz Cherry Brandy, 3 dash(es) Benedictine, 1 dash(es), 1 dash(es) Lemon Juice Grenadine, Fill glass(es) Club Soda. Directions/Comments: Shake the first five ingredients in a mixer. Pour into a collins glass and top with Club Soda.
7  Dale, 1999; Henderson, 2001: 16; Powell, 2002: 90.

The 1991 Concept Plan provided a vision for Singapore's physical development for the twenty-first century.[8] Singapore was divided into 55 planning areas, for each of which a Development Guide Plan (GDP) was prepared. These plans translated the broad vision of the Concept Plan into detailed proposals. The GDPs consisted of six sections: Introduction, Existing Conditions, Planning Analysis, Visions and Objectives, Planning Strategies and Planning Proposals. Does this constitute a homogenisation of planning and development? The common answer is that since Singapore has only limited land, it is incumbent upon the planners to optimise its use.

Samantha checked into Raffles. A Helena Rubinstein ginseng bath would prepare her for the city.

## Orchard road and beyond

Samantha started her shopping spree with a healthy snack in the basement restaurant of Wisma Atria. The view from Wisma Atria to Ngee Ann is probably a showcase of what has contributed most to the perception of Singapore as a location of global urbanity. Few public spaces in Singapore have resisted the homogenising forces of consumerism.[9] There are, of course, pockets of resistance. Shopping in Sungei Road, Pasar Lane and Pitt Street differs much from the ubiquitous emporia along Orchard Road. Shops there survived several clean-ups and still offer *pi caw sai* ('very, very cheap') items. In March 1996, notices were erected stating that the traders' occupation of the site was illegal. These notices are now gone, but the traders remain. Again, it is a battle between created memories and historiographies[10] and people's infinite ability to improvise and adapt to new conditions.

This ability is particularly challenged when it comes to occupying the 'void deck'; apparently 'void' decks seem to be a uniquely Singaporean phenomenon. It originated in the housing designs of the 1970s and today there are more than 2000.[11] A 'void deck' is essentially the first floor of a building, which is left free to serve a variety of requirements.[12] Some of these spaces acquired permanent functions as kindergartens, childcare centres or clubs for senior citizens. Others were used on a more temporary basis for weddings, festivals and funeral rites. The void deck was designed to deliver a stronger sense of belonging, to promote social interaction and cohesion. However, they failed, because they never quite managed to look inviting.[13] On the contrary, the overwhelming impression is one of emptiness governed by rules.[14]

---

8  About the development plans see Powell, 1994: 30, more general, Grant, 1999: 1–5.
9  Voyce, 2005: 537.
10  Raban, 1974: 10.
11  Powell, 2002: 96.
12  Widodo, 2003: 58.
13  Hill and Fee, 1995: 27.
14  Powell, 2002: 96.

Orchard Road welcomes everyone and prostitutes itself to anyone. In a way, Orchard Road is a theme park (see the section on Sentosa), but also a social experiment. As a theme park it only has a single theme: shopping. But this theme is also an experiment in constant development. After the independence, and in view of the development in some neighbouring countries, there has been the perceived need to unify the multiethnic population in the form of a consumerist nation. The city geography has facilitated this experiment, not only because it has been easier to perform societal planning in an environment in which city-planning and nation-building fell together, but also because the main road of the city could operate as a showcase for what it means to be Singaporean.

'Calling Orchard Road a shopping district is like calling the Grand Canyon a big ditch.'[15] It is a temple of shopping which, at weekends, seems to attract half of Singapore to its stores, cafes, cinemas and the sheer atmosphere of 'town'. In a way, Orchard Road is the indigenous Singaporean culture. However, it is important to see that this is not simply based on the vanity of shopping, but on the need to shape a cultural identity. In eminent contrast to many other areas of life in Singapore, there are hardly any regulations on shopping. Still, even in its status as a symbol of deregulation, Orchard Road is restricted: a Speaker's Corner in Hong Lim Park, where people can speak without being subjected to the otherwise strict censorship laws. But in contrast to its London counterpart, people who wish to speak must first register at the police station next to the Speakers' Corner and avoid topics that could inflame religious or racial hostility. Furthermore, they are forced to compete with the din of traffic and nearby construction work, not being allowed to use sound amplification themselves because the government has retained a firm stance on prohibiting it. Speakers' Corner is therefore usually empty. How simple shopping is in comparison to that!

Unlike many roads in Singapore, Orchard Road is not named after any specific person. Instead, it takes its name from the many nutmeg plantations, pepper farms and fruit orchards that used to line the street in the 1830s. As the city progressed inland from the Padang area, the plantations of Orchard Road gave way to residential developments, still visible at the northern end. Commercial development was initiated to provide residents with fresh food. In 1958, CK Tang opened the first department store. During the boom years of the 1960s and 1970s, more and more hotels and shopping facilities completed the image, many of them replacing the stars of earlier times, such as the Cairnhill Steak House and the Mont'dor Cafe.

New stars do not only appear on Orchard Road: the Mass Rapid Transport (MRT) began to map the Singaporean landscape. Whereas Samantha refused to take the underground in Manhattan and preferred to take a cab, the Singaporean

---

15 'Singapore Rising', Traveller May/June 2001, www.offtherails.com/spore.html, accessed 28 January 2005.

version of subterranean travel was a far more pleasant view. Samantha took the MRT from Somerset to City Hall. Travelling without the fear of being mugged was a new feeling. At the time of its initial construction, the MRT project was considered the largest public work project in Singaporean history.[16] The MRT is also the birthplace of a law which has contributed to Singapore's image as an ultra-clean city: this is none else but the ban on the production and sale of chewing gum. The ban originally applied only to the MRT system and only later was it extended to the whole city. There are a number of different stories as to why the ban was first introduced, but the most likely explanation is that some youngsters tried to block the sensors of the doors on MRT trains, which endangered the national dream of a smooth-running public transport system. Ironically, it is the cigarette or rather its antagonist, the nicotine chewing gum, which helped to lift this ban, at least if one can present a prescription.

The search for the latest Gucci handbag made it inevitable that Samantha walked up and down Orchard Road several times. Even so, there was still time to turn into some of the smaller residential streets at the Northern end of the street. The interlacing of modernity and colonial style is one of Singapore's leitmotifs. Law is no different. It is still unclear to what extent the present Singaporean legal system relies on the colonial heritage of the English law. In 1993, the *Application of the English Law Act* tried to offer some legal certainty,[17] and consequently has been hailed as a landmark statute that eradicates uncertainties surrounding the applicability of English law.[18] Still, it can be envisaged that the transplantation of English law will continue to be of legal relevance. Meanwhile, there is an increasing number of alternative influences on the Singaporean legal system: the *Evidence Act*, for example, is of Indian origin,[19] and the Singapore *Companies Act* contains Australian influences.[20] In contrast, Singaporean land law is uniquely Singaporean.[21] This is also true of the Singaporean constitution.

Regardless of the various influences, the strong focus on the inherited Westminster model remains, with a separation of powers and, in particular, its independent and relatively efficient judiciary. Earlier backlog problems with cases have been resolved.[22] Additionally, Singaporean commercial law constantly establishes new platforms for Alternative Dispute Resolutions (ADR).[23] Both traditional courts and ADR panels endorse strict case-management which relies on many resources, technological as well as human, in order to speed up the

---

16 Cervero, 1998: 164.
17 No 35 of 1993; now Cap 7 A 1994 Rev. Ed.
18 Phang, 2000: 28.
19 Cap 97, 1997 Rev Ed.
20 Cap 50, 1994 Rev Ed.
21 Tan, 1997b: 12.
22 How, 1998: 211.
23 Phang, 2000: 35.

procedures. This becomes obvious in the design of some Subordinate Courts for specific purposes, for example the Bail and Witness Videolink Courts and the Night Courts, which deal with statutory offences every evening of the week.[24] Few complaints can therefore be made about the efficiency of the Singaporean judiciary.[25]

In Frederic Jameson's analysis of late capitalism, van Gogh's 'Peasant Shoes' speak to us by including the possibility of disclosure, of origin. They are instruments of human labour, 'broken and worn'.[26] In Warhol's 'Diamond Dust Shoes', on the other hand, an x-ray gloss look negates any hierarchy and uniqueness. The image represents the final form of commodity reification: strolling along Orchard Road, one cannot miss it even if one tried.[27] DKNY stores, Swatch boutiques and Starbucks shops and products strive for difference as if to provide diversity, choice and liberty.

This blend of international brands and Singaporean uniqueness has helped to establish Singapore's reputation as a prototype of global urbanity.[28] If one does not associate consumerism with shallowness, but appreciates the intellectual tasks linked to it, Singapore is indeed more than a Potemkin Metropolis.[29] This begs the question of whether there is any specific Singaporean or even Asian postmodernism.[30] As William Lim stated, Singapore as a city is not the grand narrative Western or European cities can be. It is rather a palimpsest incorporating a number of different writings; and even Orchard Road with its global façade is no exception. One reason for this construction is the difficult relationship between interior and exterior in Singapore. Colonial architects were torn between the desire to provide office and living space, similar to that in England, and the need to provide good circulation in a tropical climate. Faced with these potentially conflicting requirements, their designs were often quite playful, for example, rooms which looked like European living rooms, but lacked walls, or marble sinks in the bathroom facing the rain forest. The new Gallery Hotel uses this blur of inside and outside. The hotel is the most obvious emblem of the Quay's transition, from warehouses and godowns to a rather hip area comprising designer hotel and luxury apartments. From the outside, it is difficult to identify the rationale behind the hotel's design: the entrance is uncelebrated, the lobby offbeat, and an art installation sends conflicting signals.[31] Under these circumstances, the market-place is clearly not the palladium of democracy as in the Ancient Greek city-states.

---

24  Ng and Tin, 2001: 6.
25  Blöchlinger, 2000: 598.
26  Jameson, 1985: 75.
27  Thai, 2002: 162.
28  For an optimistic view: Marshall, 2003: 14.
39  Koolhaas and Mau, 1995: 1010.
30  Lim, 2003: 11.
31  Powell, 2002: 102; for redevelopment and civil society, see: Tay *et al.*, 2000: 49.

Assembly points are more roofed-in now. In Ng Ang, Paragon and more recently in Suntec City, they are also air-conditioned. It has been said that this air-conditioned environment is an emblem for the political and social climate in Singapore and its society 'with a unique blend of comfort and central control, where people have mastered their environment, but at the cost of individual autonomy and unsustainability'.[32] When asked what, in his view, was the invention of the Millennium, State founder Lee Kwan Yew himself chose, certainly by design and not by accident, the air-conditioning.[33] Without air-conditioning he would never have been able to establish the threatening, but also fascinating experiment of living in comfort *and* control. From the mall orgy in Orchard Road to the precise selection of the bookstores, people have been willing to accept such exercise, because control means comfort – which explained why Samantha always found the air-conditioning conveniently set at temperatures which required her to wear her Prada stola.

## City lights and sights

A private city tour with Donald, the hotel manager who moved to Singapore from the Bronx in the late 1980s, showed Samantha some of the highlights of Singapore. At the Singapore River, the ubiquitous boat cruise was on the agenda – 30 minutes on high heels on a seesaw boat floating through a stinking sewer – no, thank you. Instead, Samantha walked up the river passing by Robertson Quay, where a number of men were watching a Premier League match at a beach bar. The seemingly spontaneous explosion of life and energy along Mohamed Sultan Road, previously a decrepit strip of abandoned shops and houses and now considered a showcase for qualities such as tolerance, multiplicity and diversity,[34] was quite a contrast to the tidy Orchard Road.[35]

Many of Singapore's main sights contain remnants of its colonial heritage. In the Civic District, the patterns envisaged by Raffles are still evident in City Hall, Parliament House and the Supreme Court.[36] Today, however, these buildings are occupied by Singaporean officials and not by colonial administrators. Still, they can be perceived as symbols of domination and control.[37] The Supreme Court's relocation to a new Norman Foster building is meant to 'equip Singapore's legal system for the demands of the new century...It will allow the Supreme Court to administer justice in a more effective and efficient way.'[38] And more just?

The Court of Appeal, the highest court in Singapore, is placed in a dramatic metal disc, the highest part of the building mirroring the dome of the existing

---

32  George, 2000: 76.
33  Escobar, 2001.
34  Lim, 2002: 14.
35  About the project, see: Van Schaik, 2002: 5 and Lim, 2002.
36  Edwards and Keys, 1988: 33; also Yeoh, 1996: 16.
37  Henderson, 2001: 12.
38  www.supcourt.gov.sg, accessed 10 January 2005.

building. This portrays 'the justice of the future', which seems to be envisaged as very different from present day justice. One reform prescribes that the routes for judges and the public are kept separate from the accused. Does this not reveal that there is little confidence in the very strength of the legal system? At least, there will be technology everywhere. Wireless hotspots will enable lawyers and court users (an interesting term) to use their laptops, and these, together with other high-tech gadgets, will become an integral part of the multimedia communications within and without the court. Samantha remembered a smart UCLA professor of Iranian origin, who, based on a thorough research of Heidegger's and Benjamin's texts, had explained to her the rift between justice and progress.

In addition to the colonial sights, there are ethnic sights such as Chinatown and Little India. These sites are symbolic of one of Singapore's largest societal projects – the building of a multi-ethnic state. Achieving a balance between each of the various ethnic and religious groups has been one of the country's biggest projects since independence in 1965 and, in stark contrast to a number of neighbouring countries, this seems to have happened without any major clashes.[39] The price to be paid has been manifold. The project of nation-building from a population previously only united by common suppression by colonial elites, has had an indelible impact on the shaping of law and policies in Singapore. For example, a strong emphasis on the needs of the community over those of the individual, which is often cited as a general trait of Asian law, was of particular use in a society which could not draw together its diverse population under the banner of a shared culture or religion.[40]

In 1990, the Malay village Geylang Serai was rebuilt. During the 1840s, Geylang Serai was a Malay enclave established after the British had dispersed the Malay floating village at the mouth of Singapore.[41] A further manifestation of the revival of some Malay traditions is the establishment of mediation programmes for resolving neighbour conflicts in which mediators act like Malay village elders (although the mediators are equipped with IT facilities and mediation often takes place through Internet chat rooms). This is linked to the broader idea of creating specific jurisdictions for different ethnic groups.[42]

The idea fits quite well with the concept of a legal system, which, institutionally as well as substantially, tries to pay attention to Asian values. What these values are all about, can be a puzzling matter: quite similar to the task of finding an appropriate explanation for the use of *lah* at the end of sentences in Singaporean English. Glorified by some, they might also be exploited to cover human rights infringements.[43] One of the values is undoubtedly the strong focus

39  Tan, 2004: 65.
40  Tay, 1996; Tan, 2002: 1; 743.
41  Gopalakrishnan and Perera, 1983: 40.
42  Ramraj, 2003: 225.
43  For the Singaporean context see Bell, 2000: 218–219.

on the community. Therefore, it seems logical to hand more judiciary powers to the community. On the other hand, the rights of the constitution must be seen as exit rights, which allow individuals to escape the iron grip of a community. The compromise has been to create community courts, such as the Syariah Court (Malay for Shari'ah), which has jurisdiction throughout Singapore (provided all parties are Muslim) in certain restricted areas such as marriage, divorce and property division after divorce.[44] The Muslim law is usually applied according to Malay customs, except where the parties are Muslims from Pakistan, India or the Middle East. Even this compromise position is potentially problematic in the context of women's rights, Art 12 of the Constitution on equality, and international law.[45]

In a city with over 70 per cent Chinese, there seems no obvious need for a Chinatown. Chinatown actually dates back to the early British settlements, when Sir Raffles divided the city into districts based on ethnic groups to keep racial tensions to a minimum. Back then, the Chinese immigrants were still a minority: only about 3,000 Chinese immigrants from mainland China, most of them penniless and half-starving. The British did not provide any police protection in Chinatown; this was the responsibility of the Chinese guilds.[46] Later, when the Chinese population grew bigger, Chinatown was slated for demolition. However, the government recognised both the people's desire and the historical importance of the area, and as a result it even extended the MRT into the refurbished Chinatown.

Many of the buildings in Chinatown are former brothels. Surprisingly, Samantha heard, prostitution as such was never prohibited in Singapore, even though there were a number of offences related to it, for example pimping.[47] Today, it is the temples and shops which attract visitors, rather than brothels and opium cafés. Like in many South East Asian states, the ethnic-Chinese population grows constantly. But only here, after Singapore gained independence from Malaysia, the Chinese became politically engaged in the nation-building process.[48] Even though they could have always moved to China or at least Hong Kong, as the charming old gambler Mr Chow did after breaking up with Lulu,[49] most of them decided to carry on enjoying the comfortable life in Singapore.

Close to Little India, in the direction of Arab and Victoria Street, one finds Bugis Street. At first glance Samantha only saw the chronically congested bus stop at Victoria Street; but then she spotted the neon sign 'Welcome to New Bugis Street 2005' and finally Bugis Square Fountain. Next to this street, thronged with people amusing themselves, old Bugis Street lies quietly, also

---

44  Administration of the Muslim Law Act (Cap. 3), 19.
45  Li-ann, 1997: 296.
46  Chinese guilds in relation to law city structures are discussed at Jankowiak, 1998: 373.
47  An overview about how prostitution has been regulated historically at Warren, 1994: 77.
48  See Suryadinata,1990: 24.
49  According to the Chinese citizenship law: Suryadinata, 2002: 172.

known as Hak-Kai (Dark Street).[50] Bugis Junction and its shopping arcade have established themselves as the place where J-Pop CDs, Japanese TV drama serial VCDs and Harajuku-style street wear can be purchased. A Japanese occupation of a different kind? Already in the nineteenth century, Middle Road was known as 'Japan Street' with its sizeable Japanese population, Japanese primary school and Japanese prostitutes.

Some reconstructed façades are intended to create the atmosphere of an old Bugis Street neighbourhood. 'Bugis Street' is also the title of a movie about the drag queens that populated the former red light district in the 1960s – a movie banned in Thailand. Who would have thought that? Mariam, a 63-year-old Malaysian transsexual, lived in Bugis Street between 1935 and 1985. She could tell of times when things were very much different from today. Post-op transsexuals were allowed to change their names and gender on their identity card and could marry. All this changed in 1996: the Registration Department only allows the addition of an alias to the original name, while the passport has to state the holder's sex in correlation to the birth certificate, which cannot be altered after the first year.[51]

New Bugis Street, together with Sim Lim Square, have also been in the heart of the piracy business. After the frequent raids in the late 1990s, however, it became more difficult to buy CDs and DVDs here. Most people relied on friends abroad to send them material censored in Singapore. Still, it remains a busy place, especially in the evening when there is a constant flux of people waiting, chatting, coming and going. With the exception of Orchard Road, this must be the busiest spot in town.[52] And with fewer posers. Samantha could not help but wonder: could there ever be a new 'Bugis Street' period again, in a Singapore whose projected image is frozen as a net of strict regulations and law-abiding citizens?

However, this image is rather outdated today. The copy of the Business Traveller Magazine Samantha had studied aboard contained pictures of a packed dance bar, in which pixie-faced girls in hot pants performed wet t-shirt shows while spectators clambered onto the stage to join in the fun.[53] And a glossy women's magazine cover at Borders, the sprawling bookstore on Orchard Road, screamed the headlines 'I bought my boyfriend a girl for a threesome', 'Have the best sex of your life', and 'Why should he have all the fun?' It is obvious that, in Singapore as much as elsewhere, certain paradigms have shifted since the late sixties. It seems that with the ongoing convalescence from the 1997 Asian flu, and the slower economic growth in comparison to China or Malaysia, a climate of uncertainty has been created, which forces Singapore to re-evaluate its strengths

---

50  Hin and Lin, 2002: 145.
51  http://jenellrose.com/htmlpostings/Transsexual_News_Archieve2.htm, accessed 20 January 2005.
52  Hin and Lin, 2002: 148.
53  Logartha, 2004: 17.

and weaknesses, just as she had to do in the halcyon chapter of her young history, when Singapore was forced to stand alone after leaving the federation with Malaysia.

The law seems to be heading along the same lines: the fact that bar-top dancing is finally allowed, is an encouraging although potentially problematic sign that the formerly squeaky-clean city has joined the real, bad world. The strict rules on chewing gum sales got a nice loophole through the introduction of 'medical chewing gum'. Bungee jumping near Clarke Quay, firecrackers during Chinese New Year, and Cosmopolitan (the magazine now, not the drink) invading the bookshelves: they all represent a big change in the law. Why? 'Because the government says so' commented a cynical stockbroker, who had tried to convince Samantha about the size of his manhood, while she was thinking that the chewing gum rules were actually quite handy for high heels.

A lot of truth in it, and it is kind of ironic that it took a few years of bad economic news to encourage social liberties, rather than the other way, as investors in China always want us to believe. 'Singapore needs a few little Bohemians', Prime Minister Goh Choik Tong has said recently. And even if he put some emphasis on 'few little', the artistic scenery grew impressively since the late 1990s. The law, as always, is lagging behind: oral sex,[54] Playboy and Penthouse are still banned, and there are regulations against spitting and forgetting to flush the toilet. Anyhow, the recent changes in law even received the blessing of the founding father Lee Kuan Yew: 'I am of a different generation; I don't think these changes necessarily add to civilized living. But if it adds to tourism and makes for buzz, well, so be it.'[55] Still, it is clear that the government sets the agenda, rendering political liberalisation a goal yet to be achieved. In spite of the proclaimed freedom of speech (Art 14 of the Constitution), the flow of Internet information is still controlled by the Singapore Broadcasting Authority.[56] Similarly, in spite of the right to freedom of religion (Art 15 of the Constitution), Jehovah's Witnesses are banned under the Societies Act from practicing their faith. It is no surprise that civil rights watchdog Freedomhouse rates the situation of civil liberties in Singapore as only partly free.[57]

Nevertheless, the journey of a thousand miles begins with the first step. And it might be no coincidence that one of the major landmarks, the bombastic Merlion statue, was moved at a distance of 120 metres in 2002. Away from the colonial spot by the Esplanade Bridge, and with the help of a barge and two DEMAGAC1600S cranes plus a team of 20 engineers, it is now facing the new cultural epicentre of Singapore, the Esplanade at the Bay. There is a lot of effort

---

54 'Unless it is performed as part of a foreplay'; has been qualified as unnatural act under s 377 of the Singapore Criminal Code. These offences are under review, see China Daily, 1 July 2004.
55 Quoted at: Logartha, 2004: 17.
56 Hwa and Min, 1998: 13.
57 www.freedomhouse.org/research/freeworld/2003/countryratings/singapore.htm, accessed 12 January 2005.

involved in moving a society even to a short distance. As the day drew to a close, Samantha realised she still had many sights left to visit; two days simply were not enough to discover a city, which is, after all, a country.

## 'Look, stranger, at this island now' (WH Auden) – Sentosa

Sentosa was the first attraction this morning. The tour agent had arranged an entry on the cable car from Mount Faber. While on Keppel Road, the taxi to Sentosa drove by a surprisingly derelict-looking building. What once must have been an impressing art-déco building, it just stood there now, looking rather desolate. The driver explained that the building still belonged to Malaysia. It was originally built by the British colonial government in 1923 as a station of the railway connection between Singapore and Malaysia. The current situation, of which the banner 'Welcome to Malaysia' on the station building was an obvious sign, exemplifies the complicated relationship between the two countries. As a territorial state, Malaysia had many resources that Singapore lacked: water, agriculture and people. But a stronger liaison was hindered by political discrepancies.

They had tried it once. In 1965, in order to combat the challenge of Communism in South East Asia, a pompous alliance of the Malaysian kernel state, Sarawak and Sabah – the latter to prevent domination by ethnic Chinese – had been established.[58] But the efforts needed to shape a uniform economic policy as well as other forms of cooperation had turned out to be more costly than the gains of a long-term relationship. Samantha understood that very well.

The railway station was a memento of the divorce, which took place only two years after the merging.[59] In 2001, the Malaysian Deputy Prime Minister Abdullah, the apparent heir of veteran Prime Minister Mahathir Mohamad, and the Singapore Prime Minister Goh Chok Tong began the day with a round of golf (an important tool of diplomacy in Southeast Asia) and agreed that the railway station should be moved back to the Malaysian border. Nothing has happened since, just like many times before that, and the railway station looks like a scarecrow. Not at all what architect Rem Koolhaas had in mind when he said: 'Cities like Singapore probably represent the truly generic condition of the contemporary city: history has been almost completely blotted out, the entire territory has become completely artificial, the urban tissue does not endure in any kind of stability beyond a relatively short period of existence.'[60] But here the history had not been blotted out at all.

By comparison, Sentosa was far less straightforward. The British had handed the military installation over to the Singaporean government in 1967. It was converted into a theme park by the Sentosa Development Corporation (SDC).

58  There is hardly any post-1965 literature. Still valuable: Hanna, 1965: 12.
59  About the Singapore – Malaysia conflict: Baker, 1999: 65.
60  Koolhaas, 2000: 280.

The government took the issue of fun quite seriously in designing the park. According to the masterplan the theme is the rich history and culture that made Singapore 'the global symbol of hope that it is today'.[61] One of the central features was the Merlion statue, towering over a musical fountain. One aspect of military history covered is Fort Siloso, a major stronghold of the British guarding the Western access to the harbour. However, the exposition primarily concerns the Battle of Singapore which saw Japan overrunning Singapore and Malaysia, and led to a British surrender.

Today the site of the surrender of the Japanese at City Hall – just opposite the Supreme Court – is a tourist attraction; but the cruelty during this period may have contributed to the occasional tendency of Singaporeans to look back on the earlier British colonial period with rose-tinted spectacles.[62] The Japanese occupation is often completely neglected in narratives of Singaporean history.[63] This is an omission, because, at least retroactively, the period helps to explain a number of features of the Singaporean legal system, such as the approach to constitutional law.[64] It is likely that the structure of the constitution and the courts would have remained unchanged if Singapore had not been invaded by Japanese troops under Lieutenant-General Tomoyuki Yamashita in February 1942.[65] Justice had to be dispensed according to the rules and regulations of the Japanese conquerors, but it was not easy to find out what these rules were. Several governmental or military bodies had the power to make laws, and many laws were quite obscure: year 1942 became 2602, streets were renamed, the time adjusted to Tokyo time and new banknotes, nicknamed 'coconut' notes, were issued. Without always complying with the legislative hierarchy, these bodies issued streams of often contradictory regulations, laws and notices.[66] Singapore courts ceased to function when the occupation began. A Court of Justice of the Nippon Army replaced them in April 1942, after which some of them were re-opened. This was meant to be the introduction to the Japanese legal system. The new apex of the judicial system was the Syonan Supreme Court (Syonan Koto-Hoin), opened on 29 May 1942; it never sat.[67]

## Leaving Singapore, never easy?

Even though Samantha had not made contact with one of the more obscure regulations in Singaporean law, like the fine for not flushing the toilet, the fact

61 www.brcweb.com/products/master-plans/examples/sentosa-island-resort.htm, accessed 30 January 2005. About master plans in land law: Tan, 1997: 482.
62 Goh, 1981: xx.
63 Phang, 2000: 23.
64 Goh, 1981: xxi.
65 Tan, 1989: 5.
66 Goh, 1981: xxi.
67 Tan, 1989: 6.

that the idea of law and order was essential to the city seemed obvious. In contrast to a number of other countries in the region, there is even a well-developed construction law, which favours planned development over aimless growth. Additionally, the liability of building consultants has been enhanced by the courts.[68] In the absence of statutory law and with a view to consumer protection, the courts established a net of duties of care. But there is also a tighter statutory law than in the United Kingdom. Legislative initiatives attempt to control the construction and design of buildings. Both, the Building Control Act 2003, and the Planning Act 2003, tried to influence the use and design of buildings.

At the current time, a reasonable balance seems to have been struck in Singapore, with both the liberal sixties and the harsh seventies a thing of the past. The majority of Singaporeans are, nevertheless, aware that this balance is still a fragile one. This uncertainty may well have been encouraged by the prevailing discourse on economic efficiency and development, and the lack of a discourse on the true values of law and justice. At these moments, when the law, rather than being targeted, handy and practical, is dallying, impractical and elegant, the law can actually be beautiful. Not dissimilar to her Ungaro pantsuit, Samantha thought.

One of the common afternoon showers was coming down. The cab turned into Raffles Boulevard to get onto the motorway to Changi Airport. The taxi driver turned up the Chopin piano music coming from the radio. Back to Manhattan, Samantha thought. Another special island.

## Bibliography

Baker, J (1999) *Crossroads: A Popular History of Malaysia and Singapore*, Singapore: Times Books

Bell, D A (2000) *East Meets West*, Princeton, NJ: Princeton University Press

Blöchlinger, K (2000) 'Primus Inter Pares', 8(3) *Pacific Rim Law & Policy Journal* 591–618

Cervero, R (1998) *The Transit Metropolis*, Washington, DC: Island Press

Dale, O J (1999) *Urban Planning in Singapore: The Transformation of a City*, Kuala Lumpur: Oxford University Press

Edwards, N and Keys, P (1988) *Singapore, A Guide to Buildings, Streets, Places*, Singapore: Times Books

Escobar, P (2001) 'Singapore, The Roving Eye', *Asia Times* 18 May 2001

George, C (2000) *Singapore, the Air-conditioned Nation*, Singapore: Landmarks Books

Goh, K L (1981) 'Legal History of the Japanese Occupation in Singapore', 1 *Malayan Law Journal* xx–xxiv

Gopalakrishnan, V and Perera, A (1983) Singapore Changing Landscapes, Singapore: FEP International

Grant, M (1999) *Singapore Planning Law*, Singapore: Butterworths Asia

68  Pillay, 2001: 358.

Hanna, W A (1965) *The Separation of Singapore from Malaysia*, New York: American Universities Field Staff

Henderson, J C (2001) 'Conserving Cultural Heritage: Raffles Hotel in Singapore', 7(1) *International Journal of Heritage Studies* 11–35

Hill, M and Fee, L K (1995) *The Politics of Nation Building in Singapore*, London and New York: Routledge

Hin, H W and Lin, T K (2002) 'Mapping Bugis', in Lim, W (ed.), *Postmodern Singapore*, Singapore: Select, 142–157

How, Y P (1998) *Speeches and Judgements of Chief Justice Yong Pung How*, Singapore: FT Law and Tax Asia Pacific

Hwa, A P and Min, Y T (1998) *Mass Media Laws and Regulations in Singapore*, Singapore: Asian Media and Communication Centre

Jameson, F (1985) 'Architecture and the Critique of Ideology', in Ockman, J (ed.), *Architecture Criticism Ideology*, Princeton, NJ: Princeton Architectural Press, 51–87

Jankowiak, W (1998) 'Research Trends in the Study of Chinese Cities', 10(1) *City & Society* 369–395

Koolhaas, R (2000) *Mutations*, Bordeaux: ACTAR

Koolhaas, R and Mau, B (1995) 'Singapore: Portrait of a Potemkin Metropolis', in Sigler, J (ed.), *S, M, L, XL*, Rotterdam: 010 Publishers

Kurlantzick, J (2000/2001) 'Love My Nanny: Singapore's Tongue-tied Populace', XVII(4) *World Policy Journal* 311–356

Li-ann, T (1997) 'The Impact of Internationalisation on Domestic Governance: Gender Egalitarianism and the Transformative Potential of CEDAW', 1(1) *The Singapore Journal of International & Comparative Law* 278–350

Lim, W (2002) 'Creative Rebells', in Lim, W (ed.), *Postmodern Singapore*, Singapore: Select, 4–17

Lim, W (2003) 'Spaces of Indeterminacy', in Lim, W (ed.), *Alternative (Post)Modernity*, Singapore: Select, 11–18

Logartha, M (2004) 'Oh behave, Singapore', *Business Traveller Magazine*, March 2004, 5

Marshall, R (2003) *Emerging Urbanity: Global Urban Projects in the Asia Pacific Rim*, London: Spon Press

Mass Rapid Transit Corporation (1988) *The MRT Story*, Singapore: Wah Mee Press

Ng, A and Tin, E (2001) 'Leading Change in the Singapore's Magistracy', www.aija.org.au/Mag01/singapore.pdf, accessed 28 January 2005

Phang, A (2000) 'The Singapore Legal System', 21(1) *History, Theory and Practice* 23–37

Pillay, M (2001) 'Building Consultants' Exposure and Liability under Singapore Law', 13 *Singapore Academy of Law Journal* 358–405

Powell, R (1994) *Living Legacy: Singapore's Architectural Heritage Renewed*, Singapore: Select

Powell, R (2002) 'Fragments of a Postmodern Landscape', in Powell, R (ed.), *Postmodern Singapore*, Singapore: Select

Raban, J (1974) *Soft City*, London: Harvill

Ramraj, V (2003) 'The Post-September 11 Fallout in Singapore and Malaysia: Prospects for an Accommodative Liberalism', 2(2) *Singapore Journal of Legal Studies* 459–482

Suryadinata, L (1990) 'National Ideology and Nation-Building in Multi-ethnic States', in Quah, J S T (ed.), *Search of Singapore's National Values*, Singapore: Institute of Policy Studies, 24–44

Suryadinata, L (2002) 'China's Citizenship Law and Chinese in Southeast Asia', in Hooker, M B (ed.), *Law & the Chinese in Southeast Asia*, Singapore: Institute of Southeast Asian Studies, 169–202

Tan, E (2002) 'We v. I, Communitarian Legalism in Singapore', 4(1) *The Australian Journal of Asian Law* 1–29

Tan, E (2004) 'We, the Citizens of Singapore', in Lai Ah Eng (ed.), Beyond Rituals and Riots, Singapore: East Universities Press

Tan, K Y L (1989) 'The Evolution of Singapore's Modern Constitution: Development from 1945 to the Present Day', 1(1) *Academy of Law Journal* 101–127

Tan, P L (1997a) *Asian Legal Systems: Law, Society and Pluralism in East Asia*, Singapore: Butterworths

Tan, S Y (1997b) *Principles of Singapore Land Law*, Singapore: Butterworths

Tay, S (1996) 'Human Rights, Culture, and the Singaporean Example', 41(2) *McGill Law Journal* 743–780

Tay, S, Baharudin, Z and George, C (2000) 'The Role of Civil Service and Civil Society', *The Strait Times*, 17 February, 49

Thai, B W C (2002) 'A Few Good Men and their Phallic Jet Stream', in: Lim, W (ed.), *Postmodern Singapore*, Singapore: Select, 158–172

Van Schaik, L (2002) 'Poetics in Architecture', 72(2) *Architectural Design* 34–52

Voyce, M (2005) 'Neoliberalism, Shopping Malls and the End of Property', in Freeman, M (ed.), *Law and Popular Culture*, Oxford: Oxford University Press, 537–559

Waller, J (2003) *Drinkology – The Art and Science of the Cocktail*, New York: Stewart, Tabori and Chang

Warren, J F (1994) 'Chinese Prostitution in Singapore', in Jaschok, M and Miers, S (eds), *Women and Chinese Patriarchy*, Hong Kong: University Press

Widodo, J (2003) 'Modernism in Singapore', 29(1) *DOCOMOMO Journal* 54–60

Yeoh, B (1996) *Contesting Space: Power Relations and the Urban Built Environment in Colonial Singapore*, Kuala Lumpur: OUP

## Chapter 6

# Panjim

## Realms of law and imagination

*Jason Keith Fernandes* *

### Introduction: the madness in the method

A capital city is not simply a city, but also the site of State power. It is the physical space where the power of the State is made manifest through the erection of monuments, the construction of public buildings, the naming of streets and localities. It is also the place where groups, with different ideas as to what the State and/or society should be like, vie with each other to capture State power. This story centres on Panjim, home to around 62,000 inhabitants, located at the mouth of the river Mandovi, capital to the west coast Indian state of Goa. Panjim has been the capital almost since its inception, and in the process has been witness to both these processes of the constitution of the State; namely the physical manifestation of power and the battle for the capturing of power. It was among the places where the Portuguese colonial enterprise, itself marked by nostalgia for the Age of the Discoveries, forged a unique form of colonial relations which would leave its own impress on the politics of the city. In postcolonial times, the fantasies created in part by differing colonial encounters and the exigencies of the global economy have also led Panjim to become a site where identity, in the wide sense of the imagination of the self, is keenly battled for.

While speaking of Panjim, there are three concerns that I wish to address: first, the nature of legality of the social field in conditions of interlegality, constructed through the dialectical relations between various groups. Second, that while the role of imagination in constructing our world is recognised, we tend to see its role as overwhelmingly negative and still struggle to operationalise it in a positive manner. Third, that reflections on the colonial experience and post-colonial condition are based largely on the experience of British colonialism, which tend to wipe away the nuances born from other colonial experiences and their ramifications in the postcolonial world.

* I dedicate this essay to Alito Siqueira, the wise man in the corner, for the times spent in conversation and the introduction to thinking about the colonial experience differently. Shukran also to Rahul Srivastava for hours spent in discussion and helping this chapter evolve.

It is my argument that the physicality and the idea of the particular city are constructed greatly through the two processes of the constitution of the State, namely the manifestation and capturing of power, both of which are aspects of what Appadurai would call the 'social imagination'.[1] This social imagination can be said to have, at the very least, two components, 'nostalgia' (schematically, an imagination of our past) and 'fantasy' (an imagination of the other and the alternative, at times based on nostalgia, and in this manner also offering a blueprint for the future).[2]

The positive role that nostalgia and fantasy play in the construction of the city arguably requires much defence before we proceed to the particularities of Panjim. And for no small reason, for in the words of David Lowenthal, nostalgia is often accused as being 'ersatz, vulgar, demeaning, misguided, inauthentic, sacrilegious, retrograde, reactionary, criminal, fraudulent, sinister, and morbid'. And it is not just nostalgia that attracts such slurs from the establishment, but also the variety of terms that could broadly be linked to the imagination. It is as if the works of the mind are capable only of leading away from the real, the true, the factual. And yet, as Lowenthal seeks to establish with the help of a great number of examples drawing from heritage issues, as well as quotes from Peter Shaffer's play *Lettice and Lovage*, 'fantasy floods in where fact leaves a vacuum'.[3] We need fantasy, because, rather than being the opposite of truth, fantasy is in fact its complement, giving our lives a more lasting shape. For such a reason then, 'fabrication is no sin, but a virtue'.[4]

The role of the imagination and the manner in which it helps ground and make more real, as it were, the lived reality of our times, has been amply demonstrated in a number of works. Two examples, both relevant to the present discussion, come to mind: first, that of the nation-state, which Benedict Anderson described as an imagined yet tangible community, so much so that its members would be willing to shed very real blood and lives for the sake of the idea.[5] The second, Hobsbawm's *Invented Traditions*, points out that traditions often presumed to be ancient, are really recent inventions created to suit the needs of the day.[6] While Anderson naturalises the idea of imagination as structuring and indeed creative of our political (and legal) world, this has not been, by his own admission, the position he began from. Rather, he began from a position where the imagination of these emerging nations as antique appeared as little more than 'Machiavellian hocus-pocus, or...bourgeoise fantasy, or...disinterred historical truth', until he realised that in the case of these new nations, 'supposing "antiquity" [was] at a certain historical juncture the necessary consequence of their novelty'.[7] To repeat

---

1 Appadurai, 1996.
2 Srivastava, 2005: 36–47.
3 Lowenthal, 1998: 8.
4 Ibid.
5 Anderson, 1991.
6 Hobsbawm and Ranger, 1983.
7 Anderson, 1991: xiv.

Lowenthal's words, fantasy flooded in where fact left a vacuum. Hobsbawm too points to the very 'real' function that invented traditions perform for society. And yet, despite the role imagination plays in the world, one still feels a certain unease with this idea of the imagined and the artifice involved in the structuring of the world. There is definitely a sense of reproach and the need to be aware that they aren't really real.

A number of the critiques of modernity point to the elevation of scientific rationality as the single determiner of the real, and the subsequent division of the world into a series of binarisms, such as knowledge, reality and fact, versus ignorance, illusion and fantasy. Blaming such binary rationality for the disenchantment of the world and the ensuing lack of meaning that seems to accost the lives of contemporary subjects, Nandy[8] highlights the need for what Santos calls the 're-enchantment of common-sense',[9] a plea for the reintroduction of fantasy into our lives and the belief in dreams and utopias. Imagination is deeply implicated in the constitution of our world. Critiquing Anderson's idea of the nation-state, Marilyn Strathern points out that any community, however small, requires a certain amount of imagination so that even a group of individuals can be constituted as a community.[10]

Given that our world is therefore constituted in large part through the process of imagination, it is my argument that law, as the other side of scientific rationality,[11] defines which imagination is fantasy, and which real. The fantasy is then projected as false consciousness and therefore unreal. The law is able to maintain this crucial arbitral position primarily since it represents itself as autonomous and value-neutral, a representation which, in terms of scientific discourse, could be described as fantasy, owing to the very strong and sustained examples of how the law is neither autonomous nor value-neutral.

In his account of the legality of the modern capitalist state, Santos exposes law's representation as fantasy. Pointing to the situation of interlegality that our society experiences, he explains how the legality of our world is being formed through the inter-penetration and combination of various legalities, powers and knowledges that inhere in the six structural places which he identifies.[12] State law, which represents itself as the single legality for society, in fact operates in combination with the other legalities present in the field. However, like a number of other legal pluralists, he sees the State as the dominant partner in this combination, a theoretical position resulting from his construction of community, which he sees as opposite to, and in some respects, outside the State.[13] There is much work however, that indicates that the community, or society, participates in

---

8  Nandy, 2000.

9  Santos, 1995: 52–53.

10  Strathern, 1990.

11  Santos, 1995: 56.

12  Namely, the *household* place, the workplace, the market place, the *community* place, the *citizenplace* and the world place.

13  Fernandes, 2005: 15–16.

the construction of the State and its legality, not merely as a silent and submissive partner, but actively; capable at times of sloughing the liberal State's values and normativities, to allow for, as we shall see later, the inscription of values that go against the grain of the modern liberal state.[14] Nonetheless, to use Santos's words, since there is also a legal canon which establishes what law is, it is necessary for these non-State partners of legality to be sufficiently embroiled in the power structure of the State in order to partake of some amount of legitimacy for their offerings of normativities. Perhaps as a result of constructing community as the other to the State, the community too seems to share in the monolithic character that is attributed to the State. One way around this singular construction of community, and simultaneously around a similar construction of the State (and logically its legality), would be to adopt Bourdieu's reading of the social field,[15] and see both these terms as aggregations of competing fields, all in dialectical relationships with each other.[16]

Such a reading of legality as constructed through the interactions of multiple groups within the social field vying for a better position vis-à-vis State power, would allow us to see through the various processes born of their dialectical relationships. It shows us how the imaginations and fantasies of these various groups are cast as veritable truth when encapsulated within law, and then physically realised to shape the materiality of the city, both in its solid tangibility, and its conceptual physicality.

The following section illustrates the first of my propositions: that the moment of Panjim's declaration as capital is the moment when a particular fantasy is cast as veritable truth. However, since it is not the practices of Portugal that constitute the basis of the international legal order, this imagination is branded a fantasy, allowing for the fantasy of the British colonisers and their successors, the postcolonial nation state of India, to define reality.

## Into the mirror: fantasy into fact, fact to fantasy

Our story of the playing out and the concrete realisation of the many fantasies that populate the field commences when, on 21 March 1843, it pleased the reigning monarch of Portugal Rainha Dona Maria II, to declare,

> We the Queen make it known that given the condition of ruin and almost total abandonment in which the old city of Goa, Capital of Portuguese India,

---

14  For example, Fuller and Bénéï, 2001.

15  Bourdieu is very emphatic that we need to disaggregate the State, and if we are to disaggregate the State, then we must also necessarily disaggregate this idea of the community as well. The plea for disaggregation being one that I sense both Appadurai (1996) and Strathern (1990) use when they argue against such closed terms as culture and society.

16  Bourdieu and Wacquant, 1992: 112–114.

finds itself, though it still preserves the Primatial See and the Arsenal; and because of the ever-growing settlements in Pangim, a town noted for its beautiful buildings and as the headquarters of the Governor-General, all the Courts and main offices of the State of India (Estado da India); I hereby concede to it the status and honour that it deserves. Pangim is linked by means of long and majestic bridge to the densely populated and important village of Ribandar, which is contiguous to the City of Goa. All these shall together constitute the Capital of Portuguese India, whose glorious name is immortally linked with the historic memories of these new conquests.... And thus, from the day of publication of this Charter, the settlement of Pangim shall be deemed a city, with the designation of Nova Goa. It shall comprehend the littoral left of the Mandovi, from the mouth of that River up to Daugim bridge; and it shall have a three fold division of the wards: **Pangim**, stretching from Santa Ines Bridge to that of Cruz which links Pangim and Ribandar, having on its left side Gate of Fontainhos; **Ribandar** from the said Cruz bridge up to the Church of St. Peter which is enclosed by Chimbel; and lastly, **Goa**, stretching from the Church of the Mother of God at Daugim, onwards; it is enclosed by the demarcations and the entrance to the Old City. The new city shall have all the privileges and rights similar to those of other cities and possessions of the kingdom; and shall be permitted to compete with them in all ways; its citizens shall have the same prominence that is enjoyed by those of others. All Courts, Authorities, officials; and the people at large who read this Charter are ordered to fulfil it; and from now on to treat the settlement as city, and to grant to its citizens and residents all those privileges, immunities and freedom enjoyed by other cities; and never to violate it, either fully or partly . . . [17]

What is remarkable about the Charter is not so much that Pangim was seemingly created by a declaration, springing into life like Athena from the head of Zeus. Indeed, as the declaration itself shows quite clearly, Pangim was already a town of some substance: the viceroy had shifted his residence in 1759, and the process of shifting other administrative buildings and actually reclaiming the swamps around the growing settlement to make it liveable followed in 1830 under the Viceroy Dom Manuel de Portugal e Castro following this move. Nor is the issue that the declaration re-altered the geography of the region, drawing the hamlet of Pangim from the village of Taleigao, whose part it used to be, to create in its place an imperial capital – though this status alteration and the subsequent relationship between Pangim and Taleigao deserves a chapter in itself. To be sure, it appears that this little city has been able to assert an identity of her own vis-à-vis the law, always enjoying a plethora of names besides the ones that the

---

17 Published in the *Boletim do Governo Da Estado Da India*, Saturday 27 May 1843, and subsequently translated in Samarth, 1983.

law chose for her. Thus, while the Queen deemed this agglomeration of three hamlets to be Nova Goa, since the seat of the law was Pangim, Pangim was what it was called, with a later Anglicisation – currently popular – calling her Panjim. The city was subsequently rechristened Cidade de Goa,[18] and following Goa's integration into the Indian Union in 1961, the name was changed to Panaji – the postcolonial State's version of the vernacular pronunciation. And, throughout this rebaptising extravaganza, the popular name of the city remains *Ponje* – itself a challenge to the Statist version of the vernacular.

But I digress... Because what was (and still remains) remarkable in this establishment of a city in a colonial possession, was the granting to the city of a status similar to that of any city in the kingdom, and to its citizens, the rights, privileges and opportunities available to any citizen in the kingdom. The imaginary that allowed the citizens of Panjim, two oceans and 5,000 kilometres away from Lisbon, to be seen as similar to the citizens of any part of the kingdom, was a result of a pre-enlightenment conceptualisation of the relation between colonised/ coloniser: not as the usual polarisation between them, but as a difference that could be, and ought to be, erased, as the colonised Caliban, along with his physical space and body, was absorbed into the body of the coloniser Prospero.[19]

Such conceptualisation called for either miscegenation, or for the acquisition of the Catholic faith and use of the Portuguese language, and what could be understood to be Western European manners. The options now available were seized by those Goans who could, and were subsequently able to participate in the Empire in a manner quite contrary to that of their counterparts in British India, who were forever subjects – never citizens – of the colonial state. This absorptive character of Portuguese nationalism and colonialism was expressed as State law in 1757, when the Marquis de Pombal conferred the privileges of citizenship to the colonised in the Portuguese Indies. Following the establishment of the constitutional monarchy in Portugal a few years after Pombal's declaration, a Goan, Bernado Peres da Silva, was appointed as Prefect to introduce changes in the set-up of Goa.[20] Similarly, other Goans found themselves in the State pyramid, obtaining titles, crests and positions in the armed forces, the judiciary and as Governors in the African territories. This practice of absorption and participation in the Empire saved the Goan from the daily fate of Caliban and allowed for what Santos calls 'a comforting reading of colonialism',[21] like that of Luso-Tropicalism[22] – which

---

18  Portaria published in the Boletim do Estado da India, 22 May 1947.
19  Personal communication with Alito Siqueira. The imagery of Caliban and Prospero that I use in this essay has been drawn from Santos (2002) – an influence that runs through the whole chapter.
20  deMenezes, 1978: 118
21  Santos, 2002: 12.
22  The term 'Luso-Tropicalism' was introduced by the Brazilian sociologist Gilberto Freyre to describe the colonial process of transformation and incorporation of non-European cultures and spaces. See Madureira, 1994.

incidentally Gilberto Freyre introduced in Portugal after his stay in Goa[23] – which allowed this segment of the assimilated or aspiring assimilationists to see themselves as Portuguese and part of the Portuguese family spread from Minho to Timor.[24]

The nostalgic remembrance of the exploits of the great heroes of Portugal from the time of the Great Discoveries is said to have aided the formation of the Portuguese national character.[25] In a similar manner, the said remembrance was used to inscribe Portugal into Goa. The physical space of the city was sought to be absorbed into the idea of Portugal through the process of naming and the erection of monuments to the glories of this Portuguese past. In 1847, soon after its recognition as the capital, Panjim saw in one of its main squares the erection of a memorial to Afonso da Albuquerque, the conqueror of Goa and a star of the Portuguese Age of Discoveries. The conquest of Goa itself was markedly referred to in the Queen's declaration, thus inextricably tying Goa and its capital to the imagination and constitution of Portugal itself. Perhaps unsurprisingly, following the conquest of Goa by the Indian State, this very square was named *Azad Maidan* ('Freedom Square'). A monument to the martyrs of Goan Liberation was erected on the site, while the monument to Albuquerque was used to house the remains of T. B. Cunha, hailed as the Father of Goan nationalism. Although a legal pronouncement may have changed the signifier of this landmark for the people of Panjim, the impress of the power of the State over the people via the erection and naming of a monument remained, thus allowing the signified to carry on unaffected even in postcolonial times.

Similar to Albuquerque's commemoration, the occasion of the shifting of the remains of Vasco-da-Gama to Lisbon proved cause for the establishment of an institute intended for intellectual activity, the *Institut Vasco-da-Gama*. In time, the entrance hall to the *Institut* would be clad in *azulejos* (typical Portuguese blue-and-white handpainted tiles), depicting scenes from the *Os Lusiadas*, Camões's epic poem to Portugal's age of glory.[26] With the establishment of the Republic in Portugal in 1910, one of the principal streets of the city was renamed *31st January Road*, in memory of the first and unsuccessful Republican outburst in Porto. In more recent times, the same street would be the bone of contention regarding the continued remembrance of the colonial presence. Perhaps it is of no mean significance that the coat of arms of the city incorporated, along with the wheel of St Catherine (on whose feast day Albuquerque wrested the old city

---

23 Madureira, 1994: 170.
24 Minho is a city in mainland Portugal, and Timor a former Portuguese island possession in Southeast Asia.
25 Cusack, 2003: 3.
26 While it is common to point to *Os Lusiadas* as Camões's effort to convert Portugal's national adventure into epic, Jeremy Lawrance (2004: 8) points out, with some relevance to the present discussion, that his task was really more profound: he sought to convert it to myth, casting it as predestined by history.

of Goa from its earlier overlord), the coat of arms of Dom Afonso Henrique, to whom goes the credit of establishing the kingdom of Portugal.

This process of absorption and identification was perhaps most emphatically stressed during the *Estado Novo* inaugurated by Salazar. At the time, in view of Portugal's attempt to compete with the other super-Prosperos over in Europe, as well as the threat posed through the process and demands for decolonisation, every broadcast from the radio station perched on Altinho, the hillock above Pangim, would begin with the assertion *Aqui e Portugal* ('This is Portugal').[27] This relation between the colonial city and the metropolis was aptly summed in the words of Cortesão:

> Goa symbolises one of the greatest services we have performed for humanity and one of the illustrative paradigms of the place we have earned in the history of civilisation…We have always considered, and will continue to consider her as an integral part of Portugal even if it is governed by usurpers [i.e., even after the forcible ejection of the Portuguese from Goa in 1961]. [28]

Cortesão's statement is simply another indication of how this imaginary of absorption into the mother-country was seen by the international system: no more than a fantasy. The reason for this dismissal is that the Portuguese imaginary of absorption, namely the constitution of the colonised as citizen rather than subject, was clearly different from the practice of the northern European colonial powers, especially the British, whose practice of colonialism was linked with capitalist exploitation, and whose scientised racism defined not just the rules of ideal colonialism but international law and practice as well. Interestingly, the British, who exercised a near colonial grip on the Portuguese[29] as well as on the territory of Goa,[30] were in the thrall of their own fantasy regarding the Portuguese. Thanks to their policy of miscegenation, or perhaps owing to the colonising Briton's fear of racial admixture, the Portuguese were deemed to be never quite as European as the others on the continent: Calibanised Prosperos[31] in the realm of the super-Prosperos. By not linking their colonialism with organised capitalism, the Portuguese were seen not only as ineffective colonisers, but as the personification of sloth. So powerful were these fantasies that the representations of the Portuguese by the British and other northern colonials would also rub off on their colonised people as well. Compare the following representation of Goa and Goans by the German traveller Count Hubner in 1880:

> Pangim or Nova Goa is a small and beautiful city spread along the riverside … Very few ladies are to be seen but many a gentleman of white

27 Newman, 2001: 58.
28 Madureira, 1994: 169.
29 Madureira, 1994: 152 and Santos, 2002: 11.
30 Couto, 2004: 291.
31 Santos, 2002.

complexion though quite livid but all dressed in European style. I would take it for Lamego, Viseu or any other venerable city of Portugal, with its noblemen simply dragging along, as if convalescing and leaving a hospital.[32]

Beautiful and identified with Portugal, the local confounds the viewer: is he white? Or does the livid colour account for racial mixture? Nonetheless, he is dressed in European-styled clothes. The degree to which the Goan was seen as having imbibed the degenerate qualities of the Portuguese national character, was perhaps most forcefully put forth by T B Cunha, the so-called Father of Goan nationalism, in his famous pamphlet *The Denationalisation of Goans*. One of its themes is the 'backwardness' of the Portuguese in their colonisation, and the impact of this culture on the Goans, who, having patterned themselves on the Portuguese, are not just physically and morally degraded, but incapable of creative and original works.[33]

The result is a case of double representation of the physical space and its inhabitants: first by their colonisers as *Goa Portuguesa*; and then, by the British who impute the character of the colonisers onto that of the colonised, with all the subsequent criticism. What is perhaps most interesting though, is that the image of *Goa Dourada* ('Golden Goa'), born out of both Portuguese and Goan nostalgia, and the now-clichéd image of the Goan as carefree and given to merry-making, got entrenched after the forced departure of the Portuguese[34] as the *saudades*[35] of the assimilated locals mixed with the exotic gaze that the postcolonial British-Indian[36] inherited from their British paramount.

It has been suggested that it was perhaps this image of a Westernised and different-from-India Goa that made Goa a haven for the western hippies in the 1960s and 1970s.[37] From those days, tales are told of buses destined for Berlin and the United Kingdom (via the overland route) that could be seen at *Mapuça*, a small town less than 30 kilometres from Panjim. The presence of the hippy culture only added to the exotic character of Goa, with a number of more local tourists coming to the land where the white person walked naked and 'free'. The State was quick to seize the opportunity for revenue generation, and by 1986 it had been decided to exploit Goa for the purposes of tourism. In an industry known for the packaging of dreams and fantasies, Goa has now come to be represented as one of the world's pleasure peripheries, a cultural space for leisure

---

32  *Cf.* Samarth, 1983: 7.
33  Cunha, 1961.
34  As referred to earlier, the Portuguese were forcibly ejected from Goa through the Indian army's conquest of this Portuguese territory.
35  *Saudades* roughly translates from Portuguese into English as nostalgia and combines a sense of longing, memory and love.
36  I seek here to make a distinction, based on colonial experience, between British-India and Portuguese India.
37  Routledge, 2000: 2652.

consumption divorced from the needs and concerns of everyday life[38] – an unreal world, where fantasy could reign supreme.

Expectedly, the State and tourist industry have been making a very 'real' profit, leading among other things to the overexploitation of Goa's beach belt, arguably on the verge of ecological collapse. Others, on the other hand, express the need to exploit more effectively both the tourist potential of Goa's towns and her countryside – a sentiment neatly put in an analysis of Panjim's tourist potential where it was indicated that 'nine out of ten tourists who visit Goa visit Panaji (Panjim). They come here to shop or to stay the night before they move on to other destinations. Whatever the reasons, the importance of Panaji as a city with tremendous tourism potential cannot be ignored.'[39] Incidentally, the latter dovetails with the state government's emphasis that what is required for Goa is 'High quality, Low volume' tourism, rather than the backpack or charter tourism that Goa now plays host to.[40] Simultaneously, marking the persistent othering of Goa as a piece of Europe in India, and the growth of an Indian middle class, a large number of Indian and foreign elite have made Goa a temporary or permanent home and work place,[41] creating a market in 'heritage' real estate that has now to be preserved, both for the creation of profit as well as for the preservation of the fantasy to which the immigrant has moved. It is these fantasies and their very concrete and tangible manifestations that have woven themselves together to make Panjim an extremely contested space.

Building on the theme that imagination is crucial to the construction of our world, I have illustrated how nostalgia has been used to imagine Goa and the Goans as a part of the Portuguese family. It is thus becoming obvious that Panjim is a product of nostalgia and imagination, powerfully materialised by the creation of conditions for the Goan to participate in the managing of the empire. Owing to Portugal's marginal position in the world system and its inability effectively to have a say in the establishment of the global (legal) order, this imagination was branded a fantasy; while the fantasies of the northern European colonisers, notably that of Britain, with the sanction of law, emerge as fact.

Remarkably, such 'facts', together with the newer fantasies referred to earlier, are in need of initial and continuing validation. This can only happen through their insertion into the law. It is obvious that these fantasies influence the manner in which the city is imagined. This insertion into the law is uniquely manifested in the way the physicality of the city is being structured: thus, the relation between the law and the city becomes variably one of freezing its physicality,

---

38  Citing Rao, 1996, in Routledge, 2000: 2652.
39  Department of Tourism, 1997: 18.
40  Routledge, 2000: 2650.
41  An example of the kind of fantasies and requirements involved in the selection of Goa as 'home' by this elite can be found in Mundkur (2004) and Poggendorf-Kakar (2004).

consenting to its restructuring or erasing its past. It is on the process through which these fantasies, individually and combined, are inserted into the law, that I shall focus presently.

## Imagining the city into shape

The heady constellation of the fantasy of Goa as a part of Europe, the continued and increased exploitation of Goa as a tourist space, and the Indian middle classes' desire for order and growth, has been perfectly captured in the coming into power of the Bharatiya Janata Party (BJP) led coalition government in 2000. A national political party, the BJP is the political arm of the Rashtriya Swayamsevak Sangh (RSS), an extreme right organisation which, during its first steps in the late 1970s, found its support base among the economically vulnerable and socially insecure Hindu urban salaried middle classes and small businessmen of north and central India. It has expanded its base since then,[42] as it now articulates a Brahmanical ideology that promises to wipe away national feelings of shame, and create 'a perfectly organised state of... society wherein each individual has been moulded into a model of ideal Hindu manhood [*sic*] and made into a living limb of the corporate personality of society'.[43] The RSS's main thrust is the restoration of Hindu (and in their reading, Indian) pride through the development of the country, a project that was evinced quite clearly when in May 1998, soon after their forming the national government, they exploded a nuclear bomb and thus joined the ranks of the world's nuclear powers. To put this in terms of a metaphor I have used earlier, the colonial encounter for British India, resulted in the British Indian subject being constructed as a Caliban, whose salvation lay in the hands of Prospero, their British colonisers. What the entire project of the postcolonial development state and especially those of the Hindu right displays is Caliban's attempt to undo this construction, and reconstruct himself as a macho Prospero.

In Goa, it was Manohar Parrikar, the chief minister of this BJP dominated government, a committed member of the RSS and the legislative representative for Panjim, who was to play a major role in a massive re-engineering of the city's looks. Indeed, in his project several fantasies were played out: not just of the tourist and immigrant segments of Goa's social field, but also those of the Hindu right obsessed with national culture cast in a definitely Brahmanical Hindu mould, and the avenging of the shame brought on by colonialism. Thus, the Chief Minister accommodated not only the authoritarian nature of RSS politics, but the alternative possibilities as well, as in this brief period the law was embodied in his very person. Contravening notions of good governance while at the same time representing to be committed to it, the word of the Chief Minister

---

42  Spitz Jr, 1997 and Kumar, 1999.
43  Golwalkar, 1966: 61.

was law, and his dictate duly complied with, as he responded to the jostling between the various groups who in their attempt to physically mark the city, sought to have their fantasies and imaginaries too inserted into the space of the State: heritage *wallahs*,[44] the tourist industry, the Hindu right, and the Goan, (particularly the Panjim middle class and the nostalgic Goan elite). Nostalgia was used somewhat perversely when in a personal communication with me it was pointed out that if the Chief Minister was now the embodiment of law, Parrikar was also an embodiment of Salazar himself![45] This was definitely not a stretch of the imagination, for segments of this nostalgic middle class saw the times of Salazar as the best thing that Portugal had given to Goa, and had initially welcomed Parrikar's absolutist style of functioning, as they acclaimed his efficiency and 'good governance'.

At the time of Parrikar's coming into power, the middle class of Panjim alongside the tourist industry were in full mobilisation and lobbying to ensure that hawkers were ousted from Panjim's public face and perhaps rehabilitated elsewhere. The need for neatness and order, as well as the poor image that these hawkers would and did create for the tourist visiting Panjim, were mentioned in the numerous memoranda submitted to government agencies, in newspaper articles, and ultimately in a petition presented before the High Court.[46] The lobbying group succeeded in their effort to evict the hawkers and *gaddas*[47] from their various locations in the city, and limiting them to only three areas. This state of affairs speaks loudly for the power of this very vocal collective of groups, as well as of their projected fantasy of what the city should be: faithful to the projected likeness of Panjim to cities in Western Europe, and aspiring towards Singapore or those in the United States. Using the appeal of this fantasy to get the hawkers and vendors evicted by the offices of the State is indicative of the manner in which law is constituted through fantasies from communities with power.

With a view to woo the middle classes of Goa (and more importantly those of Panjim, who formed his electoral base), and prove the capacity for 'good governance' that the BJP was capable of, the Chief Minister singled out Panjim for a total image revamp. It was therefore decided that a liquid expanse of the city, popularly called a lake, would now be officially developed into such, while cleansed of the surrounding vegetation and complete with jogging track, fountains and other such delights in which the urban populace would be able to

44 *Wallah* in Hindi translates into 'person', here in plural.
45 Personal communication with a senior Government employee who requested anonymity.
46 *Nazareth Cabral v Panjim Municipal Council*, Writ Petition No.438/1995, the High Court of Bombay at Panaji, from the documentation of the People Movement for Civic Action (PMCS), Panjim.
47 *Gadda* is the local term for what could best be described as a 'movable' shop. Elaborations of hand carts, which can be boarded up when closed, these contraptions are fitted with wheels that theoretically allow them to be wheeled around the city. More often than not, once rolled into a space most often a side-walk, they never move again.

take pleasure. In the process of this work, comparisons to European cities abounded and the entire project of refurbishing Panjim hinged on the reification of Panjim's Lusitanian image.[48] It involved sprucing up the building that housed the first medical college in Asia, the renovation of the riverside promenade renamed the *Corniche*, the erection of lampposts that added more than a feel of Iberia to the town, and the painting of public buildings in the city with colours typical to provincial Portuguese towns. Indeed, Panjim had never been as Lusitanian as it was at the end of the year 2004, when it played host to the International Film Festival of India. The event was shifted that year to Goa in order to draw attention to the possibilities of the area as more than a sun, surf and sand holiday destination, and offering tangible proof for the stated objective and underlying desire to see Panjim as another, better Cannes...

This entire project saw a number of fantasies being worked out simultaneously. At this point, I would like to focus primarily on two. The first, inspired by the British Indian colonial experience, involved the need to compete with Europe and the West, and fulfil Caliban's desire to prove his ability to be, if not actually Prospero, at least *like* Prospero, working out thereby the inferiority that had been written through British colonial discourse into imagination of the (British) Indian self. The other projection involves the resurrection of the very Prospero image of Goa, indeed a slowly but surely dying image, since the imaginary introduced by the Portuguese colonialism was increasingly being displaced by that of postcolonial (British) India.

The latter fantasy was in no small part supported by the heritage *wallahs*, the most prominent group amongst which included, not surprisingly, eminent members of the tourist industry, architects and immigrants captured by Goa's 'natural' charm and laid-back atmosphere: a smooth combination of longing and desire, business interest and personal aggrandisement. Seeking to preserve Panjim's heritage, the group organised a number of 'high-visibility' campaigns that managed to make the city and state administration sit up and take notice. This involved the promotion of 'local' art and culture, as well as the organisation of two *Fontainhos Festivals*. *Fontainhos*, currently celebrated as a heritage precinct and 'Asia's only Latin Quarter', has become in the last three years the space where the soul of the city, her fate, is debated, determined and, as we shall see, fought for. In conversation with a member of this heritage group I pointed out that the appellation of 'Latin quarter' is one most popularly associated with the Parisian neighbourhood of the same name, famous for its Bohemian lifestyle. The gentleman amiably agreed with me and in support of the appellation referred to the lore that the *fidalgos*, the Portuguese nobility in the Portuguese Indies, were

---

48 'Lusitania' was the name of an ancient Roman province approximately including current Portugal, named after the Lusitani people. It is used as an indicator for Portugal, probably since in *Os Lusiadas*, Camões presents the Portuguese people as descendants from Lusus, companion of Dionysus and mythical founder of Lusitania.

known for their womanising and pleasure seeking.[49] Another member credited the origin of the name to the early 1960s, when litanies and rosaries were habitually sung in Latin! The latter explanation exemplifies the fascinating manner in which nostalgia, fantasy and fiction combine to structure a reality that rakes in the tourist dollars and creates a legitimate ground to protect the physical constituents of the city. A blander description of the area would describe *Fontainhos* as just another area of the city, though admittedly one of the older ones, that managed to retain its external physical structure ever since the Portuguese left, owing to the conservation order imposed by the city government.[50] The *Fontainhos* festival contributed to the area's tourist explosion, and several physical manifestations of this new state of affairs attest to it: the unearthing of earlier Portuguese street names *Povo do Lisboa, Rua Natal, Cruzador San Raphael*, figure on typical *azulejos* fixed on the walls; houses are painted in colours reminiscent of provincial Portugal and converted into guest-houses; ornaments evoking Portugal can be found everywhere in the area – one memorable anecdote involves the placing of a terracotta *Galo de Barcelos*, that ubiquitous symbol of Portugal, above the pillar of a well, and its subsequent christening as *Galo de Goa*.

This celebration of *Goa Portuguesa* however, supported both by the State and powerful lobbyists, ruffled a few feathers. These parts of society have for some time protested against the representation of Goa as Portuguese, insisting on its character as Indian, hence *Goa Indica*.[51] Such protests against the writing or remembrance of histories that do not subscribe to the saffron-rights view of history, have become a recurrent feature in India. The protest reached a high symbolic point when, on 18 June 2004, some of the *azulejos* in *Fontainhos* along *31st January Road*, along with a newly restored commemorative marker built by the Portuguese, in another part of the city, were destroyed.

Panjim is an all-round exemplification of the manner in which imaginations born of the colonial encounter and the new global economy have been sought to be inserted into an urban legal discourse. These imaginations have impacted on the physicality of Panjim in no small way: clearing the streets of the city of hawkers and vendors, reifying Panjim's Lusitanian image, forcing segments of the city to remain frozen in time, while opening up other portions so that the city may eventually become 'like Singapore'. These imaginations are inserted into law, through constellations of various groups; the middle class, the nostalgic elite, rightist groups, politicians, heritage groups, each with their own fantasy that seek political support through collaboration with the others. This insertion of fantasies into the law problematises in turn the law's representation of itself as

---

49 It is now perhaps superfluous to point out that this is once more a notion fed entirely by the British fantasies of the nature of the Portuguese national character.

50 Indicated in the Outline Development Plan 1990 for Panjim City, under the Planning and Development Authority (Development Plan) Regulations, 1989, for the Goa, Daman and Diu Town and Country Planning Act, 1974.

51 Angley, 1994.

value-neutral and objective, and gives us scope to theorise on the nature of legality.

## Conclusion: reality bites

The date of 18 June 1946 has gained significance among Goan historians as the day when the 'national' movement against the Portuguese in Goa is credited to have begun. What was perhaps most frightening through this entire episode was that it was witnessed by policemen on duty, who simply stood by and watched as street signs were being smashed by the saffron activists. This vandalisation and the silent participation of the policemen in the entire episode was pointed out most forcefully in the press, and in itself tickles the 'natural' assumption that the police are a neutral entity obliged and committed to upholding an equally objective law. In a number of instances in India, the police have been seen to be partisan in their dealing with riots, be it in her early years,[52] or more recently during the Gujarat pogrom, or the riots in Bombay.[53] This occurrence presents us with the opportunity to unmask the fantasy encouraged by the law with regard to the police, namely an independent police force upholding an objective and impersonal law, when in reality what the police invariably do is take sides in any dispute, their position determined by the content of the law. Disabusing us of this notion of an autonomous and shaping (rather than being shaped) law, Julia Eckert suggests that the various organisations involved as actors in governmental roles, be they administrative, charitable, judicial or others, generate their own versions of legality and are intent on capturing the state, feeding their 'unnamed law' into the container of the state and its legality, shaping thus the legal order.[54]

A similar example is provided in the manner in which the middle class of Panjim has been able to represent to the State that it was 'right' that hawkers and vendors be removed from places where they had set up shop. Politics then, like Bourdieu encourages us to think – and as evidenced through our earlier discussion of Panjim – can be, and is, widely understood as a game and control of government institutions and its resources, be it through its capacity to define history, to list and protect heritage buildings, or simply to ensure a flow of commissions to favoured organisations and individuals.[55] In this sense, the police can be seen, not as errant and problematic functionaries of the state and the law they serve to uphold, but as indicators of the active role that the State takes in any dispute. They are, to be flippant, perfect gauges for the current disposition of the law, indicating the actor that contributes most significantly to the current composition of the law, a perfect weathervane if you like, of which way the wind blows.

---

52  Nandy, 2002.
53  Hansen, 2001.
54  Eckert, 2002.
55  Hansen, 2001: 62.

It is in such instances of urban conflict that it becomes obvious why State practice, in its wider manifestation rather than just in its black-letter law format, should equally be seen as an instrumental form of legality. The law is created, not just out of the fantasy of dominant communities or groups, but also along the way in which the apparatus of the State and these legislations and their trappings are used as containers to obtain results. In this chapter I sought to show that when it comes to the operation of legality in the space of the city, freezing our understanding of legality as emerging from black-letter law is no longer adequate.

Panjim represents a fascinating snapshot of the interaction of the multiple fantasies, especially in the way they seek to reformulate the physical space of the city. What emerges crucially about these interactions is that they could be both conflictual and conflating. In the case of the founding moment of Panjim, and subsequently during the Portuguese rule, Panjim is imagined to be a part of Portugal, and her citizens Portuguese. However, owing to its conflict with the imagination of the colonial British who wielded the balance of power, this imagination was and unfortunately continues to be dismissed as mere fantasy, false consciousness. This dismissal is crucial as it offers us insights into the role of law and the capture of power in determining which imagination will be deemed reality and which false consciousness. The arguments of the rights of the hawkers and vendors are deemed fantasies that cannot be taken seriously until Panjim, and the state whose capital it is, becomes a 'Singapore' in its own right. The combinations of fantasies, on the other hand, also gives us insights into the manner in which the city is permitted to develop. For example, the alliance between the fantasies and politics of the heritage groups, the tourism industry, the real estate market and the burgeoning middle class, allow for one portion of Panjim to be frozen in time, even as it legalises the filling of the rice-fields of Taleigao to accommodate the growing influx into the city. Fantasy and nostalgia can therefore be seen as the very 'real' constituent of the city and our world, actively shaping our experience of it, as well as its material constitution. This calls for a recognition and operationalisation of this phenomenon, rather than restricting ourselves to a response that sees it as false consciousness.

To end on a different note, a tad flippantly, but nonetheless concerned with the politics of Panjim: it appears that while we are busy seeking to exorcise the other from ourselves (and never quite succeed in doing so), we forget that there is another player in the social imagination who may have gained more than bargained for. Portugal's other has been successfully exorcised, and Portugal has been converted into the original Prospero. In the process of constituting the image of Europe via Portugal in Panjim, we have exorcised the ghost of the other from the Portuguese soul. The influence of the Moors, Portugal's original 'contaminant', is removed, as Portugal is now created, from within the realm of Caliban, as the Prospero it has always aspired to be. In the *Jardin Municipal* of Panjim, the palms that provided the echo of the Islamic garden now lie clogged and threatened amidst the rubble of construction associated with the rebuilding of Panjim in the image of Europe. If it was colonial law that lifted the Goan out of the morass of Calibanism, it is also through law and the operations of the state that Portugal has been lifted out, in Goa, from its Caliban identity, and raised to the height of the other super-Prosperos of the continent it shares with them.

## Bibliography

Anderson, B (1991) *Imagined Communities*, London: Verso

Angley, P (1994) *Goa: Concepts and Misconcepts*, Mumbai: Goa Hindu Association

Appadurai, A (1996) *Modernity at Large*, Delhi: Oxford University Press

Azavedo, C (1997) 'Historical Growth', *Panaji*, documentation of a seminar organised by North Goa Planning and Development Authority

Betts, J E (eds) (1997) *Festschrift in Honor of Charles Speel*, Monmouth, IL: Monmouth College, www.sikhlionz.com/rsssolution.htm (accessed on 29 November 2006)

Bourdieu, P and Wacquant, L J D (1992) *An Invitation to Reflexive Sociology*, Chicago, IL: The University of Chicago Press

Couto, M (2004) *Goa – A Daughter's Story*, New Delhi: Viking/Penguin Books

Cunha, T B (1961) 'The Denationalization of Goans', *Goa's Freedom Struggle*, Bombay: Dr. T.B. Cunha Memorial Committee, 55–98

Cusack, I (2003) *Nationalism and the Colonial Imprint: The Stamps of Portugal and Lusophone Africa and Asia*, www.psa.ac.uk/cps/2003/Igor%20Cusack.pdf

daFonseca, J N (1986) *An Historical and Archaeological Sketch of the City of Goa*, New Delhi: Asian Educational Services

deMenezes, A (1983) *Goa: A Brief Historical Sketch*, Panaji: AMA Travel Publications

de Noronha, O (1993) '150 years of a Capital City', *Goa Today*, 22 May

Dept. of Tourism (1997) 'Tourism Potential', in *Panaji*, documentation of a seminar organised by North Goa Planning and Development Authority

deSouza, P R (ed.) (2000) 'Pragmatic Politics in Goa: 1987–99', *Contemporary India: Transitions*, New Delhi: Sage Publications

Eckert, J (2002) *Governing Laws: On the Appropriation and Adaptation of Control in Mumbai*, Working Paper No. 33, Halle/Salle: Max Planck Institute for Social Anthropology

Fernandes, J K (2005) 'State and Community: Partners in Legality', unpublished thesis, International Institute for the Sociology of Law, Oñati, Spain

Fuller, C J and Bénéï, V (eds) (2001) *The Everyday State and Society in Modern India*, London: Hurst and Company

Golwalkar, M S (1966) *Bunch of Thoughts*, Bangalore: Jagarana Prakashana

Hansen, T B (2001) 'Governance and Myths of State in Mumbai', in Fuller, C J and Bénéï, V (eds), *The Everyday State and Society in Modern India*, London: Hurst and Company

Hobsbawm, E and Ranger, T (1983) *The Invention of Tradition*, Cambridge: Cambridge University Press

Kumar, S (1999) 'BJP's Defeat in Vidhan Sabha Elections, 1998: Widespread Erosion of Support Base', *Economic and Political Weekly*, www.epw.org.in/showArticles.php?root=1999&leaf=01&filename=2944&filetype = html (accessed on 29 November 2006)

Lawrance, J (2004) *The Search for India: Spanish and Portuguese Exploration at the Start of the Modern Age*, RB Tate Lecture, Nottingham, 3 March

Lowenthal, D (1998) 'Fabricating Heritage', 10(1) *History & Memory*, http://iupjournals.org/history/ham10-1.html (accessed on 29 November 2006)

Madureira, L (1994) 'Tropical Sex Fantasies and the Ambassador's Other Death: The Difference in Portuguese Colonialism', 28 *Cultural Critique*, Autumn 1994, 149–173

Mundkur, B (2004) 'An Outsider in Goa', 543(Nov) *Seminar* 79–83

Nandy, A (2000) 'Freud, Modernity and Postcolonial Violence', 4(5–6) *The Little Magazine*, www.littlemag.com/looking/ashisnandy.html (accessed on 29 November 2006)

Nandy, A (2002) 'The Death of an Empire', in Vasudevan, R, Sundaram, R, Bagchi, J, Narula, M, Lovink, G and Sengupta, S (eds), *Sarai Reader: The Cities of Everyday Life*, New Delhi: Sarai, CSDS and The Society for Old and New Media

Newman, R S (2001) '*Konkani Mai* Ascends the Throne', in Newman, R S (ed.), *Of Umbrellas, Goddesses and Dreams*, Mapusa: Other India Bookstore

Noronha, P (1997) 'Heritage Lost', *Panaji*, documentation of a seminar organised by North Goa Planning and Development Authority

Pandit, H (2003) *Walking in Goa*, Mumbai: Eminence Designs Pvt. Ltd.

Poggendorf-Kakar, K (2004) 'A Personal View', 543(Nov) *Seminar* 77–78

Rao, A (1996) 'The Fourth Periphery and the Two Conventions', 2(4) *The Eye* 28–32

Routledge, P (2000) 'Consuming Goa: Tourist Site as Dispensable Space', *Economic and Political Weekly*, 22 July 2000, 2647–2656, www.epw.org.in/showArticles.php?root=2000&leaf=07&filename=1555&filetype=pdf (accessed on 29 November 2006)

Samarth, A (1983) *Nova Goa: A Historical Glimpse, Collection of Essays*, Panjim: Hotel Nova Goa, 2–11

Santos, B de Sousa (1995) *Toward a New Common Sense: Law, Science and Politics in the Paradigmatic Transition*, London: Routledge

Santos, B de Sousa (2002) 'Between Prospero and Caliban: Colonialism, Postcolonialism, and Inter-identity', 39(2) *Luso-Brazilian Review* 9–43

Spitz Sr, D (1997) 'The RSS and Hindu Militancy in the 1980's', in Sienkewicz, T J and

Srivastava, R (2005) 'The Fantasy of Heritage', X(ii) *Art India* 36–47

Strathern, M (1990) 'The Concept of Society is Theoretically Obsolete', in Ingold, T (ed.), *A Debate Held in the Muriel Stott Centre, John Rylands University Library of Manchester, 28 October 1989*, London: Publishing Solutions

## Case

*Nazareth Cabral v Panjim Municipal Council* Writ Petition No.438/1995, the High Court of Bombay at Panaji, from the documentation of the People Movement for Civic Action (PMCS), Panjim

# Part III

# Legality/illegality/legitimacy

Chapter 7

# Athens

## The boundless city and the crisis of law

*Julia H Chryssostalis**

This said, it is pointless trying to decide whether Zenobia is to be classified among happy cities or among the unhappy. It makes no sense to divide cities into these two species, but rather into another two: those that through the years and the changes continue to give their form to desires, and those in which desires either erase the city or are erased by it.

(Italo Calvino, *Invisible Cities*)[1]

## Athens

Even if Calvino is right and there are no happy and unhappy cities, only cities that give their form to desires and cities erased by desires, Athens presents us with an impossible conundrum. As the most celebrated *polis* in the world and the name most associated with the classical aesthetic of reason, harmony and the law of *Logos*, Athens has inspired city making, planning and building for centuries, and provided a point of reference for movements as diverse as neo-classicism and modernism.[2] Yet at the same time, *Athens* is also the name for the formless urban landscape of mundane apartment buildings and permanently crammed streets,

* I wish to thank Alex Deliyannis for providing leads to valuable Greek material and for enabling my access to the library of the National Centre for the Enviroment and Sustainable Development [*Ethniko Kentro Perivallontos Kai Aeiforou Anaptyxis*]; Patrick Hanafin for inspiration, sustenance, and creative distraction; and Andreas Philippopoulos-Mihalopoulos for his friendship and unfailing faith that this piece would be written.

1 Calvino, 1997: 35.
2 Let us not forget, after all, that *Athens* names one of the key modernist texts on architecture, the Athens Charter, that is, the results of the 4th *Congrès Internationaux d' Architecture Moderne* (CIAM), which took place in the summer of 1933 aboard a cruise ship sailing between Marseilles and Athens. Initially published as a set of 'Constatations' (Observations) in *Technika Chronika – Les Annales techniques* 44–46 (November 1933), the journal of the Greek Technical Chamber, it was later incorporated in Le Corbusier's *The Athens Charter* published in 1943. A major modernist manifesto and a defining text for town planning after the Second World War, it provides the clearest statement of the modernist vision of the 'functional city', that is, a city ordered and organised on the basis of four functions: dwelling, which is seen as the most important, work, leisure and circulation. On the 1933 congress (CIAM 4) and the 'Athens Charter' see further, Mumford, 2002: 73–91.

which swallowing up both city and non-city with equal fervour, today extends over the entire basin of Attica and beyond. In other words, under the name of *Athens* we find united a regulative idea for the perfectly formed city in both civic and urban terms, as well as a hopelessly unruly urban reality in which the city is repeatedly re-built (through a series of building booms), re-modelled (through major infrastructural projects) and re-membered (through various conservation and renovation projects), but at the same time also perpetually lost.

Then again, when we are talking of loss in this case, what exactly is it that is being lost here? Is it a certain specificity of the city of Athens *vis-à-vis* other cities, or is it Athens as a *city* that is being lost? And when we start asking this sort of questions about the character or nature of *a* city, are we not also asking implicitly a host of other questions, such as

> what are the laws and constitutions that make a city a city, that prevent it from becoming something else, even as it inevitably undergoes transformation and change? What would it mean to establish the borders of a city, to define and limit it in order to confer an identity upon it? How is a city lost, destroyed, abandoned, and then rebuilt from its ruins, sometimes in other places and in memory of its name and patrimony? What would it mean for a city to remain identical to itself or for it to remain internally consistent? Is this possible, or must a city always remain open to transformation, to the changes that alter and displace it?[3]

These questions are particularly apposite in the case of Athens, as 'Athens' names a city without which it would be impossible to think the city, a city to which, as Aldo Rossi notes, we ultimately trace our very memory of the city,[4] and to which we constantly return as one of its *loci classici*. For according to Rossi, even

> if Rome is responsible for supplying the general principles of urbanism, and thus for the cities that were constructed according to rational principles throughout the Roman world, it is Greece [and Athens in particular] where the fundamentals of the constitution of the city lie, as well as a type of urban beauty, of an architecture of the city.[5]

There is little doubt that to the Western mind Athens signifies more than a city, the utopian, picture perfect of the marriage of *polis* and *asty*, *civitas* and *urbs*. At once iconic – 'the purest experience of humanity'[6] says Rossi – and mythical – '[f]or a brief generation in Athens the ways of the gods, the ways of nature, and the

---

3  Cadava and Levy, 2003: xv.
4  Rossi, 1984: 134.
5  Ibid.
6  Ibid. at 137.

ways of men came close to a common point',[7] writes Lewis Mumford in *The City in History* – it is a place which is central to the modern imaginary, a place in which Europe locates its *archē* and which modernity has invested with the value of an 'origin' (of philosophy, democracy, the arts and the sciences). As a repository of perfect forms and eternal values, Athens is thus also a place standing outside of place and time, ideal and impossible. Dislodged from its actual location, disembodied and atemporal, it is a symbol, a place of the mind, repeatedly fantasised about and infinitely appropriated, a dreamscape which belongs to the Western collective unconscious; one of those places that is well known and feels immediately familiar[8] but at the same time, when confronted with, is difficult to take in. Like Freud on the Acropolis,[9] one feels equally surprised that it *should* be there – '[s]o all this really *does* exist just as we learnt at school![10] Freud catches himself thinking – and that it should *not* be there; an astonishing thought, Freud continues, since he 'had been unaware that the real existence of Athens, the Acropolis, and the landscape around it had ever been objects of doubt'.[11]

Indeed, Athens, as one commentator puts it, 'is famous for being *old*'.[12] And yet, surprising as this may be (for it shows, more than anything else perhaps, how deeply embedded a certain idea of Athens is in the modern unconscious), Athens is not an old city in the way that, say, Rome is old, or Istanbul, or Thessaloniki for that matter. These are cities which have always been cities,[13] whereas in the case of Athens there is a profound discontinuity marking its urban

---

7  Mumford, 1991: 194.
8  'To arrive there is a homecoming', Hugh Leonard, the Irish playwright, says in a piece for the *New York Times Magazine* (Leonard, 2004: 165).
9  Freud, 1964.
10  Ibid. at 241 (emphasis in the original).
11  Ibid. As Freud goes on to explain, of course, this incredulity has to be sought in his own relation to Athens, that is, in the meaning that Athens has for *him*. For ultimately his doubt is not about the real existence of Athens but about whether or not *he* '*should* ever see Athens' (Ibid. at 246; my emphasis). Though very personal, Freud's account of his encounter with Athens is of wider significance. It shows how one does not come to Athens simply with a set of images but with a specific way of relating to the city already forged. In other words, the city has meaning not only at the collective, symbolic level but also at the profoundly individual level of fantasy, which ultimately determines the way one comes to it, irrespective of whether or not one ever actually reaches it. Take for instance, Karl Friedrich Schinkel, the eminent nineteenth-century architect and committed neo-classicist, who was commissioned to design a palace for King Otto on the Acropolis. Although intensely preoccupied with Athens throughout his professional life, his so-called 'Greek abstinence', meant that he never travelled to Athens and continued to dwell in the Athens of his designs instead. Or Hélène Cixous, who, while writing about Prague, mentions Athens as another of those cities about which she had repeatedly dreamed of but could not imagine herself in 'in the flesh' (Cixous, 1997: 304). Or Jacques Derrida, who, while in Athens, finds himself wondering why it took him so long to visit, why he was yielding to Greece so late in life (Derrida, 1996: 46 (French text); 15 (Greek text)).
12  Roderick Beaton, 'Foreword', in Llewellyn Smith, 2004: viii.
13  Ibid.

history. The arrival of Christianity in the fourth century, which eventually led to the closing down of the theatres and the schools of philosophy, along with long periods of instability during the Middle Ages,[14] meant that by the end of the twelfth-century Athens had declined to such a degree that one could hardly say it existed, let alone call it a city. Michael Acominatus, Metropolitan of Athens (c. 1175–1204) writes:

> You cannot look upon Athens without tears. Not that the city has lost her ancient glory, it is too long since that was taken from her. Now she has lost the very form, appearance and character of a city. Everywhere you see walls stripped and demolished, houses razed to the ground, their sites ploughed under.[15]

Moreover, this picture of destruction and desolation does not represent a brief, isolated moment in the city's history. This *is* the picture of the city from the twelfth century onwards, despite a brief spell of prosperity between 1263 and 1305. It is telling that, in 1573, the German humanist Martin Crusius (Kraus) writes to a correspondent in Constantinople to ask whether or not Athens still existed,[16] and it is not an accident that during this period Athens seems to have lost even its name, being referred to as 'Setines'.

When it gets rediscovered by Western travellers in the eighteenth century,[17] it has a population of around 12,000 and the image 'that emerges...is of a small, sleepy Greek Ottoman town cut off from the great movements of ideas and of commerce',[18] with 'mean and straggling'[19] houses that are built close to the Acropolis and streets that 'are very irregular',[20] narrow and crooked. The ancient ruins are of course still there, although

> the Parthenon ha[s] been converted into a mosque, complete with a minaret. The Areios Pagos – meeting place in the ancient assembly – [is] empty and overgrown. The agora, where Socrates had pursued his interrogations and poisoned himself in a prison cell, [lies] buried beneath a thriving Turkish

14  On the history of the city during the Middle Ages, see Stoneman, 2004: 161–196.
15  Cited in Llewellyn Smith, 2004: 108. On this point see also ibid. at 173.
16  'The German historians', he says, 'are writing that Athens has been totally destroyed and that nothing is left but for a few fishermen's huts' (cited in Lydakis, 2004: 4).
17  Two architects, James ('Athenian') Stuart and Nicholas Revett were probably the most influential. They arrived in Athens in 1751, with their trip funded by the Society of Dilettanti, to study the Architecture of Athens 'for the improvement of the arts in England'. Their *Antiquities of Athens Measured and Delineated*, which came out in three parts between 1762 and 1794, was a constant point of reference for Greek revival architecture in Edinburgh and throughout Britain.
18  Llewellyn Smith, 2004: 117. See also more generally, 112–126.
19  Richard Chandler, *Travels in Asia Minor and Greece: Or An Account of a Tour, Made at the expense of the Society of Dilettanti*, cited in Llewellyn Smith, 2004: 116.
20  Ibid.

neighbourhood. The Attic plain has been given over to the cultivation of grains and olives.[21]

Then, in the nineteenth century, during the Greek War of Independence, Athens turned into a major battleground, which meant that, by 1827, with the end of the siege of the Acropolis, little was left of the town. The population had left, taking refuge in the neighbouring countryside and islands. Of the buildings, only 60 houses remained standing, most of them severely damaged, the rest being completely destroyed, and it was only after *all* the fighting had ended[22] that people started slowly returning and rebuilding their houses. According to one British traveller, still in 1832

> [t]he town of Athens is... lying in ruins. The streets are almost deserted: nearly all the houses are without roofs. The churches are reduced to bare walls and heaps of stones and mortar. There is but one church in which the service is performed. A few new wooden houses, one or two of more solid structure, and the two lines of planked sheds which form the bazaar are all the inhabited dwellings that Athens can now boast.... In this state of modern desolation... [t]he least ruined objects here, are some of the ruins themselves.[23]

Of this not much had changed when, a couple of years later, on the 1/13 of December 1834, Athens became by Royal Decree[24] officially the capital of Greece.

## Modern Athens

To this day, Athens has not stopped being built. Viewed from a distance, the dense mass of little greyish boxes lining the Attic basin looks like a giant fungal carpet spreading further and further up the slopes of the surrounding mountains[25] and encroaching on the shores of the Saronic Gulf, all the way from Eleusis and Piraeus

---

21 Faubion, 1993: 24–25.

22 Although the last battle was fought in March 1829, the War of Independence formally came to an end with the signing of the London Protocol in February 1830. The Protocol recognised Greek independence under the guarantee of Britain, France and Russia.

23 Christopher Wordsworth, *Athens and Attica: Journal of a Residence There*, cited in Llewellyn Smith, 2004: 128.

24 Royal Decree [hereafter RD] of 1/13 September 1834 'On the transfer of the capital to Athens', (*Ephemeris tis Kyverniseos* [Government Gazette] 16/28 September 1834). The actual transfer was set to take place three months later, on the 1/13 December 1834.

25 These are Mounts Hymettos, Penteli, Parnitha and Aigaleo. Tellingly, one of the priorities of 'Attica SOS', the action plan set up by the Ministry for the Environment, Regional Planning and Public Works in 1994, involved protecting the mountains against the all-devouring automatism of the city to expand. On this, see further 'Attica SOS' at www.minenv.gr/4/44/4401/g440120.html (accessed on 27 November 2006).

to Sounion.[26] With a population of almost 4,000,000 (in other words, over a third of the overall population of Greece), the city keeps extending in every direction, irrespective of physical and official boundaries. What is now called 'the Metropolitan Area of Wider Athens' is an urban complex that dominates the entire region and defines the forms and norms of urban life throughout Greece. For right from the very beginning of the Greek state, planning legislation for Athens has served as a model for other cities and towns, while at the same time the tropes of the 'Athenian urban model' are being reproduced in cities and towns throughout Greece. This is also why one should read the 'metropolitan' designation here literally – Athens as normative urban matrix (*metro*-polis) for the rest of the country.

As far as the material history of the city's development is concerned, it is invariably told as a tragedy: a story of grand designs, weak rulers and impotent laws, of dislocated people and uncontrolled urbanisation, of rapid growth and environmental degradation. Set out in four acts,[27] the first covers the years from 1833 to 1922. This is when, from destroyed Ottoman town, Athens was gradually transformed into the bustling neo-classical capital of an expanding kingdom[28] with irredentist ambitions.[29] With a layout designed by German and German-trained architects[30] following international neo-classical ideals of urban form and beauty; a morphology in which neo-classicism constituted both the official architectural language and 'a widely-disseminated architectural idiom in vernacular use';[31] the antiquities excavated, restored, purged from later 'additions' and fenced off from the fabric of daily life, ready for visitors to see and admire; and a new, magnificent civic architecture 'bestow[ing] a stamp of grandeur and

26 Needless to say, the sea need not be the limit here. According to Prevelakis (2002), if things continue like this, it is only a matter of time before the city extends not only further east to the plain of Mesogeia, where the new airport is now located, but also further to the south, to the nearby islands of Aegina and Salamina.
27 Cf. Stoneman, 2004 and Condaratos and Wang, 1999. For a different approach, see Burgel, 1981 and Burgel, 2005.
28 During this period, Greece is granted significant territorial gains: the Ionian islands (1864), Thessaly and Arta (1881), Crete, Macedonia, Ioannina and islands of the Aegean (1913), Western Thrace (1919), Eastern Thrace, the rest of the Aegean islands, and the right to administer the greater Smyrna area in Asia Minor, pending a plebiscite (1920). See further, Koliopoulos and Veremis, 2002.
29 These ambitions (and the expansionist policy that actively pursued them) were encapsulated in the 'Great Idea' (*Megali Idea*) – the dream of an imperial 'Greece of two continents and five seas'. See further, Koliopoulos and Veremis, 2002.
30 These were Stamatis Kleanthis and Eduard Schaubert, who designed the first plan for the 'New City of Athens', and Leo von Klenze, who subsequently modified it. Kleanthis and Schaubert had studied under Schinkel in Berlin, while von Klenze had studied in Berlin and Paris and was already an established figure in European architecture when he arrived in Athens. His projects include the Munich Glyptothek and Pinakothek, the Walhalla and St Petersburg's Hermitage.
31 Giacumacatos, 1999: 27. Although neo-classical architecture was introduced by the Bavarian court in the 1830s, as Biris points out,

> [t]he course of Athenian neo-classicism is a unique phenomenon in the history of modern architecture which, both in the aesthetic cohesion of its expressive media and in its

permanence to the city and its institutions',[32] while at the same time concealing the internal fragility of the new state, the building of the 'New City of Athens' in the nineteenth century came to symbolise 'the country's rebirth, connection with antiquity, and entry into the family of Europe'.[33] By the turn of the century, its population had risen to 125,000. 'It boasted several paved, straight, wide streets, which were tree-planted, lit at night and even sprinkled with water on hot summer days',[34] elegant two-storey mansions with gardens at the back, cafes and theatres, as well as a host of new, imposing buildings, which included the palace, the parliament, the cathedral, the archaeological museum, the Athenian trilogy (university, academy, library) and many private residences of wealthy Greeks of the diaspora. As Bastea notes,

> [t]he extraordinary investment represented in the building program, at both the civic and the residential level, coupled with the development of arts and letters in Athens, gradually strengthened the position of the capital among the Greeks within and outside the national borders.[35]

and consolidated it as the cultural epicentre of Hellenism.[36] At the same time, the well-preserved classical antiquities coupled with the stylistic similarities between its urban vocabulary and that of other European capitals, underlined Athen's connection to Europe.

So did it matter that the initial plans by Kleanthis and Schaubert[37] were never fully implemented, not even in the watered-down version set out by von Klenze? Did it matter that, while the extensive planning and building programme of this

---

unprecedented duration – amounting to at least seven decades, down to about 1910 – consistently responded to the ideological and more generally cultural demands of the modern Greek society of the time'.

(Biris, 1999: 15)

On Athenian neo-classicism, see further Giacumacatos, 1999 and Biris, 1999.

32  Bastea, 2000: 147. It should be noted that a number of these grandiose buildings were built with funds provided by wealthy Greeks of the diaspora.

33  Ibid. 118.

34  Ibid. 146.

35  Ibid.

36  As Filippidis observes, 'Athens was not designed merely to be the capital of a petty state: it was to be the chief city of an empire, along the lines of the other colonialist capitals of Europe' (Filippidis, 1999: 67).

37  RD 6/18 July 1833, 'On the Rebuilding of the City of Athens, and the Transfer of the Seat of the Government There' (reprinted in *Ephemeris tis Kyverniseos* [Government Gazette] 26, 1867), approved the designs for the New City of Athens submitted by Kleanthis and Schaubert, and also declared Athens the capital of the 'Greek nation'. For their vision of the city, see further Kleanthes and Shaubert, 2000.

period was supported by a number of royal decrees,[38] 'the actual development of the city continuously deviated from the plans, and the officials themselves were often unable to define the building lines and issue construction permits'?[39] Did it matter that ownership rights and lack of funds for the necessary expropriations often resulted in narrower streets and smaller squares? Did it matter that, while the authorities failed time after time to finalise the city's plans, building continued without building permits or that building continued even when it was expressly prohibited (as in the case of the archaeological zone)? And did it matter that, as a result, 'city extensions continued to be approved in a piecemeal fashion with little concern for public spaces and other civic functions'?[40] According to Filippidis, it is in the mannerisms and compromises characterising the building of the city during this period that we find the 'seeds' of all of Athens' 'unhappy futures'.[41]

'Act Two' of the city's expansion drama covers the years from 1922 to 1950. A particularly difficult time for Greece at all levels, social, political and economic, it opens with the defeat of the Greek army in Anatolia (1922), and the ensuing refugee crisis, and is marked by economic dictatorship (1936–1941), war and foreign occupation (1940–1944), and civil war (1946–1949). During this period, Athens experienced the first wave of large-scale urbanisation. The arrival of approximately 400,000 refugees in the aftermath of the Asia Minor events[42] was to transform not only the size of its population but also its social fabric, its topography and its urban landscape.

One should note that by the early 1920s, Athens and Piraeus were already facing a housing problem. For years there had been practically no extensions to the city

---

38  These defined the city's regulatory and partial plans, approved even minor alterations, and detailed the guidelines for the rebuilding of the new capital. They included RD of 6/18 July 1833, 'On the Rebuilding of the City of Athens, etc', n. 37 earlier; RD of 6/18 March 1833 'On Penalties for Violations Regarding Public Cleanliness [Requirements] for Waste Food [Disposal] and Building Works'; RD of 3/15 May 1835 'On the Hygienic Building of Towns and Villages' (*Ephemeris tis Kyverniseos* [Government Gazette] 19, 1835); RD of 9/21 April 1836 'On the Implementation of the Plan of Athens' (*Ephemeris tis Kyverniseos* [Government Gazette] 20, 1836); and RD of 12/24 November 1836 'On Additions to the Decree on the Plan of Athens' (*Ephemeris tis Kyverniseos* [Government Gazette] 91, 1836); RD of 28 September/10 October 1837 'On a change of the 12/24 November Royal Decree About Plot Sections in the City of Athens' (*Ephemeris tis Kyverniseos* [Government Gazette] 35, 1837); RD of 3/15 June 1842 'On Amendments to the 9/21 April 1836 Decree on the Athens Plan' (*Ephemeris tis Kyverniseos* [Government Gazette] 14, 1842); RD of 31 October 1856 'On the Definition of the Zone of the City of Athens' (*Ephemeris tis Kyverniseos* [Government Gazette] 74, 1856).
39  Bastea, 2000: 106. RD of 9 October 1852, 'On the Demolition of Buildings that Do Not Follow the Plan' (*Ephemeris tis Kyverniseos* [Government Gazette] 54, 1852) provided for a rudimentary 'conflict resolution process' for such cases.
40  Bastea, 2000: 113. Between 1836 and 1920, 565 decrees were passed, which approved city extensions in areas previously developed illegally (Fotiou, 1989: 79).
41  Filippidis, 1982: 26. For an insightful analysis and a detailed account of Athens' urban development during this period, see Bastea, 2000.
42  In August 1922 alone, Greece received a total of 1,069,957 refugees, of whom 225,000 settled in Athens and Piraeus. More arrived in the months that followed (Constantopoulos, 1999: 82).

plan, and the increasing numbers of workers employed in the growing industry around the capital lived in appalling conditions in rented accommodation. So when the refugees arrived, the situation was already bad. They were initially 'housed' in makeshift camps set on the bare hills around Athens or on waste grounds in the fringes of the two cities – 'so that the social life of the city remained undisturbed', as the Refugee Settlement Commission put it.[43] State provision for accommodation on a more permanent basis took two forms. One involved the construction of low cost housing complexes at the edge of Athens and Piraeus.[44] The other involved 'the construction of properly-designed suburbs – such as Nea Smyrni – for the housing, on a private basis, of such refugees as [can] afford it.'[45] Given the extent of the crisis, though, it is clear that the publicly funded housing projects were unable to cover the housing needs of the refugees. What happened then is that the makeshift camps progressively turned into settlements, which in turn 'solidified' into districts outside the city plan. These then gradually received new waves of settlers: first workers with their families, and subsequently people fleeing the fighting of the civil war and the ensuing persecution of the anti-communist campaign. Thus, already by the early 1940s, Athens and Piraeus were no longer two separate urban entities but had become a single urban complex of over 1,000,000,[46] which continued to grow in the immediate post-war years. Moreover, as the drift to the city during the 1950s and 1960s intensified, the effect of illegal building, particularly on the western side of Athens, was 'the formation of entire urban extensions...adjoining the industrial zone along the Kifissos River'.[47]

Two aspects of this expansion need to be underlined here. The first is that right from the start the city's growth was accompanied by the establishment of a distinct socio-economic division between its eastern and its western part. On the east, there was the affluent, established, middle-class city, whereas on the west, there was the poor, working-class, precarious non-city, a mere 'urban extension' at the very edge of the city's land and law. The second aspect of this expansion is that the 'wild' urbanisation[48] of this period coincides with the introduction of

---

43 Cited in Leontidou, 1985: 79. Areas at the edge of the city used for this purpose included Kaisariani, Vyronas, Kokkinia, Nea Ionia, and Anavyssos and Nea Fokaia towards Sounio.

44 Initially, the designs for these housing complexes 'were imported and accompanied by support from international organisations, but towards the end of the period plans were also produced by Greek architects in line with the prevailing modern idiom' (Filippidis, 1999: 67). According to Leontidou, the concerted efforts to provide housing for the refugees under the direction of the Refugee Settlement Commission, which was set up by the Greek Government under the auspices of the League of Nations, was the only instance in which Greece had an active national housing policy (Leontidou, 1985: 80).

45 Filippidis, 1999: 68.

46 Leontidou, 1985: 79; Prevelakis, 2002: 50–52.

47 Filippidis, 1999: 68.

48 Leontidou, 1985: 78. The Greek word Leontidou uses here is '*agria*' which can be translated both as 'uncontrolled, uncontained, undomesticated' and as 'ferocious'. Both meanings are equally applicable in this case.

a whole new legislative framework about city planning and building meant to organise and modernise urban space and systematise the way it was dealt with. In connection to planning, Legislative Decree [*Nomothetiko Diatagma*] of 17 July 1923 'On the Planning and Building of the Cities, Towns, and Settlements of the State', required all urban development to proceed on the basis of prior, specifically drafted city and town plans, and also provided a set of basic rules regulating all phases of planning: drafting, approval and implementation.[49] In addition, a number of measures were introduced in order to implement recently elaborated city plans and to respond to the appearance of what was then a novel architectural type: the apartment building or *polykatoikia*,[50] which was to transform the urban landscape not only of Athens but of the Greek city in general. To begin with, Law 3741/1929, 'On Horizontal Ownership', made possible the individual ownership of a portion (in other words, of an a-*part*-ment) of a multi-storey building and regulated the property rights of the building's co-owners.[51] Further, the Presidential Decree of 22 April 1929 'On the General Building Regulation' consolidated and modified existing planning and building provisions, thereby unifying the regulation of urban space, provided for multi-storey building and the ratios of built and non-built space, and detailed the architectural and structural features of the modern apartment building.[52] Finally, the Royal Decree of 22 May 1934 'On Maximum Permitted Building Heights and Residential Sectors in Athens',[53] which amended the Royal Decree of 7 September 1922 'On Building Heights', divided the city into nine residential

---

49 This was an important piece of legislation at a number of levels. Symbolically, it established (urban) planning as a requirement for urban development and, by aligning itself with similar attempts to organise urban growth in other European countries, it sought to underline the country's modern and progressive orientation. On a practical level, it provided the city plans that were being drafted at the time (most notably those for Athens and Thessaloniki) with the legal tools for their implementation. For a brief presentation and criticism of the 1923 Decree, see further Christophilopoulos, 2002: 46–49; and Sakellaropoulos, 2003: 285–289.

50 The term was coined by Kyprianos Biris, and translates as 'multi-residence' (Constantopoulos, 1999: 82). According to Fotiou (1989: 80), the first apartment block appeared in Athens in 1917. It had seven storeys, it was located on Syntagma Square and preceded both the first general provision for permitted building heights (RD of 27 November 1919) and the introduction of a General Building Regulation (Presidential Decree [*Proedriko Diatagma* (hereafter PD)] of 22 April 1929) providing for multi-storey building.

51 'Horizontal ownership', introduced by Law 3741/1927, constitutes an exception for Greek property law, which is ruled by the Roman Law principle of *superficies solo cedit*, according to which ownership of a portion of land will also include ownership of all the buildings that have been constructed on it (Art 954 (Greek) Civil Code). This 'exception', which allows the individual ownership of a portion of the building combined with the joint ownership of the land, is now regulated by Arts 1002 and 1117 of the Civil Code, Law 3741/1927 and Legislative Decree [hereafter LD] 1024/1971 'On Divided Property'.

52 For a detailed examination and analysis of the 1929 Building Regulation, see Sakellaropoulos, 2003: 296–326.

53 *Ephemeris tis Kyverniseos* [Government Gazette] 167A, 1934.

sectors and determined maximum and minimum permitted heights for each, ensuring that multi-storey building remained fairly low-rise.[54]

The question that emerges here is the following: how does the fact of the existence of a series of laws aiming at modernising, unifying and controlling urban space and its development, sit with the reality of a city that is expanding outside all plans and building laws?[55] Given the city's *de facto* division, it is tempting, of course, to say that the city's growth develops along two parallel lines: one inside and one outside the city's plan and law, mirroring each other perfectly in the topography of east and west. This may well appear to be true, especially when one looks on the one hand, at the urban settlements in western Athens, which as a result of their illegal character lacked even basic services and amenities, and, on the other hand, the well-groomed suburbs that were being developed in the eastern part of the city along the model of European 'garden cities'. However, a closer look at the city inside the plan and its law reveals a much more complicated picture, not only because the *urban* space of the lawful city is not 'smoothly' lawful, since it both holds pockets of illegal building and bears the traces of such pockets, but because the *legal* space of the lawful city is also not smooth or unified. A number of examples can help illustrate this.[56]

Take for instance the provisions concerning the minimum permitted size of building plots in the General Building Regulation of 1929. In the case of Athens, an exception was made which meant that the coming into effect of these provisions was postponed every two months from the date of commencement of the Building Regulation. This postponement continued over a 10 year-period until, in 1941,[57] the provisions' effect was suspended indefinitely. Finally, a new set of provisions was brought in by the 1955 Building Regulation. Throughout this period, therefore, the size of building plots in Athens was regulated, at least technically, by the provisions of the earlier legislation of 1922.[58] However, at the same time, new extensions to the city plan, which were bringing 'within' the plan and its law areas that had been previously developed 'without', would introduce new permitted minimum sizes for the building plots. In some cases, the new permitted minimum sizes would be introduced in express deviation from the rules, but these would be neither the 1929 rules, which applied to the rest of the country, nor the 1922 rules, which applied to Athens, but a set of even earlier rules of 1834.[59] As a result, not only is there

54 The maximum height was set at 23 metres, or seven storeys, and this was only limited to the buildings in the northern section of the commercial 'triangle'. On the 1934 Decree, see further Sakellaropoulos, 2003: 351–359.
55 For an attempt to explain this coincidence, see Mantouvalou and Balla, 2003.
56 Here, I am indebted to the detailed discussion of the building legislation of this period provided in Sakellaropoulos, 2003.
57 RD of 17 March 1941.
58 RD of 7 September 1922 'On Structural Building Features, Maximum Permitted Heights, and Residential Sectors of the City of Athens'.
59 This particular case was that of the district of Kallithea, which was brought in the city plan by virtue of the Decree of 26 April 1933.

a differential implementation of the General Building Regulation, but also a fragmentation of the terms and conditions with which various urban areas are incorporated into the city's 'official' fabric, which in turn looks more and more like a set of patches that have been linked in a discontinuous and jerky way.

Consider a further example. As already mentioned, the 1934 Royal Decree on maximum permitted heights divided the city into nine residential sectors and designated maximum and minimum building heights for each. On one level, the decree maintained the basic reading of the city in terms of (commercial and residential) centre and (residential) periphery established in earlier legislation, despite the proliferation of city sectors that it introduced. On another level, however, by differentiating these areas internally into separate sectors, the implementing decree promoted an unofficial and fragmented reworking of the city. This reworking was not only unplanned but ran counter to the basic provisions of both the 1923 Planning Legislative Decree and the 1929 Building Regulation. This was achieved in two ways. First, by allowing different building heights within the same block, it cancelled the block as the basic unit of urban planning on which the regulatory framework of both decrees relied. Second, a formalistic interpretation of the 1934 decree and the 1929 Regulation validated this move, while allowing, on the basis of the 1929 Regulation itself, changes to the permitted heights to be made by a normal, rather than a legislative, decree.[60] It was now possible to amend the provisions of the General Building Regulation under this much less demanding 'procedure' – a practice that was widely used in the years to come and which meant in effect the transformation of implementation into a 'technique' of cancellation[61] of the general regulatory framework with regard to planning and building.

'Act Three' of the city's growth covers the period from 1950 to 1975 – in other words, the years of post-war reconstruction and of dictatorship during which the city goes through a new metamorphosis, marked by a new wave of *über*-urbanisation and explosive growth. As the drift to the cities continued in the post-war years, Athens' population grew in the 1960s from 1,800,000 to 2,500,000. New houses continued to be built either illegally outside the city plan, or legally inside the plan, on the *quid pro quo* system (*antiparochē*). Under this system, the owner of a plot of land and/or house agrees with a developer to exchange the plot for two, three or more apartments in an apartment block, which the developer is to build on the plot.[62] This is an arrangement, which is unique to the building market in Greece, and has proven able to satisfy both parties in equal measure to this day. It is not difficult to see why. On the one hand, the owner of the plot is able to secure housing for his/her family members in the future and steady revenue from renting the apartments he/she is not using. On the other, the developer is able to obtain land without having to spend money

---

60  Council of State, Decision (Voulevma) 75/135.

61  'To use Kassimatis' apt formulation. See Kassimatis, 1981.

62  Hence the title of Skopeteas' documentary film on Greek society and architecture in Greek fiction films (Skopeteas, 2004), *For Five Apartments and a Shop*.

for it, which he can then put into the construction of the building. In addition, as his share of the apartments is often sold in advance from the preliminary plans, his financial participation in the project remains small thus maximising his profit.[63]

On a broader picture, given that legislation in Greece right from the start has allowed the construction of buildings on fairly small plots, the use of the *quid pro quo* system has meant the construction of large numbers of buildings without correspondingly large sums of capital. In this way, part of the housing problem was dealt with without disbursement on the part of the state. Moreover, as the government saw the building trade as a lever for economic recovery, it supported the *quid pro quo* system by introducing legislation, which increased the permitted number of floors among other things.[64] As convincingly argued,[65] this increase marks an important shift in the way the urban environment is viewed under the new General Building Regulation of 1955. For, in contrast to the earlier building legislation, which saw the building as a homogeneous volume, the relative autonomisation of the floor under the new provisions meant that the building was now viewed as a mere aggregate of floors, namely useful surfaces. And this, in turn, meant that the determining factor of building now became the maximisation of the profitability of the plot. As a result, 'the apartment block acquired an unmistakably commercial orientation and its morphology was [standardised] and commercialised',[66] while the construction of apartment buildings flourished as never before – so much so that today the apartment building constitutes 'the public urban face of the Greek cities'.[67]

Throughout this period, Athens had become an enormous worksite. Under the signs of a ruthless 'development' and an anxious 'modernisation', the city was being rebuilt house by house employing a vulgarised vocabulary of modernism. As the neo-classical buildings were being pulled down one by one and replaced by apartment blocks built exclusively in reinforced concrete and plastered with stucco, and obeying a typical width and pattern, the city 'came to be a cumulatively produced entity – often a mere jumble – of independent and separate building units (apartment blocks) without any organisation whatsoever'.[68] In a certain sense, we have here the modern city produced as an 'unconscious achievement...woven, one could say, on the loom of the 19th century fabric, with the woof of a disciplined

---

63  We should also add here that until very recently the *quid pro quo* system was not taxed. The only charge was a 3.5 per cent stamp duty that was paid by the landowner. This changed after Law 3427/2005 introduced a 19 per cent VAT charge on the sale of all new buildings whose building permits were issued after 31 December 2005.

64  RD of 30 September 1955, 'On the General Building Regulation of the State', *Ephemeris tis Kyverniseos* [Government Gazette] 266A', 1955.

65  Sakellaropoulos, 2003: 326 ff.

66  Constantopoulos, 1999: 80. To a large extent, this is also what differentiates the post-war version of the apartment building from the one developed during the inter-war period. For a discussion of the differences between the two, see Constantopoulos, 1999 and Fotiou, 1989.

67  Giacumacatos, 1999: 36.

68  Constantopoulos, 1999: 80.

modern building regulation which determines both the coverage of the site and the height of the constructions'.[69]

By the early 1970s, though, the total lack of planning and control over building activities and the growing use of the motor car, coupled with a series of measures introduced during the seven-year-dictatorship allowing significant increases in the coverage ratio of the plot and the permitted heights of buildings,[70] led to the severe environmental degradation of the city. Unacceptable density indicators, crammed conditions, absence of green spaces, pollution, lack of infrastructures and the loss of a number of important buildings of earlier times,[71] became the defining features of the crisis of Athens' modernity.

Finally, 'Act Four' covers the years from 1975 until today. By this stage, the city had acquired its current form, and the effects of its 'wild' urbanisation had become impossible to ignore. Athens of course was not the only 'victim' of rapid growth. Other cities all over Greece suffered irreversible damage to their urban fabric as the 'Athenian model' metastasised everywhere, while previously 'undeveloped' areas were being 'discovered' and taken over by tourist and industrial facilities, which were set up without any consideration of their environmental impact. At the same time, illegal building continued unopposed. Given the scale of the problem, the response came at a number of levels and sought to intervene with a variety of measures.

To begin with, a new provision in the 1975 Constitution[72] placed the environment (natural, cultural and urban) under the protection of the state and set out the general principles and directions of spatial and urban planning. Further, a series of laws were introduced, dealing with spatial and regional planning,[73] urban planning and illegal building,[74] building regulations,[75]

---

69  Frampton, 1987: 15; English trans. Y. Aesopos available on www.minenv.gr/hellenikon-competition/oa/en/frampton_en.htm (accessed on 27 November 2006).

70  See for instance Compulsory Law [Anagkastikos Nomos] 395/1968. The effects of these measures were immediate at both the micro- and the macro-levels. So, for example, at the level of the individual building, it became now possible to build 'skyscrapers', while with regards to building in general, these measures powered the spread of the 'Athenian model' to the rest of the country (Filippidis, 1999: 70) .

71  Despite the introduction of legislation to protect them. Law 1469/1950 concerned the conservation of post-1830 buildings, artworks and landscapes of particular beauty.

72  Art 24 of the 1975/1986/2001 Constitution.

73  These were Law 360/1976 'On Spatial Planning and the Environment', which remained largely unimplemented, and Law 2742/1999 'On Spatial Planning and Sustainable Development'. See further Christophilopoulos, 2002 and Oikonomou, 2002.

74  These were Law 947/1979 'On Urban Areas', which amended the LD of 17 July 1923, yet, remained largely unimplemented; Law 1337/1983 'On the Extension of City and Town Plans', which was complemented by the provisions of Law 2508/1997 'On Sustainable Urban Development of the Cities and Towns of the Country'; and the regulatory plans for Athens (Law 1515/1985) and Thessaloniki (Law 1561/1985). Also Law 1337/1983 and PD 267/1998 dealt specifically with illegal building. See further Christophilopoulos, 1999 and 2002. In connection to illegal building in particular, Law 720/1977 (Art 1) introduced the possibility for the owner of the illegal building to have it legalised by paying a fee. The provision was deemed unconstitutional by the Council Of State (decisions 247/1980 and 1876/1980) and never implemented.

75  This was Law 1577/1985 'On the General Building Regulation'.

environmental protection,[76] and sustainable development.[77] In addition, an environmentally aware Council of State[78] took an increasingly active role in enforcing the new constitutional stipulation by reviewing legislation that would have an adverse effect on the environment or that did not comply with the obligation to subject further plans for development (urban, industrial, infrastructural and so on) to a careful examination of their environmental impact.

Yet, once more, despite this extensive legal programme, on the ground, the city continued to develop on the basis of its established patterns: the *quid pro quo* system and illegal building. On the one hand, as conditions in central Athens reached crisis point, more and more people moved to the suburbs which enthusiastically submitted to the rule of the apartment building.[79] At the same time, in previously illegally developed areas that had been in the meantime legalised, the old houses were also being pulled down and replaced by apartment buildings. On the other hand, new houses continued to be built illegally outside the city plan or in areas where building was prohibited, such as those classified as woodland. It is important to note here that until this point in time, illegal building had operated as an unofficial social housing policy of sorts,[80] allowing people with no financial means to have a roof over their heads. From the 1980s onwards, though, it becomes a generalised phenomenon involving all types of dwellings (primary homes, luxury villas and holiday residences), tourist facilities and recently even shopping malls.[81]

As a result of the law's inability to control and contain the city and successfully regulate urban space on the big scale, during this period there is a marked inward turn to small-scale interventions to the urban fabric.[82] This takes a number of forms, including the listing and preservation of single buildings, the pedestrianisation of certain central commercial roads (Voukourestiou, Ermou) and the remodelling of neglected areas, starting with the renewal of the Old City of Athens (or Plaka)[83] and followed for other parts of the centre (Thiseio, Metaxourgeio and Psyrri).

Finally, arguably the most spectacular development in 'Act Four' of the story of this notoriously chaotic, congested and polluted city (over 55 per cent of all Greek cars are in Athens, along with approximately 50 per cent of Greek industry) is the comprehensive makeover the city underwent in preparation of the

---

76 These were Law 360/1976 'On Spatial Planning and the Environment', which remained largely unimplemented, and Law 1650/1986 'On Environmental Protection' as amended by Law 2742/1999 on sustainable development.

77 Law 2742/1999.

78 The Fifth Chamber of the Court deals specifically with matters concerning Art 24 of the Constitution.

79 On this, see further, Kazeros and Lefas (2003).

80 Mantouvalou and Balla, 2003.

81 See further, Christophilopoulos, 1999; On the case of 'The Mall', see Telloglou, 2004.

82 Filippidis, 1999: 71.

83 'The key elements in the "cleaning up" of the area were the introduction, for each city block, of permitted land uses and the banning of the motor traffic for much of the road network' (ibid.).

2004 Olympic Games.[84] This involved major infrastructural works that had been on the cards since the mid-1970s – an airport to the north-east of the city, a high-speed ring motorway, a metro system and a tram network – as well as a whole series of other large and small scale interventions, such as the creation of an 'archaeological park' connecting the main ancient sights,[85] the renovation and improvement of the museums and galleries, the redesigning of the city's main squares, the redecorating of the buildings' façades and the removal of large poster advertisements from the city centre.[86] As a result, there is now a significantly improved road and transport network, certain parts of central Athens, particularly those in the immediate vicinity of the 'archaeological park', are in a process of regeneration, the old divide between eastern and western parts of town is being addressed, and the city seems to have re(dis)covered its seafront[87] along with a new sense of euphoria about itself. At the same time, however, it is also clear that the aims of the capital's Olympic makeover were far more ambitious than a simple set of 'improvements'. While showcasing the city's past, freshening up its image and making an immediate difference to the capital's everyday life, the makeover also involved reorganising the city's substance, remapping its topography, rebranding its identity and producing a forward-looking, unified and coherent narrative. By this the capital emerges not only as a transformed city, but more importantly as a city ready for the challenges that lie ahead, a city that can manage its differences and contradictions while maintaining a distinct identity; not a metropolis[88] therefore, but allegedly a new kind of city altogether, a '*metapolis* of the 21st century'.[89]

At this point, it is tempting to ask: Is this actually the case or is it simply a matter of the 'queen's' new clothes? How deep can even the most ambitious 'facelift' run? Reading through the 2005 Ombudsman's report on 'Quality of Life' makes one think that little has actually changed as regards the ways in which the city is growing.[90]

## Boundless city

It is perhaps difficult today to imagine that modern Athens started its life as a work of fiction. As we saw, when it became the Greek capital in 1834, it was still

---

84  Law 2947/2001 'Matters Concerning the Hosting of the Olympic Games, and the Works for the Games Infrastructure'.

85  This is a project that had started much earlier. The body in charge was set up by a joint decision (45810/24 November/15 October 1997) of the Ministers for Culture, the Environment and Public Works, and Finance, on the basis of Art 5, Law 2229/1994, which amended Law 1418/84.

86  Law 2833/2000, Law 2947/2001 and Law 3057/2002. See further Telloglou, 2004.

87  On this, see further, Telloglou: 2004, 125–162.

88  On the problematic of the metropolis, see Cacciari, 1993.

89  www.culture2000.tee.gr/ATHENS/ENGLISH/main2.html accessed on 27 November 2006. For a darker vision of the notion of 'metapolis', see Aesopos and Simaioforidis, 2001.

90  Synigoros tou Politi, 2005: 111–136.

a city only on paper, a city that had no being outside the law and the city plans, a completely imagined, if not hallucinated, city. To a large extent, therefore, the drama of the city's growth is also the story of law's defeated authorial ambitions to produce the city as an artefact, an object formed and normed, fashioned to the smallest detail. Despite law's attempts to author the urban text, to contain and control it, this has resisted law's authoring and has not stopped writing itself. In this sense, Athens presents us with a case of failed legal 'architectography',[91] in which the law, while seeking to architect the urban text, is constantly displaced from the position of *archē*, or sole authority of the city's building, that it seeks to occupy. Viewed differently, one could argue here that this displacement marks the transition from the city as architectural object to the city as post-metropolitan space, as urban expanse, as a series of urban settlements[92] – the making of Athens in the plural.

This does not mean of course that the law resigns from its ambition to make the city, to control and contain it, and pose as the only master of its space and territory. In the Greek context, the ritual of the 'city extension' has consistently provided the setup in which the law, by retrospectively legalising illegally developed urban areas can engage in its performance of omnipotence, whereby the unlawful is 'magically' transformed into lawful, and unilaterally the law extends its reach. No matter that this operation in the end works only to prove law's impotence in the face of the city's expansionist automatism. For, by reinstituting its own transgression as law, the law silently accepts and performs its own self-suspension, while, by authorising its differential application and instituting parallel legalities, it cancels out its own general regulatory programmes concerning building, town and spatial planning.[93]

Rather, what the failure of the law as the author of the city means is that the city is written and rewritten according to automatisms and regularities which relate to an altogether different set of laws. The city plan and its *nomos* can only glimpse such a set of laws in the symptomatologies of transgression that mark the city's making. This in turn would mean, though, that the constitutive act of the city 'is not the act of tracing boundaries, but their negation or cancellation'.[94]

## Bibliography

Aesopos, Y and Simaioforidis, Y (eds) (2001) *Meta-polis 2001. The Modern (Greek) City*, Athens: Metapolis Press

Agamben, G (1998) *Homo Sacer: Sovereign Power and Bare Life* (trans. Heller-Roazen, D), Stanford, CA: Stanford University Press

91 Marin, 2001: 203.
92 Cf. here Tzirtzilakis, 1999: 106.
93 On the point of the weakening of the law as boundary (or *nomos*) more generally in the boundless/infinite city, see Cacciari, 2004.
94 Agamben, 1998: 85.

Bastea, E (2000) *The Creation of Modern Athens: Planning the Myth*, Cambridge: Cambridge University Press

Biris, M (1999) 'From Late Neo-Clacissism to the Emergence of Modernism: 1990–1930', in Condaratos, S and Wang, W (eds), *Greece, 20th-Century Architecture*, Munich: Prestel, 15–26

Burgel, G (1981) *Croissance urbaine et développement capitaliste. Le 'miracle' Athénien*, Paris: Editions du Centre National de la Recherche Scientifique

Burgel, G (ed.) (1989) *H Neoelliniki Poli* [The Modern Greek City], *Athens: Exantas*

Burgel, G (2005) 'Athènes: une métropole contemporaine exemplaire?', *Cemoti* 24 – Métropoles et métropolisation', available at http://cemoti.revues.org/document1460. html (accessed on 27 November 2006)

Cacciari, M (1993) *Architecture and Nihilism: On the Philosophy of Modern Architecture*, (trans. Sartarelli, S), New Haven, CT: Yale University Press

Cacciari, M (2004) 'Nomadi in Prigione', in Bonomi, A and Abruzzese, A (eds), *La Città, 51–58 Infinita*, Milano: La Triennale di Milano/Bruno Mondadori, 51–58

Cadava, E and Levy, A (2003) 'Introduction', in Cadava, E and Levy, A (eds), *Cities Without Citizens*, Philadelphia, PA: Slought Books, xv–xviii

Calvino, I (1997) *Invisible Cities* (trans. William Weaver), London: Vintage

Christophilopoulos, D (1999) *To Dikaio tis Domisis. Tomos B: Afthaireti Domisi* [Building Law. Vol 2: Illegal Building], Athens: Sakkoulas

Christophilopoulos, D (2002) *Politistiko Perivallon – Chorikos Schediasmos kai Viosimi Anaptyxi* [Cultural Environment: Spatial Planning and Sustainable Development], Athens: Sakkoulas

Cixous, H (1997) 'Attacks on the Castle', in Leach, N (ed.), *Rethinking Architecture: A Reader in Cultural Theory*, London: Routledge, 303–308

Condaratos, S and Wang, W (eds) (1999) *Greece, 20th-Century Architecture*, Munich: Prestel

Constantopoulos, E (1999) From City-Dwelling to Multi-Dwelling', in Condaratos, S and Wang, W (eds), *Greece, 20th-Century Architecture*, Munich: Prestel, 79–88

Derrida, J (1996) 'Demeure, Athènes', in Bonhomme, J F, *Athènes à l' hombre de l' Acropole*, with text by J Derrida, Athens: Olkos (In French and Greek), 7–35 Greek text; 39–64 French text

Faubion, J D (1993) *Modern Greek Lessons. A Primer in Historical Constructivism*, Princeton, NJ: Princeton University Press

Filippidis, D (1982) 'Urbanisme coloniale en Grèce', *Urbi* 6: 25–30

Filippidis, D (1999) 'Town Planning in Greece', in Condaratos, S and Wang, W (eds), *Greece, 20th-Century Architecture*, Munich: Prestel, 65–74

Fotiou, Th (1989) 'Architectonika Protypa stin Synchroni Athina. I Periptosi tis Astikis Polykatoikias, i Morfologia tis Polis' [Architectural Models in Modern Athens. The Case of the Urban Apartment Block and the Morphology of the City], in Burgel, G (ed.), *H Neoelliniki Poli* [The Modern Greek City], Athens: Exantas, 79–95

Frampton, K (1987) *Modern Architecture: A Critical History* (Greek translation, ed. Kourkoulas, A, trans. Androulakis, T and Pangalou, M), Athens: Themelio

Freud, S (1964) 'A Disturbance of Memory on the Acropolis', in Strachey, J (ed.), *Complete Psychological Works of Sigmund Freud*, Vol 22, London: Hogarth Press, 237–248

Giacumacatos, A (1999) 'From Conservatism to Populism, Pausing at Modernism: The Architecture of the Inter-War Period', in Condaratos, S and Wang, W (eds), *Greece, 20th-Century Architecture*, Munich: Prestel, 27–39

Kassimatis, G (1981) 'I "Ektelesi" ton nomon os techiki mataiosis tis thelisis tis Voulis' ['Legal "Implementation" as a Technique of Cancellation of Parliament's Will'], *Politiki* 1: 95–103

Kazeros, N and Lefas, P (eds) (2003) *Choris Oria. Oi Achaneis Ektaseis ton Athinaikon Proastion* [Without Limits. The Endless Spaces of the Athenian Suburbs], Athens: Futura

Kleanthes, S and Shaubert, E (2000) [1832] 'Explanation of the Plan for the City of New Athens' published as an 'Appendix', in Bastea, *The Creation of Modern Athens. Planning the Myth*, Cambridge: Cambridge University Press, 217–223

Koliopoulos, J and Veremis, T (2002) *Greece: The Modern Sequel: From 1821 to the Present*, London: C. Hurst ad Co

Leonard, H (2004) 'O, Greece!', in Kerper, B (ed.), *Athens: The Collected Traveller*, New York: Fodor's/Random House, 164–172

Leontidou, L (1985) 'Poleodomiki Organosi kai koinonikoi metaschimatismoi stin Athina 1914–1985' [Urban Development and Social Transformation in Athens 1914–1985], in Ypourgeio Politismou [Ministry of Culture] (ed.), *H Athina opos (den) fainetai 1840–1985* [Athens (Dis) Appearing 1840–1985], Exhibition Catalogue, Athens, 78–83

Llewellyn Smith, M (2004) *Athens: A Cultural and Literary History*, Oxford: Signal Books

Lydakis, S (2004) 'O City of Athens, Thou Who Wert the Nurse of Wisdom' ['Eros Athinon, ton palai thryloumenon'], in *Kathimerini: Epta Hmeres*, 4 April 2004

Mantouvalou, M and Balla, E (2003) 'O (Mi?) Schediasmos tou Astikou Chorou: Koinonkoi Prosdiorismoi kai Politikes Diastaseis' ['(Non?) Planning of the Urban Space: Social Determinations and Political Dimensions'], available at www.nomosphysis. org.gr/articles, (accessed on 27 November 2006)

Marin, L (2001) 'The City in Its Map and Portrait', in *On Representations* (trans. Poe Rter, C), Stanford, CA: Stanford University Press, 202–218

Mumford, E (2002) *The CIAM Discourse on Urbanism 1928–1960*, Cambridge, MA: MIT Press

Mumford, L (1991) *The City in History: Its Origins, Its Transformations and Its Prospects*, London: Penguin Books

Oikonomou, D (2002) 'To thesmiko plaisio tis chorotaksias kai oi peripeteies tou' ['The Legislative Framework for Spatial Planning and its Adventures'], *Aeichoros* 1(1): 116–127

Prevelakis, G (2002) 'O mitropolitikos schediasmos stin Ellada: I periptosi tis Athinas' [Metropolitan Planning in Greece: The Case of Athens], *Aeichoros* 1(1): 50–59

Rossi, A (1984) *The Architecture of the City* (trans. Ghirardo, D and Ockman, J), Cambridge, MA: MIT Press

Sakellaropoulos, C (2003) *Moderna Architectoniki kai Politiki tis Astikis Anoikodomisis. Athina 1945–1960* [Modern Architecture and Urban Reconstruction Policy. Athens 1945–1960], Athens: Papazissis

Skopeteas, Y (dir.) (2004) *For Five Apartments and a Shop!* A Documentary Film About Architecture and Society in Athens as Shown in Greek Fiction Films *(1924–2004)*, script by Philippidis, D and Skopeteas, Y, Athens: Benaki Museum

Stoneman, R (2004) *A Traveller's History of Athens*, London: Phoenix/Windrush Press

Synigoros tou Politi [Ombudsman] (2005) *Annual Report,* available at www.synigoros.gr/annual_05/04_apologismos_p2.pdf (accessed on 27 November 2006)

Telloglou, T (2004) *H Poli ton Agonon* [The City of the Games], Athens: Estia

Tzirtzilakis, Y (1999) 'Belated Neighbour or Familiar Stranger? Positioning the Models for the Reception of Greek Architecture', in Condaratos, S and Wang, W (eds), *Greece, 20th-Century Architecture*, Munich: Prestel, 101–108

Ypourgeio Politismou [Ministry of Culture] (ed.) (1985), *H Athina opos (den) fainetai 1840–1985* [Athens (Dis) Appearing 1840–1985], Exhibition Catalogue, Athens

# Chapter 8

# Mexico City

The city and its law in eight episodes,
1940–2005

*Antonio Azuela**

## Introduction

This chapter is about the relation between the law and a city that has increased its population 7 times in 50 years, has undergone profound changes in its political system and has suffered economic crises much worse than the earthquake that destroyed 3,000 of its buildings in 1985. An attempt to tell that story through a mere description of statutes and by-laws that supposedly rule urban processes would give us only a very small part of that story; or rather, it can give us only a single moment of it: the one in which inspired political actors (in their role as legislators) enact the urban world as (they think) it should be. Instead, I intend to explore the *legal experience* of this urban society, that is, the way people use the law (or is forced to tolerate it) in the wide range of social interactions that occur in the urban context. The problem, of course, is that such legal experience is a vast and complex reality, and it would be impossible to render a reasonable accout of that universe *as a whole* in a few pages. Indeed, in the work of the urban theorist Richard Ingersoll, we encounter the idea that the impossibility of analysing the totality of a contemporary metropolitan agglomeration finds its solution in the language of film-making: the *jumpcut* is the way in which a story is told in pieces, sometimes abruptly taking us back and forth in time and from one place to another. Cinema-goers rarely have more than 90 minutes to consider a story; yet film-makers manage to deliver one. The story 'as a whole' is something we reconstruct in our minds and with our own cultural background; what they give us is just a series of images put together through the *jumpcut* technique; this is also the way we experience the huge urban agglomerations of our time.[1]

In what follows, I offer to the reader an idea of the relation between Mexico City and the law, through the description of eight 'legal landmarks' of the city's history in the last 60 years. Through what might be called a small collection of

* Instituto de Investigaciones Sociales. Universidad Nacional Autónoma de México. Dedicated to Irene Azuela, a *Chilanga* who is also a Londoner. I wish to express my warmest thanks to Arturo Valladares and Camilo Saavedra for providing useful comments to a first draft of this chapter.
1 Ingersoll, 1996.

vignettes, I illustrate the multiple dimensions of that relation. This endeavour presupposes the abandonment of two (predictably similar) ideas: that the city is a coherent whole, just like an organism; and that the law is a system, that is also a coherent whole. The notion that a city is an organism (an old biological metaphor which is hard to sustain when one considers, *inter alia*, contemporary environmental parameters)[2] must be replaced with the recognition of the fragmented character of contemporary metropolis.

On the other hand, the idea of the law as a coherent system weakens when, instead of looking at the logical connections between norms, we analyse social practices in which the law is central to actors' discourses; coherence becomes the least interesting concept by which to describe what we see. Moreover, when we consider the urban experience *and* the legal experience together, the word 'fragmentation' gives way to a stronger one: *dislocation*. Not only are the parts of the whole separated from each other, but they are positively *dislocated:* no longer is it possible to imagine a way of reestablishing a meaningful connection between them.

## 1946: the invention of regularisation

During the Second World War, Mexico City was growing at an unprecedented rate, both in population[3] and in industrial production.[4] One of the most relevant changes taking place was the emergence of the *colonias proletarias*, which became the dominant form of urban habitat for the poor. Looking at this phenomenon from the unusual point of view of the *Diario Oficial de la Federación* (the Mexican 'Registrar'), one finds an interesting legal fact: in six years, 71 decrees signed by the President of the Republic expropriated suburban areas in order to 'create population centres for workers'.

The practice of expropriating land for the urban poor resembles the agrarian reform that distributed half the national territory to peasants throughout the twentieth century.[5] It may thus seem strange that this practice by the city's government was never proclaimed as part of the official programme of the Mexican revolution. However, the fact is that those expropriations had, to a large extent, a fictional character. Not because land was not really occupied by the urban poor;

---

2  Obviously, most large cities' energy balance includes flows coming from afar. Also, their internal fragmentation makes it possible that, within the same 'city', hundreds of thousands may be exposed to horrible tragedies, whereas those in the rest of the urban agglomeration experience (when tragedies occur) the same kind of emotions they can feel with distant tsunamis or with the death of a Pope.

3  During that decade, the city's population went from 1.7 to just over 3 million, an annual growth rate of 5.87 per cent, Negrete, 2000: 248.

4  For the general evolution of the city, see generally Garza, 2000.

5  As with agrarian reform, these urban policies included mechanisms to integrate the masses into corporatist organisations. See the analysis of the *Reglamento de Colonias* in Azuela and Cruz, 1989.

rather, because in many cases the poor had already occupied the land – be it in the form of land invasion or illegal subdivisions – by the time the expropriation decrees were issued. When aerial photographs of those years are analysed in relation to the dates of the expropriation decrees, one discovers that many of the latter were issued long after houses had appeared on the land that was expropriated for 'creating' those workers' neighbourhoods.[6] For almost six years, government officials had been trying to pretend they controlled the process, when in fact they were only reacting to a *de facto* situation. This was recognised at the end of the *sexenio* (the six-year term of the presidency), as the final report of the city government states that during the period 107 *colonias* were *regularised* – with a list that included those that had been allegedly created by decree. It was the first time the word 'regularisation' was used in official discourse.

As we shall see, land tenure regularisation became public policy in the 1970s, but its social foundations were well established by the 1940s. In the beginning, it took some time for the government to recognise regularisation as an acceptable practice, but its political potential became clear at once. As in the rest of the underdeveloped urbanising world, the Mexican state was (and still is) unable to guarantee access to land for the urban poor. But in Mexico irregular urbanisation was integrated into the political system in a remarkably extensive fashion. It is well known that granting government tolerance towards illegal urbanisation in exchange for loyalty at electoral times has been a profitable political transaction in many parts of the world, but in Mexico City the use of legal devices to sanctify this tolerance was part and parcel of the process. The ideology of the Mexican Revolution permeated the legal practice of the government to such an extent, that legal pluralism was an internal tension of state practice, rather than a tension between state law and practices outside it.[7]

## 1952: the end of planning as urban renovation

Nowadays, urban processes that contravene land use regulations are seen as the clearest evidence that there is no such thing as a rule of law in this country. But a less simplistic image emerges when we look at specific episodes of the history of planning in the city. By the early 1950s, the 1933 Planning Act (*Ley de Planificación*), influenced by CIAM,[8] used the word *planificación* for the opening (or widening) of roads in the city's core. Following Le Corbusier's ideas, the way of dealing with a congested and 'unhealthy' urban environment was to tear buildings down and to open wide roads for better ventilation – and cars. Nowadays, this is seen as an atrocity against the richest historical centre of the

---

6  Azuela and Cruz, 1989.

7  For another account of the way people use the law in urban processes in Mexico, see the splendid article by Jones, 1998.

8  The Internatsional Congress of Architecture, dominated by modernist urban theories.

continent,[9] but by 1950 three major renovation projects had already destroyed parts of the centre and a social protest began to emerge through a coalition of conservationists and house owners.

Interestingly, the Planning Act created a 'Planning Commission', a sort of planning board with representatives of professional bodies (engineers, architects), house owners' associations and government officials. Since all urban projects had to be approved by the Commission, this body became the field of the confrontation between those who wanted to preserve the city, and 'planners' – that is, those in favour of road opening. The latter used the Planning Act and its 'instrument'; the former used the law on monuments and historic buildings. In one of the sessions, one of the planners said that

> ...if, really, colonial monuments cannot be touched and no betterment is allowed for the city, then there is no point in the existence of a Planning Commission at all.[10]

That was the sort of technocratic approach with which planning was associated. But what I want to convey here is that the law was used by social actors even in an authoritarian political context. That was the period of an undisputed political domination by the official party (the *Partido Revolucionario Institutional* or PRI); a party that for decades fascinated political analysts with its capacity to stay in power through what appeared an eternal and invincible machine. In spite of such an authoritarian context, social resistance to urban projects used the law and did it successfully: with the decisive support from one paper,[11] in 1953 the government projects were abandoned and, since then, it is unthinkable to promote urban renovation actions that affect what we proudly call the *centro histórico*.

## 1964: Tlatelolco and its hypermodern property arrangement

In pre-hispanic times, Tlatelolco was a small town close to Mexico-Tenochtitlan, the capital of the Mexica (also known as the Aztec) empire. Since the early 1960s, the area has been occupied by a public housing project, with more than 150,000 people living in 102 ultra-modernist buildings. Tlatelolco was to become the symbol of two tragic moments in Mexico's contemporary history: the massacre of students in 1968, and the earthquake of 1985, in which hundreds of people died and dozens of buildings were destroyed. In 1964, in the project's opening ceremony, the speech of the main responsible comprised two elements that reflect the optimism of those days. On the one hand, he announced that a

---

9   This is true at least in terms of colonial architecture.
10  Quoted in García Cortés, 1972: 261.
11  One of Mexico city's major papers, *El Universal*, covered the story and its role was crucial in forcing the government to stop renovation projects. True, newspapers had not enough freedom to criticise the President, but they could influence urban policies, as in this case, García Cortés, 1972.

team of competent engineers had already taken care of the 'slight leaning' that had been detected in one of the buildings. On the other hand, he praised the innovative system of property rights that was being used, namely, the certificate of participation (or *certificado de participación inmobiliaria*) that Mexican lawyers had devised in order to facilitate transactions over individual apartments, following the inspiration of trust management in the United States of America. Like today's law-and-economics gurus, so obsessed with 'getting the institutions right' through a specific 'property arrangement' for every social problem, lawyers working for banks (including in this case a state-owned one) thought they had found the smart legal formula that could give both economic efficiency and the personal sense of security that property titles are supposed to provide.

Years later, it became obvious that both legal and civil engineering had failed. Many buildings did not resist the 1985 earthquake and the legal formula had worked against the interests of the state. As all apartments were part of a trust fund, and this fund was the government's responsibility, certificate holders (i.e. home owners) did not care about having their apartments insured and the federal government had to pay for the reconstruction after the earthquake. The residents of the Tlatelolco project were the only middle class sector of the city that obtained a state subsidy for the *entire* cost of the reconstruction, whereas at the lowest extreme of the social scale, some 12,000 households had to borrow with market-based interest rates in order to get a new house in one of the reconstruction programmes: just another instance of perverse effects of a property system.

In any case, the fact is that in the first half of the 1960s the Mexican elite still had a very strong sense of confidence in the future; a confidence that was seriously damaged in 1968, and then almost totally destroyed in 1985. Legal institutions were in the middle of that process.

## 1973: the institutionalisation of regularisation

In the planning agenda of the 1970s, one of the most salient issues was (and still is) the formation of the so-called irregular settlements in the urban periphery. As in other parts of the developing world, those settlements were created through the illegal subdivision of land and, less frequently, through its direct occupation by settlers – appropriately known in Mexico as *colonos*.[12] Eventually, it was possible for the government to control land invasions, as well as illegal subdivisions by private landowners. What has proved strikingly enduring is the selling of land belonging to *ejidos*. An *ejido* is a corporation of peasants that received land as part of the agrarian reform.[13] Land is owned collectively but cultivated individually by

12  The experience of spending years, and sometimes decades, in a hostile territory without urban services is a true colonisation process.
13  In some cases, the agrarian reform recognised the rights held by communities from colonial times – the latter are not called *ejidos*, but *comunidades*. There are some 30,000 of those two forms of agrarian corporations and they own 52 per cent of the national territory.

*ejidatarios*, that is, the members of the corporation. Each *ejidatario* has individual rights over a piece or land (*parcela*) which forms the basis of the household economy. Up to 1992, agrarian law denied both *ejidatarios* as individuals and *ejidos* as corporations the right to sell their land. Although this has been a matter of intense debate,[14] the *ejido* was a paternalistic landownership system in which only the President of the Republic was authorised to make land transactions – through the power to expropriate land. According to agrarian law, private land sales were non-existent (*inexistentes*). Thus, in the urbanisation process, transactions through which *colonos* had bought an un-serviced plot of land from *ejidatarios* were not recognised. Agrarian legislation provided for severe sanctions for *ejidatarios* if they sold their lands, but those sanctions were never applied.

By the early 1970s, the situation was ripe for an institutional innovation: since its creation in 1973–1974, the Commission for Land Tenure Regularisation ('Corett')[15] has conducted the most comprehensive programme of land regularisation in the developing world; a programme that cannot come to an end because it has created the conditions for the institutionalisation of this specific form of urbanisation.[16] Every participant in the illegal urbanisation of *ejido* lands knows that, eventually, *colonos* will get a property title from Corett. The system is very simple: once an irregular settlement is created, Corett promotes an expropriation procedure.[17] Then Corett sells to the *colonos* the plots they had bought 'outside the law'. It is like the dream of economic liberalism, since original transactions are not subject to any restriction – if only because they are illegal. There are only three problems: first, *colonos* have to pay twice for having access to (un-serviced) land;[18] second, in many instances *ejidatarios* create settlements in high-risk areas; and, third, in the whole process the government can act as a benevolent agent that forgives settlers for their improper behaviour, and places their needs above the idea of enforcing the law – no one seems to notice that it is not settlers, but *ejidatarios*, who have broken the law.[19]

There is an obvious political rationale in the government's tolerance towards the illegal selling of land by *ejidatarios*. The *ejidatarios* are the core of the 'peasant sector' of the PRI and throughout the century they constituted a very important part of the social support of the regime, something that Echeverría's

---

14 Most of those who see themselves in the left, consider the reform that allowed *ejidatarios* to sell their lands as just one more example of privatisation policies. In my opinion, there is enough evidence that such reform strengthened the position of *ejidos* vis-à-vis the state.
15 Comisión para la regularización de la tenencia de la tierra.
16 Smolka, 2000.
17 Getting the President's signature is not a problem, since he will be happy to appear as the benevolent king that grants property rights to settlers. Since 1988, titles are handed out in a folder with the president's name on the front page.
18 They pay for the non-existent original operation when they must acquire their plots from Corett.
19 The prohibition to sell the land is in this case clearly addressed to the owner, not to those who buy it in good faith.

administration tried to maintain and even nourish at any cost. In the long run, this institutionalised tolerance undermined state authority, by strengthening the position of *ejidos*. They became corporatist enclaves in which public authorities have very little to say as to the way *ejidatarios* use their lands.[20]

## 1976: the short life of planning as social justice: the Human Settlements General Act

One of the aspects of President Luis Echeverría's administration was the so-called democratic opening (*apertura democrática*) which consisted of the cooption of former student leaders into the government ranks. That was the origin of a generation of professionals that constructed the planning institutions of the country in the last quarter of the century. From 1970 to 1975, urban policies began to take shape in different government agencies and, by the time the Vancouver Conference on Human Settlements was called upon, the Mexican government was ready with a model statute, the Human Settlements General Act (*Ley General de Asentamientos Humanos* or LGAH). The President arrived at the conference in June 1976 with an exemplary legal piece, but at the cost of a very intense political conflict in the country.

The LGAH expressed the expectations of that particular generation of urban planners and urban lawyers – my generation. Not only did it create a 'rational' planning system, with a state-of-the-art version of planning theories, but it seemed, above all, to provide for legal instruments in order to bring to the urban arena one of the dearest principles of the Mexican Revolution: the *social function* of private property – a principle that was not recognised by Constitutions in many Latin American countries until the 1990s. Since 1917, Art 27 of the Mexican Constitution proclaims the principle that the general interests of society are above private property rights. It was also the basis for a comprehensive agrarian reform, public ownership over strategic natural resources, and wide regulatory powers of the state over the economy in general. But it was only in 1976 that urbanisation processes became the subject of a programme in which the social function of property was to be the core idea of urban law and policy.

Under a pragmatic interpretation, the LGAH appears as nothing more than the typical planning legislation of a capitalist country in the second half of the century. No more harmful for property interests than planning in Rooseveltian America or even in Franco's Spain.[21] However, the rhetoric, both of the legal text and of President Echeverría's propaganda regarding his initiative, made it look like a step towards socialism. Private business's organisations launched a campaign against

---

20  For an insightful account of the strategies of rural communities towards urbanisation in the periphery of Mexico City, see Cruz, 2001.

21  Indeed, the favourite reading of those interested in urban law in those days was the Spanish legal literature, and the model was the Land Act (*Ley del Suelo y Ordenación Urbana*) of 1956.

the bill arguing that it had been drafted by 'Chilean advisors that had worked for Allende', and even spreading the rumour that the Government's intentions was to place homeless people into any spare room that 'decent families' may possibly have in their houses. The President's response was also strong: he denounced entrepreneurs as a 'plutocratic and fascist minority' for opposing his bill.[22] The confrontation went on until the end of Echeverria's administration in December 1976. The political climate was so harsh that it incubated the rumour that the President was ready to organise a *coup d'état* in order to stay in power indefinitely – indeed, the rumour appeared as the main instrument of the political right.[23]

Three decades later, the whole thing looks like an appalling comedy of errors. The truth is that Echeverria's relations with private capital had deteriorated so much that anything could have sparked off a conflict in the last year of his *sexenio*. But it can also be understood as an interesting ideological debate about the tension between planning and private property in urban development. LGAH has been the basis for contemporary land use planning in Mexico. We cannot offer a comprehensive analysis of the question here, but we can acknowledge that the issue of social justice was not part of the legacy. Most Mexican cities have plans now, as does Mexico City, but the prestige of social justice for planning was seriously damaged. The idea of delivering social justice through planning law fell into irreparable disrepute and is now subject to the accusation of 'populism' or 'statism'.

## 1985: an earthquake with two epicentres

It was 7.30 am on the 19 September 1985, when an earthquake of 8.2 on the Richter scale hit Mexico City and other parts of the country. Nobody knows how many people died, but calculations range from 20,000 to 35,000. Around 3,000 buildings collapsed, and the worst-hit part of the city was its historical centre. Many thousands were found overnight living on the streets, and a few days after the initial shock the question was what the future of the city's centre and its inhabitants would be.

By then, the city centre's population was predominantly poor and (except for those living in public housing projects such as Tlatelolco) most were tenants in deteriorated buildings. Given that a large part of the latter were subject to rent controls (*rentas congeladas*), the obvious fear after the earthquake was that property owners would take advantage of the opportunity to evict tenants. Some visionaries also advocated the possibility of 'renovating' the centre; this time it was not buildings they wanted to get rid of, but people.

It would be unfair to say that driving people out of the centre was the government's project. But people had good reasons for being afraid of being expelled to the periphery. Thus, a huge social movement began to emerge as two myths of Mexican politics collapsed. First, people did not follow the leaders of

22  Azuela, 1989.
23  Monsiváis, 1980.

the PRI. The so-called official party had lost every chance of doing its historical job of organising the masses, and the new leaders had to appear as 'independent' to get any credibility – the Mexican Leviathan was publicly naked. Second, thousands of people from the rest of the metropolitan region poured into the centre to help in all sort of tasks, with a certain feeling of disobedience against the government's claims that everything was 'under control'. *Chilangos*, as they call us derogatively in the rest of the country, realised that Mexico City's immense urban community did not fit in the cliché of indifference and individualism that large cities usually convey. The word *solidarity* permeated the symbolic space, and the phrase *civil society*, until then used only by Gramscian intellectuals, rapidly became part of the political vocabulary of the whole country. Leaving aside the many implications of this collective experience, three legal landmarks are worth recalling from those days.

*An expropriation:* In the previous two years, President Miguel de la Madrid had been engaged in the redefinition of the role of the state in the economy. After Echeverría's government, things had got even worse with his successor José López Portillo, who nationalised all the banks as part of another conflict with private capital. Thus, by 1985, the word 'expropriation' was an anathema, as it evoked one of the legal instruments through which an authoritarian regime was built. But after the earthquake, it was precisely an expropriation that people were demanding in order to avoid being displaced from the city centre.

In post-war Europe, reconstruction took place through 'compulsory purchase' – a euphemism for expropriation, when read from the point of view of Mexican legal culture. But in Mexico that same action evoked a memory of the times that modernisation policies wanted to avoid – the nationalisation of the banks was too recent and the new political elite wanted to assure private capital that expropriation was out of the agenda. The problem was that hundreds of thousands were (literally) on the streets asking the government to expropriate the ruins where they used to live and develop housing projects in the centre. Sociologists that had been following urban social movements that, up to the earthquake, took place mainly in the urban periphery, would habitually locate those movements also in the periphery of the political system. But now they were witnessing a huge movement in the very centre – in both senses.

On 11 October 1985, and just before the urban disaster became a disaster for the political system as well, the President, De la Madrid, issued a decree through which more than 4,000 buildings were expropriated in order to conduct a housing programme: *Renovación Habitacional Popular*. Although some voices bemoaned that gesture as a return to populist politics, its immediate effect was to calm down the public unrest. Overnight, a social movement that had brought some 150,000 people to the gates of the presidential house, adopted the shape of a disciplined queue in front of whatever state agency was to be created in order to *administer* the reconstruction.[24]

24  For an account of this process, see Azuela, 1987.

*A new social pact:* Social discipline did not last long. *Damnificados* (those injured by the earthquake in one way or another) were not ready to accept just any proposal the government would have for the reconstruction – *inter alia*, financial conditions for the payment of new houses could be hard for poor tenants. The conflict was aggravated because the initial response of the government displayed the typical authoritarian attitude of the old political style. In March 1986, a new team was appointed to conduct the negotiations with a different approach, and two months later an agreement called *convenio de concertación* was signed between the government and dozens of social organisations. The political meaning of this agreement was much stronger than its legal status: it was the first time that a post-revolutionary government openly recognised as legitimate interlocutors social organisations that were not part of the PRI. *Concertación* was not only the catchword for a new political style: governing through agreements was the source of a new form of legitimacy that departed from the old idea of following general rules enacted by the legislative power.

*A new legislative body:* It is difficult to assert the specific impact of the political aftermath of the earthquake on Mexico's democratic transition. But there can be no doubt that it was a turning point in the city's political system. One year after the earthquake, the *Asamblea de Representantes* was created. For the first time in the history of the Federal District, there was a mechanism for the representation of the capital's polity. Since then, *Chilangos* are not second-class citizens anymore.

The *Asamblea's* powers were increased in 1996, when it became *Asamblea Legislativa.* Amongst other changes, it gained an important role in the process of lawmaking for the city. Finally, the times in which the President of the Republic ruled the city through an appointed functionary ended in 1997, when the first *Jefe de Gobierno* was elected and President Ernesto Zedillo conceded to the triumph of Cuauhtémoc Cárdenas.

When one considers together the three legal events that followed the earthquake, the complexity of the relation between the law and the life of the city becomes apparent. An instrument of the old regime (the expropriation) was used in order to reestablish social order in the city; a contractual mechanism (the *convenio de concertación*, so different to the classical ideal of the rule of law) was necessary to recognise social forces that the old PRI could not accommodate; and a legislative assembly, based on the principles of modern democracy (the *Asamblea de Representantes*), was to become a source of legitimate lawmaking. Regardless of the theoretical tag we can put on this (legal pluralism, interlegality), the coexistence of three different instruments illustrate the density of legal practices in the complex set of social relations in the city. Far from a lawless land, this appears as an ebullient social landscape that never stops from producing rules, norms and legal gestures of all sorts.

## 1998–2002: metropolitan planning in times of political pluralism

Apart from being the moral leader of the Mexican left since 1988, Cuauhtémoc Cárdenas is an engineer. An active member of the planning movement since the late 1960s, he shares the vision of urban development that one can find in the Human Settlements Act (*supra*). Thus, when he became the first elected mayor of the capital city in 1997, he promoted the review of urban development plans at several levels. It is interesting to note two of those planning initiatives, as they were put to the test in the following years. On the one hand, some 30 local plans (*planes parciales*) for particularly problematic areas were put together after a painful process of public participation. Public participation was an exercise in which different views and interests were taken into account *before* drafting the plans. About half of them relate to areas of the urban periphery, where it has been particularly difficult to find a balance between the views and the interests of three groups of actors: environmental NGOs that oppose every form of urban expansion over rural areas; members of rural communities, who do not want to be 'swallowed' by that expansion; and groups of *solicitantes de vivienda*, that is, social organisations that seek a plot of land to develop housing projects in the urban periphery, the only land they can afford. Most local plans were approved by the *Asamblea Legislativa*. And therefore they embody a combination of *concertación social* with the legitimacy of lawmaking through formal political representation.[25]

On the other hand, the Cárdenas administration promoted a Metropolitan Programme for Urban Development; that is, a programme that included more than 30 municipalities of the State of Mexico, where almost 9,000,000 people live. A constructive attitude on the part of all main actors (i.e. the planning authorities at federal level, the State of Mexico and of course Mexico City) produced what had been impossible in the times of the one-party system: a legally binding metropolitan development plan. There was an issue, however, on which they could not reach a consensus: the location of the new airport. Everyone could see that in a few years it would be necessary, but the federal government had not made a decision as to where to build it. A wise solution to this uncertainty was to state in the programme, quite explicitly, that the question had to remain open.

In 2000, the country's political landscape changed radically: Vicente Fox (from the right wing *Partido de Acción Nacional*) defeated the PRI in the presidential election, and Andrés Manuel López Obrador (AMLO), the candidate of the Partido de la Revolución Democrática (PRD), became the new *Jefe de Gobierno* in Mexico City. The PRI retained most state governments and a strong position in Congress.

25 Ziccardi, 2003.

Conflicts between Fox and AMLO have marked Mexican political life since then and, most interestingly, urban issues have been the motive – as well as the excuse. Two examples will suffice to illustrate the weakness of planning law facing those conflicts.

One of the first decisions AMLO adopted was to stop the issuing of planning permits in the urban periphery. Listening to the old argument that there is no more water to sustain urban growth, and without any public consultation, he published what became famous as the *Bando Dos* (Edict number two),[26] a simple announcement that no new urban projects would be authorised outside the central areas of the City. In the long run, it is possible that this will help to increase densities in those areas that had been losing population during the last decades. But there were two problems with this *Bando*: the decision ignored three years of public participation in planning from the Cárdenas administration. At the same time, and perhaps more importantly, it was the first gesture in which AMLO showed a lack of respect to the law, since he was clearly exerting the land use regulation powers that are by law reserved to the *Asamblea*.

AMLO had not been alone in ignoring planning laws. The main infrastructure project of President Fox's administration was the new airport for Mexico City. The governors of Mexico and Hidalgo battled over 'winning' the decision for their states. But after the Federal Government announced its decision to build the airport in the state of Mexico, it had to face a fierce upheaval of *ejidatarios*, who opposed the expropriation of their land. As a result of this, in April 2002, the project was abandoned. Many things could be said about this episode, which was, not only the first drawback of the Fox administration, but above all, a clear indication of the strength of the *ejido* property system *vis-á-vis* state institutions. The point is that the Federal Government was so determined to conduct the process in a technocratic way, that it ignored the Metropolitan Urban Development Programme approved by the Metropolitan Commission only three years before. The Commission was created as a forum for public deliberation on metropolitan issues. In other words, Fox too violated urban laws in his haste to begin the construction of the new airport, regardless of the obligation of public consultation that is recognised in the generally progressive national planning legislation.

These are only two examples in which planning law has been ignored by political actors. In both cases, actors did not employ the law in order to defend their views – not even their interests. The local government (AMLO) did not request a public discussion on the airport issue in the metropolitan commission. At the same time, those affected by the *Bando Dos* (including housing organisations and landowners in the urban periphery who could have benefited from their projects) decided not to challenge the *Bando* through legal means.

---

26 *Bando* is an old terminology for proclamations of different kinds. For example, the results of an election are announced through *Bandos*, but they are not supposed to bear a normative content by themselves.

All these conflicts have been overshadowed by an emergent political phenomenon: AMLO's social policies, in combination with his amazing political talents, have made him the most popular politician in the country – in Mexico City he enjoys an approval of more than 80 per cent of the population and at national level he has been ahead in the surveys for the presidency for almost two years. This takes us to our last vignette, which involves some serious *jumpcut*.

## 2004–2005: from a petty expropriation to a political crisis

On 7 April 2005, a legal event in Mexico City hit the front pages of many papers outside the country. For example, *The Boston Globe* reported that 'Mexico's lower house of Congress is expected to vote today to impeach the enormously popular mayor of Mexico City, Andres Manuel Lopez Obrador, in one of the most divisive moments in the nation's recent history.'[27] As it happened, the *Cámara de Diputados* stripped AMLO of his immunity. In the language of the law, this meant he could then be subjected to trial for contempt of court. In the language of politics, it meant he would not be able to contend for the Presidency in 2006, because (again in the language of the law) those who are subject to criminal charges cannot exercise their political rights – with this I want to stress the circularity between law and politics. It was the first time in the country's history that an urban conflict led to a major political crisis at national level. For more than two years, the relation between the *Jefe de Gobierno* and President Fox had deteriorated to such an extent, that it became the main issue in Mexican public life. In March 2004, the gap widened as a series of videotapes showed high level officials of the AMLO government taking money from a private entrepreneur who was making millions with public works.[28] A great divide in public opinion developed and it had to do with the relation between law and politics. On one side, for those who see AMLO as an irresponsible populist leader, he represents a threat to Mexico's democratic order because he shows no respect for the law; for those on his side, on the other hand, the whole thing was a 'conspiracy' to kick him out of the presidential race; just another example of the selective use of the law as a means to get rid of difficult political adversaries.[29]

This is not the place to explain in what sense there is some truth in both sides. But it is interesting to note that, in the legal arena, it was not the corruption cases that were being discussed, but a typically urban conflict: an expropriation decree

---

27  The Boston Globe, 7 April 2005.
28  Carlos Ahumada, the contractor, appeared in one of the videos handing money to René Bejarano, a close collaborator of AMLO and one of the leaders of the tenants' movement after the 1985 earthquake. They both went to jail.
29  On this point, see Escalante, 1999: 39.

that had been issued in order to open an unimportant road, which was challenged by the landowners through an *amparo* suit.[30] An injunction was issued by a federal judge ordering the local government to stop works on the site.[31] It is not entirely clear what the specific conduct of AMLO was in the case, but in two occasions federal courts ruled that his administration had failed to comply with the injunction. After one of those judges denounced the situation to the General Attorney (i.e. the law enforcement agency of the Federal Government), the latter referred the case to the *Cámara de Diputados* in order to obtain impeachment. As many political analysts say, his absence from the presidential election would have seriously damaged the legitimacy of our incipient democracy. That morning, before speaking to the *Cámara de Diputados* as part of the impeachment process, he gathered almost half a million people on the city's central square and launched a movement of social resistance to defend his cause.

It is of course impossible to ascertain the many implications of this episode, but there are two elements that should be mentioned for the purpose of the present argument. First, considering that the original conflict (the opening of a secondary road) is of a lesser importance compared with the great dilemmas of contemporary urbanism, it is remarkable that the legal system was not capable of dealing with it efficiently.[32] The courts were not only unable to appease the conflict, they actually made it worse. The courts' inability to explain to the general public the facts, the nature and the meaning of the conflict is indeed worrying. When the Supreme Court tried to offer such an explanation through a long insert that appeared in seven national newspapers, most people (including many lawyers) were unable to make any sense of it.[33] It is no surprise that, as in any political conflict, people take sides regardless of the arguments of the other party. But when legal discourse is unintelligible, eccentrics who want to have an independent opinion on the basis of public information end up greatly frustrated.

Second, there is a profound ambiguity in AMLO's conduct towards the law. In previous expropriation cases, his reluctance to follow courts' decisions revealed with clarity to what extent the judiciary has been the place of numerous frauds;[34] surely, he deserves credit for that. But at the same time, he repeats over and over

---

30  *Jucio de amparo* is the name of the legal recourse that private persons have in order to obtain judicial protection from government's actions that violate constitutionally protected rights.
31  The expropriation decree had been issued by the local government before the AMLO administration. It is no surprise that a federal judge find weaknesses in those kinds of decrees.
32  For a good analysis of the case, see Roldán-Xopa, 2004.
33  For a collection of opinions on this case in the Mexican press, see the newsletter Foren(sic) at www.unam.mx/iisunam
34  In the famous Paraje San Juan case, a judge ordered the payment of an absurdly large amount of money as compensation for an expropriation. It was only after AMLO refused to pay, that the Supreme Court overruled the judge's decision. The principle of *res judicata* had to be broken in order to amend what had been disclosed thanks to AMLO's reluctance to follow a judicial decision.

that the Supreme Court 'cannot be above the people' ('people', in his discourse, does not include those who disagree with him); in his scheme, substantive justice is on one side, while the law on the other. Thus, he declared that even if he was entitled to remain free on bail, he would go to jail because he had no intention of using any legal resource against an injustice.

It is not enough to recognise a political strategy there; of course protests would have been much more effective with him in jail. Rather, the point is his reluctance to give an explanation in the language of law. When confronted with the direct accusation that he ignored at least four requests by judges in the El Encino case (in order to stop public works on the site), his explanation had no clear meaning in the realm of law. His only answer was that he did no wrong, that he never gave orders to disobey the judge and that he just wanted to build a road to connect a hospital. Interestingly, he never made clear whether he answered to those requests and what exact explanation he gave. The dislocation between form and content seems irreparable. The accusation is put in such a formalistic and procedural language that it was impossible to see the substance of the case; but the substantive character of AMLO's answer was delivered in such terms, that it was very difficult to accommodate in a legal argument. Instead, his *dignity* as a social leader (a form of moral superiority) appeared as the argument for explaining both his reluctance to defend himself with legal means and for *not* explaining his conduct as the head of the local government.

After the impeachment, AMLO left his office and appointed a close collaborator in his place in order to avoid being accused of another crime. While he waited to be arrested, he led a large social mobilisation against the impeachment. Almost 1,000,000 people marched in Mexico City,[35] the international press unanimously sustained that a presidential election would not be legitimate without AMLO, and President Fox began to experience social protest in person: at every public appearance someone would show him a banner with a *no al desafuero – that is, against the impeachment*. Two weeks later, in an unexpected move, Fox solemnly announced in a nationwide TV broadcast that he had 'accepted the resignation' of the General Attorney and ordered a 'review' of the case. The political crisis, together with the legal case, dissolved into thin air, as the new team announced that there was not enough evidence to prosecute AMLO for contempt of court. Although this 'political solution' was decried by some, most analysts praised it as proof that the President was rising to the level of a real head-of-state.

It is difficult to say whether this episode will leave a mark in Mexican legal culture. But if there is any, it will probably be the reiteration of a generalised idea: that the law is an instrument in the hands of those with power, much more than a means to defend legitimate interests.

---

35  Many who did not support AMLO's policies joined the march as a protest for what was seen as a 'factious' use of the law.

## Final remarks

The *jumpcut* technique I have followed in this essay is only one way of illustrating the complexity of the relation between the law and a city like Mexico. To be sure, there is nothing new in the recognition of such complexity; suffice it to recall the old insight of E P Thompson, whose historical research found that the law was 'at every bloody level' of social reality.[36] This is particularly relevant in Mexico's public debate, where the main question is usually posed in an oversimplified (binary) way: is there (or is there not) an 'authentic' rule of law here? This is a heroic question that, as citizens, we can ask ourselves from time to time. But from an analytical point of view, its simplicity casts more shadows than light on the understanding of the meaning of law in society. Instead, I have tried to show that people use the law in many different ways. Whether we like it or not, there is not a single kit of analytical categories to find a general meaning to this 'untidy' universe. The flow of legal practices that occur in Mexico City is as overwhelming as the endless stream of human movement and interaction through which the city is socially constructed everyday. The legal experience of the city is at times as confusing as its smells and sounds. It is not easy to distinguish noise from music, destruction from construction. Likewise, it is hard to explain the kind of social order that produces (and is produced by) such practices.

There are, however, some risks in this approach: it can encourage one to adopt images like the old adage that Mexico is 'a surrealist country', a local joke that is rarely confronted with serious thinking. The recognition of complexity, paradox and contradiction should not prevent us from trying to see some general effects of major socio-legal processes. In this respect, the impeachment of Andrés Manuel López Obrador (as well as the subsequent decision not to prosecute him), the most relevant legal event of the city's history in many years, should lead us to at least one major question: to what extent will this episode change social attitudes and expectations in relation to the legal system? Beyond the propensity of most observers to conflate their own opinions with that of the majority, this should be a central empirical question for socio-legal research in the years to come.

## Bibliography

Azuela, A (1987) 'De Inquilinos a Propietarios. Derecho y Política en el Programa de Renovación Habitacional Popular', 2(1) *Estudios Demográficos y Urbanos* 53–73

Azuela, A (1989) *La Ciudad, la Propiedad Privada y el Derecho*, Mexico: El Colegio de México

Azuela, A and Cruz, M S (1989) 'La Institucionalización de las Colonias Populares y la Política Urbana del DDF 1940–1946', 4(9) *Sociológica*, January–April, 111–133

36  Thompson, 1978.

Cruz-Rodríguez, M S (2001) *Propiedad, Poblamiento y Periferia Rural en la Zona Metropolitana de la Ciudad de México*, Mexico: Universidad Autónoma Metropolitana – Azcapotzalco

Escalante, F (1999) *La Democracia Mafiosa*, Mexico: Reflexiones sobre el Cambio, AC Serie Política y Sociedad

García Cortés, A (1972) *La Reforma Urbana de México. Crónica de la Comisión de Planificación del D. F*, Mexico: Bay Gráfica y Ediciones

Garza, G (ed.) (2000) *La Ciudad de México en el Fin del Segundo Milenio*, Mexico: El Colegio de México

Ingersoll, R (1996) 'Tres Tesis sobre la Ciudad', 185 *Revista de Occidente*, October, 11–44

Jones, G A (1998) 'Resistance and the Rule of Law in Mexico', 29(3) *Development and Change* 499–523

Monsiváis, C (1980) 'La Ofensiva Ideological de la Derecha', in González Casanova, P and Florescano, E (eds), *México, Hoy*, Mexico: Siglo Veintiuno Editores

Monsiváis, C (2002) 'El Vigor de la Agonía. La Ciudad de México en los Albores del Siglo XXI', 44(IV) *Letras Libres* 12–17

Negrete, M E (2000) 'Dinámica Demográfica', in Garza, G (ed.), *La Ciudad de México en el Fin del Segundo Milenio*, Mexico: El Colegio de México

Roldán-Xopa, J (2004) *El Desafuero de Andrés Manuel López Obrador ¿Qué es la Legalidad?* Mexico: Huber Editor

Smolka, M (2000) 'Los Mercados de Suelo en América Latina', 12(5) *Landlines*, September, Cambridge, MA: The Lincoln Institute of Land Policy

Thompson, E P (1978) *The Poverty of Theory*, London: Merlin

Varley, A (1985) *Ya Somos Dueños. Ejido Land Development and Regularisation in Mexico City*, PhD Dissertation, University of London

Ziccardi, A (2003) *Planeación Participativa en el Espacio Local. Cinco Programas Parciales de Desarrollo Urbano en el Distrito Federal*, Mexico: UNAM

# Chapter 9

# Law and the poor
## The case of Dar es Salaam

*Patrick McAuslan*

## Introduction: Dar es Salaam 1961–2005: then and now

As a prelude to this chapter, it may be of interest to explain how I found myself in Dar es Salaam in September 1961, so beginning a life-long interest in, and intellectual involvement with, many periods of living in the city. During my time at Oxford University, I had met with several Tanganyikans who extolled the virtues of their country. I had had the opportunity to hear the late President Nyerere talking about his hopes and plans for an independent Tanganyika (as it then was).[1] As I was in the last stages of my final year at Oxford, the Denning Report on Legal Education in East Africa[2] was published and it was quickly announced that the new University College of Dar es Salaam would have as its first Faculty a Faculty of Law to provide legal education for the three countries of Kenya, Tanganyika and Uganda. I applied for one of the three posts and was fortunate to be successful.[3] Three days after completing my Bar Finals, I flew out to Uganda (as Makerere University College was temporarily providing administrative support for Dar es Salaam) and then on to Dar where I arrived on 27 September. Less than a fortnight later I was in the classroom with 14 students from Kenya, Tanganyika and Uganda, teaching Legal Systems of East Africa and

---

1 I recall hearing Nyerere explaining that he must be the only person ever to have won every seat in a contested election and finish up as leader of the opposition as the colonial government could, under the then 'multi-racial' constitution, nominate sufficient members to the legislature to obtain a majority.

2 *Report of the Committee on Legal Education for Students from Africa*, Cmnd. 1255 (HMSO, London 1961). There were 21 members on the Committee, a roll-call of the English legal establishment. Only 3 members were academics and only one, E R Dew, did not have some prestigious initials after his name. He must have been a solicitor. No lawyers from the Scottish legal profession were on the Committee. Scottish Law Schools however played a major role in the development of legal education in Botswana, Lesotho and Swaziland as Scots law is or was thought to be closer to the Roman-Dutch law applied in those countries.

3 The other two members were also law graduates from Oxford; A B Weston as Professor and Dean and William Twining as Senior Lecturer. The first Cambridge graduate to join the Faculty P J Nkamo-Mugerwa (who later became Attorney-General in Uganda) was dismayed and very critical that we had not included Roman Law in the curriculum.

the Law of Contract. I moved into teaching Land Law in 1965. I stayed at the College until April 1966 but have been back to Dar numerous times since then.

When I first arrived in Dar es Salaam on the eve of Tanganyika's independence, I entered a town of some 90,000 people. When I arrived in Dar es Salaam in May 2005, I entered a city of over 3,000,000 people.

In 1961, the town still had recognisable neighbourhoods where different African tribal groups lived; housing was not a significant problem for most of the residents and there was a relaxed approach to the law and housing. There was an informal and semi-formal sector of the economy which even then was quite significant but as Leslie's (1963) survey clearly showed, was not thought to be any sort of 'problem'. Consider these two quotations:

> In Dar es Salaam, the greatest possible freedom is given to the house-builder to build as he thinks best. Building regulations, overcrowding laws and so on have never been made to apply to houses built by Africans for Africans in non-permanent materials... it is often said the housing must be regulated or it will go steadily downhill, ending in a slum town of shanties... Where as now land is unlimited and provided that plots can be demarcated and distributed quickly enough... houses will continue to be built rapidly and to good standards... There has been an enormous amount of improvement of shanty dwellings converting them into normal Swahili six-room houses with high roofs and big rooms... the current danger is in fact not of too low a standard of building but of too high... Strict rules have never been enforced in Dar es Salaam although the law does provide powers to control building and living standards to a fairly strict degree. In practice prosecutions for overcrowding are undertaken only when such overcrowding is a real danger to health; they have been few: as a result it has been possible for Africans to own houses in the heart of town as well as on its outskirts.[4]

> It would be pure guess-work to put a figure to the overall underemployment: but if to the crude 'unemployment' figure of 18%, one adds what is believed to be a substantial margin for underemployment, a resulting figure of a quarter or even more of the working-age males as being on any given day temporarily free from the necessity for working to earn a living is not in conflict with one's own observation... The ease with which one may live in town without an income makes it possible for those without work to remain long after they should have given up hope of getting employment and returned whence they came...[5]

In 2005, at least 70 per cent of the residents were living in unauthorised urban settlements, technically illegal housing and subject therefore to planning by the

4 Leslie, 1963: 155–156, 178.
5 Ibid. 204–205.

bulldozer; a mode of planning that despite the fine words of housing and land policy documents is still a feature of urban planning in Tanzania. Similarly, the informal sector of the economy provides at least 70 per cent of the work undertaken by the residents of the city and of the income generated by that work.

In 1961, Dar es Salaam was governed by a Municipal Council. After a somewhat chequered start bedevilled by colonial policies of 'multi-racialism' which required equal numbers of councillors from the three communities resident in the municipality (Europeans (about 5 per cent of the population) Asians (about 20 per cent of the population) and Africans (about 75 per cent of the population) and representation of Africans by a mixture of appointed councillors and (European) District Commissioners), elections without such restrictions were held in January 1960 and an entirely elected council of 24 councillors had been elected. They had elected the first African mayor of the municipality. At independence in December 1961, Dar es Salaam had been raised to the status of a city. In 2005, Dar es Salaam with around a 98 per cent African population had a three-tier structure of local government, a City Council, 3 Municipal Councils and 70 Ward Councils.

In the space of 44 years, there have been dramatic and far-reaching social and economic changes in the city. From being a city whose economy, society and governance had been shaped by and existed for the most part for non-Africans, the city has become one now lived in and shaped by Africans, but Africans of two very different strata of society. On the one had, there is the urban elite – the politicians, the public servants, the small but visible private sector economic elite of professionals and business people, and on the other there are ordinary people, for the most part poor, struggling to find somewhere to live, something to work at and some income to survive on.

What role has the law played in Dar es Salaam in the 44 years covered by this vignette? Has it kept pace with the dramatic changes in society and economy? Has it facilitated the changes? Or has it lagged behind and acted as a brake and an obstruction to change? Is it, as it was in colonial times, still a law for the urban minority or is it a law which the urban majority can respond to and use to better themselves? In the space of a short chapter, these important questions cannot be given anything like full and comprehensive answers. Only parts of the law can be examined and I intend to concentrate principally on urban planning and land.

## Urban planning 1961–1990

In 1961, the Town and Country Planning Ordinance was five years old. It was a slightly modified version of the colonial model law produced in the Colonial Office of the British Government in the early 1950s, and was based on an amalgam of the English 1932 and 1947 Town and Country Planning Acts. It had been applied to areas in Dar es Salaam and four other towns by 1961. Under the Ordinance, within the areas to which it had been applied, an Area Planning Committee prepared a general planning scheme and submitted it to the Minister for his approval. After the scheme had been approved and published, all development in the area to which it related was required to conform to the provisions of the scheme. In order to enable the scheme to be carried out, the Ordinance provided for land within the area to be acquired compulsorily.

In 1961, Dar es Salaam was very clearly, in practice, divided into African, Asian and European areas. The African areas lay behind the Mnazi Mmoja, an open space where many political rallies took place in the run-up to independence, in Kariakoo,[6] Ilala and beyond. The Asian area commenced in front of Mnazi Mmoja and was the commercial centre of Dar es Salaam together with Asian residential areas. The Asian residential areas extended to Upanga, a mile or so from the commercial centre. Then came Selander Bridge. Beyond the bridge lay Oyster Bay, the low-density area where the European administrators, professionals and higher class commercial persons – bankers, industrialists, lawyers, doctors, accountants and so on – lived. The facilities and infrastructure of the three areas reflected the priorities of those who made the decisions about who got what.

When the independence movement – the Tanganyika African National Union (TANU) – took power in 1960, they announced that one of their early priorities would be to reverse the flow of urban investment and begin a process of investing in the African areas of Dar. As a sign that they meant business, they built the new Party Headquarters on Lumumba Street, the street that divided Kariokoo from the Mnazi Mmoja and the Asian areas of the city. The Party overstretched itself financially in building its headquarters and willingly leased the building to the new University College of Dar es Salaam which commenced with a Faculty of Law to serve all East Africa and took its first students in September 1961. I had been appointed a lecturer in the new faculty and on my arrival in Dar in September, was also asked to become the warden of the new College. The 14 students and myself lived and worked in the TANU building during our first year, as good an introduction to urban life in an African city as one could ever hope for.[7]

In 2006, the Town and Country Planning Act will reach its fiftieth anniversary. It will be the only colonial town and country planning law left in Anglophone Africa, Mauritius having finally replaced its 1954 colonial law with a new Physical Planning Act in 2004. The Party Headquarters, now very much run down, is still occupied by the University of Dar es Salaam (as the University College became in 1967). The original urban structure of Dar es Salaam remains very much what it was in 1961. Kariakoo and behind are still overwhelmingly African. The commercial centre of Dar is still dominated by Asian traders

6 This is a phonetic spelling of Carrier Corps, the military porters of the 1914–1918 war that were stationed in that area of Dar es Salaam.
7 The following year we all moved to a Salvation Army encampment at Mgulani. That was not so pleasant.

who continue to live in Upanga. The centre has spread and now accommodates several large office blocks for insurance companies, lawyers' offices, embassies, various parastatal headquarters. Only Oyster Bay has changed significantly. Now African politicians, administrators, business people and professionals have joined the expatriate community of aid officials, embassy staff, long-term consultants and expatriate business people in Oyster Bay which now also has some up-market hotels and small but tasteful shopping centres, restaurants and slipways for yachts.

In 1976, I organised and took part in a conference on Urban Legal Problems in Eastern Africa. I wrote then:

> What can be said of the introduction of the Town and Country Planning Acts into these countries. Let it be assumed that the introduction was well meant: that it was genuinely believed that this legislation was a *sine qua non* of orderly urban development and was entirely value-free; nonetheless the mind boggles at the naivety of these beliefs. The introduction of development plans provided an even better opportunity than existed under public health regulations to entrench racial segregation under the guise of low density, and high density residential areas; open spaces; market areas and commercial zones... Nor has the influence of this legislation ceased at independence...[8]

Tanzania, alas, provides an excellent illustration of this continuation of colonial style planning under a colonial style planning law. A National Capital Master Plan produced for Dar es Salaam by Canadian consultants in the early 1970s proposed the following policies for the urban majority – already a decade after independence, the urban majority were 'illegal':

> The removal of existing settlements that are in embryo and likely to be *tomorrow's problems* (italics added).
>
> The removal of existing areas that conflict with the Master Plan, particularly in the first stages of implementation.
>
> The employment of a staff or enforcement officers who actually ensure that squatters are moved from the land and are resettled in accordance with a pre-determined residential layout in other areas.
>
> No compensation should be given for the costs of resettlement and disturbance of squatters where it is proven that illegal development has taken place after an appointed day since the coming into force of new controlling legislation which should be enacted as soon as possible.[9]

8  Kanyeihamba and McAuslan, 1978: 20.
9  Ibid. 23.

Such policies would not have been suggested if planners and politicians had not been of the same mind on the matter. Fortunately the lack of funds prevented these ridiculous and socially regressive policies from being carried out but the philosophy behind them – that the urban majority are 'in the way' of the development of the city beautiful and must be made to conform to 'The Plan' is still very much alive in parts of the Tanzanian Government.[10]

In 1977, there was a move to review and replace the old Town and Country Planning Ordinance. I was invited to comment on the new draft Bill. My conclusions were that the new Bill was no more than a rehash of the existing law and had made absolutely no attempt to bring the law into line with existing Tanzanian policies on land use, social development or democracy. Perhaps my comments were a little naïve. Within planning circles, the draft was very much in accord with existing Tanzanian policies on urban development as the Master Plans being produced for Dar es Salaam and Dodoma showed. In the event, the existing law continued in operation.

## The Habitat Agenda: a new approach to urban planning

The Master Plan of the 1970s was developed in the heyday of Tanzania's socialist era, when top-down central policies to guide and if necessary compel the country and its citizenry into better times was the norm. But 25 years on, when I was involved as a consultant in advising on the reorganisation of local government in Dar es Salaam, nothing had changed on the urban planning front. This was despite the fact that major and fundamental changes had taken place at the international level with respect to policies about urban planning and development and at the national level with respect to land tenure.

First, the international level. At the UN City Summit in Istanbul in June 1996, participating governments, of which Tanzania was one, agreed to a Global Plan of Action (GPA) and the Habitat Agenda, a set of policy prescriptions designed to chart the way forward to new and more people-friendly approaches to urban development for the new millennium. At the risk of oversimplification of a complex, densely packed and significant document, the fundamental principle which informs all the detail and helps make sense of the Habitat Agenda is that of *enablement*. In order however to make sense of enablement, to understand how it has been used in the Agenda, it needs to be broken down into three parts – market enablement, political enablement and community enablement.[11]

10  The same Canadian planning firm was chosen to prepare the Master Plan for the new capital of Dodoma. It was the same type of plan. See McAuslan, 2003: chapter 7, for a discussion of that plan.

11  In making this distinction, I follow the framework developed by *The Challenge of Sustainable Cities* (1997), a publication which was the product of a conference held as part of the world-wide preparations for Habitat II.

Market enablement involves the withdrawal of the state from the provision of many goods and services, that is, in the urban sector, provision of housing and utility services should be privatised. It involves deregulation, particularly of the market for land and of the use of land since attempts to regulate and control land supply and use via state bureaucracies stifle initiatives, limits competition, increases costs and contributes to corruption. Governments should be confined to facilitating and promoting the formal and informal business sectors and markets and monitoring their performance. Legal, institutional and financial arrangements should be put in place to achieve this.

Political enablement involves the transformation of the structure and functions of central and local government, the relations between them and their relations with the market and the community. It is achieved through decentralisation at both political and administrative levels, democratisation, managerial and institutional reforms, the use of NGOs for governance functions, particularly in the delivery of services and the adoption of enablement strategies towards the market for urban goods and services. But there is more to it. The reasons for political enablement are similar to market enablement; centralised governments are inefficient, inequitable, prone to rent-seeking behaviour, proliferate overlapping agencies and lack accountability. Equally however, local governments are also inefficient, unaccountable, and lack financial resources and discipline so political enablement is also directed to rolling back the local state. Powers are to be decentralised but they would also be restructured to emphasise the enablement approach.

Community enablement in the words of *The Challenge of Sustainable Cities*:

> ...can be defined as a strategy adopted by central and local government to coordinate and facilitate the efforts of community- and neighbourhood-based organisations to initiate, plan and implement their sown projects according to the principles of self-determination, self-organization and self-management....
>
> This position contrasts sharply with previous attitudes and policies towards community participation...[12]

These had seen communities, especially those of the urban poor, as the objects of planning which had proceeded on a top-down basis and which too often selected communities and neighbourhoods to be benefited on subjective, political or 'technical' criteria. There had also been considerable suspicion of community organisations working in poor areas or having as their objective the enablement of the poor. These were, and in many countries still are, regarded as subversive.

The similarities between the Agenda and this model are plain. Chapter III of the Agenda is Commitments. Commitment C of the Agenda is headed Enablement and Participation and stresses the central role of enablement in the future

---

12 Burgess *et al.*, 1997: 151.

management of human settlements. References to enablement however recur constantly in this chapter. Commitment A: 'Adequate shelter for all' commits governments to recognise that they have an obligation to '*enable* people to obtain shelter and to protect and improve dwellings and neighbourhoods'. Commitment B: 'Sustainable human settlements' commits governments to 'creating an *enabling* international and domestic environment for economic development, social development and environmental protection...' Commitment E: 'Financing shelter and human settlements' commits governments to 'strengthening regulatory and legal frameworks to *enable* markets to work, overcome market failure and facilitate independent initiative and creativity...' (my italics).

## Reforming the land laws of Tanzania: putting the Habitat Agenda into action

What is very striking about the GPA is the stress laid on the central role of law in its implementation, particularly at the national level. Governments were expected to review their laws and bring them into line with the policies they had signed up to. In respect of Tanzania, we can look at land tenure and urban planning. In the case of land tenure, Tanzania has created, via a Land Act, 1999 and a Village Land Act, 1999, a legal framework for the operation of an equitable and efficient land market with proper regulatory procedures in place to ensure that those entering the market for the first time are not taken advantage of, and with a high degree of decentralisation to small communities to manage their own land.

The primary source and authority for the shape and content of the Tanzanian legislation is the National Land Policy (NLP), adopted by Parliament in June 1995 which clearly paid some attention to the policies being developed within Habitat in preparation for the City Summit. The philosophy behind the NLP may be stated in the following six propositions:

- The overriding role of land as a major national resource which must be used and managed in the national interest;
- The primary importance of providing for security of tenure and title to all citizens;
- The need for transparency and accountability in the exercise of public power over land, in terminology well known to lawyers, for openness, fairness and impartiality in the public administration of land;
- The need to create the conditions for the operation of an efficient *and equitable* land market;
- The need to bring about a greater involvement of the citizenry, both directly and through their representatives, in the management of land;
- The importance of providing an appropriate Tanzanian legal framework for, and mechanisms for dispute-settlement and the redress of grievances in relation to, land management.

The Land Act and the Village Land Act drafted in 1996[13] gave legislative effect to these principles.

## Sustainable cities: the failure of the Habitat Agenda to alter urban planning

We may turn now to urban planning law and bring the level of discussion down from the national to the city. I want to consider the situation of Dar es Salaam and show the contrast between new GPA-friendly land laws enacted by central government or GPA-friendly urban management policies espoused by central government and what happens at the local level. In 1996 Dar es Salaam was being run by a central government appointed Commission; the elected City Council had been dismissed for corruption and incompetence in 1996. The initial period of the Commission was to be one year and in early 1997 a joint national and international team of consultants, of which I was the team leader, was appointed to advise on the modalities of the conversion of a unitary City Council into a three-tier structure of 70 ward councils, 3 Municipal Councils and an upper tier City Council on the basis that this was to take place as soon as possible so that elected and more responsive local government could be restored to the city.

No official communication was made to the team during its work between February and June to suggest that the basis on which it was proceeding was not correct so that the report that emerged set out mechanisms, including legal changes, which would have allowed elections to new local authorities to take place in early 1998 with the new authorities beginning to exercise their new powers around March 1998. One week after the team submitted its report, the Government announced that the Commission's life was to be extended to 1999 from 1 July and it was later extended by a further year to 2000. The reasons given for this were that major changes were underway across the board in local government so that the necessary legal changes in the governance of Dar es Salaam would be accommodated within general reformatory legislation and all local government elections would take place in 2000 on the basis of the new legislation.[14]

The extension of the powers of the Commission in Dar es Salaam gave the green light both to a return to a heavy-handed, insensitive and bullying approach to the exercise of powers against the urban poor by the Commission and to central government planners to revert to the use of the bulldozer as the principal tool of urban planning. Tripp shows how the early 1980s saw the attempted forcible

---

13 McAuslan, 2003: chapter 11, for a discussion of the development of these laws. I was the principal consultant involved in their drafting.

14 The Danish aid agency DANIDA had funded the whole consultancy on the clear basis that it would lead to the rapid restoration of elected local government in Dar es Salaam. The agency was not very impressed by the Government's going back on that deal.

movement of the allegedly unemployed from Dar es Salaam through draconian legislation modelled on colonial precedents.[15] Those operating in the informal sector were deemed to be unemployed and even those in employment who were walking in the streets during the day could be charged with being 'engaged in a frolic of his [*sic*] own at a time he is supposed to be engaged in activities connected to or relating to the business of his employment'. 'If we don't disturb loiterers, they will disturb us!' thundered the late President Nyerere. Tripp notes that 'the campaign was destined to fail when the government resorted to coercion against city dwellers with little regard for the realities faced by the urban poor.' From the mid 1980s onwards, government changed tack and began to recognise the informal sector, inviting those working in it to 'come out of hiding' to help the nation by undertaking productive activities. As Tripp says, there was an element of absurdity in the notion that 95 per cent of the population of Dar es Salaam should come out of hiding, but the changed approach was welcome.

Some 10–12 years on, the Commission seemed intent on putting the clock back. It began to conduct a campaign against the informal sector, evicting traders from areas they had previously been allowed to operate in; destroying a large number of stalls used by informal sector traders, even those who had licences to be where they were, and destroying their goods as well. Youths were rounded up and ordered back to 'their' villages, without regard to whether they originally came from a village in the first place. The Commission was impervious to complaints about its conduct and seemed completely unwilling to contemplate any action except demolition of stalls when faced with allegedly illegal informal sector activity.

At the same time, large scale demolitions of houses, shops and stalls were undertaken by central government planners in pursuit of enforcing the 1979 Master Plan of Dar es Salaam and of road widening. In the latter case, the government made clear that it was not proposing to pay any compensation as the road reserve should not have been built on in the first place. As more than one dispossessee pointed out, government stood by and did nothing to deter those building for well over 15 years how now could it refuse compensation? There were harrowing tales in the press of people reduced to scavenging on rubbish dumps because they had lost both house and livelihood. As was pointed out by some commentators, the government seemed to be reverting to the behaviour of the First Phase government (a.k.a. President Nyerere's governments) when legal niceties and rights were not allowed to stand in the way of 'development' and development meant officials ordering the people about.

It may be argued that it is unfair to single out Dar es Salaam; many other cities in Africa are no different. True; indeed at the same time as the unelected City Commission in Dar es Salaam was harassing the informal sector, the elected City Council in Nairobi was destroying a famous informal sector tourist market in

15  Tripp, 1997.

the centre of Nairobi with losses amounting to tens of thousands of shillings for the traders and this was done despite a court order restraining the council from so acting. Tripp recounts similar offensives against the urban poor in Ghana, Nigeria and Zambia.

What makes Dar es Salaam special however is this. In 1991, the city authorities of Dar es Salaam had asked UN-Habitat for a grant of 3,000,000 dollars to finance a new Master Plan to replace the existing 20-year Master Plan that was out of date after 10 years. The request was refused[16] and an alternative was offered. In 1990 the UNCHS/World Bank/UNDP Urban Management Programme had launched the Sustainable Cities Project (SCP), a new participative approach to city planning with all stakeholders involved in the process of small-scale neighbourhood planning and an end to grandiose master planning, and its inevitable corollary, the bulldozer.

An SCP was offered to and accepted by the Dar es Salaam City Council. An SCP office was established in the City Council with a full-time Habitat official working alongside first, the City Council and then the Commission. Large sums of money were leveraged by the project and it is held out as a major success. What emerges from the saga recounted earlier, however, is that despite more than six years of efforts by a specific Habitat project which was in fact used as a model for the Habitat Agenda, attitudes to planning and the urban poor on the part of the political and administrative elites in the Government had not changed one iota.

Two Tanzanian scholars drew attention to the hostility of the planners to the SCP:

> The custodians of Land-Use Planning as practised within the legislative framework of the 1956 Town and Country Planning Ordinance have argued that the EMSD and EPMD[17] as produced and presented to them in November 1997 did not constitute the planning output of the SDP…it would miss their required long-term (10–20 year) land-use plan…that is not dissimilar to the earlier city master plans…These practitioners comprising the law enforcers in town and country planning from both central and local government have regarded the EPM process…to be wasteful in terms of both time and other resources and thereby an interference with their routines…for instance the ongoing unilateral action of the Dar es Salaam City Council [this is incorrect; it was the City Commission at the time of writing] to demolish kiosks used by informal sector operators in the name of law enforcement…The position of this group of practitioners is anti-EPM since it discourages partnership and

---

16 By me. At the time I was the Land Management Adviser to UN-Habitat and the Urban Management Programme. I was on a mission to Dar es Salaam when the request was made. I could not see the case for spending so much money on a process which was designed to repeat failure. For the Urban Management Programme see Wegelin, 1994 and McAuslan, 1997.

17 Environmental Management Strategy for Dar es Salaam and Environmental Planning and Management for Dar es Salaam.

participation amongst the city stakeholders...So in Dar es Salaam land use planners apply (at any cost) various law-enforcement instruments to fight such humble operators of informal-sector income generating and housing activities.[18]

## Estate agency: whose priorities; consumers or producers?

Two final illustrations of the continued regressive approach to the urban poor in Dar es Salaam may be given. In 2004–2005, I was involved in a consultancy to develop a law on estate agency in Tanzania. This is not probably the most pressing urban problem that Tanzania has but it was one that officials in the relevant Ministry wanted tackled. A key issue here is what to do about *dalali* agents, very prevalent in Dar es Salaam:

> The brokers are everywhere if you want them with their official business premises by the roadsides – on verandas or in tree-shades...Their only business investment is to buy a mobile phone. To contact the 'dalali' you find them from the classified free-of-charge announcements in the newspapers... In a good week the dalali may bag two million shillings, non-taxable income.[19]

Dalali agents may have little formal education but they are effective at their work in bringing buyers and sellers, would-be landlords and tenants together and their services in the land and housing market are widely used by rich and poor alike. But for some officials and some university-educated estate agents, dalali agents are charlatans and crooks who should be chased out of business as they are preventing the development of the profession of estate agency. What is best for the consumer, especially the poor consumer, is less important than using the law to boost the status and income of the professional or would-be professional middle class. The proposals in the draft Bill were to accept dalali agents and try to create a situation where over time the two halves of the service could learn to work with each other. What will ultimately emerge is not yet known.

## Mortgage law reform: to him that hath shall be given

The second illustration comes from the amendment to the Land Act which revised the chapter of the Act on Mortgages. Although not a specifically Dar es Salaam problem, in the nature of things, there are more would-be mortgagors in Dar than elsewhere, so changes in the law would have a disproportionate effect in Dar.

18  Halla and Majani, 1999.
19  Ahabwe, 2004, 'Highly Earning, Non-taxable Jobs', *Sunday Citizen*, 14 November.

The Land (Amendment) Act 2004 repealed and replaced Chapter X of the Land Act – the chapter on mortgages – with a new law on mortgages avowedly designed to alter the balance between mortgagee and mortgagors by increasing the powers and reducing the limitations on those powers of the mortgagee with respect to defaulting mortgagors. The extent to which this new mortgage law is likely to succeed in its avowed aim will become clearer as it is commented on but the genesis of the new law is as instructive in locating it in its context as was the overview of the Land Act as a whole in locating it in its context.

The Land Act 1999 was brought into force in May 2001. From very early on in its life, some of the banks in Tanzania took exception to the new law on mortgages. They objected to the abolition of foreclosure and the apparent granting of powers to the courts to re-open mortgages, the making of which, or the terms of which, were prima facie oppressive, illegal or discriminatory. They objected to the numerous time limits for actions to be taken which they considered hindered their exercise of discretion and gave too many opportunities for defaulting mortgagors to escape the consequences of their default. They objected too to the willingness of the courts to grant injunctions to prevent actions for possession and sale for non-meritorious reasons. Finally, they objected to the new concept of 'small mortgages'.

The use of the word 'apparent' in the aforementioned paragraph is deliberate. The relevant sections of the old Chapter X – sections 141 and 142 – were an attempt to codify the existing judicial precedents on these matters which were already a part of the law of Tanzania. No or very few new powers of intervention were being granted to the courts by those sections. As for foreclosure, it was being replaced by the much more efficient statute-based remedies of possession and sale in many countries in the Commonwealth and Tanzania was not unique in moving in this direction.

The objection to small mortgages was the most incomprehensible. First, the concept was a response to numerous reports of the lack of an appropriate vehicle for making small loans to peasant smallholders who wished to move, via small loans taken out for short periods, to growing cash crops. Ditto for small *jua kali* business people and people wanting small revolving loans for improving their accommodation. Second, small mortgages were a facility. There was never any suggestion that banks would be compelled to lend on small mortgages, so that if banks did not like them they would not have offered them. There was no need to insist on their abolition. Third, all the evidence from other developing countries is that poor people taking out small loans for short periods with banks have a much better repayment record than middle and upper class borrowers, so that the small mortgage facility was a potential money-spinner for the banks.

The banks pursued their objection with the World Bank. An official in the World Bank consulted the author on the matter. The author wrote a memorandum in May 2002 for that official in which he pointed out these matters and explained that, compared to the old law which Chapter X of the Land Act was replacing, the remedies provided by the new law and the time-scale within which these remedies could be activated were much superior with respect to mortgages other than small mortgages and the remedies for small mortgages followed the model of other countries where, for instance, residential mortgages were often given special protection.

Whatever the impact of that memorandum on the official, the World Bank had clearly got the bit between its teeth. At an investors' conference in Tanzania in July 2002, the President of the World Bank strongly urged the need for reform of the law on mortgages. The President of Tanzania agreed saying that there were general clauses in the land law which had not encouraged potential investors in commercial agriculture. 'Agricultural specialists say that at present, the land laws are very complicated and makes the question of ownership a difficult one.'[20] A Financial Sector Assessment mission from the World Bank in September 2003 increased the pressure for change:

> The comparative absence of longer-term credit is often remarked and blamed on the Land Act 1999. Undoubtedly this altered the balance of protection away from the lenders and towards the borrower and introduced many uncertainties. There has been continuous pressure from the banks for extensive changes in this law to allow them to secure lending on landed property with greater assurance. It is unlikely that much expansion of longer-term finance can be expected without some amendments to the land law, though it will not be a panacea as it is not only in Tanzania that financiers

20 Tanzania: land reform needed for agricultural investment. www.irinnews.org./report.asp? Report ID=28923 UN Office for Humanitarian Affairs reporting the conference of 22 July 2002. It is difficult to know what part of the land laws were complicated and made the question of ownership a difficult one. Apart from 1 per cent of the land that was alienated in freehold to German settlers during the German colonial period (1884–1916) there has never been private ownership of the land in Tanzania or its predecessor Tanganyika. The Land Act 1999 maintains that position. Information derived from interviews in November 2004 was to the effect that a serious problem of double allocation of land which bedevilled the system under the old law and so made the question of ownership a difficult one was now a thing of the past thanks to the Land Act's clear rules on who had the power to allocate land. It may be that these 'specialists' are concerned because it is now much more difficult to grab land from villages and peasant farmers than was the case under the old law, so that creating vast commercial farms out of village and peasant land without the full co-operation of villages and villagers is probably a thing of the past. It may however, be that the concern was precisely that Chapter X of the Land Act 1999 made it easier for banks to take possession of land from defaulting mortgagors (other than mortgagors with small mortgages) than had previously been the case. As we will see, the new Chapter X introduced by the Land (Amendment) Act 2004 makes it harder for banks to repossess land in use as agricultural or pastoral land. This will undoubtedly benefit large-scale landowners. One suspects that these 'specialists' and even the President of the World Bank himself had not familiarised themselves with the new land law but had focused on the fact that Tanzania does not permit freehold ownership of land and has put some hurdles in the way of foreign investors acquiring rights of occupancy. It is unlikely too that the World Bank (or indeed at the time the TBA) understood what the underlying law of mortgages of Tanzania was or how the new law fitted into and made use of that law.

are reluctant to commit funds to uncertain ventures even if secured by a mortgage on real estate.[21]

The Government of Tanzania agreed to revise the new law. The Attorney-General took the lead[22] and made arrangements with a City of London firm of solicitors to rewrite the law on mortgages. This they duly did and the Land (Amendment) Act 2004 is the result. The firm argued in their commentary on their draft Bill that the aim of the Bill was to provide a modernised law of mortgages for Tanzania. The law they were replacing was derived from an English Law Commission Report of 1991 containing a new draft Land Mortgages Bill and a New Zealand Law Commission Report of 1994 containing a draft of a New Property Law Act which included a chapter on mortgages,[23] both laws being adjusted to take account of the needs of Tanzania. Those parts of the new Chapter X that altered the law owe a good deal to the English Law of Property Act 1925 with important additions introduced in 1970 and 1973. What is most significant is that while small mortgages have been abolished, restrictions on mortgagees taking enforcement actions against defaulting mortgagors have been increased; enforcement actions against all defaulting mortgagors of residential, agricultural and pastoral property must first go to court. This reform will benefit all those with regular mortgages – the urban middle and upper classes while it is the less well-off who will lose out by the reforms.

## Conclusions

Much colonial planning law was inspired by a fear of the masses: the military cantonment in cities in the Indian sub-continent set between the colonial city and the indigenous city; the 'green belts' created in African cities between the settlers' and officials' city and the African urban areas were there not solely for public health reasons – the official reason – but to distance the colonial and European presence from the people. Similarly the development of legal regimes which denied the indigenous population any legal tenure in the city, this made it easier to remove them as and when the colonial authorities saw fit with a minimum of expense and fuss. These planning and legal regimes still exist. Mukoko, in putting forward his

---

21  Financial Sector Assessment Report (2003) para 6. (World Bank, Washington DC). The effect of this comment and seeming support for the banks' position was rather spoilt by the preceding paragraph which noted that large swathes of the economy were working with little formal credit and put this down to poor physical infrastructure and the fact that a high fraction of the population reside in remote rural areas. 'Neither banks nor microfinance institutions (MFIs) have made any significant headway finding secure and cost-effective ways of lending to these areas.' These challenges and the failure of banks to address them long pre-dated the Land Act 1999.

22  It was put to the author that the A–G acted without much consultation with the Ministry responsible for lands which fully understood the scope of the law on mortgages and saw nothing untoward about it.

23  Law Commission (1994) *A New Property Law Act: Report No. 29* (Wellington).

proposals to bring about an integration of the African city – densification of the 'modern' high-income areas of the cities – states that this may be opposed by 'politicians motivated by their desire to keep popular masses at bay'. The continuation of the colonial approach to planning laws is not the product of inertia; it is deliberate.

The most depressing conclusion which may be drawn from this case study is that Tanzanian urban administrators and politicians, to judge from the law and its operation, appear to be more opposed to facilitating the urban poor's getting a toe-hold into the legal city than the old colonial administrators which, if Leslie is to be believed,[24] had a more relaxed attitude to self-help and the informal sector. The old colonial laws are being used, or in some cases reinforced, to oppress the urban poor. Thus, whereas the old building regulations did not apply to self-build African housing, the 2001 Building Regulations have been characterised as 'not appropriate for low-income settlements, the home of the majority of the urban poor. The regulations are irrelevant because they are based on specifications.'[25] Fortunately urban administration in Dar es Salaam remains inefficient and under-resourced; this allows the urban poor to continue to survive in an inhospitable social and economic climate. It is a sad commentary on the Government, however, that while one of its citizens is the Director-General of UN-Habitat,[26] it continues to lag behind in putting into action the precepts of the Habitat Agenda.

## Bibliography

Briggs, J and Mwamfupe, D (2000) 'Peri-urban Development in an Era of Structural Adjustment in Africa: The City of Dar es Salaam', 37(4) *Urban Studies* 797–809

Burgess, R, Carmona, M and Kolstee, T (1997) *The Challenge of Sustainable Cities: Neoliberalism and Urban Strategies in Developing Countries*, London: Zed Books

Halla, F and Majani, B (1999) 'The Environmental Planning and Management Process and the Conflict over Outputs in Dar es Salaam', 23(3) *HABITAT International* 339–350

Kanyeihamba, G W and McAuslan, J P W B (1978) *Urban Legal Problems in Eastern Africa*, Uppsala: Scandinavian Institute of African Studies

Leslie, J A K (1963) *A Survey of Dar es Salaam*, Oxford: Oxford U.P. for the East African Institute of Social Research

Lusugga Kironde, J M (2000) 'Understanding Land Markets in African Urban Areas: The case of Dar es Salaam, Tanzania', 24(2) *HABITAT International* 151–165

McAuslan, P (1997) 'The Making of the Urban Management Programme: Memoirs of a Mendicant Bureaucrat', 34(10) *Urban Studies* 1705–1727

McAuslan, P (2003) *Bringing the Law Back In: Essays in Land, Law and Development*, Aldershot: Ashgate

Max, J A O (1991) *The Development of Local Government in Tanzania*, Dar es Salaam: Educational Publishers and Distributors

24  Leslie, 1963
25  Sheuya, 2004: 198.
26  Mrs Anna Kajumulo Tibaijuka. See her Report on Zimbabwe's slum clearance programme (2005) for her views on such activities.

Ministry of Foreign Affairs/DANIDA The United Republic of Tanzania, Prime Minister's Office Dar es Salaam City Commission (1997) *Preparation of the Strategic Plan for the Restructuring of the City Council of Dar es Salaam*, Dar es Salaam: COWI

Sheuya, S (2004) *Housing Transformations and Urban Livelihoods in Informal Settlements: The Case of Dar es Salaam*, Dortmund: SPRING Research Series

Taylor, J C (1963) *The Political Development of Tanganyika*, California: Stanford University Press

Tibaijuka, A K (2005) *Report of the Fact-Finding Mission to Zimbabwe to Assess the Scope and Impact of Operation Murambatsvina by the UN Special Envoy on Human Settlements in Zimbabwe*, New York: UN

Tripp, A M (1997) *Changing the Rules: The Politics of Liberalisation and the Informal Economy in Tanzania*, Berkeley, CA: University of California Press.

Wegelin, E (1994) 'Everything You Always Wanted to Know about the Urban Management Programme (but were afraid to ask)', 18(4) *Habitat International* 127–237

# Part IV

# The other intramuros

# Chapter 10

# Toronto

## A 'multicultural' urban order

*Mariana Valverde**

The city of Toronto's website contains a statement on 'Cultural diversity', reading as follows:

> Multiculturalism – it's what sets Toronto apart from other big North American cities. Toronto is home to virtually all of the world's culture groups and is the city where more than 100 languages are spoken.
>
> Once primarily a British and protestant city, immigration has played a dynamic role in the changing face of Toronto since the end of the Second World War. Today, 42 percent of all Canadian immigrants choose Toronto as their destination and as such, Toronto's visible minority population now accounts for more than 40% of the population compared to 11% nationwide. ... The world has brought its best to Toronto and in return, the city has embraced the many cultures of the world. Toronto has bilingual street signs, specialty stores, ethnic restaurants, ethnic publications, and a variety of ethnic shopping centres.[1]

The Toronto we-are-multicultural myth could be debunked by documenting the continuing hegemony of Protestant white males in the financial services industry (Toronto's main economic engine) and in the corridors of state power. But in the spirit of Roland Barthes,[2] I do not set out to speak truth against power here: I do not wish to claim that the multicultural myth is 'a lie'. It is real, as William James would say, since it has considerable real effects. Instead of debunking, then, I undertake the more genealogical task of documenting some of the myriad daily practices that produce Toronto's myth. But departing from Barthes's semiological method and static signs, I focus on social interactions. Research for this article involved observing hearings at the Toronto Licensing Tribunal (about 20 hours in

* Heartfelt thanks to Davina Cooper, Susan Coutin, Dena Demos, Lorne Sossin, Bill Maurer and Audrey Macklin for their thoughts and comments.
1 www.city.toronto.on.ca, Nov. 2004.
2 Barthes, 1973.

person and about 40 hours via a research assistant) and conducting interviews with tribunal members and with staff from the Municipal Licensing and Standards (MLS) branch. I also draw from preliminary research findings in other sites of urban law/administration. This research, supplemented by a considerable amount of personal experience, is here used to document the ways in which some low-level legal and administrative processes run by the municipality function as sites for the production of Toronto's distinct brand of multiculturalism.

It needs to be noted at the outset that when I say 'production' I do not for a minute imply that multiculturalism has been successfully produced. Foucault once said that to say we live in a disciplinary society does not mean to say we are all actually disciplined; and I would apply this to multiculturalism. Toronto's multiculturalism is an ever-shifting, never achieved process that involves, among many other things, the elaboration of techniques for managing tensions and conflicts without necessarily solving them – or even naming them. In the study that follows, we shall see that in keeping with the Toronto/Canadian ethic of niceness, hostility against non-European new immigrants is rarely directly and forcefully expressed, especially in official and public settings, despite the fact that my interviews with city officials show that hostility exists. Everyday occurrences that might become flashpoints or catalysts for the overt expression of 'race struggle'[3] are immediately channelled into certain discursive, administrative, and legal paths that are not obviously racialised and not obviously political – indeed, not even obviously conflictual.

One of the effects of the operation of the creaky but not wholly dysfunctional Toronto administrative and legal system is the constitution of micro-fields in which conflicts turning on ethnicity, culture, immigration status and class are worked through (usually indirectly), managed and re-created. The phrase 'the production of multiculturalism', therefore, designates not one process that can be said to be either successful or not, but rather a fluid and open-ended set of processes. In the following cases we shall see that overt racism against new immigrants of colour is rare, and not voiced in public official settings: but a distinctly European Christian theory of the self is nevertheless presupposed and recreated in low-level legal-administrative settings.

## The Toronto Licensing Tribunal

All businesses required to obtain a licence from the municipality, from hair salons to massage parlours, can potentially end up at the tribunal. Some businesses are governed more closely by having to justify, in person before the tribunal, a transfer of ownership: 'adult entertainment parlours' are among these. But what the tribunal hears most of the time consists of appeals of licence denials and suspensions. And the vast majority of appeals going to a full oral hearing involve taxi drivers.

3 Foucault, 2003.

A very large proportion of newer drivers are recent immigrants from Somalia, India (especially the Punjab), Nigeria and a handful of other countries mainly in the horn of Africa. The Municipal Licensing and Standards workforce, by contrast, are mainly either 'old Anglos' or first- or second-generation European 'ethnics', although with a substantial sprinkling of Asians and some African-Canadians. The tribunal itself, at the time of my research, was made up of six individuals, five of whom were male, and all of whom were white and not noticeably 'ethnic'. The hearings – held by a three-member panel – also regularly feature interpreters. (These are provided free of cost – against the provincial rules for this sort of tribunal, which specify that only French-English interpretation is to be provided at no cost; the interpretation budget is thus a silent statement of the city's commitment to multiculturalism.) Occasionally, lawyers or agents for the taxi driver are also present; all the ones I saw were white. The cast of characters is completed by two clerks, one stenographer (all three of these being white women), and an elderly white gentleman who pours glasses of water, dispenses Kleenex when needed, and occasionally swears in the witnesses.

Having provided some information about the subpopulations involved in various roles at the tribunal, let us examine a few specific cases. These are not chosen because they are 'representative': in this, as in other low-level legal venues, the representative case would be an adjournment or a matter that gets settled informally in the offices across the hall.[4] They are chosen precisely because they are unusually elaborate: but neither the process nor the outcome seem out of keeping with what happens in the cases that are dealt with more summarily.

## Babies, papers and other contested legal signs

A would-be taxi driver dressed in a suit and tie, accompanied by an elegant wife and an adorable toddler, appeared before the tribunal one winter day (in January 2004) to try to persuade the tribunal to overturn the bureaucratic refusal to issue him a licence. He is represented by 'an agent'. The (untypical) presence of an agent combines with the unusually elegant attire and bodily demeanour of the applicant and his wife to create the impression that the driver in question belongs to that large group of educated middle class African immigrants who end up driving taxis on Toronto streets because their credentials are not recognised in Canada. This initial impression is corroborated as two mobile phones go off within minutes of each other and, as people glance at their own purses or briefcases, these turn out to belong to the applicant and to his wife.

The city solicitor starts off, as is usually the case. The solicitor (a young woman who I judged to be a first-generation Canadian of Southern European descent) begins by arguing that every single word of the proceedings needs to be translated. The tribunal chair suggests that perhaps the interpreter could merely

4  See Yngvesson, 1988.

stand by just in case: 'it might expedite things to proceed without the interpreter'. The city lawyer, who often prolongs her questioning in time-consuming ways that seem to me quite unnecessary, invokes the spectre of judicial review: 'we won't know what he understands until the judicial review comes in'. The tribunal, minimally trained in law and thus always apprehensive, gives in to this, and so everything is translated. The interpreter is thus sworn in. Because she is sworn in by one of the full-time female clerks – who, alert to multiculturalism, regularly offers Punjabi and African taxi drivers the opportunity to affirm rather than swear on a Bible – the interpreter is sworn in by affirmation. In other cases, it is 'Joe', the elderly volunteer, who administers the oath: he always uses what appears to be his own personal Bible, bound in white leatherette. At no time during my observation or during the interviews did anyone ever note, much less criticise, the lack of uniformity in oath-administering practices.[5] The oath thus functions as a site for the delivery of rather contradictory messages about multiculturalism.

The city solicitor calls up a manager from the licensing unit, a first-generation Eastern European ethnic. The manager explains that Mr S's application for a new licence was turned down, three months before the date of the hearing, on the basis that Mr S had a 'serious record of conviction'. Since a criminal conviction is not (contrary to the wishes of most staff interviewed) an absolute bar to obtaining a cab licence, when Mr S applied for his licence and the bureaucrats discovered the conviction, they called Mr S in for an interview. At that interview (the manager testifies) the applicant stated that the conviction for sexual assault stemmed from an incident at a cigar shop where the applicant was employed as store manager. The applicant had received an employment application from a woman. The woman reportedly agreed to an interview 'on the spot', and this took place in a stockroom in the back of the store. In the interview with the city manager, the applicant indicated that the woman picked up 'an adult magazine', looked through it, and looked at Mr S 'suggestively'. The result was 'a liaison' – in the words of an interpreter who had been translating for the applicant during the interview at the office. (The manager was using notes taken during that interview). A couple of days after this 'liaison', he was arrested. After some complicated moves, involving police laying extra charges to pressure Mr S into pleading guilty to one charge, Mr S pleaded guilty and received a non-custodial sentence – which involved (according now to Mr S's own testimony) having his penis tested for susceptibility to pornographic images at the local psychiatric institute.

While this testimony is going on, the three tribunal members and others present take surreptitious looks at the applicant's wife. The awkwardness created

---

5  In most Canadian courtrooms witnesses are given the choice to affirm or to swear, usually on a Christian Bible. Other objects identified with truth telling are sometimes used – eagle feathers are sometimes offered to Aboriginal witnesses. There seems to be no general policy on this.

by hearing sordid sexual details being recounted in the presence of the applicant's wife and child remains subterranean for a long time: but it breaks through the surface and becomes actionable, as it were, when the adorable toddler suddenly bursts into tears. The tribunal ignores the crying for some time; but eventually one of the members asks 'Joe' – the dispenser of glasses of water – to have the woman and the 'unhappy little fellow' escorted out of the room. This is done. The crying, however, is still audible, and so the tribunal chair asks Joe to accompany the wife and child further away, 'preferably to the lower level of the building'.

The applicant, who appears oblivious to Canadian norms regarding the presence of (crying) children, and equally oblivious to the awkwardness caused for others by his wife being present throughout the testimony, asks through the interpreter to be allowed to go out and console the child, who is 'crying because he's away from me'. The tribunal Chair bristles at this request: 'you cannot leave in the middle of testimony.' Nothing more is said, but the tribunal members look stony-faced. In general, tribunal members are very understanding about breaches of administrative law procedure, but not so about breaches of Canadian courtroom norms.

On their part, the agent and the applicant first try to argue that the plea bargain did not amount to an admission of real guilt but rather a pragmatic choice made under pressure. Then they proceed to introduce documents that have nothing to do either with driving abilities or with the sexual assault charge. One of these documents is a letter of reference written by a 'British lady' who was a doctor with UNICEF and worked in Sudan, in a school that Mr S attended as a young refugee from Eritrea. The city solicitor begins to object vigorously to the irrelevant and previously 'unseen documents' being entered in evidence. The agent, however, continues to produce them – a school diploma; a 1993 letter from a previous employer and so on. The city lawyer objects again. The tribunal chair intervenes to side with the city, criticising the agent for wasting time with 'impertinent documents'.

The agent then declares: 'At the end of the day this is a case about character. My client's character. And I want to present his character.' This ringing statement is in keeping with the importance that determinations of character – especially honesty – play in this tribunal's adjudicating work.[6] The agent has probably had previous clients whose cases turned on 'character'. But the tribunal chair, annoyed by the time wasted on documents of little relevance, counters that 'matters pertaining to character are important but not critical in this case'. 'We don't want to restrict you from presenting evidence but want…maybe we can expedite this with the help of the city solicitor…' The solicitor begins by saying: 'It is not my awareness that character is the issue in this proceeding…' But then she contradicts herself, adding 'with the very obvious exception of the

---

6 My thanks to Audrey Macklin for many enlightening conversations on this point. See Macklin, 1998; Coutin, 2003.

sexual assault'. In fact, she had previously spent a great deal of time going over the intentions and the morals of the would-be taxi driver.

Eventually the tribunal decides, against the judgement of the city staff, to grant him a cab driver's licence, conditional upon providing a copy of his criminal record every year for three years. Despite the tribunal's previous objections to highlighting 'character', the oral reasons turn out to be all about character: but it is now the (absent) female complainant's character that suddenly emerges as a legal factor. 'Without in any way diminishing the seriousness of a sexual assault charge, based on the evidence you gave us we accept that there may have been some leading on that you misinterpreted by the young woman...'

A one-time observer might have concluded that collective sexism determined the outcome. However, interviews with tribunal members and city licensing staff about the licensing process in general suggest that although it is certainly true that female passenger safety is not foremost in tribunal's deliberations – in addition to Mr S, two other cab drivers with some history of violence against women managed to get their licences during my research time – nevertheless, from the point of view of the participants, the decision appeared primarily as another skirmish in the long war between the administration and the tribunal. The gendered risks to female passengers were here mainly a weapon in a struggle between the bureaucracy (which favoured strict bans against convicted criminals driving taxis) and a tribunal intent on preserving its discretion and autonomy. But let us return to the hearing room.

Comparing Mr S to other less legally fortunate taxi drivers, it becomes apparent that, however uncomfortable some people might have been when noticing that the wife and child were listening to sordid sexual details, Mr S's ready willingness to admit that some kind of impropriety – though not rape – had taken place when he 'interviewed' the female job applicant at his cigar shop was an important factor in his favour. A case heard in December of 2003 is particularly informative about the extreme importance, not of character in general but, more specifically, of European Christian notions of truth-telling and individual honesty.

In that hearing, a Punjabi-speaking applicant for a cab driver's licence, who had several convictions for driving infractions on his regular provincial driving licence and had been caught driving a cab without a cab licence, ended up being subjected to a very lengthy examination regarding not his driving but rather his commitment to truth-telling. The city solicitor focused her quasi-prosecution of Mr M on the authenticity of the form certifying medical fitness to drive a taxi that Mr M submitted to the bureaucracy. A great deal of time was spent on repetitive questions, some of which were obviously misunderstood (despite the interpreter's presence). But I finally concluded that 'the facts of the case' were that Mr M had visited a doctor – a professional from the same ethnic group – and had obtained a hand-written note on letterhead certifying his fitness to drive a cab; but he had not gone back to the doctor's office to obtain the doctor's signature on the correct bureaucratic form. Mr M failed to see that it would have served him better to admit quickly that he did indeed forge the doctor's signature because he did not want to pay the fee that the doctor would demand for his signature on the right piece of paper. He insisted on strenuously denying having forged the signature – only to break down in tears when he realised the game was over. Understanding that he now had to explain why he forged the signature, but still refusing to openly admit his fault, he pleaded by saying that 'I only had two choices: suicide myself or drive a cab without a licence…I could not find any other work and I was desperate.' The tribunal members look particularly stony faced at the mention of suicide; it is all too clear – to everyone except Mr M – that the members do not appreciate what looks to white Canadians (including myself) as an attempt at emotional blackmail.

Given that forgery has now been established, what would normally be a routine discussion of the applicant's claim to have improved himself by paying for a driving course – errant taxi drivers know that taking a 'refresher' driving course at their own expense is useful legal capital – turns into a fraud investigation. A recess is called so that the driving school that provided Mr M with a letter can be checked out in the city licensing department's computer. The school turns out itself not to be licensed, which for the bureaucracy means that it does not exist. The manager states: 'I am confident, from my [computer database] search, that this school is not licensed. It does not exist.' This remarkable faith in the creative powers of licensing is not shared by the tribunal, however. The tribunal chair points out that the school might exist. 'Why didn't you make a phone call to the number on the letterhead?' the manager is asked. She does not answer.

The inquiry into the authenticity of the driving school's letter thus ends up in a sort of draw. But although the school's semi-legal spectral status is not blamed on the cabbie, the spectre of forgery – deliberate deception and fraud – is not dispelled. At the conclusion of the hearing, the city solicitor chooses to leave Mr M's appalling driving record unmentioned, focussing wholly on the question of truth and confession. 'The fact that Mr M has difficulty stating the truth is central to this', she states in her concluding submission. 'Mr M has not been truthful with this tribunal. He therefore cannot be considered trustworthy.' He cannot be 'trusted to honour bylaws' because he did something 'extremely dishonest' with the medical certificate. 'He has breached the law and has a problem with his integrity and will continue to do so.' 'We have no proof that he will honour the law.'

The impression is thus created – by the only person in the room who is actually licensed by the Law Society to practice law – that administrative law is all about honour and repentance, not about formal compliance with the bylaws and with the conditions of the licence. In responding, the agent too decides to remain on the (Christian) terrain of repentance and forgiveness. Earlier, the agent had made a great deal out of the fact that his client was 'desperate' to drive a cab because he refused to contemplate asking for social assistance, being too proud to collect welfare. At the final stage, he again tries to build up his client's probity rather than play a more strictly legal game. 'If you look at the overall picture and at his demeanour', he argues, 'you'll see that he has shown remorse. He will not do this again...He should be given a license with severe restrictions. ...He has learnt his lesson and will pull his bootstraps up.'

This was an unfortunate closing submission. Remorse was precisely what Mr M failed to convincingly produce. His unrepentant presentation of self could have resulted from the simple fact that he didn't think that his minor infraction regarding the medical certificate was truly shameful. He had actually visited the doctor in question for a medical exam, so he was not lying about that: he had merely failed to get the right signature on the right physical piece of paper. Or perhaps, unfamiliar with this tribunal's obsession with the legal value of confessing one's sins and receiving absolution and penance, he assumed that his legal fortunes would be worsened rather than improved if he admitted having committed a deception or lie. Most importantly, he did not receive the necessary legal-cultural advice from his agent during the hearing.

The appearance of remorselessness was thus overdetermined. The tribunal's wholly predictable decision was that Mr M should not be granted a licence to drive a cab in Toronto because he has not demonstrated 'honesty and integrity'. 'In general, his explanation appears to be lacking in conviction and his answers are misleading.'

### 'We look at the whole man': quasi-judicial discretion as an inquiry into the soul

What sealed Mr M's fate was not his awful driving record, but rather his failure to confess and ask for forgiveness To further probe the tribunal members' sense of themselves as experts on honesty and repentance, it is useful to look at a contrasting case. The case that can best illustrate this featured a white working-class English-speaking tow-truck driver who was relatively forthright about rather questionable conduct in a hearing that I witnessed the week before Mr M's appearance.

The first thing that was notable about Mr C, the tow-truck driver, was that he appeared in his blue jeans and was remarkably at ease in the unfamiliar environment of the hearing room: the Black and South Asian new immigrants who appear regarding taxi driving licences look largely ill at ease, by contrast, and are in most cases 'dressed up' for the occasion. They are also often accompanied by family members, agents, interpreters and some other unidentified supporters. Mr C brought one friend/agent, but no other retinue. While the blue jeans and down-home working-class language (complete with the 'f' word) might have come across as signs of lack of respect, they also functioned as signs of authenticity and integrity: here is a man who does not have a lawyer, does not dress up, and talks plain – a man who is, basically, himself.

An MLS officer suggested in his testimony that Mr C had beaten up a competitor, another tow-truck driver, who showed up at the scene of an accident. He could not positively state he had seen the assault with his own eyes, but he mentioned that Mr C had been criminally charged by a police officer who came on the scene later. Under cross-examination, Mr C ended up admitting to spitting on the other guy, but claimed that the other driver had punched him first, and declared he would plead not guilty at his upcoming trial.

The hearing became rather disjointed, and it was impossible to ascertain the facts with any degree of certainty, in part because the police officer who had laid the charge was not present (a sore point with city staff). Despite this lack of clarity, I am sure I was not the only person present who went away concluding that the tow-truck business is one in which physical violence and intimidation are common, and that, in particular, it was highly likely that Mr C was prone to violence. But instead of ending up looking like some kind of biker tough, Mr C was able to play his working-class status to advantage – in stark contrast with the taxi drivers, who never tried to 'play the race card' or otherwise use their minority status as a form of legal capital. During cross-examination, Mr C burst out: 'Why are you asking me all these questions ... I don't have a lawyer with me and you're asking me all these questions and I think I might be incriminating myself since I haven't even had my trial yet'. Unbeknownst to Mr C, not having a lawyer worked to his advantage: tribunal members always provided procedural help and legal explanations to unrepresented applicants, but became unhelpful and even confrontational when a lawyer was present.

In keeping with this preference for unrepresented 'authentic' applicants, the tribunal chair, far from chastising the tow-truck driver for his outburst, patiently explained to him that administrative proceedings regarding a licence are totally separate from the criminal process. This is in fact legally correct – as was highlighted by a licensing manager in an interview about this case. When asked why the city tried to take away Mr C's licence before rather than after his criminal trial, the manager stated: 'our mandate is to protect the public. We're not concerned with the outcome of his criminal case. He didn't dispute the fact that he punched the other guy and that was our point. We can't have guys out there licensed by the city beating other people up.'[7]

The staff member's keenness to use the regulatory capacities of administrative law to discipline the space of the city in ways that are not within the purview of the criminal law was not shared by the tribunal, however. Instead of concluding that Mr C, whether guilty of the criminal offence of assault or not, was, on the preponderance of the evidence, a violent man who had a questionable claim to a city-issued licence, the tribunal chose to treat him as a normal boy who just needed a talking-to about his temper. After the tribunal told him that their decision was to reinstate the licence, a tribunal member (one who routinely sides

---

7 The procedural bible that applies to all administrative tribunals in the province of Ontario is the *Statutory Powers Procedure Act*. Only one of the four tribunal members interviewed specifically mentioned being very familiar with the Act, but the hearings I witnessed were not in conflict with the Act.

with the applicants rather than with the city) gave him a short fatherly sermon. Turning to the rugged-good-looking Mr C, the (male) tribunal member stated: 'Your licence will be reinstated immediately, Mr C. That means you can go to work on Monday. Tomorrow even, if you're ready.' But 'from now on, if something on the street upsets you, don't react. As you've found out, it isn't worth it. Don't let your anger get the better of you. If trouble comes calling, just walk away. Try to exercise some self-control.' No doubt accustomed from his school days to this sort of boys-will-be-boys rap on the knuckle, Mr C knows exactly how to respond. 'I will,' he says, looking directly into the tribunal member's eye. 'Thank you.'

It is important to note, however, that the recourse to non-legal statements and behaviours as forms of legal capital is not limited to Anglo-Canadians who know the cultural codes. Applicants from non-European and largely non-Christian backgrounds do not limit themselves to trying to prove formal compliance. As we have seen, some applicants bring a wife and/or a child. Some burst into tears and beg to be given a licence so they could feed their children. Some talked about the cost of school fees for their children in Pakistan; and some tried talking about dying fathers. The supplement to bureaucratic law they seem to be looking for, however, does not involve confession, forgiveness and repentance, but rather something like the exercise of a sovereign mercy that looks at the circumstances of the person and takes pity on them because of these (outward) circumstances.

Along these lines, an unrepresented Nigerian cab driver, when told that he had the right to question and cross-examine the city's witness, did not proceed to the questioning: instead, he talked about being 'sick'. To compound this breach of the norms, he pulled up his shirt to reveal some kind of electrical monitor on his chest. This did not go over well. 'You currently have seven demerit points', the man was told by the tribunal chair even before he could pull his shirt back down. The literal production of a sign of illness did not produce mercy and compassion. On the contrary, it made the tribunal eager to get back to a bureaucratic line of reasoning – reasoning that they themselves often neglect and even disparage, but which was here seen as the correct way to get the proceedings from being derailed by exhibitions of a sick body. It was a confession, not a pity-evoking wound, that the tribunal wanted to see.

When asked why the tribunal puts so much emphasis on truth telling and repentance, a senior member made the remarkable statement that the bureaucracy looks at rules and texts, but the tribunal looks at 'the whole man'. Even a convicted murderer, I was told, should not be categorically banned from the taxi business; it all depends on the particulars. When pressed to think about whether expecting people to admit to lies or mistakes in a formal state venue might be ethnocentric, this adjudicator merely repeated that 'lying through their teeth' is the worst thing that an applicant can do at the tribunal. 'The tribunal doesn't like that,' I was told – as if a fact about a legal process were being reported to me by a third person, when of course the tribunal's dislikes had been largely produced by the very person sitting with me in a coffee-shop.

This same member, when asked about the city's bylaws about street food vending, had proudly volunteered the statement that 'We're not a Protestant city any more.' But while waxing eloquent about how Toronto would be improved by the free, unregulated provision of burritos and falafels on city sidewalks to replace the compulsory hot dogs imposed by current bylaws, this former (leftwing) politician was unable to reflect critically about the Christian theory of the relation between the ability to find and name one's sins and one's claim to discretionary forgiveness.

The ethnographic research at the licensing tribunal did not reveal any instances of overt ethnocentrism, other than a comment by an Italian-Canadian city employee about the difficulty of pronouncing 'ethnic' names, meaning African names. But interviews with tribunal members and city staff brought to the fore certain fears and hatreds that in Toronto usually remain unspoken. (These fears and hatreds were undoubtedly voiced in my presence because in the Toronto municipal governance context I look like one of 'us'.) One city manager who had a great deal of experience in bylaw enforcement and licensing was thoroughly laid-back for about the first hour of the interview; but he suddenly became agitated when explaining that one of the few things that would send a taxi driver 'directly to the tribunal' (that is, that would cause an immediate suspension of the licence, which would then be appealed) was a refusal to pick up a blind passenger. Perplexed, I asked why taxi drivers would not want to pick up blind people. The response was: 'Muslims don't like dogs.' Many taxi drivers refuse to have guide dogs in their vehicles because they are somehow impure: they don't want to pay for their taxi to be cleaned afterward. The indignation with which this claim was made was quite out-of-keeping with his laid-back, I've-seen-it-all style. No taxi driver that I saw at the tribunal, however, had had a licence suspended because of this kind of breach of human rights norms, and I did not hear of any such cases during interviews.

In pursuit of more information about cross-cultural communication at the tribunal, a white 'old Canadian' tribunal member who had had decades of experience within the city was asked whether it would be possible that taxi drivers are disadvantaged procedurally because they are not used to the Canadian legal system. The interviewee misinterpreted my query. Instead of producing the standard Torontonian liberal apology for not knowing enough about other cultures, he proceeded to assert that the ethnic groups from which taxi drivers are drawn include those that 'don't respect women'. They are 'Middle Eastern', he added. Given that I did not see a single Middle Eastern taxi driver during my research, I can only conclude that by 'Middle Eastern' he meant 'Muslim'. The easy slippage between Muslim religion, 'Middle Eastern' ethnicity/nationality, and risks to women passengers' safety is of course powerfully overdetermined by the anti-Muslim discourses that European and North American societies have nurtured in the early years of the twenty-first century. But what was perhaps distinctly Torontonian about the statement is that it was not uttered in an angry voice, and it was not preceded or followed by any overtly racist remark. It was made as a factual statement. Muslims do not like dogs; Middle Easterners do not respect women. That's why 'we' regulate taxi drivers' licences.

## Concluding remarks

The factual claim that taxi drivers are largely 'Middle Eastern' and therefore 'don't respect women' is, needless to say, factual only in form. This is hardly remarkable; as has been noted by countless philosophers of language, factual claims are rarely 'just' factual. But what is notable here is that even the most blatantly ethnocentric remarks that I heard during my research were not framed as arguments in political and cultural struggles, but rather as merely factual statements. Muslim taxi drivers do not like dogs. That is a fact. So is the 'fact' that confessing one's sins is a powerful form of legal capital for errant taxi and tow-truck drivers. The exercise in examination of conscience and remorse that the tribunal expects of these errant souls is not regarded as culturally specific or religiously biased. It is seen as a universal truth technology – and one with an equally universal legal cash value. We European immigrants are not imposing our values, the tribunal members seem to be saying, since the incitement to confess and repent is not an ethnocentric preference but rather an essential feature of administrative law as such.

In possession of an apparently universal means for converting determinations of moral character into legal currency, Toronto's officials can remain blithely confident that they can 'embrace' multiculturalism, as the city website states, and celebrate it without fears about the sort of ethnic violence that mars other cities. We eat different foods, engage in different gender practices, and believe in different gods. But we are all supposed to share a belief in the same model of soul: the truth-telling, inward-focussed soul of the properly self-fashioned person, one who is not afraid to recount and confess his sins. The existence and the desirability of this (Christian) soul appears as a bedrock or background fact – not as a norm. Because it is not seen as a norm or a value, questions of ethnocentrism do not even arise.

In his monumental genealogy of the modern inward-focussed self, Charles Taylor tells us that this transmutation of a religious norm into a social fact goes back many centuries: 'It is hardly an exaggeration to say that it was Augustine who introduced the inwardness of radical reflexivity and bequeathed it to the Western tradition of though.'[8] The inwardness of radical reflexivity associated with the Protestant Reformation and with counter-reformation Catholicism alike is still alive and well in one minor legal site that manages to produce multiculturalism and Christian hegemony at the same time – and with the same techniques.

8  Taylor, 1989: 191.

# Bibliography

Barthes, R (1973) *Mythologies*, London: Paladin

Coutin, S (2003) 'Suspension of Deportation Hearings and Measures of "Americanness"', 8(2) *Journal of Latin American Anthropology* 58–95

Foucault, M (2003) *Society Must be Defended*, New York: Picador

Macklin, A (1998) 'Truth and Consequences: Credibility in Refugee Determination', International Association of Refugee Law Judges, Realities of Refugee Determination on the Eve of a New Millennium (Haarlem: IARLJ 1999)

Taylor, C (1989) *Sources of the Self*, Cambridge: Cambridge University Press

Yngvesson, B (1988) 'Making Law at the Doorway: The Clerk, the Court, and the Construction of Community in a New England Town', 22(4) *Law and Society Review* 409–447

# Chapter 11

# Sydney

## Aspiration, asylum and the denial of the 'right to the city'

*Chris Butler*

### Sydney: aspiration and asylum

As the largest urban conurbation in one of the most highly urbanised countries in the world, Sydney has often been heralded as providing the classic definition of Australian city life. The predominant place that it occupies in the national imagination can be at least partly attributed to its sheer size. With a population of approximately 4 million people, Sydney accommodates a fifth of all Australians, and its sprawling western regions that stretch well into the Blue Mountains provide the paradigmatic model of Australian suburbia writ large. At the level of the symbolic, Sydney's cultural significance also derives from the ways in which its geographical features now embody both the essence and the dichotomies of the classic Australian polis. It is a city which combines the show and spectacle of the Gay and Lesbian Mardi Gras with the ludic pleasures of its coastal setting, and the mundane, everyday life of suburbia. It is also a city which, despite its importance, is not quite the national capital, yet for many purposes continues to be treated as such by financial markets and media organisations.[1] For international 'spectators', Sydney is the home to those quintessentially Australian icons – the Opera House and the Harbour Bridge, while its hosting of the 2000 Olympic Games has often been proclaimed as an event which inaugurated its status as a truly 'global' city.

This relatively superficial caricature of Sydney is at least able to draw out some of the ways in which the city simultaneously enacts a national suburban mythology while becoming increasingly integrated into an internationalised economic system. For Peter Murphy and Sophie Watson, these 'spatial contradictions' demonstrate how Sydney is increasingly marked by a heterogeneous and fragmented play of surfaces, engendered by cultural, sexual and gendered forms of difference.[2] While there is much truth in this portrayal, it also elides the ways in which this city provides the

---

1 This treatment appears to be endorsed by the choice of the Prime Minister John Howard to live in Sydney, rather than in 'The Lodge' — the traditional Canberra residence for the national leader.

2 Murphy and Watson, 1997. The term 'spatial contradictions' is taken from the work of Henri Lefebvre, 1991: 331 and 1976: 17–18.

central reference point for many of the obsessions that occupy current national political discourse.

Perhaps the best example is to be found in the widespread public fascination with and involvement in speculative investment in the housing market. While certainly a national phenomenon, in many respects Sydney continues to provide a general measure for all Australians of the affordability of home-ownership and the prospects for material advancement in a globalised economy. Fears about the prospects for home ownership and the possibility of increasing interest rates have provided an important subtext for the last two national election campaigns: in 2001 and in 2004. So-called aspirational voters in outer suburban areas of Sydney have been often identified as a new class of constituent: the 'Howard battlers', who are increasingly prepared to support a conservative national government in return for the subsidies and tax relief that now attach to home ownership.

Whether or not it is possible to identify the existence of this group as a new voting bloc at the national level, it is clear that there have been significant changes to Sydney's human geography over the past 20 years. In the past, the city has been commonly portrayed in terms of a contradiction between the cosmopolitan urban centre and the mundane and deprived existence of the western suburbs.[3] This centre-west dichotomy is now breaking down with the rise of affluent, increasingly privatised and ethnically homogeneous enclaves emerging in the outer suburbs. These developments are premised upon limitations on the capacity of all social groups to share city services, and raise serious questions about the restrictions they place on urban citizenship.[4] Such changes in the human landscape of Sydney reflect and, to an extent have helped to fuel an ideological climate that has extended the political currency of fear.

This can also be seen in the second issue which played a prominent part in the election of 2001 – the treatment of refugees and asylum seekers. From the moment the *MV Tampa* sailed into view in August 2001, carrying its tragic cargo of 433 stranded passengers, the Australian government worked single-mindedly to capitalise on several years of preparation in the demonising of asylum seekers.[5] Hence the real and imagined threats to national security in the wake of the recently announced 'war on terror' could be linked to asylum seekers by framing government actions in terms of 'border security'. However, the treatment of asylum seekers and their concerns were barely acknowledged in formal terms in the most recent election campaign in 2004, despite the ongoing deprivations suffered by those in detention and those who face long periods of insecurity on temporary protection visas. As this issue remains at the margins of mainstream political debate, it is important to consider the ways in which the treatment of these people by the Australian State has been conceptualised.

---

3  Symonds, 1997.
4  Gleeson, 2003.
5  For a comprehensive account of the politicisation of the asylum-seeker issue during the 2001 election see Marr and Wilkinson, 2003.

My aim in this chapter is to juxtapose the increasingly privatised and hierarchical nature of Sydney's suburban landscape, with Australia's treatment of those asylum seekers who can establish their status as refugees, but whose access to social services and support is denied. The desires for material affluence and security amongst a certain 'aspirational' constituency in Sydney can be easily compared with the limited forms of social support provided to refugees. But I also want to show how the social inequality between these groups can be understood as a spatial problem which can be at least partly addressed by a spatialised political agenda. Accordingly, I will explore the model of governance that has been set up by Australia's refugee regime in a way that has not been previously considered, by drawing on the work of Henri Lefebvre. In particular I will suggest that his notion of the 'right to the city' is an entitlement that flows from the *inhabitance* of urban space and should be extended to those provided with temporary forms of refugee protection in Australia.

## Sydney's spatial contradictions

Sydney's emergence as Australia's 'premier' capital city in national, political and cultural discourse has a spatial dimension. Since the Second World War, cultural studies of Sydney have emphasised the spatial contradictions between the urban centre and its suburban periphery – the legendary western suburbs. The growth of the western regions of the city throughout the middle decades of the twentieth century was at one level promoted and encouraged by state planning authorities who at least partly carried the mantle of an earlier generation of planners, resolute in the belief that the medical, hygienic and technical problems of urban life could be solved by low-density residential development. However, armed with the knowledge that the large-scale housing developments in Sydney's west were a far cry from Ebenezer Howard's aesthetic model for *garden cities*,[6] the same planners viewed these new housing estates with some caution, as bringing with them the potential for an unwanted American-style import – urban sprawl.[7]

The growth of the suburbs in the post-war era did not occur without challenge within Australian cultural criticism either. Perhaps the best known denunciation of the banality, anti-intellectualism and narrow personal self-interest supposedly fostered by the suburban plot is provided by Allan Ashbolt's classic 'Godzone' piece. He identifies in the 'mechanised pagan chorus' of synchronised weekend lawn mowing, all the limitations and narrow acquisitiveness of everyday Australian life:

> Behold the man – the Australian man of today – on Sunday mornings in the suburbs, when the high-decibel drone of the motor mower is calling the faithful

6  Howard, 1902.
7  Johnson, 1997.

to worship. A block of land, a brick veneer, and the motor mower beside him in the wilderness – what more does he want to sustain him, except a Holden to polish, a beer with the boys, marital sex on Saturday nights...[8]

An important element to this critique of suburbia was a suspicion and rejection of the bush myth imagined to be represented in the suburbs. While an earlier generation extolled the partial 'retreat to nature' through the suburban plot, the bush connection has been one of the sources of the rejection of the suburbs within Australian cultural criticism. For these objectors, the suburban retreat to the bush marks the corruption of the enlightenment values embodied in urban 'civilisation'. The suburb has thereby been associated with a collective turning of the back on the urban as the centre of culture. The cultural historian Humphrey McQueen explains this objection in the following terms:

> Contemporary Australia is significant neither for its empty outback, nor for the concentration of its population in capital cities, nor for suburban living. More distinctive is the importance that suburbia occupies in the national mentality, where it is at once enshrined as the ideal way of life and mocked as the enemy of culture and innovation. If city life seemed dull, the suburbs were perceived as irredeemably flat so that 'suburban' defined not just a place to live, but also a refusal to think, or to feel.[9]

In relation to Sydney, this claim is most forcefully made in the almost visceral denigrations of the outer suburbs as 'other'.[10] Michael Symonds situates western Sydney's place in this discourse in terms of Hegel's narration of the tale of *Antigone*.[11] In Hegel's reading, the home is a mini-cosmos of particularity and the site of a natural or divine law which is juxtaposed with the secular, universal human law of the city centre. A necessary part of the formation of the modern subject involves its disenchantment with nature and a move towards the centre. But within this myth, there is always the possibility of a 'return home' to an 'enchanted history of nature'. However, the outer suburbs (and particularl Sydney's west in Symonds's analysis) seem beyond this dialectic – spaces 'where modern subjectivity is denied'.[12] Containing nothing to disenchant, they are incapable of constituting a true home. Through a process of self-formation, the centre has worked tirelessly to turn its back on the harsh and barren interior of the western suburbs.

8  Ashbolt, 1965: 373.
9  McQueen, 1988: 38–39.
10  Powell, 1993.
11  Symonds, 1997.
12  Ibid. 84–5.

The image of the western suburbs as a cultural wasteland is the very past Sydney had to expel in order to establish its reputation as a city centre. In this sense, the western suburbs become Sydney's historical waste.[13]

As Symonds notes, nature occasionally reappears in the city, in romanticised aesthetic forms such as native gardens and commodified Aboriginal culture, but the outer suburbs with their 'fibro' houses and treeless housing estates – like the sparse and desolate landscapes in the paintings of Russell Drysdale – 'function as a much-mocked reminder of what has been left behind'.[14]

However, it is not such a simple matter to bracket the suburbs outside the urban as this critique appears to suggest. The city may appear to have exploded, but this has been accompanied by a corresponding urbanisation of the periphery. In a Lefebvrean sense, the relationship between centre and periphery should not be seen as the product of an inevitable, evolutionary development, but as logically and strategically generated by historical struggles over the production of space. In Sydney, this can be most clearly observed in the tensions between the desire of social democratic governments since the Second World War to increase public infrastructure in the western suburbs, and the simultaneous recognition of a need to preserve development-free greenbelt areas as the city expanded. Spatial conflicts over issues such as this ensure that suburbia never truly escapes the urban,[15] and the geographical associations which have often been made between suburbia and the bush have always been more symbolic than real. They mask deeper fears of an intellectual and cultural wasteland perceived to lie outside the inner city.

Indeed, the spatial dialectic between centre and periphery in Sydney has been complicated by geographical developments over the last two decades. Of particular interest is the way in which newer outer suburbs have expanded on the western fringe. The 'first wave' of post-war housing developments occurred in what are now the middle ring suburbs of Sydney's west and were designed as affordable housing, targeted towards lower income households.

By contrast, these newest fringe suburbs are a distinctly novel phenomenon in the history of Australian urbanisation, catering as they do for primarily middle-income, 'aspirational' households seeking to escape the deprivation and disadvantage that now characterise the ageing middle regions of the west. These so-called McMansion suburbs with their 'large, car-dependent homes on small plots – are now a dominant feature of the new suburban landscape'[16] in western Sydney.

Many of these new residential developments are master-planned estates designed as a celebration of 'the pleasures of order, homogeneity and amenity...as the rightful

13  Ibid. 88.
14  Ibid. 90; see also Symonds, 1993: 69.
15  Lefebvre, 1996a: 79.
16  Randolph, 2003: 13.

reward for individual effort'.[17] However, despite the strong perception of these estates as essentially privatised worlds, their very existence is dependent upon a complex web of public subsidies in the form of tax breaks, and their location near major public facilities and infrastructure, such as parks, main roads and recreation centres. Hence, private developers are able to capitalise on the amenities that are the result of decades of public planning and investment in order to market these new estates as 'landscapes of self-reliance'.[18] In addition, the Howard government has displayed its preference for large-scale public subsidisation of 'private' housing investments through its $7000 grant to first home-owners and its generous taxation provisions for owners of investment properties.

Recent empirical research has revealed that the residents of these new estates in western Sydney have been largely driven to move there by a desire to separate themselves from the deprived and declining areas of the middle west.[19] These residents emphasised their fears of insecurity and the threats of potential social disorder associated with living in close proximity to public housing estates and other obvious identifiers of poverty. This geographical shift to the outer west by those who can afford to move has increased social polarisation and heightened socio-economic inequalities within western Sydney itself, and reveals the way in which the previously established dialectical relation between Sydney's centre and its periphery is progressively giving way to a more complex spatial formation. As the suburban west becomes integrated into the booming housing economy of central Sydney, it is producing an increasingly divided suburban structure, with new areas of great affluence loosely surrounding regions of great disadvantage and despair.

## Aspiration against asylum

Gabrielle Gwyther's research also reveals darker fears which have helped motivate residents to leave the suburbs of the middle west. In particular she identifies concerns about the arrival of non-English speaking migrants in western Sydney since the early 1970s as pivotal to many residents' decisions to seek the security and sanctuary of the 'privatopias' of the outer west.[20] This takes on a greater importance in light of the role that Sydney plays in current debates about immigration, and reveals deep anxieties about its future as a city of plenty for 'true' Australians. Since as early as the mid-1990s, the former New South Wales Labor Premier Bob Carr had asserted that Sydney was being swamped by inappropriately high levels of immigration. Carr consistently argued for the need to limit the influx of new arrivals to Sydney for both environmental and economic reasons.[21] His rhetoric

17  Gleeson, 2003: 63.
18  Gleeson, 2005: 64.
19  Gwyther, 2003.
20  Ibid., 2005: 65.
21  For example see Carr, 2002a and 2002b.

helped to fuel Sydney home-owners' fears that immigration contributes to rising housing prices and that Sydney residents bear an unfair burden of subsidising the housing and social services costs of the thousands of people who settle in Sydney each year.

Carr's anti-immigration stance made it easier to connect the range of aspirations and anxieties about home ownership and material advancement that afflict modern Sydney life with a distinctly racist fear of the outsiders who have intruded into the 'national home'. The geographical outcome of these fears can be seen in the fragmentation and explosion of the outer western suburbs as (predominantly) Australian-born residents seek the security of homogeneous and well-serviced estates away from the poverty and uncertainty of the older middle ring suburbs.

If housing has dominated the wider Australian political landscape in recent years, the flip-side to the portrayal of Sydney as the central locus of national obsessions with home ownership has been the imagined dangers posed to the integrity of the nation by the outsider in the form of asylum seekers and refugees. As is the case with many countries, during the last decade, the Australian government has devoted considerable energy to portraying the movements of asylum seekers as an onslaught by an undeserving multitudinous 'other'. Faced with an increase in the unauthorised arrival of boatloads of asylum seekers from Iraq and Afghanistan in the late 1990s, the government felt the need to sharpen its attacks on these unwanted and untrustworthy intruders into the national lounge room. In the words of the former Immigration Minister Philip Ruddock, asylum seekers arriving in Australia in this manner can be best characterised as 'those who have the money (and deceitfully pretend destitution), those who break our law, those who are prepared to deal with people-smugglers and criminals'.[22]

This increasing demonisation of asylum seekers by the Howard government cannot be explained properly without understanding it as a tactic to attract the votes of supporters of the explicitly racist One-Nation party. However, as mentioned previously, fears about the rise in the numbers of asylum seekers and immigration in general have by no means been the sole preserve of the conservative side of politics. With concerns about being swamped by the multitude dominating the political environment, the Australian government found it relatively easy to radically overhaul its refugee processing system and implement a range of punitive measures to deny services, support and recognition to the outsider in our midst. This occurred in October 1999, when the government amended the *Migration Regulations* 1994 (Cth) in order to create a secondary category of refugee visa: the temporary protection visa (TPV).[23]

The TPV is targeted at those who arrive in Australia without authorisation and make 'onshore' applications for asylum. It is designed to be distinguished from

---

22 Quoted in Duncanson, 2003: 33. For more comprehensive analyses of the political rhetoric utilised in relation to this issue see Mares, 2002 and Corlett, 2000.

23 Visa subclass 785.

those applications by asylum seekers who 'join the queue' and apply for refugee status 'off-shore'. Successful applicants in the latter category are issued with a permanent protection visa, which entitles them to settle permanently in Australia, gain settlement support and sponsor family members to join them. By contrast, TPV holders are only issued a protection visa for three years, which is accompanied by a reduced level of entitlements and the denial of a range of settlement services which are normally publicly provided to refugees. It seems clear that the TPV regime is an attempt to punish those refugee claimants who have arrived in Australia by irregular means, and is designed to function as a deterrent to others who might be thinking of following suit.

Holders of TPVs are bluntly denied the right to family reunion – including the prospect of reuniting with a spouse or children. Unlike refugees on permanent protection visas, they have no automatic right of return if they leave the country. Some of the most important services that are restricted or denied to TPV holders include limitations on the range of social security benefits that they may access and their ineligibility for federal government funded English language programs and interpretation services. Children on TPVs have access to public schools in New South Wales, but there is an effective exclusion from involvement in tertiary education due to the federal government's imposition of full fees for these people. While TPV holders are permitted to work, the temporary nature of their visa status and their difficulty in accessing affordable English-language tuition are strong obstacles preventing them from finding continuing and decently-paid employment.

For refugees on permanent protection visas, there are a range of migrant resource centres and other community-based organisations funded by the Department of Immigration, Multicultural and Indigenous Affairs (DIMIA) which can assist with settlement services such as housing, the provision of material goods, skills training and educational support. Under the rules governing the funding of these organisations, they are prevented from providing such services to TPV holders, which leads these people to overwhelmingly seek assistance from relatives, friends or acquaintances, or unfunded organisations with little resources and only volunteers to provide assistance.[24] Lastly but crucially, TPV holders in Sydney (as with the rest of New South Wales) are denied access to public housing and other forms of housing assistance, the effect of which is magnified by the extremely high cost of accommodation in the private rental market in Sydney.

While very few TPV holders are released from detention centres into the Sydney community, a very high proportion of these people gravitate towards the middle western suburbs of Sydney from other parts of Australia. But unlike governments in other states (most notably Queensland),[25] the New South Wales state government's concerns about the concentration of refugees in Sydney has led to an informal collaboration with the federal government's punitive denial of services to TPV

---

24  Barnes, 2003: 2.
25  Mann, 2001.

holders. Its rationale appears to be that provision of services to these people will attract more refugees to Sydney and exacerbate the already disproportionately high financial burden that is carried by New South Wales in resettling refugees. However, there is no evidence that people living on TPVs have moved there primarily to seek publicly provided services, but rather do so in the search for employment, and to live near people they know and communities they feel connected to. The vast majority of TPV holders from Afghanistan and Iraq live in the areas of Auburn, Fairfield, and parts of Blacktown, Bankstown, Liverpool and Parramatta.[26] These are precisely the areas of decline and deprivation that the so-called aspirational residents are moving away from. So, in addition to the restrictions on benefits and services that these people have to live with, they are also spatially disadvantaged by the environments in which their communities have been forced to settle. It appears that the entitlement to a full urban life in Sydney is increasingly preserved for those who can afford to buy their own sanctuary.

In political and economic terms, the legal regime that governs successful asylum claims can be understood as a weapon in the forefront of a battle to defend the Australian polis against the destabilising winds that accompany neoliberal globalisation. As a way of deflecting responsibility from the Australian government's aggressive free market dogmatism, the negative impacts of what is known locally as 'economic rationalism' have been shifted to those who arrive here in leaky boats without prior invitation. In this narrative, Australia's economic strength and security are not perceived to be directly threatened by large-scale economic agents, who are instead welcomed (as evidenced by the recent accession to the United States–Australia Free Trade Agreement). Rather the threat is transposed and attached to an undeserving multitude arriving on our shores by illegal means in order to take advantage of Australia's supposedly generous social provisions and high standard of living.

In another register, the TPV regime serves as a demonstration of the triumph of a cultural nationalist parochialism over the cosmopolitanism that has supposedly accompanied the official version of Australian multiculturalism for the past three decades. It defines the regulation of asylum claims in terms of national sovereignty and the need for the State to act as a 'spatial manager' – patrolling the borders for impurities which might pollute the national home.[27] But even when refugee status can be established, the Australian State reserves the right to impose restrictions on the entitlement to partake in a truly social life, depending upon a person's mode of entering the country. The social, economic and psychological effects on TPV holders of their social exclusion and the ever present threat of deportation have now been extensively documented in a number of places.[28] Less thoroughly examined is the question of how best to understand the citizenship rights of those whose

26  Barnes, 2003: 6–7.
27  Hage, 1998: 38.
28  Mann, 2001; Mansouri and Bagdas, 2002; Barnes, 2003; Leach and Mansouri, 2003 and 2004; Marston, 2003.

presence in Australia depends upon the continued validity of a 36-month protection visa. In the next section I will consider how the treatment of those on TPVs can be characterised as a direct denial of a type of urban citizenship which is depicted by Henri Lefebvre as the 'right to the city'.

## Asylum seekers and the 'right to the city'

The work of Henri Lefebvre has been of profound importance in the development of critical approaches geography over the past three decades. His 1974 book *The Production of Space* is a classic account of the ways in which capitalism has been able to survive and consolidate its hold over lived in experience, primarily by occupying and *producing* space. Here I would like to draw on an earlier and much less well-known work in which he issued his first major intervention into debates over the nature of urban space. Written just prior to the momentous events of May 1968, *The Right to the City* (*Le Droit à la Ville*) is partly a philosophical history of the capitalist city and partly a manifesto for a new form of urban living. Despite the fact that over a third of a century has passed since it was written, many of the ideas in the book are keenly relevant to contemporary concerns about the politics and governance of the urban environment. I will argue that the treatment of refugees through the TPV regime can be explained in Lefebvrean terms as a denial of the right to the city.

In order to comprehend fully Lefebvre's conceptualisation of this right, it is necessary to recognise the crucial role the *urban* occupies in his social theory. For Lefebvre, the urban is not simply a product of processes of industrial production and capital accumulation. It is 'more or less the *oeuvre* of its citizens'[29] – a work of art that is constantly being remade anew. The characteristic of the urban as a space of encounter allows differences to flourish and generates the contemporary conditions for creative human communities. Groups and individuals who are prevented from fully participating in this collective, creative act, are denied the right to the city. For Lefebvre, the right to the city is neither a natural nor a contractual right,[30] but is grounded in the entitlement to physically occupy urban space. It emerges from the essential qualities of the urban – as a space of centrality, gathering and convergence.[31] It 'gathers the interests...of the whole society and firstly of all those who *inhabit*'.[32]

Here Lefebvre not only draws attention to basic questions such as the adequacy of housing, but also emphasises the importance of the right to the full use or *appropriation* of space by those who dwell within the city. Importantly, for

29  Lefebvre, 1996a: 117.
30  Lefebvre, 1996b: 194.
31  Ibid. 195; Lefebvre, 1996a: 131.
32  Ibid. 158.

Lefebvre, the right to the city extends beyond a visitation license or a right of return to the centre by those groups who have been expelled to the peripheries.[33] It is, at once, a right not to be expelled from the city and social life, and a rejection of enforced segregation to the urban peripheries with the daily hardships that afflict these areas. As he argues,

> To exclude the *urban* from groups, classes, individuals, is also to exclude them from civilization, if not from society itself. The right to the city legitimates the refusal to allow oneself to be removed from urban reality by a discriminatory and segregative organization. (It) proclaims the inevitable crisis of city centres based on segregation ... which reject towards peripheral spaces all those who do not participate in political privileges.[34]

Segregation here refers to both market-driven processes which accentuate social divisions and spatial polarisation within cities, and the enforced relocation of marginalised groups into ghettos by deliberate State action. Indeed, these latter forms of segregation are encouraged by urban governance regimes which prioritise the exchange value of space, and produce land speculation and higher housing costs. This is precisely what has happened in the transformation of the western suburbs of Sydney over the last two decades, as shifting priorities in public investment have facilitated the move of the middle class into pockets of privilege in the outer west. The way in which these new nodes of power, wealth and advantage have established themselves amidst the increasingly maligned and neglected middle west demonstrates the increasing complexity of the centre-periphery dialectic that Lefebvre identifies. But even more importantly, his analysis of the political nature of spatial change may be the source of a powerful counter-move directed against the increasingly privatised and polarised urban landscapes of Australian cities. By emphasising the importance of *use values* in the everyday occupation and inhabitance of urban space and the necessity of a right to the *appropriation* of space by those who inhabit the city, Lefebvre's thought provides a challenge to the dominance of exchange values in the priorities of regimes of urban governance.

Holders of TPVs living in western Sydney are denied the right to the city in multiple ways. At the very least, the inhabitance and appropriation of space implies a right to adequate housing,[35] which is deliberately made inaccessible by the restrictions on housing assistance placed on this social group by the New South Wales government. In addition, these people experience spatial segregation at two levels. Most obviously, they are forced to inhabit the most deprived and

33  Ibid. See also Kofman and Lebas, 1996: 19.
34  Lefebvre, 1996b: 195.
35  Mitchell, 2003: 19.

marginalised areas of the middle western suburbs. But their isolation and exclusion is exacerbated by a legal regime that imposes extra restrictions on their capacity to access public services. Their ability to participate fully in urban life and to appropriate the space they inhabit is clearly circumscribed by their access to English language services, labour market skills programs and other forms of educational support and their lack of entitlement to family reunion in the future. As Lefebvre makes clear, the right to the city must be accompanied by the provision of adequate services which 'bring the citizen out of isolation' and allows all who dwell within the city to contribute to its social reproduction.[36]

A number of writers have recently proposed Lefebvre's 'right to the city' as a potential basis for the replacement of formal notions of political citizenship with a broader notion of 'urban citizenship'.[37] Lefebvre himself explicitly articulates the connection between 'the *democratic* character of a regime' and its attitude towards 'urban liberties' and resistance to spatial exclusion.[38] The right to the city foreshadows a *spatial* citizenship which should 'modify, concretize and make more practical the rights of the citizen as an urban dweller and user of multiple services' and protect workers, immigrants and the 'marginal' from dispersal and being trapped in ghettos.[39] Australian suburbia may be regarded as an unlikely site for the inauguration of this new form of citizenship. Tim Rowse has described how for both its defenders and detractors, 'suburbia is a society without history or politics'.[40] It remains largely dominated by exchange values in the form of an acquisitive consumerism and high levels of private home-ownership. But it is in the midst of such apparent quietude that the contradictions of space occasionally make themselves felt.

In particular, the struggles of TPV holders to access basic social services can be understood as forms of spatial resistance, which assert their right to fully inhabit the city and participate in its reproduction as *oeuvre*. Such struggles clearly link the concerns of refugees with others who have been marginalised and excluded by existing geographical transformations in western Sydney. By grounding itself in demands for the appropriation of space by its inhabitants, the right to the city not only provides a way of moving beyond intractable definitional arguments about the content of international instruments such as the *Refugee Convention*,[41] but also provides a political means of resisting the current trend towards a form of urban citizenship structured by the logics of privatism and individual self-reliance.

---

36  Lefebvre, 2003: 253.
37  McCann, 1999: 180–181; Oakley and Verity, 2002; Purcell, 2002a; Purcell, 2002b; Purcell, 2003.
38  Lefebvre, 1996a: 141.
39  Kofman and Lebas, 1996: 34.
40  Rowse, 1978: 12.
41  For a critique of the discourse of rights in this area see Dauvergne, 2000. There are also some connections between Lefebvre's formulation of the right to the city in these terms and Ghassan Hage's call for a 'multiculturalism of inhabitance'; see Hage, 1997: 144–145.

## The city as refuge or the 'right to the city'?

In an essay originally published in 1997, Jacques Derrida considered the 'problem' of the right to asylum in Europe and the developed world more generally.[42] Noting that this right has been progressively reduced to a specifically *juridical* concept, Derrida suggests the possibility of 'look(ing) to the city, rather than to the state',[43] as the source of protection for asylum seekers. He raises the prospect of 'cities of refuge' as autonomous sites of a new cosmopolitanism capable of enlivening the historical duty of hospitality. In meditating on the difficulties facing such an endeavour, he draws on the history of hospitality in the Hebraic, medieval and Kantian-cosmopolitan traditions to identify a recurring contradiction

> between the Law of an unconditional hospitality, offered *a priori* to every other...*whoever they may be*...and the conditional laws of a right to hospitality, without which the unconditional Law of hospitality would be in danger of remaining a pious and irresponsible desire...[44]

This neatly encapsulates the competing standpoints in the politics of immigration and refugee law – between the supposedly 'utopian' resistance to State policies by refugee activists, and the conditions that the State places on its hospitality. Elsewhere, Derrida has written at length of how the latter position is driven by fears that the host is permanently at risk of becoming the *hostage* to the foreign guest in their midst.[45] These fears have been most clearly articulated in the notoriously blunt statement which became the Liberal Party election slogan for the 2001 federal election: 'We will decide who comes to this country and the circumstances in which they come.'[46] Nevertheless, for those seeking asylum and particularly for those who have gained recognition of their plight through being granted temporary sanctuary, there is still a need, indeed a necessity to dream, as Derrida puts it, 'of another set of rights, of another politics of the city'.[47]

In this chapter I have suggested one way of responding to Derrida's challenge. Rather than focusing on a particular city as the site of refuge, I have argued that a right to the city extends to all those who inhabit urban space. People living in Sydney on TPVs should be entitled, by virtue of their inhabitance of the city, to the full use and enjoyment of social services, in order that they can participate in the ongoing creation of the city as *oeuvre*. Although acknowledging the legitimacy of their claims for asylum, the State has imposed a range of discriminatory limitations

---

42  Derrida, 2001. I would like to thank Anna Farmer for her helpful and thorough research assistance for this section of the chapter.

43  Ibid. 6, 10.

44  Ibid. 22–23.

45  See for example Derrida, 2000: 53–55 and also Derrida, 1997.

46  Prime Minister John Howard, formally launching the Liberal Party election campaign, 28 October 2001, quoted in Marr and Wilkinson, 2003: 246.

47  Ibid. 8.

on the capacity of TPV holders to participate fully in the production of their social space. This group certainly experiences the punitive nature of this legal regime most directly, but it is important to recognise that it is also an attack on the city of Sydney itself. It is part of an attempt to restrict participation in the spatial reproduction of the urban to those who benefit from the segregation of the city and the prioritisation of the value of exchange over social use. An assertion of the right to the city should therefore be understood, not as placing the host-state in danger of becoming a hostage to the outsider, but as a necessary political strategy to link the oppression of TPV holders to the spatial demands of other marginalised inhabitants of urban space. Accordingly, the defence of the spatial rights of those living in the shadow of temporary protection can play a crucial part in the construction of newer, more inclusive forms of spatial citizenship in Australian cities.

The asylum-seeker story is one not only of legal arguments over the content and failure of international human rights norms – the promise of justice and its denial – it is also a story of space and political struggles over the rights to occupy it. This is obviously so in relation to the jurisdictional questions embodied in the crossing of borders,[48] and it is also deeply embedded in the Australian government's policies of mandatory detention, symbolised by the desert 'camp', isolated and detached from urban life. However, less attention has been paid to the spatial politics that structure the lives of those asylum seekers who are granted refuge and freed from detention. For those living in cities under the shadow of temporary protection, their experiences are framed through the limited form of spatial citizenship to which they are entitled. This can be seen most dramatically in the case of those TPV holders who live in Sydney's western suburbs.

This urban region, once seen by many as a place of plenty and opportunity, is now increasingly dominated by an ideology of privatism and a spatial logic which generates pockets of poverty alongside great wealth and social investment. The treatment of those holding TPVs in Sydney is a reinstatement of these spatial inequities, demonstrating how difficult it is for some to participate and share in the currently dominant model of urban citizenship. It provides a sobering reminder that if Sydney is to emerge as a truly global city, it must be welcoming to more than flows of capital and the gaze of the world. It must also necessarily be open to human flows whose social rights are grounded in their inhabitance of space. As Lefebvre proclaims: 'the right to the city is like a cry and a demand...(it is) a transformed and renewed right to urban life.'[49] The continuing electoral success of the Howard government suggests that it is a cry that is yet to fully resonate with a majority of Australians, but will continue to cast a spectre over the everyday politics of western Sydney into the foreseeable future.

---

48 *Ruddock v Vadarlis* [2001] FCA 1329.
49 Lefebvre, 1996a: 158.

# Bibliography

Ashbolt, A (1965) 'Godzone 3: Myth and Reality', 25(4) *Meanjin* 373–388

Barnes, D (2003) *A Life Devoid of Meaning: Living on a Temporary Protection Visa in Western Sydney*, Blacktown: Western Sydney Regional Organisation of Councils

Carr, R (2002a) 'Is Population the Key to Growth?', *Address to the Australian Davos Connection Leadership Retreat*, Hayman Island, 6 September

Carr, R (2002b) 'Planning Sydney's Future', *Address to the Urban Development Institute of Australia Conference*, Sydney, 8 November

Corlett, D (2000) 'Politics, Symbolism and the Asylum Seeker Issue', 23(3) *UNSW Law Journal* 13–32

Dauvergne, C (2000) 'The Dilemma of Rights Discourses for Refugees', 23(3) *UNSW Law Journal* 56–74

Derrida, J (1997) *Adieu to Emmanuel Levinas*, Stanford, CA: Stanford University Press

Derrida, J (2000) *Of Hospitality*, Stanford, CA: Stanford, University Press

Derrida, J (2001) 'On Cosmopolitanism', in *On Cosmopolitanism and Forgiveness*, London: Routledge

Duncanson, I (2003) 'Telling the Refugee Story: The "Ordinary Australian", the State of Australia', 14(1) *Law and Critique* 29–43

Gleeson, B (2003) 'What's Driving Suburban Australia? Fear in the Tank, Hope on the Horizon', 2 *Griffith Review* 55–71, Summer 2003/2004

Gwyther, G (2005) 'Paradise Planned:Community Formation and the Master Planned Estate', 23(1) *Urban Policy and Research* 57–72

Hage, G (1997) 'At Home in the Entrails of the West: Multiculturalism, "Ethnic Food" and Migrant Home-building', in Grace, H, Hage, G, Johnson, L, Langworth, J and Symonds, M (eds), *Home/world: Space, Community and Marginality in Sydney's West*, Annandale: Pluto Press

Hage, G (1998) *White Nation: Fantasies of White Supremacy in a Multicultural Society*, Annandale: Pluto Press

Howard, E (1902) *Garden Cities of Tomorrow*, London: Swan Sonnenschein

Johnson, L (1997) 'Feral suburbia', in Grace, H, Hage, G, Johnson, L, Langworth, J and Symonds, M (eds), *Home/world: Space Community and Marginality in Sydney's West*, Annandale: Pluto Press

Kofman, E and Lebas, E (1996) 'Lost in Transposition', in Lefebvre, H, *Writings on Cities*, Oxford: Blackwell

Leach, M and Mansouri, F (2003) *Critical Perspectives on Refugee Policy in Australia*, Burwood: Deakin University

Leach, M and Mansouri, F (2004) *Lives in Limbo: Voices of Refugees Under Temporary Protection*, Sydney: UNSW Press

Lefebvre, H (1976) *The Survival of Capitalism: The Reproduction of the Relations of Production*, London: Allison and Busby

Lefebvre, H (1991) *The Production of Space*, Oxford: Blackwell

Lefebvre, H (1996a) 'The Right to the City', in *Writings on Cities*, Oxford: Blackwell

Lefebvre, H (1996b) 'Space and Politics', in *Writings on Cities*, Oxford: Blackwell

Lefebvre, H (2003) 'From the Social Pact to the Contract of Citizenship', in *Key Writings*, London: Continuum

Mann, R (2001) *Temporary Protection Visa Holders in Queensland*, Brisbane: Multicultural Affairs Queensland, Department of Premier and Cabinet

Mansouri, F and Bagdas, M (2002) *The Politics of Social Exclusion: Refugees on Temporary Protection Visas in Victoria*, Geelong: Deakin University

Mares, P (2002) *Borderline: Australia's Response to Refugees and Asylum Seekers in the Wake of the Tampa*, Sydney: UNSW Press

Marr, D and Wilkinson, M (2003) *Dark Victory*, Crows Nest (NSW): Allen & Unwin

Marston, G (2003) *Temporary Protection, Permanent Uncertainty: The Experience of Refugees Living on Temporary Protection Visas*, Melbourne: RMIT University

McCann, E (1999) 'Race, Protest, and Public Space: Contextualizing Lefebvre in the US City', 31(2) *Antipode* 163–184

McQueen, H (1988) *Suburbs of the Sacred: Transforming Australian Beliefs and Values*, Ringwood: Penguin

Mitchell, D (2003) *The Right to the City: Social Justice and the Fight for Public Space*, New York: The Guilford Press

Murphy, P and Watson, S (1997) *Surface City: Sydney at the Millennium*, Annandale: Pluto Press

Oakley, S and Verity, F (2002) 'Whose Right to the City?: The Politics of Urban Citizenship', paper presented at the *International Sociological Association Conference*, Brisbane, 7–13 July

Powell, D (1993) *Out West: Perceptions of Sydney's Western Suburbs*, St Leonards: Allen & Unwin

Purcell, M (2002a) 'Excavating Lefebvre: The Right to the City and its Urban Politics of the Inhabitant', 58 *Geo Journal* 99–108

Purcell, M (2002b) 'Globalization, Urban Enfranchisement, and the Right to the City: Towards an Urban Politics of the Inhabitant', paper presented at the *Rights to the City Conference*, Rome, 29 May–1 June

Purcell, M (2003) 'Citizenship and the Right to the Global City: Reimagining the Capitalist World Order', 27(3) *International Journal of Urban and Regional Research* 564–590

Randolph, B (2003) *The Changing Australian City: An Overview and Research Agenda*, University of Western Sydney, Urban Frontiers Program, Issues Paper No. 16

Rowse, T (1978) 'Heaven and a Hills Hoist: Australian Critics on Suburbia', 37(1) *Meanjin* 3–13

Symonds, M (1993) 'Imagined Colonies: On the Social Construction of Sydney's Western Suburbs', 1 *Community/Plural* 63–72

Symonds, M (1997) 'Outside the Spaces of Modernity: Western Sydney and the Logic of the European City', in Grace, H, Hage, G, Johnson, L, Langworth, J and Symonds, M (eds), *Home/World: Space, Community and Marginality in Sydney's West*, Annandale: Pluto Press

Chapter 12

# Johannesburg
## A tale of two cases

*Johan van der Walt*

## Introduction

The white and black populations of Johannesburg had been living apart for most of the history of the city when the Group Areas Act of the apartheid era was abolished in 1994. It was to be expected that the abolishment of this act would not lead to an easy and simple integration of the cities of South Africa. Years of separation from and suppression of the Black majority left the White minority scared and distrustful as to what the end of official racial segregation would bring to their doorsteps. They took recourse to the one enclave of separate existence that 'post-apartheid' Johannesburg could be expected still to afford them, at least for a while, namely, the economic exclusivity of the already expensive and soon to be drastically more and more expensive properties in the neighbourhoods and suburbs towards the north of Johannesburg. Thus began the white flight and capital flight from central Johannesburg to the new business districts of Sandton and Midrand to the north of Johannesburg. This flight, however, could not shake off the wave of crime that quite expectedly followed it as if drawn in by a slipstream. Hence, also the ever-increasing number of gated neighbourhoods[1] and high security office parks, within the boundaries of which, well-off 'citizens' of Johannesburg spend their lives. Exposure to life outside these boundaries, that is, exposure to the city and to city life as such, exposure to and meeting with strangers in streets, parks and other public spaces have become

---

1 Towards February 2004 there were roughly 300 gated neighbourhoods or 'communities' in Johannesburg. See Landman, 2004. See also Beall *et al.*, 2002; Beale, 2002. Neighbourhood enclosures are of course not something particular to Johannesburg. For discussions of the increase of neighbourhood enclosures across the world, see Webster *et al.*, 2002: 315–320; Macleod, 2003. The legal basis of neighbourhood enclosures in Johannesburg can be found in the Gauteng Local Rationalisation of Government Affairs Act of 1998. The act allows for access restrictions and even road closures, but also sets strict conditions as far as free and unhindered access is concerned. There is, nevertheless, considerable evidence of non-compliance with these conditions and the city lacks the capacity to effectively monitor compliance, as the South African Human Rights Commission (2005: 26) would find in its report on boom gates and gated communities of 2005. See also footnote 27 in this chapter.

a negligible margin of average existence in Johannesburg today. This essay will explore the possibility of restoring city life in Johannesburg, city life understood as the encounter with and experience of the different lives of those who do not belong to the familiar circle of friends and family, an encounter without which a truly post-apartheid Johannesburg will never become a reality.

## The regeneration of the central business district and the regeneration of public life

There are several public and private initiatives afoot to bring about the restoration and regeneration of the old city centre of Johannesburg. The first initiative that must be mentioned in this regard is the initiative of the national government to restore the old centres of all South African cities ruined by white and capital flight by amending the Income Tax Act 58 of 1962 by the Revenue Laws Amendment Act of 2003. Section 33 of the Amendment Act provides for the insertion of section 13quat into the Income Tax Act of 1962. Section 13quat provides for, and specifies income deductions of, substantial percentages of costs pertaining to the erection, extension, addition or improvement of any commercial or residential building within an urban development zone that is to be used solely for purposes of the taxpayer's trade. The percentages of costs thus deductible begin with 20 per cent of erection, extension or improvement costs in the first year of occupancy of the building and 5 per cent of that cost in each of the following sixteen years.[2] In the case of extensions, additions or improvements of old buildings of which the existing structural or exterior framework is preserved, the percentages of costs deductible begin with 20 per cent in the first year and 20 per cent for each of the four succeeding years of occupancy.[3] All the specified deductions are subject to the continued occupancy of the building for purposes of the taxpayer's trade.[4]

This urban development project launched by the national government in co-operation with local municipalities must certainly be welcomed as a significant step towards the restoration of city life in Johannesburg. The decision of the City Council in 2002 to stop and reverse the urban sprawl around Johannesburg by delineating a boundary around the city beyond which no bulk services will be provided, must also be welcomed in this regard.[5] Likewise must one welcome all the business or private initiatives that have been launched to restore the infrastructure of the inner city, combat crime and thus turn around the tide of inner city decay. These initiatives, however, do not themselves guarantee the return of

2 See section 13quat(2) and (3)(a).
3 See section 13quat(2) and (3)(b).
4 See section 13quat(5)(a) and (b).
5 Thale, 2002. One of the express goals of the decision is to encourage denser suburbs and inner city development.

city life to central Johannesburg. There are already visible signs that the inner city development may ultimately turn into no more than a financially attractive and therefore opportunistic incorporation of old Johannesburg into the corporate culture of Sandton and the northern suburbs. Already does the development of the inner city begin to take on the form of a series of high-security enclaves within which members and employees of huge companies can work in the secluded corporate environment of the employer without it ever being necessary to venture into and experience the open realm and exteriority of the city. As Lindsay Bremner puts the matter strikingly:

> Simulating their suburban counterparts, these new [corporate] monoliths have absorbed and privatised all the paraphernalia that usually make a city buzz – coffee shops, magazine stands, bookstalls, stationers, chemists, hairdressers. For those inside, the city has ceased to exist; for those outside, the city is a pretty desperate place.[6]

The return of city life to Johannesburg will ultimately turn on the cultivation of a public-minded concern with an exposure to otherness, with the brushing of shoulders with strangers,[7] and with learning about their very different sorrows and joys, despite the risks and discomforts involved in these public encounters. The following section will now expound briefly the theoretical background that would inform such a cultivation of city life as public life.

## City life as public life

The understanding of city life as an encounter with strangers and with the fates of the different lives of others posited above as a precondition for a post-apartheid Johannesburg is inspired firstly by the work of Jean-Luc Nancy. Nancy does not understand community in terms of some form of communion or oneness that turns on common values and common cultural backgrounds. His thoughts on community resist the idea of a community that puts itself to work, so to speak, on the basis of common principles with regard to which we already share a consensus, common principles to which we have already agreed. Nancy

---

6  Bremner, 2004: 54–58.
7  I am indebted to Louise du Toit for this metaphor of urban civilisation as 'a brushing of shoulders'. As she once explained to me on a busy street in Prague: The Afrikaans word for civilisation is 'beskawing' which relates to 'skawing', the substantive form of the verb 'skaaf', of which the English equivalents could be the verb 'chafe' and its corresponding substantive 'chafing' or the verb 'plane' and its substantive 'planing'. The brushing of shoulders with strangers on the often over-crowded streets of cities can of course also have the irritating and aggravating potential of 'chafing', but this invariably takes place when we enter the streets, not for the sake of entering the streets, but in rushed pursuit of some or other private goal. It is the extent to which our lives are dominated by these urgent private concerns that makes us lose sight of the city as the potential site of a smoothing down of rough edges that may bring out the gloss of a deeper humanity in us.

understands community as that which occurs in the experience of difference and otherness, in the experience of the exteriority that takes place in the encounter with the other. The communality and communication of community cannot be experienced in the communion or oneness of what is already held in common, that is, held in common in advance. The common or communality that unites us in advance is never marked by language. This understanding of communality turns on a silent selfness or self-identity (*ipseité*) of consensus, a selfness or self-identity that is silent for reasons of the absence of any necessity to communicate it. What is held in common can only be *experienced* and *communicated* when a lack of communion calls for the communication and experience of what we have in common (*en commun*). The experience of community turns on the experience of a lack of community. Community turns on the unworking of community, not the working or putting to work of community. Community concerns an inoperative community.[8]

Gerald Frug articulates an understanding of city life that resonates deeply with Nancy's understanding of the inoperative community. Frug's understanding of city life relies on Iris Young's 'ideal of city life'. Young articulates this ideal as follows:

> By 'city life' I mean a form of social relations which I define as the being together of strangers. In the city persons and groups interact within spaces they all experience themselves as belonging to, but without those interactions dissolving into unity or commonness... City dwelling situates one's own identity and activity in relation to a horizon of a vast variety of other activity, and the awareness... [of] this unknown, unfamiliar activity affects the conditions of one's own.... City dwellers are thus together, bound to one another, in what should be and sometimes is a single polity. Their being together entails some common problems and common interests, but they do not create a community of shared final ends, of mutual identification and reciprocity.[9]

Frug elaborates further Young's ideal of city life:

> The hard work in community building – and the task I think cities should undertake – is to deal with the differences within the group. For me, this task requires not cultivating a feeling of oneness with others but increasing the capacity of all metropolitan residents – African American as well as white, gay as well as fundamentalist, rich as well as poor – to live in a world filled with those they find unfamiliar, strange, even offensive.[10]

8 Nancy, 1999.
9 Young, 1990: 237–238, as quoted by Frug, 1999: 11.
10 Ibid.

It is from this understanding of city life that Frug takes issue with the impoverished understanding of local autonomy in American local government law. Frug's fascinating account of the history of the city and the eventual splitting of the public and private concerns of cities in the nineteenth century must be taken into account in order to come to grips with his views regarding the impoverished understanding of local autonomy in American local government law. This history begins with an analysis of the ambivalent public/private status of the medieval towns that liberated themselves from the feudal order from the eleventh century onwards. The legal structures of these towns were that of corporations whose economic strength developed to a level that allowed them to exercise a degree of power and liberty *vis-à-vis* the king and other feudal lords. This power and liberty allowed them considerable autonomy as far as the management or government of the local affairs of the town was concerned. This autonomy comprised the public authority to govern and regulate local affairs and the private liberty to pursue and advance its own financial interests.

However, these public and private aspects of the corporate autonomy of the medieval town were never really distinguished as such. It is only in the nineteenth century that legal doctrine began to distinguish between the public and private powers of cities and eventually divided the city into the two separate corporate identities of private and public corporations. In the process, the public or governmental powers of the erstwhile towns became restricted to public corporations whose governmental or regulatory capacities were fully subjected to the political power of the state and federal government. The only remnant of the local autonomy of the erstwhile towns thus became restricted to the liberty of private corporations to pursue their private interests. This development came to a head in American law in 1819 with the judgement of the United States Supreme Court in *Trustees of Dartmouth College v Woodward*. Justice Story decided the question regarding the status of local government with reference to the fundamental criterion of the protection of private property. The distinction between public and private corporations thus came to turn expressly on the question whether they pursued private or public interests, hence the eventual understanding of the city as a public corporation with no essential private interests and hence also the understanding of the city as stripped of all political autonomy *vis-à-vis* state governments.[11] Autonomy would henceforth be associated exclusively with private property concerns. It is this conception of local government, argues Frug, that ultimately gave rise to the powerlessness of American cities to promote public values that resist the increasing dominance of private property concerns in the regulation of local affairs.

> State control has reduced the importance of cities as instruments of public policy and thereby diminished the opportunity for widespread participation

---

11 See *Trustees of Dartmouth College v Woodward*, 1819; See also Frug, 1999: 41.

in public decision making, a form of participation that is achievable only at the local level. At the same time, local government law's privatized version of local autonomy has channelled the decisions that cities are allowed to make into vehicles for separating and dividing different kinds of people rather than bringing them together, withdrawal from public life rather than engagement with others, and the multiplication of private spaces instead of walkable streets and public parks.[12]

In contrast to this privatised understanding of local autonomy, Frug proposes an understanding of local authority that would promote the public encounter of different kinds of people:

> City power can become a vehicle for facilitating the ability of different kinds of people – of strangers who share only the fact that they live in the same geographic area – to learn to live with, even collaborate with, each other. Its value can be seen in terms of connecting metropolitan residents rather than separating them. Reconceiving city power in this way requires rethinking the legal conception of a city from the ground up. And this involves, first of all, rejecting the legal system's attempt to build city power on the image of the autonomous individual and the nation-state. The legal system treats autonomous individuals and nation-states not only as interested in pursuing their own self-interest, but as able to discover what their self-interest is in an unproblematic way: they can do so simply by looking within themselves. In other words, it treats them as having what theorists have called a 'centered' sense of self. By adopting a similar understanding of city power, local government law has imagined that power can be decentralized in America by moving a portion of it from the national government to the local level without changing its nature. It seeks to decentralize power simply by recentering it – by moving its location – rather than by decentering it, that is, by questioning the sharp self/other distinction embodied in the notion of the centered subject.... By building decentralization on theories of the subject other than that of the autonomous individual, I seek to defend what I consider to be the values of decentralization: the freedom gained from the ability to participate in the basic societal decisions that affect one's life, the creativity generated by the capacity to experiment in solving public problems, and the energy derived from democratic forms of organization.[13]

Frug's understanding of city life echoes the Nancean understanding of community in terms of the communality or 'in common' that does not precede, but results from the experience of difference and lack of community. Space constraints prevent me

---

12 Frug, 1999: 8–9.
13 Frug, 1999: 9–10.

from engaging further with his remarkable work on city making in what follows. Doing so would require going into a detailed comparison of American and South African local government law, especially as far as issues such as exclusionary zoning of suburbs and the regulation of gentrification of inner cities are concerned. Again, I cannot attempt to do this here. Suffice it therefore, to restrict this engagement with Frug's arguments regarding zoning law and urban planning to a brief statement of the City of Johannesburg's vision regarding urban planning and development for the next three decades and the executive role the City Council aims to play in this planning and development.

## *Joburg 2030*

The City Council has articulated its vision as regards urban planning and development in a broad plan of economic development plan titled *Joburg 2030*.[14] The plan is divided in a Foundation Section, a Vision Section and a Strategy Section. The Foundation Section expounds 'a theoretical paradigm of the key ingredients and casualties for creating and nurturing the City in order that it may generate a "better life" for all its citizens.'[15] The Vision Section aims to 'paint a picture of what the city may look like in 2030'. It offers a 'description of a City we would be glad to imagine our children and grandchildren living in'.[16] The Strategy Section 'sets an agenda for resource allocation and resource planning for the short, medium and long term so that the goals set by the Vision may be reached by the year 2030'. As far as urban development is concerned, the City will have to contend with the legacy of apartheid urban planning (or lack of planning). The concern of apartheid urban planning having been little more than the basic aim of racial separation, post-apartheid Johannesburg inherited from the apartheid era a dysfunctional urban development that stands in need of radical transformation. Johannesburg is very spread out and has poor transport systems. The need to travel far from home to work has a negative impact on productivity in the city and the provision of basic services such as electricity, water, sewerage and garbage removal is expensive and inefficient. To change this, the Council has already decided in 2002 to lay down development boundaries so as to stop and reverse urban sprawl and densify neighbourhood populations.[17] The overall plan is to restructure development within these boundaries along two main public transport and key business development lines that would cross the city from north to south and east to west.[18] The '[h]istorically black townships will be redeveloped and upgraded' so as to 'become new suburbs designed like historically white suburbs'. There will be 'fewer poorer communities and they will be concentrated so that

14  *Joburg 2030*, 2002.
15  Prologue to *Joburg 2030*, 2002.
16  Ibid.
17  Thale, 2002.
18  *Joburg 2030*, 2002: 7 (*Executive Summary*).

their special needs can be met'. 'Residential housing will be closer to business opportunities, shopping and public transport.' 'Outdoor life will be more pleasant and there will be rivers, dams, parks and outdoor relaxation facilities.'[19]

The City Council sees its own role in the overall urban and economic development of Johannesburg as follows:

> Strategically, *Joburg 2030* incorporates three crucial shifts from the perspective of the City Council. First the Council will need to redimension itself. Traditionally the Council has essentially been an administrator and a provider of utility services. In the future the City Council will need to become an agent for economic growth. Second the Council will need to shift outwards its fundamental delivery horizon with respect to achieving a better City.... Finally, to achieve its vision, the Council will need to reposition itself in relation to other spheres of government. Increased support, co-operation and co-ordination from the National and Provincial tiers of government will be crucial to the success of this strategy.[20]

Three paragraphs from the Strategy Section are most significant in this regard:

> [A]s the Council redimensions itself from a mere administrator and service provider to an agent of economic growth, so too will it need to increase its exposure with the departments in spheres of government with which it has not previously needed to be in contact. For example, there has been little need to co-ordinate and mutually agree on approaches to sectoral development with the Department of Trade and Industry (DTI) in the past. The new Strategy makes it clear that such a relationship would be mutually beneficial both to DTI and the Council.[21]

> Due to the lack of a long-term, coherent strategy for the City, Council's interactions with other spheres of government have been dominated by joint co-operative projects or narrowly defined specific interventions that have generally arisen from strategic decisions taken at provincial or national level. The Council has not previously been in a position to engage substantively at a strategic level in many areas and has seldom taken the lead in a new strategic direction or approach. This situation is now about to change and, armed with a strong agenda and Strategy, the level and content of intergovernmental relations can now be strengthened.[22]

The political confidence of the City Council that these two passages exude, stems from the realisation that Johannesburg is a formidable economic force in

---

19 *Joburg 2030*, 2002: 5–6 (*Short Version*); See also ibid. 7–8 (*Executive Summary*).
20 Ibid. 2 (*Executive Summary*).
21 *Joburg 2030*, 2002: 145.
22 Ibid.

the broader South African context. The passage that precedes these two passages directly makes this realisation quite clear:

> [T]he City of Johannesburg is economically important at a national level. The City contributes 16 percent of national GNP, 12 percent of national employment, 20 percent of national exports and is home to the head offices of 94% of listed and foreign companies trading in South Africa. As such the health of the City's economy has a direct bearing on national economic performance, as well as perceptions regarding South Africa as an investment destination. At a provincial level, Johannesburg contributes 84 percent of Gauteng's provincial GGP and is home to the provincial legislature. Thus the economic performance of the province is intimately connected with the economic performance of the City. Given the economic significance of the City of Johannesburg, it is appropriate that it take the lead in fostering better relations with the other two spheres of government.[23]

These three passages from the Strategy Section resonate remarkably with Frug's explication of the political power and freedom of medieval cities *vis-à-vis* the King and other feudal lords that resulted from the increasing economic power of these cities. It is nevertheless important to note that the political confidence of the Johannesburg City Council articulated in these passages relates predominantly, if not exclusively, to its role as an agent for economic growth. Apart from fighting crime and poverty, neither the Vision Section nor the Strategy Section mentions anything about the political goals and aspirations of the city beyond that of economic development and growth. The vision articulated as far as public spaces such as parks and other outdoor facilities are concerned is heartening to the extent that these spaces and facilities may well foster more inter-personal exchanges between strangers of the kind that Young and Frug take to be crucial for the learning about otherness that should inform city life. More densely populated neighbourhoods and a more functional public transport system will also contribute to the brushing of shoulders with strangers that is so crucial for urban civilisation and urban civility. But the urban development plan expounded in *Joburg 2030* can hardly be said to articulate a vision as regards the cultural and political life and lifestyles of a future Johannesburg that goes beyond the basic concerns with residential accommodation, earning one's living and entertainment facilities. '[W]ork[ing] hard by day and play[ing] hard by night' is as far as *Joburg 2030*'s lifestyle vision for a future Johannesburg goes.[24]

---

23  Ibid.

24  *Joburg 2030*, 2002: 113 (*Vision*). This 'playing hard' will not necessarily be devoid of cultural experiences, since the Council does envisage a 'diverse and full cultural events calendar'. Cultural events and experiences can nevertheless, easily regress to a matter of passive consumption in contexts that do not allow for active public participation in the destiny of the city.

The vision statement says nothing about structural changes in urban development that will bring more variation into neighbourhood patterns that are as yet still predominantly characterised by a bleak black-white division. The plan to redevelop and upgrade '[h]istorically black townships' so as to 'become new suburbs designed like historically white suburbs' does also not say much about the need ultimately to unite a city that is racially still deeply divided by four decades of institutionalised apartheid.[25] White suburbs in South Africa are characteristically the abodes of people who live predominantly *apart* from one another and interact with no one outside the closed circles of family and intimate friends. The white suburb is hardly the basis for imagining a *post-apartheid* Johannesburg. Even less so is the deeper withdrawal into private little heavens of domesticity that marks the lifestyles of those living in the ever-increasing number of security estates and gated neighbourhoods in and around Johannesburg. One cannot sociologically imagine that these fearful ones will ever be inclined to make use of the improved public transport facilities of the future Johannesburg or frequent its parks and outdoor facilities. As regards the latter, most of the security estates will in any case have their own little green belts. Exposure to the city outside will be from within the enclave of the family car on the road between the outer gates of gated neighbourhoods and security estates and the gates of office parks, shopping malls and schools. The vision articulated in *Joburg 2030* includes nothing apart from its intent to fight crime that may come to discourage and eventually reverse this emaciation of citizenship in a future Johannesburg. It offers no express concern with the rehabilitation of citizenship in Johannesburg.

This lack of political vision in *Joburg 2030* as regards values other than economic growth is not all that surprising. These values would require the introduction of legal principles and rules that would in many respects contradict the values that inform the increasing withdrawal into private lives devoid of public exposure. We have of course learnt from Duncan Kennedy that the law is full of contradictions[26] and the introduction into the legal system of values that are more public-spirited is not a problem as such. The problem relates only to the limited legislative scope that local government enjoys as far as introducing such public-spirited rules and principles are concerned. The privatist orientation of South African law does certainly not begin with the legislative ordinances of local government. It is deeply embedded in a private law system that constitutes one of the main stays of the national legal system. The rules and principles of private law can only be changed by means of national legislation or by the reinterpretation of existing private law rules by the common law and ultimately constitutional judiciary of South Africa. Whatever political clout the city of Johannesburg might gain as a result of its economic strength, its legislative autonomy will remain that of

25  See Beall *et al.*, 2002.
26  Kennedy, 1979 and 1987.

a third tier of government. It will not be able to make law that contradicts provincial or national law. It will still be deeply marked by the erosion of the public power of cities that Frug traces to nineteenth-century local government law in America.

It is important to note that the South African Human Rights Commission conducted hearings to determine the constitutionality of gated neighbourhoods during October 2003 (at the time that I was completing this essay).[27] The issue of gated neighbourhoods in South Africa will ultimately come to turn on the tension between private law and constitutional rights of ownership and freedom of contract, on the one hand, and the restrictions of these rights in view of the rights of others and public concerns in general. This would not only apply to the gating of neighbourhoods in the suburbs, but also to areas of restricted access in the inner city. To bring to mind again the development that Lindsay Bremner already identifies in downtown Johannesburg: if a company would buy up a whole block of office buildings in the urban development zone demarcated by the Johannesburg municipality, renovate and improve them, and in the end restrict access to them so as to only allow employees and clients inside these inner city 'office parks', this national and urban regeneration initiative would ultimately contribute nothing towards restoring the city as public space where strangers would brush shoulders and learn about the different lives of others. There is nothing in the Revenue Laws Amendment Act that would discourage, let alone prohibit, this privatisation of the inner city of Johannesburg, despite the fact that the income deductions involved in the construction of these 'office parks' actually mean that they would to a considerable extent be funded by public money.

What scope would this privatisation of downtown Johannesburg leave for freedom of public expression? Suppose civil society organisations or labour unions would want to arrange a public protest against some or other practice of the company who owns the 'office park' or of one of the businesses that occupies premises within these parks. What would they be allowed to do? Would they be allowed to enter the park so as to effectively make known their presence and protest? This is most unlikely. Would they be allowed to demonstrate and picket around the entrances to the park? It is against the background of these questions that two High Court cases decided in Johannesburg in the 1990s as regards the right to public expression are of fundamental significance for the rehabilitation of public life in the city. In the first of these cases, *Deneys Reitz v SA Commercial Catering and Allied Workers Union*, decided in 1991, the court granted an interdict

---

27 The Commission published its report on these hearings in March 2005. The principal findings of the Commission reflected substantial apprehension with regards to boom gates and gated communities. It considered these booms and gated communities to cause 'social division, dysfunctional cities' and a cause of 'further polarisation' of our society while its 'proposed benefits' remained 'in doubt and the subject of considerable debate'. It also considered them to have the potential to, and to indeed violate, a number of constitutional rights. For a full statement of the Commission's findings and recommendations in this regard, See South African Human Rights Commission, 2005: 26. See also note 1 in this chapter.

against the decision of a labour union to launch a programme of public protest against the anti-union practices of a firm of attorneys. The labour union planned, among other things, to picket outside the offices of the attorneys. The interdict was granted on the ground that the protest would infringe the rights to subjective comfort of employees and clients of the attorneys when they passed by the picketers to enter and exit the offices of the attorneys. The reasoning of the court clearly sought to extend the considerations of peace and quiet, to which one is entitled in the private realm of the home, to the public space that one enters when one ventures into streets.[28]

If this kind of reasoning is to prevail in the jurisprudence regarding public expression in South Africa, one of the last chances for experiences of otherness and for insightful encounters with the different lives and concerns of others will disappear from South African cities. But fortunately, this is not the only stance the Johannesburg High Court has taken on this issue. In 1999 the same court took a much more liberal stance on the issue of public expression by adopting a mode of reasoning that is much closer to the 'clear and present danger' test developed in the United States as far as the curtailing of freedom of expression is concerned.[29] This was the case of *Four Ways Shopping Mall v SA Commercial Catering and Allied Workers Union*.[30] In this second case, the court made the granting of an interdict against intended protesting and picketing subject to concrete evidence that the protest and picketing gave or will give rise to the wrongful infringement of the rights of others. The two cases are clearly in tension with one another, so the law that actually applies in this regard remains most uncertain. There is no case law in any of the other High Court Jurisdictions in South Africa that exercises any pull on this uncertainty, nor has the Supreme Court of Appeal had an opportunity to steer the law in one way or another. The Johannesburg High Court is thus still quite free to take the lead and lay down the law regarding public expression in the City of Johannesburg. Where will it go? What direction will the Supreme Court of Appeal take should it eventually be required to decide the issue? Or will this matter ultimately be decided by the new judiciary on the block, the judges of the Constitutional Court? The very institution of the Constitutional Court may well come to inspire hope as regards the rehabilitation of public life in South African cities, especially if the aesthetics of the building in which its jurisprudence will be developed is to have any influence on this jurisprudence.

## Constitutional Hill: the Old Fort and the New Court

The citizens of Johannesburg shall always be indebted to Wessel le Roux for a brilliant and beautiful and now already widely inspiring essay on the aesthetics

---

28 *Deneys Reitz v SA Commercial Catering and Allied Workers Union* (1991), especially at 696D-F.
29 Tribe, 1988: 841–861.
30 *Four Ways Shopping Mall v SA Commercial Catering and Allied Workers Union* (1999).

of the new Constitutional Court in Johannesburg.[31] Le Roux's essay analyses the setting and architectural design of the court from the perspective of a concept of street democracy that he also infers from the work of Iris Young and Gerald Frug (among others) from which the articulation of city life as public life in this essay has taken its cue above.[32] His essay also relies on the work of Lindsay Bremner to add another voice of resistance to the privatising process of white and capital flight that have led to the destruction of public space or public spaces in central Johannesburg.[33] The brief engagement with Le Roux's essay in what follows cannot hope to do justice to its richness of the essay. It therefore only aims to highlight a number of the historical and aesthetic aspects of the new Constitutional Court discussed in the essay.

The South African Constitutional Court is built on the site of the old prison in Johannesburg known as the Old Fort. The site as a whole has now been renamed as 'Constitutional Hill'. Many prominent individuals who struggled against apartheid were incarcerated in the Old Fort prison over the years. The site was selected by the Constitutional Judges of South Africa not only on the basis of its physical accessibility and prominent location in central Johannesburg, but also and especially for reasons of its rich symbolism. As Le Roux puts it:

> The Constitutional Court judges regarded the Old Fort precinct as a truly South African centre of repression and hope, and thus as the ideal symbolic site for the construction of the Constitutional Court. The judges felt that the transformation of the old prison into a constitutional court would physically and visually dramatise the contrast between the past of 'untold suffering and injustice' and the future of 'democracy and peaceful co-existence'.[34]

The selection of the site is also symbolic as far as urban development is concerned. Le Roux continues:

> The choice made by the judges contrasts sharply with the dominant urbanisation trends operating in post-apartheid Johannesburg. Lindsay Bremner has recently described how crime has lead to a re-segregation, re-privatisation, re-militarisation and re-fortification of the Johannesburg urban environment after the collapse of formal apartheid. In the way reminiscent of urban planning during apartheid, crime has created new centres of power and locales of weakness. As white capital moves further north towards Sandton and Midrand, she explains, the 'gaps between the world of the township, the inner city and the suburb are widening. The chances that people of this city will develop a sense of shared space, of shared destiny grow slimmer by the day.'[35]

31  Le Roux, 2001.
32  Le Roux relies on Frug, 1996.
33  Le Roux relies on Bremner, 1998.
34  Le Roux, 2001: 155.
35  Ibid. 155–156 referring to and quoting Bremner, 1999.

After the site was selected, it was decided that the selection of a design for Constitutional Hill as a whole and the Court in particular should take place through a public competition. 'In order to maximise public participation, the competition was opened to individuals and institutions not registered as architects in South Africa.'[36] The winning design, avers Le Roux, 'not only invites street democratic interactions, but mirrors these interactions' in the constructions themselves:

> The design team aimed for and achieved an architectural expression of the structural dynamic of the postmodern normative ideal of city life as presented by Young, Sennet and Frug. The design thus breaks radically with both the neo-classical aesthetic (expressing the authority and power of the colonial nation state) and the functional aesthetic (expressing the authority and power of the programmatic, bureaucratic apartheid state). The symbolic significance and potency of the Constitutional Court building does not lie in the power with which it can maintain its own monumental or functional self-sufficiency, but in the non-authoritarian way it manages to relate to, and enter into dialogue with its civic environment and more importantly, the way in which it manages to encourage the people constituting its potential public to do the same.... [A] variety of accessible and open pedestrian walkways [cuts] across the site.... Parks, tree-lined walkways, libraries, museums, marketplaces, offices and living places make up Constitutional Hill. [I]t is...a fragmented aggregation of spaces, volumes and routes. The admix of pavilions, galleries, canopies and arbours gives concrete form to the openness of the democratic constitutional process. [I]t derives its symbolic significance from the vibrancy of the city life and movement between people it supports. In this urban public space, a crowd of eccentrics will be able to move through a legible landscape of buildings that alternate with squares, footpaths, courtyards and clusters of indigenous trees, none of which will dominate the urban environment. The...complex is not a grand, singular object to be appreciated and appropriated at a distance, as was the dream of the acropolitan Union Buildings complex,[37] but an urban environment encouraging participation in a street-life where it would be possible to see and meet people, all kinds of people, not just of one class, or colour or age.[38]

One cannot predict to what extent the aesthetics of Constitutional Hill will eventually influence the jurisprudence of the Constitutional Court. Le Roux has

---

36 Le Roux, 2001: 157.
37 That is, the Herbert Baker designed buildings on *Meintjies Kop* in Pretoria that still house the executive branch of the South African government.
38 Le Roux, 2001: 159–161.

his doubts in this regard.[39] But surely, the more it does, that is, the more this jurisprudence comes to embrace city life, not as a concern with the comfort of the home, but as a concern with the curiosity and courage that celebrate difference and alterity, the more the interpretation that it might one day come to give to the right to freedom of expression embodied in Art 16 of the South African Constitution will take leave of the curtailment of this right in *Deneys Reitz v SA Commercial Catering and Allied Workers Union.*

## Bibliography

Beall, J (2002) *The People Behind the Walls: Insecurity, Identity and Gate Communities in Johannesburg*, Working Paper 10, Development Research Centre LSE, at www.crisisstates.com/Publications/wp/wp10.htm (accessed on 27 November 2006).

Beall, J, Crankshaw, O and Parnell, S (2002) *Uniting a Divided City. Governance and Social Exclusion in Johannesburg*, London: Earthscan Publications

Bremner, L (1999) 'Crime and the Emerging Landscape of Post-apartheid Johannesburg', in Judin, H and Vladislavic, I (eds), *Architecture, Apartheid and After*, Cape Town: David Philip

Bremner, L (2004) *Johannesburg. One City Colliding Worlds*, Johannesburg: STE Publishers

Frug, G (1996) 'The Geography of Community', 48 *Stanford LR* 1047–1066

Frug, G (1999) *City Making. Building Communities without Building Walls*, Princeton, NJ: Princeton University Press

*Joburg 2030* (2002) at www.joburg.org.za/joburg_2030/index.stm (accessed on 27 November 2006).

Kennedy, D (1979) 'The Structure of Blackstone's Commentaries', 28 *Buffalo Law Review* 205–382

Kennedy, D (1987) 'Form and Substance in Private Law Adjudication', 89 *Harvard Law Review* 1685–1778

Landman, K (2004) 'Who Owns the Roads? Privatising Public Space in South African Cities through Neighbourhood Enclosures', at www.gatedcomsa.co.za/docs/NewOrleans Paper_v6.pdf (accessed on 27 November 2006)

Le Roux, W (2001) 'From Acropolis to Metropolis: The New Constitutional Court Building and South African Street Democracy', 16 *SA Public Law* 139–168

Macleod, G (2003) 'Privatizing the City? The Tentative Push Towards Edge Urban Developments and Gated Communities in the United Kingdom', at www.bris.ac.uk/sps/cnrpapersword/gated/macleod.doc (accessed on 27 November 2006).

Nancy, J-L (1999) *La Communauté Désoeuvrée*, Paris: Christian Bourgois

South African Human Rights Commission (2005) *Road Closures/Boom Gates*, at www.sahrc.org.za/Publications.htm (accessed on 27 November 2006).

Thale, T (2002) 'The Sprawl Stops along this Line', at www.joburg.org.za/march2002/urban_sprawl.stm (accessed on 27 November 2006).

Tribe, L (1988) *American Constitutional Law*, New York: The Foundation Press

---

39 Ibid. 168.

Webster, C J, Glasze, G and Frantz, K (2002) 'Guest Editorial', 29 *Environment and Planning B: Planning and Design* 315–320, at www.pion.co.uk/ep/epb/editorials/b12926.pdf (accessed on 27 November 2006).

Young, I (1990) *Justice and the Politics of Difference*, Princeton, NJ: Princeton University Press

## Case law

*Deneys Reitz v SA Commercial Catering and Allied Workers Union* 1991 (2) SA 685 (WLD)

*Four Ways Shopping Mall v SA Commercial Catering and Allied Workers Union* 1999 (3) SA 752 (WLD)

*Trustees of Dartmouth College v Woodward* (1819) 17 US 4 Wheat 518

# Part V

# Lines of lawscapes

# Chapter 13

# Brasília

## Utopia postponed

*Andreas Philippopoulos-Mihalopoulos*

## Landing

Flying into Brasília is the best way to appreciate the city's shape, and with it, the symbolic weight it bears. As the plane approaches, the body of the capital is revealed in all its sleek elegance, a shapely trunk with an outstretching flank on either side. Indeed, Brasília is built in the shape of an airplane, an aerodynamic, forward-looking shape dashing like an arrow on the ground, playfully mirroring the shadow of the airplane about to land.[1] This moment of reflection between the two 'airplanes' is decisive for the understanding of Brasília's role in the building of a nation. It is the moment when the mythology of utopia, as it echoes in the observer's mind flying above, is brought together with the reality of a utopian project as it features on the ground.

Brasília is a rupture in the centre of Brazil, a tear on the skin of the nation that marks as well as demarcates, divides as well as brings together, repeats as well as forgets. The omphalos of the country has been excavated in the 1950s. The umbilical cord that linked the country with whatever lied before then has been torn away triumphantly and attached instead to the collective consciousness. So, the cord is still here, mercilessly omnipresent. It is on this cord, on the line that links, on the one hand, the city in its concrete materiality, and on the other, the collective consciousness in its most ebullient modernist imagery, that Brasília is to be sought and explained. Brasília is not merely a city. Of course it is that too: but a city, being a mere point on the map, cannot rip apart, distinguish and invisibilise the way Brasília has. In its magisterial role as the constructed Capital of Brazil, Brasília operates only in conjunction with its mirror point, that of the observer's expectation who sits comfortably in the airplane above. Brasília is the sharp line

---

1  Walter Gropius's building in Dessau, Germany, which hosted the Bauhaus School also looked like an airplane. Gropius himself wrote that the air view was a principal perspective in Bauhaus and the shape of the School represented exactly this need for differentiation (each arm had distinct purposes and housed different departments) and uniformity (they all looked the same from outside) (Trachtenberg and Hyman, 1986: 523).

that links the world's imagination of what utopia is and looks like, with the reality of a utopia found, grounded, lived in and, inevitably, discredited.

The link between the expectation of the city and the city itself will be seen in its legal and generally normative dimensions. The role of the law in the line's simultaneously linking and dividing function will be described through instances of Brasília's history and geography. But during these descriptions, a hidden side of the line will slowly emerge, the line's very own shadow on the virginal ground where Brasília was built: unsurprisingly, here too law puts an appearance – arguably its most instrumental – and indulges a rather personal battle with its own limitations, expectations and fantasies about justice.

Before this, however, a question begs to be asked: why Brasília – and indeed, why now, almost 50 years after its construction? The question seems even more relevant in view of the dearth of recent literature on Brasília. It would seem that the world has forgotten about the Brazilian capital, and this may well be the case: the modernist miracle of utopia-in-practice is already passé. The world has turned its back on the dream-turned-nightmare, and with it, all the grand utopian projects. Indeed, utopias are nowadays met with doubt, consternation, even animosity: the only thing remembered is the 'intrinsic illiberality, inhumanity, amorality and inanity of the utopian words'.[2] And an applied utopia is useful only as an example of how badly dreams can end up.

Perhaps it is for all these reasons that I am interested in Brasília. My purpose here is plural. I will not deny that I am fascinated by the project's lustrous naiveté, its flirtation with the idea of a clean break, its groundbreaking encapsulation of hope not entirely devoid of a certain arrogance. All these appear enticing rather than simply totalitarian and frightening, because they operate in a specific framework: that of failure.[3] This Brazilian fallen angel shows how the line can never forget the other side of what it demarcates and inaugurates, nor can it avoid creating shadows while it only aimed at the light. And in so doing, it demonstrates law's inability to deal with utopia, even its own internalised idea of utopia. In fact, Brasília is a brutal but conclusive proof of the law's maladroit nature when it comes to its flirting with utopia. The only saving clause for law is that it is indeed impossible to capture utopia, however much Brasília was set to prove otherwise. Not only is it impossible, but it must also *remain* impossible. Utopia is to remain unfound, forever postponed and *ou*-topic ('non'-topic, nowhere to be located). As Lewis Mumford puts it, utopias are 'the only possible beacon upon the uncharted seas of the distant future',[4] and although everyone should see the beacon, nobody really would want to bump into it.

---

2 Kolnai, 1995: 8; See also Molnar, 1990; Lowenthal, 1987; Bauman, 1998; and generally on utopias and critical thinking, see Philippopoulos-Mihalopoulos, 2001 and 2005a.

3 'All attempts to a "different life" have something in common: failure.' Paquot, 1996: 61.

4 Mumford, 1923: xii.

At the same time, however, Brasília is a tangible manifestation of the resilience of the urban, even when sealed in the frozen heights of utopia. It shows how the skies of modernity can blend adequately well with ground reactions (would I dare call this reaction 'postmodern'?), and create a heady mix that constantly redefines itself (or would I dare call *this* 'postmodernity'?) while defying its own demarcating lines. And it will also become clear that the final reason for which I am interested in Brasília is precisely my personal oscillation and hesitation before the line that distinguishes the aesthetics of the light from that of its shadow, the architecturally beautiful from the urbanistically operable, the dream from its analysis.

## The line

The inspiration for Brasília's aerodynamic shape came directly from a postcard of an Amazonian Indian about to shoot an arrow into a river: the X created between the bow and its projectile, and the symbolic gesture of marking one's space with two crossing lines, prompted Lucio Costa, an already established Brazilian planner, to submit just five medium-sized cards with sketches and a brief commentary to the competition for the new capital.[5] No mechanical drawing, no model, no land-use schedule – just a bare concept, a symbol as powerful and as banal as the signature of the illiterate and the first algebraic unknown. The river was to be the River Paranoá, the mark would be the two Axes that constitute the skeleton of the city, and the Indian would represent the whole Brazilian nation, who, in awe, desire, consternation, doubt, pride, had been waiting for almost two centuries to be presented with their new capital.

The new capital has been the cornerstone of the collective imagination ever since 1789, when the pioneers of the Brazilian revolution regarded the move of the capital as the necessary gesture for the country's political and socio-economic independence from colonial influence. In 1822, the name 'Brasília' makes its first appearance in the legislative agenda.[6] Art 3 of the 1891 Constitution puts aside 14,400 km$^2$ in the *planalto central* (the central plateau of the country) for the new capital. The project to move the new capital becomes a staple of virtually all the following Constitutions (1934, 1937, 1946), with several laws and decrees arranging for Committees to investigate the area, studies on the exact location, and projects on the construction of rail links with the proposed area.[7] Finally, in 1956, the move of the capital to the heart of *planalto central* is a legal reality.[8] On 16 March 1957, the Jury for the Selection of the *Plano Piloto* of the

---

5  Epstein, 1973.
6  For a concise history of Brasília, see Schmidt, 1985; also Pordeus, 1960.
7  Decreto Legislativo N. 4.484, 18/01/1922; Lei N. 1.803, 5/1/1953; Decreto N. 32.976, 8/6/1953; Lei N. 266, 12/12/1894.
8  Lei N. 2.874, 19/9/1956.

New Capital of Brazil chooses Costa's X to become an urban reality within the impossible period of three years. Indeed, on 21 April 1960, less than 36 months from the actual beginning of the construction, Brasília is inaugurated by President Kubitschek, the political *patrão* of the project, together with Lucio Costa, the planner, and Oscar Niemeyer, the architect.

The legislative instances of the construction of and move to the new capital are incidental of an attempt to ground an essentially utopian project on some communicable format of collective consciousness, which possessed adequate authority to counteract any practical consideration.[9] The whole mythological freight of the move to the hinterland, being 'strategically' positioned in the 'heart' of the country and equidistant from existing political and financial centres, needed a strong beast of burden. Law, along with emotive politics of the kind Kubitschek excelled in, seemed to be exactly that beast. It was a short leap from there to the collective imagery, reinforced by Kubitschek's declarations that during his electorate campaign, people kept on asking when he was going to move the capital.[10] A collective desire, a slyly realised utopia, a modernist experiment, a constitutional promise, a personal capriccio or indeed a *follie-à-trois*?

Of course, good reasons were given for the move: amongst others, the economic and geopolitical development of the hitherto neglected interior as a means to national integration; the exploration and exploitation of Amazonian resources; the establishment of a modernised, corruption-free bureaucracy; the creation of a new symbol which the people of Brazil would believe in and feel proud of, and which the international community would admire; the development of a new urbanism that would deal with the traditional class stratification of Brazilian society, and so on.[11] All these reasons envisage a crossing of the line that Brasília, rooted in the collective consciousness, would carve on the expectant chastity of the Brazilian hinterland. Thus, on the one side, 'before' the line as it were, one finds the existing urban centres and the coastal 'pseudo-civilisation',[12] the colonial influence and the historically burdened past, social stratification and mushrooming *favelas*; while on the other side, a unified new Brazil with its confident centre, its luminous national architectural and cultural heritage, its attractive economy, its democratic new society – and *no* favelas! Brasília has been donned with the supreme responsibility of balancing on the very line that needs to be crossed at all costs, the line joining her geography and the expectations of national and international observers. Such a line is meant to tear apart any sense of historical and geographical continuity, and divide the nation into two

---

9  The *planalto* was a totally isolated zone in the centre of Brazil, with no road or rail connections to invariably coastal existing government centres.

10 Silva, 1971: 112. Kubitschek's presidential mandate was to end in five years, and he was keen on making the transfer of the capital irreversible – hence the record three years construction time and the consequent extortionate national debt that the construction incurred (Epstein, 1973: 48).

11 See variably Pastore, 1969; Silva, 1977; Holston, 1989; Madaleno, 1996.

12 Silveira, 1957.

self-contained chunks: society before Brasília – impoverished, colonised, dependent, disintegrated, chaotic – and society after Brasília – modernist, progressive, unified, proud, orderly. And all this would be perfectly possible because, as it has been repeatedly declared by every actor and observer of the project, Brasília is not just a city: it is the 'Capital of Hope',[13] 'not just *urbs* but *civitas*',[14] the future of world's modernism (for if Brasília failed, 'the culture of a competent global elite would have failed too'),[15] a 'political and economic renaissance',[16] a 'cyclopean monument'.[17]

Thus, the material city had to match the expectations. The urban body unleashed its modernist potential and provided for an arena of numerous planning, architectural, technological, social, legal, geopolitical observations: for a few years, the world was busily circulating along the two main axes of the city trying to unearth the Capital. And the Capital was revealed: a symptom and a symbol at the same time,[18] Brasília spanned the chasm between the old and the new, and gently pushed Brazil over its capital body and into the realm of the 'world'.

In the folds of the city, the traces of the capital were magisterially inscribed: the city (or at least what is still now called *Plano Piloto* – the 'Pilot Project') is but two grand intersecting lines, the Monumental and the Residential Axis. The city's airplane shape serves the purpose of clearly demarcating the different sectors, such as the governmental, the residential, the commercial and so on. Costa believed in the operational differentiation of urban areas, separate but interlinked with free-flowing highways and no traffic lights. At the top of the Monumental Axis, in other words the main body of the 'airplane', there are the conspicuous, all-controlling twin towers of the House of Parliament surrounded by a moat-like expanse of water, and flanked, on the one side by the superbly lyrical Supreme Federal Court, and on the other, the Planalto Palace, which hosts the president's office: the first lecture in any constitutional law course served on a plaza, aptly called 'Three Powers Square'. Linking the square with the juncture of the two axes is the Esplanade of Ministries, a vast expanse of identical, matchbox-like, Le Corbusier-style buildings with glass façades. Somewhere along the esplanade but decentred,[19] is the Cathedral, a volcano-like building with stained glass walls and floating statues of angels.

The Residential Axis, on the other hand, is divided in the North and South Wing (the wings of the 'airplane'). Each wing is divided into 110 *superquadras*,

---

13 André Malraux, de Gaulle's minister of culture, in his speech delivered in Brasília on the 29 August 1959, quoted in Shoumatoff, 1987: 55.
14 Costa, 1957: 41.
15 Pedrosa, 1981: 366.
16 Lopes, 1996: 228.
17 Silva, 1977: 65.
18 Sonne, 2003.
19 'a question both of protocol, since the church is separate from the state, as well as of scale... and vista' Costa, 1957: 42.

or 'superblocks', further divided into a series of residential apartment *blocos*. While the atmosphere of the Monumental Axis is grandiose, full of distant vistas and dramatic architecture, the Residential Axis was designed as intimate and retiring, with communal courtyards protected from the traffic, shrubs and foliage creating natural screens, churches, schools and cinemas for every four *blocos*. These uniform residences would accommodate all social strata in a democratic mix, with the minister living next to his chauffer, and without compromising on the high level of comfort and aesthetic potential.

Indeed, from conception to delivery, the city was supposed to be a paradigm of utopian democratic community: workers, architects, master-architect and master-planner all working, eating, sleeping under the same conditions, wearing the same uniforms, calling each other the same name: *candango*, the pioneer builder of Brasília. Residents would be sharing similar domestic comforts and access to public areas regardless of their social position – and to help establish this, a new urban language, peculiar to Brasília, is introduced: thus, there are no *ruas* ('streets') but *eixos* ('axes') and *vias* ('roads'). This is a manifestation of the modernist antipathy for the street,[20] especially the 'corridor' street, the one with shops, windows and balconies along its stretch, with its pivotal position in the typical Brazilian (and not only) socialisation. By eliminating 'street corners' and street life, Brasília attempts a more democratic balance between the public and the private.[21]

Further, streets were distinguished by the letters of the alphabet; addresses are not street names but acronymic descriptions of locations ('SQ 310 N – Bloco H 39' is a typical example); and every public and private venture of some calibre is known by an elaborate acronym. Everyone forgets (or never even knew) the full name, but no one will ever forget that Brasília is a 'CIAM' city,[22] and that Costa is Le Corbusier's brightest disciple.[23] CIAM, together with *La Charte d'Athènes*, dictate modernism's highest principles: purity, neutrality, order, functionality, beauty of form, functional differentiation, social equalisation, masterplan control. This is the only way in which political and social neutrality would be guaranteed, social integration assured, the possibility of an error eliminated with the employment of the perfect masterplan, and Brazil would show the world the map to utopia.

Ecce Brasília! Conceived, designed, constructed and presented 'as a whole',[24] with a maximum population of 500,000 and no possibility of growth, Brasília has

---

20  Holston, 1989.

21  An entirely public city deracinates the private control of property and replaces it with a new urban regime 'in which private property is no longer the source of public order' (Holston, 1989: 135). But public control was not to be trusted, as I discuss in the following section.

22  The acronym of the most established modernist manifesto, the *Congrès Internationaux d' Architecture Moderne*.

23  Le Corbusier, 1957; for the relation between Costa and Le Corbusier, see Shoumatoff, 1987.

24  Machado, 1985: 193.

been a *fait accompli* right from the beginning. Its urban plan was fit not just for a city, but for a whole nation. As a metaphor and as concrete reality, Brasília appeared at midnight of 21 April 1960: the lights were turned on and the spectre that has always been haunting the Brazilian dream was revealed to the thousands invited to the opening ceremony and to the watching world. Even though several things were still under construction and most of the residential sector was a building site, there was no trace of the building process in sight:[25] Brasília was to shine as the fulfilment of the Babel promise; a Babel, furthermore, that escaped the hubris because of its humble and noble intent. Brasília was given to the world as an always-already, a totalising symptom and symbol of stability, a masterplan free from the worries of any existing structure, a 'city perfect and complete...that would never develop from within',[26] an accomplished *being* with 'an adult skeleton',[27] a confident denial of *becoming*, and the uniquely tangible cathedra of modernist *non-fallitur*. Brasília, the city, was converted into Brasília, the capital.

At least this is what the plan said. But at this point, the sharp capital line becomes porous and smudgy, inviting criticisms,[28] criss-crossing, inversions, spillovers. By Costa's admission, Brasília's social integration project failed,[29] since, unsurprisingly, *civitas* was found to require more breathing space than uniform boxes with little margin for personal intervention.[30] And the world was watching. Umberto Eco – an avid spectator – wrote: 'from the socialist city that it ought to be, Brasília is transformed into the absolute image of social difference.'[31] The consequences for the symbol are far-reaching, but not as far-reaching as for the people in Brasília. It is bad enough being a figure in a utopian architectural model; it is even worse being a victim of a failed social experiment.

It is not my purpose to write another criticism of modernism at large or modernist Brasília specifically. This has been convincingly done elsewhere.[32] In what follows, I turn to the ways in which the law supported and cheered the construction of the line and the Brazilian passage. The legal presence was particularly prominent, and manifested itself mainly through what I refer to as the law's self-imposed suspension – a portentous act, which can only be legitimised (but never justified) by the fact that, during those times, the law was operating in that somnambulist state in which utopia, in its alluring guise as earthly justice, was guiding its steps.

25  Lopes, 1996: 223.
26  Berman, 1988: 7.
27  Epstein, 1973: 52.
28  See Silva, 1977, for a selection of reactions, both for and against, as well as Paviani, 1985 for a Marxist critique.
29  Although not because the plan was wrong, but simply because the plan was not fully implemented (Costa, 1968).
30  Schmidt, 1985.
31  Eco, 1968: 224.
32  Paviani, 1985; Berman, 1988; Holston, 1989.

## Its shadow

In the geometric luminosity of the crash between reality and utopia, the line cannot possibly remain intact. Its self-appointed porosity aside, the line is afflicted by all those factors that, astonishingly, were not taken into account. The closer one gets to the inauguration date, when the plane of utopia eventually lands on the ground of reality, the longer the shadows of the line. Even before the moment of the collision between the plane carrying the expectations and the 'plane' embodying utopia, the shadow had already totally shattered the line.

This has not been an easy affair. Indeed, the line was inscribed too deeply to allow for shadows. The passage from one side to the other was meant to be complete. And everything was called to assist: language, by creating new forms of urban materialities; politics, greatly through demagogy; economy, by opening new iron mines, building up the Navy, attracting foreign investment, expanding the local industry, especially automotive;[33] the society of spectacle, through monumental constructions, grandiose ceremonies and hordes of poets and global intelligentsia lining up to recite eulogies to the line;[34] And the law? Law assists the passage through a transgression entirely of its own. The law steps out of itself and creates a space within the city's materiality and history, where lawfulness and unlawfulness, just as names and addresses, are resemiologised in order to reinforce the line and assist the passage. For law, the project was taken rather personally: Brasília was not simply a new city, a new capital or a new terrain of legal acrobatics. Law's stakes were higher than most: Brasília was law's wet dream, a pulsating opportunity for self-expurgation, the chance for law to escape itself and blossom into the butterfly it has always fantasised of: justice! In the social order that Brasília was inaugurating, justice would be law's leave of absence: when there is justice, law is obsolete.[35] In an ideal society, where everything is 'architecturally' planned to guarantee perfect co-existence, conflicts are eliminated. The state caters for all needs, people follow predetermined routes in their lives, just as they follow the city avenues, and all is predefined. This is law's utopia: a perfect order, masterfully thought and executed, delivered in that immaculate state of frozen working perfection, never to develop further and open up fissures of potential conflict, an adult ideality that departs from the nest of the creator and flies securely and confidently towards its illustrious fate. This new and much improved Frankenstein harbours neither stress nor burden for its creator. It is already a fully fledged creation that allows its justly proud creator to retire. Indeed, a just city is a city that no longer needs law. No doubt, law would have to work hard to achieve this; but once achieved and the promise delivered, the law could rest, having all its actions justly legitimised. Law's utopia entails the

---

33  Shoumatoff, 1987: 38.
34  Luz, 1982.
35  This is only impressionistic. For my analysis of the circular and mutually exclusive relation between law and justice based on Derrida's undecidable and Kierkegaard's suspension, see 2003.

loss of law, the revelation of its *ou*-topos, and the annihilation of its very self-description. For if law's utopia is justice, and justice no longer needs law (or so it seems), then utopia for law implies and necessitates law's *ou*-topian vanishing into the depths of self-indulging relinquishing of the self.

Unsurprisingly though, by closing its eyes and indulging the minutiae of its fantasy, the law, just as language, economy, politics and spectacle, in fact reinforced the line's shadow and clogged the passage. Away from the frisson of utopian expectations and monumental architecture, away from the purity of the capital line, but not far from the city, things are revealed and covered up in their own undercover passage. Things like conditions of labour, the handling of the favelas, the right to the built city, and the disregard for any environmental consideration, are all part of the line's underbelly.

It should be made clear that these shadows are not to be found on the same plane as the line, nowhere around the total simultaneous space either side of it, and certainly not on the line itself (although to what extent is the shadow not part of the line?).[36] They must necessarily remain *outside*, underneath the line's totalising tear, on the ground. For, even if the line intends to distinguish between Brazil's colonial past and confident future, both these instances are designed to be simultaneously co-present and permeable. A perfunctory list of such 'legitimate' and planned transgressions would include: the urban structure of the capital, which is, if not purely French, certainly more international than traditionally Brazilian;[37] the construction of the artificial Lake Paranoá that hugs Brasília as a partial concession to the coastal *saudade*[38] of the immigrant population (who, being mostly government employees, were obliged to move to the new capital); and of course, the constant evocation of historical analogy with the patriotic past and the long mythology of the move to the mainland, which would constantly feed into the idea of a brave new future.[39] All these instances incorporate glimpses of the 'other' side of the line (external influences, the coastal culture, social stratification, historical legacy), the one that Brasília has supposedly eradicated but which remains always present even as a measure of comparison. In such a state of porous interpenetration, where the invisible is visibilised according to the needs of the already visible, there is no place for the line's shadow. The shadow's invisibility is the condition of the legitimacy of the crossing, the indispensable state of exception to an autocephalous rule that has decided to sacrifice legality for the purposes of self-legitimation.

---

36 This can be put in Luhmannian parlance as *form*: a pre-Edenic unity, which remains inoperable until the point of marking and temporal prioritisation of one of its sides. See indicatively, Luhmann, 2004, as well as Philippopoulos-Mihalopoulos, 2005b, on the significance of the form in law.

37 So much so that Brasília has often been dismissed as 'un-Brazilian' (Skidmore, 1999: 167).

38 A notoriously elusive term, which can be roughly translated as 'nostalgia' but will always leave something untranslated.

39 Holston, 1989: 211.

And legality has indeed been sacrificed on several instances. A few examples will have to suffice. For the purposes of accelerating the construction of the capital, a 1956 Act of Congress establishes the *Companhia Urbanizadora da Nova Capital do Brasil* (NOVACAP),[40] namely the *carte blanche* co-ordinator of everything concerning 'planning and execution of localisation, urbanisation and construction of the future Capital' directly and/or through public or private actors.[41] NOVACAP's unaccountability has been regularly misused: labour laws for the ad hoc recruited labour force were reinvented, omitting standard protective measures such as limitation of working hours, judicial redress, collective representation and so on.[42] The first and perhaps greatest victim of such a policy of expediency has been the natural environment, and most specifically the particularly fragile environmental balance of the *cerrado*, namely the climatic conditions in the broader Brasília region, characterised by long periods of drought. The vegetation is indigenous, sparse and especially sensitive to the effects of rapid development. Half of the region's vegetation was destroyed between 1954 and 1960,[43] variably due to uncontrolled development, high levels of pollution and frequent fires (often arsons in order to allow for more land development) favoured by the *cerrado* effect. It is perhaps needless to note that there was no environmental policy in place at the time of the construction. The future-gazing capital could not be paying attention to its excrement: no environmentally sound waste disposal system was developed,[44] nor the obvious problem of atmospheric pollution from the envisaged 'automobile city' was taken into consideration.[45] Whenever environmental policy suggestions were made, they were promptly silenced in view of the race to utopia.[46]

While the destruction of the environment is a long and insidious process without spectacular outbursts, there have been some more easily dramatised events in the domain of labour for the construction. On 8 February 1959, several workers were killed as a result of a police attack that took place in the workers' barracks in order to quench protests on the lack of water and food.[47] Even after the construction, workers who wanted to acquire full rather than temporary ownership of land (allocated at a considerable distance from the Plano Piloto) had to comply with an extortionately termed contractual procedure which regularly resulted in loss of land and whatever improvements thereon.

---

40  Art 2, Lei N. 2.874, 19/9/1956.

41  Art 3, Lei N. 2.874, 19/9/1956.

42  Lei N. 5.452, 1/5/1943, Consolidacão das Leis do Trabalho, especially Art 59 ff. For an analysis see Ribeiro, 1980; Teixeira, 1982; Souza, 1988.

43  http://www.unb.br/fau/planodecurso/EstudosAmb.doc, accessed on 20 March 2005.

44  http://www.pps.org.br/index.asp?opcao=noticias&id=23146, accessed on 12 April 2005.

45  Automobiles are now the principal source of air pollution in Brasília, http://www.distritofederal.df. gov.br/042/04202008.asp??ttCD_CHAVE=138, accessed on 22 March 2005.

46  Pellegrini-Grinover, 2000.

47  Lopes, 1996: 212.

Needless to say that this kind of contract was created ad hoc by the company and for the specific conditions of Brasília.[48] It is all the more impressive when compared to the fact that Plano Piloto apartments were usurped en masse by higher echelon officials of NOVACAP, without proper tenure procedures.[49]

NOVACAP has also been involved in the designation and gestation of workers' settlements. The most infamous was the *Cidade Libre* ('Free City') – the closest thing Brasília ever had to the Wild West.[50] Designated as an area where private companies related to the works would set up shop, the Cidade Libre was established by NOVACAP as an island of illegality and 'freedom' from the standard regulations, 'the principal space of every pleasure…at times accompanied by aggression and death' where 'the oppressed libido of the workers would explode'.[51] The Cidade Libre is the clearest embodiment of the law's suspension: a legal 'stepping out' of the habitual discourse of lawfulness and unlawfulness, and a blind eye to illegality as a means of expediting the journey to the much lauded utopian city of justice. Indeed, what is a little sacrifice of the usual legal fastidiousness, when Eden is waving from the other side?

Except of course for the fact that affairs and blind-eye necessities were constantly cropping up en route to utopia – next to Cidade Libre in fact! The first ever favela of the capital cropped up as a precarious, 8-days-set-up affair that accommodated approximately 4,000 refugees from a drought disaster in the North. NOVACAP was ready to raze it, when a peculiar game of symbols was enacted: the residents called their favela *Vila Sara Kubitschek*, after Kubitschek's wife, and, with this emotive gesture manifested through parades and banners, NOVACAP was pressured into doing the unthinkable: upgrade onomatologically the settlement, from the anathema of *favela* to the relative prestige of a *satellite city*.

Even so, utopia's frozen adulthood was not to be compromised. The settlement was moved away from the Plano Piloto.[52] It has been followed by 18 more satellite cities, mostly starting as favelas close to Plano Piloto and later being relocated at a more than safe distance. The area's social structure has been evident ever since: the poor are simply not accepted in the Plano Piloto, initially because it was reserved for government officials, and later because they could not afford it. In its excitement to facilitate its utopian state of justice and social equity, the law created a space of transition and expectation, in which it voluntarily suspended itself. It is interesting to observe, though, how law's suspension (in the temporal and spatial sense of the word) above its usual semiologisations and in that dangling state of geographical arousal, created shadows on the ground of

---

48  Holston, 1989: 284.
49  Holston, 1989; Lopes, 1996.
50  Shoumatoff, 1987; Holston, 1989.
51  Lopes, 1996: 183.
52  NOVACAP helped the Vila Sara residents to rebuild the settlement, transferred everyone and provided the basic infrastructure (health, transport, water). Vila Sara was subsequently renamed Taguatinga. Silva, 1977: 230.

utopia that came to haunt the very line at whose service the suspension was supposed to be.

## Landing postponed

Utopia has been cancelled. The shadow of the plane on the ground is the irrefutable indication that the project has never been realised as envisaged: the distance between the plane of the visitor above and the 'plane' of Brasília below, in other words the expectations of utopia and the geography of reality, remains irreducible, swamped by the shadows on the ground. Law's suspension above the streets of its utopian dream was a deluded attempt at self-fulfilment, and the Frankenstein once again turned against his creator. Shadows swarmed law's suspension and cast a *memento vanitas* for law's inability to deal with utopia.

In order to capture the utopia of the Brasílian project, the law indeed stepped out of itself and suspended its normal operations: the law suspended itself at a safe distance from the ground, siding up with the utopia from above, looking haughtily at the ground below. The law created a pool of non-law, where everything and everyone were facing expectantly (their desire for) the awakening utopia. Through the Cidade Libre, the treatment of the candangos, the satellite cities, the environmental indifference and so on, the law believed that, in suspending itself, it would reach that state of superfluity in the face of the established utopia of social justice. Thus, the law looked inside itself, circumscribed that area of self-negation and self-ignorance where no legal code could work, and delved into it in a state of oneiric suspension. But in so doing, the law made a mistake: the law actually believed that it would finally get utopia – and that was the total, self-consuming focus of its suspension. The law *focussed* on utopia, stared in utopia's Medusian eyes and, for a facetiously panting moment that lasted three whole years, believed that utopia was no longer elusive, but possible; even worse, if the pun can be forgiven, 'cornered', happily trapped somewhere between monumentalism and social integration. Confidence was quickly converted into shadows, and the shadows quickly swamped the capital line of the last utopia on earth. The link between the body of the city and the expectations of the world was severed, utopia escaped from the capital of hope, the world lost interest, and the rest is reality: Brasília is a failed utopia, a city abandoned by its residents at the weekends, a capital whose fragile skeleton is breaking under the pressure of the favelas closing in from all around.[53]

---

53 Law made a second mistake, an analysis of which would be too long for the present purposes. Epigrammatically, the law did not respect the necessary mutual exclusion between itself and justice: after the end of the journey to (whatever mirage seemed at the time as the desired) utopia, the law did not return to itself, reassert itself as it were and allow utopia, in its turn, to suspend itself. This would not only be a sign of respect to the indefatiguable circularity between law and justice, but also the *conditio sine qua non* for a certain apparition of justice. See my dealing with it (2003), albeit in the marginally different context of lesbian love.

However, Brasília as a *city*, freed from the umbilical cord of utopian expectation, is still worth a closer look if only for the process of re-appropriation, familiarisation and 'Brazilianisation' of the city by its residents. Of course, the conversion from utopia to city has been neither inclusive nor spectacular – but it would not be. The 'spectacular' parts of the city remain solid *aides-mémoire* of the failure. Take for example, the big decorative white bowl in front of the House of Parliament, especially designed for people to slide and climb in. Its destiny was, as expected, frozen in the *rigor mortis* of utopia: it had to be put out of bounds because it was covered in graffiti and its structure was damaged. The bowl is a metaphor for Brasília as utopia. The map to utopia looks easy, paved, within reach, just as Brasília looks from the airplane of the utopist getting ready to land on her ultimate destination. But Brasília on and from the ground, in all its muddy splendour of utopia *proper*, is the scale of reality: long, cold and inaccessible. One feels exposed in utopia. Just as no human figure is to be found in the great architectural utopias of the renaissance, in the same way Brasília is not made for ambling. It has no street corners, and the Brazilians never learnt to operate without them. So they had to invent them. And it is now, after the postponement of utopia, that reality begins being livable.

A few indicative examples: while all shops in superquadras are to face inside to a courtyard, a walk on the south wing commercial sector shows otherwise: the walls facing the road have been gutted and replaced by shop windows, while the courtyard windows have either been bricked up or generally fallen into desuetude. As a result, the urban spectacle has reclaimed the road and converted it into a 'street': cars and people mixing up, commercial signs, street vendors, even beggars parade in that part of the city, forgetting that they live in a frozen exemplar of utopia.[54] Likewise, residents have reacted to the transparent and 'open' nature of most of the flats in the blocos: façades are now blocked up, or at least dressed with shutters and curtains, thus manifesting the need to reassert the private even in an entirely public city. Even the monumental sector, the epicentre of utopia proper, is not left intact by the right to the city: the Esplanade of Ministries, that quintessence of the Haussmanian ideas on crowd control, has seen many a demonstration and spontaneous public eruption. This kind of events manages, even temporarily, to tear the space away from its 'radical monumentalism'[55] and render its material and quotidian presence at least as adequate as its symbolic.

On a different level, the seriously well-off elite has altogether abandoned the Plano Piloto with its communal recreational areas and clubs, and has taken advantage of the bucolic surroundings of the lake to build extravagant villas that would easily be the nightmare of any modernist. So much for social equality and uniformity – but there is nothing surprising about this. It was only to be expected

---

54  Holanda, 1985.
55  Ibid. 1985: 145.

that the city would be at least partly re-appropriated and the traditional Brazilian modes of urban organisation would progressive seep in from the 'other' side of the line, where they were thought eradicated. The kitsch villas, the Plano Piloto favelas and the satellite cities represent precisely that 'seeping in'. The line tried to circumscribe the geography of utopia, preserve its 'adult skeleton' and illusion of totalising ideality, and enclose it in a fence of legal and political suspension. The line, however, was defeated by its shadow, all those hidden things, 'life itself' which proves 'always stronger: it moves and modifies all the projects we make. It is always impossible to carry out a grand plan in the way it is initially conceived', as Costa said two decades after the project.[56]

For this reason, the plan has been somewhat modified, or at least allowed to be modified in the future. In an unexpected turn, and as part of the successful campaign to convince UNESCO on the award of the World Heritage Site title to Brasília, the Plano Piloto reasserted its nature precisely as *plano* rather than a frozen utopian accomplishment: instead of having everything about it listed as protected assets for the future, it allows for modifications to most of its constituent parts, as long as the land that each part occupies remains the same. In other words, the buildings are not protected in Brasília – what is protected is their outline and the land they occupy.[57] The *idea* of utopia remains, but disconnected to the actual city. Thus, the line previously linking expectations of utopia and city has now been moved to linking expectations and *plano*. This transition, from a solid expression of absolute protection of Brasília as a 'whole', a never-to-develop, ideal embodiment of utopia, to the protection of the *plano*, the project, the process, the 'way-to', is law's redeeming feature in the story. It would seem that the law has finally allowed utopia to escape its real entrapment.

So, is there any hope for the capital? I think so, and this is neither because I feel the need to offer a happy end, nor because I want to convince anyone to repeat the experiment. It is an unorthodox hope, though: there is no hope of recapturing utopia in Brasília – and *this* is exactly the only hope! Brasília (and the world) seems to be on its way to abandon its utopian epithet and concentrate instead on the *project*, the *city* in hand, the street corner. Even the law seems to be giving utopia a rest and allow for a trifle of the quotidian to seep in. In other words, the city has realised the need to suspend its utopian persona and engage with self-criticism on the level of society rather than on the level of symbol. Remarkably, however, when society does the same, namely suspend itself in the form of self-criticism, it gives rise to

---

56  Costa, 1977: 61.

57  The old 1960 law simply stated: 'any alteration to the Plano Piloto with regard to the urbanisation of Brasília shall be authorised by Federal Law' (Art 38, Lei N. 3.751, 13/4/1960). The new set of laws (The State law Portaria N. 314 do Secretaria da Cultura Instituto do Patrimônio Histórico e Artístico Nacional, 08/10/1992; and the Federal law: 'Brasília Revisitada', Anexo I, Decreto N. 10.829, 14/10/1987) are much more detailed. See el-Dahdah, 2004, for an interpretation of the relevant legislation with regard to the passage from city to project.

a reaction against its very self that often takes the form of utopia.[58] This can only mean one thing: that utopia may unexpectedly but reassuringly crop up, if the belief in its possibility is suspended. The only way for the utopist to reach the destination is by constantly postponing landing.

## Bibliography

Bauman, Z (1998) *Globalization: The Human Consequences*, Cambridge: Polity Press

Benhabib, S (1990) 'Postmodernism and Critical Theory: On the Interplay of Ethics, Aesthetics and Utopia in Critical Theory', 11(July–August) *Cardozo Law Review* 1435–1449

Berman, M (1988) *All that is Solid Melts into Air*, New York: Penguin

Costa, L (1957) 'Relatório do Plano Pilôto', 10(1) *Revista Brasileira dos Municípios* 41–44

Costa, L (1968) 'Brasília', 78(1) *Revista Arquitectura* 35

Costa, L (1977) 'Entrevista a Marc Emery', 6(2) *Metropolis* 3–7

Derrida, J (1992) 'Force of Law: The "Mystical Foundation of Authority"', Quaintance, M (trans.), in Cornell, D, Rosenfeld, M and Gray Carlson, D (eds), *Deconstruction and the Possibility of Justice*, New York: Routledge

Eco, U (1968) *La Struttura Assente*, Torino: Fabbri–RCS Libri

El-Dahdah, F (2004) 'Brasília – The Project of Brasília', in Robbins, E and el-Khoury, R (eds), *Shaping the City: Studies in History, Theory and Urban Design*, London: Routledge

Epstein, D (1973) *Brasilia: Plan and Reality*, Berkeley, CA: University of California Press

Goodwin, B and Taylor, K (1982), *The Polities of Utopia*, London: Grossoman

Holanda, F de (1985) 'A Morfologia Interna da Capital', in Paviani, A (ed.), *Brasília: Ideologia e Realidade*, São Paulo: Projeto

Holston, J (1989) *The Modernist City: An Anthropological Critique of Brasilia*, Chicago, IL: University of Chicago Press

Kolnai, A (1995) *The Utopian Mind*, London: Athlone Press

Le Corbusier (1957) *La Charte d'Athènes*, Paris: Editions de Minuit

Lopes, L C (1996) *Brasília: O Enigma da Esfinge*, Porto Alegre: Editora da Universidade do Rio Grande do Sul

Lowenthal, L (1987) 'The Utopian Motif is Suspended', in Jay, M (ed.), *An Unmastered Past: The Autobiographical Reflections of Leo Lowenthal*, Berkeley, CA: University of California Press

Luhmann, N (2004) *Law as a Social System*, Ziegert, K (trans.), Kastner, F, Nobles, R, Schiff, D and Zieger, R (eds), Oxford: Oxford University Press

Luz, C (1982) *Invenção da Cidade*, Brasília, Rio de Janeiro, RJ: Editora Record/Instituto Nacional do Livro, Ministério da Educação e Cultura

Machado, L Z (1985) 'Imagens do Espaço: Imagens de Vida', in Paviani, A (ed.), *Brasília: Ideologia e Realidade*, São Paulo: Projeto

Madaleno, I M (1996) 'Brasília: the Frontier Capital', 13(4) *Cities* 273–280

Molnar, T (1990) *Utopia: The Perennial Heresy*, Lanham, MD: University Press of America

Mumford, L (1923) *The Story of Utopias*, London: G. Harrap

---

58 'Utopia... is inevitably at variance with the imperfections of existing society and so, *per se*, constitutes a *critique* of social institutions.' Goodwin and Taylor, 1982: 16, original emphasis. In other words, every utopia is a product of society's self-suspension.

Paquot, T (1996) *L'Utopie ou l'Idéal Piégé*, Paris: Hatier

Pastore, J (1969) *Brasília: A Cidade e o Homem*, São Paulo: Companhia Editora Nacional

Paviani, A (1985) *Brasilia, Idevlogia e Realidade: Espaço Urbano em questão*, São Paulo: Editora Projecto/CNPQ

Pedrosa, M (1981) *Dos Murais de Portinari aos Espaços de Brasília*, São Paulo: Perspectiva

Pellegrini-Grinover, A (2000) 'A Defesa do Meio Ambiente em Juízo como conquista da Cidadania', 2(1) *Revista dos Direitos Difusos: Direito Urbanístico e Qualidade de Vida nas Cidades* 121–129

Philippopoulos-Mihalopoulos, A (2001) 'Mapping Utopias: A Voyage to Placelessness', 12(2) *Law and Critique* 135–157

Philippopoulos-Mihalopoulos, A (2003) 'The Suspension of Suspension: Settling for the Improbable', 15(3) *Law and Literature* 345–370

Philippopoulos-Mihalopoulos, A (2005a) 'Between Light and Darkness: *Earthsea* and the Name of Utopia', 8(1) *Contemporary Justice Review* 45–57

Philippopoulos-Mihalopoulos, A (2005b) 'Dealing (with) Paradoxes: on Law, Justice and Cheating', in King, M and Thornhill, C (eds), *Luhmann on Law and Politics: Critical Appraisals and Applications*, Oxford: Hart

Philippopoulos-Mihalopoulos, A (2007) *Absent Environments: Theorising Environmental Law and the City*, London: Routledge

Pordeus, I (1960) *Raízes Históricas de Brasília*, Ceará: Imprensa Oficial

Ribeiro, G S L (1980) *O Capital da Esperança*, Brasília: UnB

Schmidt, B V (1985) 'Brasília como Centro Politico', in Paviani, A (ed.), *Brasília: Ideologiae Realidade*, São Paulo: Projeto

Shoumatoff, A (1987) *The Capital of Hope: Brasilia and its People*, Albuquerque, NM: University of New Mexico Press

Silva, E (1971) *História de Brasília*, Brasília: Coordenada – Editôra de Brasília

Silveira, P de (1957) *A Nova Capital*, São Paulo: Pongetti

Skidmore, T (1999), *Brazil: Five Centuries of Change*, Oxford: Oxford University Press

Sonne, W (2003) *Representing the State: Capital City Planning in the Early Twentieth Century*, Munich: Prestel

Souza, N H B de (1988) *Construtores de Brasília*, Petrópolis: Vozes

Teixeira, H A (1982) *Brasília: O Outro Lado da Utopia*, Brasília: UnB

Trachtenberg, M and Hyman, I (1986) *Architecture: From Prehistory to Postmodernism*, New York: Prentice Hall

# Chapter 14

# Cyber cities

## Under construction

*Bela Chatterjee**

## Introduction: dis/integration

Let me start with a statement that might appear obvious: cities are material things. In trying to describe what a city is, I could say that a city is a town with a charter giving city status, or one with a cathedral;[1] but for me this is not what immediately comes to mind. In my view, the primary feature of a city is its *architecture*, spread out over miles. I try to look up to see the rare timber-framed houses leaning at improbable angles in narrow streets, or to pick out the towers of steel and glass that rise from the urban core. Alongside the visual impact of the architecture comes the noise of the 24/7 traffic, different sound systems, accents, and the clouds of pollution and dust from the streets. The architecture of a city, I would argue, is more than the sum of its buildings or the totality of the physical mass of houses, shops and offices therein, but the complex interaction between the urban design, form, meaning and function; the sum total of the connections between the physical buildings, spaces and their inhabitants.[2] Unlike the town, the architecture of the city is marked by greater diversity, scale and complexity, a showcase of the broadest spectrum of architectural realities and possibilities. The architecture represents the city's aspirations, *and* its limitations, as outlined in King's lyrical evocations:

> ...g]reat cities are labyrinths of time (past lives, hopes, dreams, despairs), lost in the incomprehensible labyrinths of space. All architecture, for its part, is (mere) translation – from the chaotic, jumbled, forever unreadable 'text' of the city (those labyrinths of space, quintessentially two-dimensional) and

* I wish to thank Suzanne McGuinness, Andreas Philippopoulos-Mihalopoulos (in particular for the title suggestion!), Steve Riley, David Sugarman, David Seymour, Kirsty Stevenson, Madeleine Jowett and Julia Chryssostalis. An earlier version of this chapter was given as part of the University of Westminster Law School seminar series in March 2005, and I am grateful to the audience for the vibrant discussion that resulted. Thanks also to Lancaster University Law School for granting me a period of study leave in order to research this chapter.
1 See further Frug in Blomley *et al.*, 2001 for a legal history of cities.
2 See further Mumford, 1937 in LeGates and Stout, 1996; Grosz, 2001.

from the architect's half-recalled memory of a million other texts (other labyrinths of time, the confusion of all things ever seen or imagined.[3]

Architecture is understood as a language, a sign system, and a way of transmitting meaning through building.[4] But more than this, it is, in the words of Heyer, 'a social art',[5] which mediates the connection between people and their environment, thus influencing how we live through the design of the spaces and dwellings in which we habitually move. Architecture, the discourse of form and structure, works actively to engage our senses,[6] responding to the fundamental needs of the body and locating us in very material ways in the equally material sites of the metropolis. As Jorge Silvetti has stated, materiality is an intrinsic, obstinate attribute of architecture, more than a technical property, indeed 'a precondition that promotes ideas, creativity, and pleasure in architecture.'[7] It is this materiality, solidity, physicality – and on such a grand scale – which is what comes to mind, when one thinks of cities, as witnessed by some of the other contributors to this volume.[8]

And yet, the city is disintegrating. By saying this, I do not mean to suggest that the city was ever stable, for as Light reminds us, '[a]s an ideal, "the city" is invented and reinvented, and cannot be treated as a static referent.'[9] However, at the same time as the city appears to be (quite literally) a concrete entity, we can also see its dissolution, disruption and disaggregation in the emergence of hyperreal spaces such as Peter Cook's 'melting architecture' and Lebbeus Woods' 'anarchitecture'.[10] Commentators have sought to critique urban architectures and chart their deconstruction,[11] as seen for example, through the 'warped spaces' described by Vidler, who traces the change from the metropolis to the megalopolis, and sees the city as fractured and distorted, evoking feelings of profound anxiety and disquiet. For him, the spaces of contemporary art and architecture become deformed sites where 'the apparently fixed laws of perspective have been transformed, transgressed, and ignored'.[12] One can identify several ways in which the city is

---

3  King, in Pile and Thrift, 2000: 134.
4  I acknowledge, of course, that there is more than one school of thought on what architecture is or might be, and that there are different definitions to describe different periods or movements, much like, for example, cubism and impressionism in art. The architecture I describe here can loosely be thought of as postmodern, but see further and more generally Jencks, 1978 and 1980; Klotz, 1988; Lloyd Wright in Gutheim, 1975; Grosz, 2001.
5  Heyer, 1966.
6  Arnheim, 1977; Mori, 2002.
7  Mori, 2002: *preface*.
8  For example, Bowring and Philippopoulos-Mihalopoulos, in this volume.
9  In Crang, LeGates and Stout, 1996; Cf. Calvino, 1997; Westwood and Williams, 1997; Crang and May, 1999: 122; Pile and Thrift, 2000; Grosz, 2001.
10  Palumbo, 2000: 38; see also Novak in Benedikt, 1991: 247–248.
11  For example, Boyer, 1996; Jewson and MacGregor, 1997; Leach, 1997; Westwood and Williams, 1997; McClung, 2000; Pile and Thrift, 2000; Rendell *et al.*, 2000; Virilio in Leach, 1997; cf. Light, in Crang, Crang and May 1999.
12  Vidler, 2000: 1.

disintegrating, literally and metaphorically, some of which are worth considering here. It is useful to note the challenge to traditional divisions – the idea of centre and periphery,[13] and the critiques and reconsiderations of materiality.[14] Attempting to decentre the city theoretically and politically, and in keeping with the postmodern shift from the centre to the margin, contemporary theorists of identity have started to interrogate the politics of location,[15] questioning the traditional discursive focus that the city has assumed and the urban models of identity that result.[16] For example, Palumbo notes how the spaces of the city become disrupted, and the margins of the city, formerly clearly conceived and sharply discernible,[17] are increasingly indistinct. 'It is more difficult', she writes, 'to identify the limits of the city (the suburbs of the countryside) and the curious presence of holes inside the city becoming more evident.'[18] For Palumbo, the city is a place of porosity, where the very integrity of urban spaces come under question, taking on the nature of 'nodes' and 'networks',[19] rather than the traditionally distinct zones of Hoyt or Burgess. The city becomes a space of confusion, a chaotic interface: 'having blurred the threshold between the city and the non-city', she writes, 'a new threshold emerges within the city, making the city itself a frontier system between worlds whose physical distance is irrelevant because it is divided by lack of measurement, or the disproportionate gap between wealth and hunger, between peace and war.'[20] Where is the centre in such a space, and does the idea of there even being a centre make sense? Such a city is a fractal space, where the ordered rules of Euclidean geometry no longer seem to apply.[21]

Thinking about the second critique of the city, that of its materiality, we can see how the city is disintegrating (and sometimes re-integrating) in the literature on postmodern architecture and design, with writers such as Mori and Puglisi suggesting that the very fabric of the city is in flux.[22] Mori, whilst critical of the moves away from materiality in architecture (i.e. through computer-aided design), describes instances where building substances can be radically denatured using new technologies. In this new architecture, materials become membranes designed to interact with their surroundings, becoming 'immaterial' or 'ultramaterial', such as plastics engineered by nanotechnology, or aerogels, based on silica but comprising of 98 per cent air.[23] Puglisi speaks of 'hyperarchitecture', where digital technologies

13 For example, Palumbo, 2000; Phillips *et al.*, 2000.
14 Pawley, 1998; Puglisi, 1999; Mori, 2002; Palumbo, 2000.
15 See hooks in Rendell *et al.*, 2000: 203–210.
16 Kramer in Bell and Valentine, 1994; Phillips *et al.*, 2000.
17 cf Light, *op cit* above.
18 Palumbo, 2000: 33–34.
19 Ibid. 47.
20 Ibid. 36.
21 Boyer, 1996: 15, 145; Virilio in Leach, 1997: 382; Sim, 2001: 311 (Mandelbrot/fractals); see also Grosz in Wolmark, 1999: 119–135.
22 Palumbo, 2000; Mori, 2002; see also Puglisi, 1999.
23 Mori, 2002.

are integral to buildings and conventional architectural rules and structurings are overturned: an architecture of fluidity where cities not only *resemble* chips and circuit boards, but *become* them. 'A new architecture has...evolved', he states, 'profoundly influenced by electronic writing, an architecture with more nerves than body...establish[ing] relations with nature that are no longer characterised by diversity, but integration.'[24] As the lines between centre and margin, material and immaterial blur, the case for the city as a purely material space seems less sure. Virilio writes 'from here on, constructed space occurs within an electronic topology where the framing of perspective and the gridwork weft of numerical images renovate the division of urban property.'[25] Puglisi echoes this mutation by quoting McLuhan, who predicts that 'all man's [*sic*] extensions, including cities, will be translated into information systems.'[26] Puglisi's vision, shared by others, suggests a somewhat paradoxical space, a city with little or no materiality, unbound by the traditional rules of architecture – in short, *a digital city*.[27]

## Architecture (1): metropolis/netropolis

Whereas the other cities described in this volume have 'real' referents firmly fixed by solid foundations and locatable by the co-ordinates of latitude and longitude, digital cities may not always have such an anchor.[28] Digital cities can exist in and through data, wires and connections, their geographies postmodern and indistinct.[29] They may exist as conceptual space, represented by computer graphics, if at all. Just as real cities differ from each other, so do digital ones. In some instances, they are intended to be 'virtual analogues'[30] to an extant city, such as the Dutch *De Digitale Stad* (Digital City) based on Amsterdam,[31] or the Finnish Helsinki Arena 2000: collaborative spaces created in partnership with city councils, telecommunications networks and citizens.[32] Dürsteler describes these cities as 'regions of cyberspace where people from communities of regional scope can interact, share information, access community digital services and exchange experiences and knowledge'.[33]

Some understand the digital city as described in the introduction to this chapter; others again see it as being closer to the postmodern, mediated city of

24 Puglisi, 1999: 61. See also Boyer, 1996; Virilio in Leach, 1997; Komninos's 'smart cities', Komninos, 2002; Pawley, 1998.
25 Virilio in Leach, 1997: 382.
26 McLuhan in Puglisi, 1999: 58.
27 In the context of this chapter I use the terms digital city and cyber city interchangeably.
28 Boyer, 1996: 145.
29 Cf. Dodge and Kitchin, 2001; Cavallaro, 2000: 133–163.
30 Phrase borrowed from Rommes, van Oost and Oudshoorn in Green and Adam, 2001: 242.
31 Rommes, Van Oost and Oudshoorn in Green and Adam, 2001; see www.dds.nl
32 Dürsteler, 2002: unpaginated. Unfortunately at the time of going to press, digital Helsinki (formerly at www.ias.trident3D.net/elisa/tes-b/3d/helsinki/wrl) was under construction, as it were.
33 Ibid.

Puglisi. Grosz, for example, suggests that the cyber city is rendered fluid and connected to us by its informational nature. 'When we are hooked up to our computer terminals,' she states,

> ...talking to each other virtually, in different locations, the city is working through us rather than between us...the invention of electronically generated media does not introduce us for the first time to virtuality but rather renders virtuality graphic...the city has never been just anything but an ongoing site of virtuality.[34]

In similar vein, M Christine Boyer suggests that the cyber city is the unstable, postmodern site located at the (dis)juncture between the 'real' and the 'virtual' city.[35] Drawing on writers and theorists such as Virilio, Baudrillard and Calvino, Boyer has remarked that the cyber city is the formless, mediated city of postmodernity which has taken on the qualities of virtual space, an 'informational matrix...where borders are crossed by a hypermedia navigator who guides travellers in riding, traversing, browsing, playing the links between different texts, images, words as they move across the grid of the electronic screen establishing new relationships in unpredictable ways.'[36] Boyer's cyber city could therefore refer to any developed city closely integrated with an electronic communications system; indeed for Boyer, the cyber city is not a distinct city or city space like *De Digitale Stad* or Helsinki Arena, but descriptive and symbolic of what all developed cities have become. '[W]e experience a loss of spatial boundaries or distinctions,' she writes, 'so that all spaces begin to look alike and implode into a continuum.'[37] Thus for Boyer, all cities are digital cities: 'the modern metropolis is being displaced by the postmodern netropolis...the space of the netropolis is cyberspace.'[38]

Novak states that the 'netropolis' is one of highly fluid forms, populations and values. 'Cyberspace is liquid' he states, '[l]iquid cyberspace, liquid architecture, liquid cities...an architecture whose form is contingent on the interests of the beholder...an architecture that opens to welcome me and closes to defend me.'[39] The issues he touches upon in the guise of belonging and defence, are those of community, cohesion and security which law (amongst other things) endeavours to create. As we chart the crisis in urban forms, it is interesting to consider how law is affected by this change, and to ask ourselves whether law too undergoes a radical mutation. It is arguably well established that architecture

---

34  Grosz, 2001: 16–17.
35  Boyer, 1996; see also Novak in Benedikt, 1991.
36  Boyer, 1996: 31.
37  Ibid. 19.
38  Boyer quoting Taylor and Saarinen, 1996: 228.
39  Novak in Benedikt, 1994: 250 (emphasis omitted).

and law are closely intertwined, the physical construction of the city and the buildings within it influencing or constraining behaviour and the nature of the subject;[40] yet how does this connection translate in the liquid architectures and 'non-space' of cyberspace? And what happens to law when the matrices that determine the structure and meaning of urban space are made fluid as in cyberspace, and when the digital city itself is distanced from territorial ties and boundaries?[41] Exciting possibilities are suggested by the deformation of the city, and possible reconfigurations of the links between body, city and law that arise because of it.[42] I am intrigued by the question of how law translates in a digital space, particularly in terms of the connections between spatiality and (juridical) order; if architecture is the law of ordered space, does it also produce the space of ordered law, and how does this work in 'spaceless' places such as the digital cities of cyberspace? Given these themes of the denatured city, body[43] and law, it is interesting to consider what forms of law emerge in the digital city, and in the following sections, I consider aspects of digital cities in the context of space, sexuality, transgression and law, while understanding digital cities to be, not merely virtual spaces, but spaces that are linked (or integrated, following Palumbo) with the physical space of the 'material' city. Keeping some distance from the more utopian ideals of the cyber city and anchoring discussion in the material (and the political) is necessary because as Grosz reminds us, 'there can be no liberation from the body, or from space, or from the real'.[44] In order to gather my thoughts on this, I have chosen to draw on the work of Lawrence Lessig, a leading writer on cyber law, and turn his theories on cyber law to focus on areas of sexual trade in cyber cities – the virtual equivalent of 'red light' areas.

## Architecture (2): digital structures of law

The emergence of cyberspace as a viable social and commercial space has led legal commentators to consider how law would work in it. Early explorations were mainly concerned with jurisprudential issues and tended to argue one of four positions: new laws would be needed; existing laws could be extended; a mixture

---

40  See for example, Foucault, 1975 and 1991; Arnheim, 1977: 286–274; Grosz, 2001.
41  It is notable that recent work by Elden (2005) suggests a critical rethinking of the concept of territory. Elden suggests that space should become the object of our analysis rather than its tool, and that territory itself be problematised. Accepting his argument (that territory gives rise to the conditions of possibility for the border rather than the other way round) has significant implications for the theorisation of space, state and city within law. Unfortunately, there is insufficient room within this chapter to explore this.
42  See further Grosz, 2001.
43  I emphasise this because as Grosz has reminded us, the body is a theme frequently forgotten from architectural and urban analysis (Grosz, 2001: xix). I wish also to use the theme of sexuality and the body to avoid what might otherwise be an abstract and apolitical discussion on the function of cyber law.
44  Grosz, 2001: 18.

of existing and new laws could be used; or types of non-legal regulation would be most apt.[45] It was noted that the transjurisdictional, virtual and transient nature of cyberspace distinguishes it from other communications media. Some suggested responses to this issue have included developing law along the lines of *Lex Mercatoria* ('Lex Electronica'), legal pluralism, or along the lines of International Law.[46] Yet elsewhere, it has been argued that, although cyberspace is transjurisdictional, transactions and users are based in geographically distinct locations, and that location therefore determines jurisdiction as it does in existing media such as faxes. However, the problem with this is that the link between the geographical location and the 'location' in cyberspace is not necessarily readily established or even direct.[47] To quote Johnson and Post, 'the rise of an electronic medium that disregards geographical boundaries throws the law into disarray by creating new phenomena that need to become the subject of clear legal rules but that cannot be governed, satisfactorily, by any current territorially based sovereign'.[48] In thinking about how the law is thrown into disarray, one of the most influential cyber law theorists, Lawrence Lessig, put forward the argument that what is most influential in regulating cyberspace is its architecture, in the form of 'code'. 'In real space' he argues, 'we recognise how laws regulate, through constitutions, statutes and other legal codes. In cyberspace we must understand how code regulates... code is cyberspace's law'.[49]

Just as architecture in real space influences one's actions through the nature and constraints of buildings, the architecture of cyberspace – the way it is built and the mindset of the builders, the structure of the system – constrains or enables certain behaviours.[50] Lessig explains that 'an analogue for architecture regulates behaviors in cyberspace – *code*. The software and hardware that makes cyberspace what it is constitutes a set of constraints on how you can behave... the code writer, as Ethan Katsch puts it, is the "architect." '[51] Although other regulatory factors, such as norms, markets and 'real' laws, play a part, Lessig argues that code is the predominant and most effective form of regulation in cyberspace, because code is a self-executing constraint.[52] Traditional laws, he argues, require subjective awareness to ensure conformity and a substantial enforcement structure. For example, entry into private space in a 'real' city is governed by the law of trespass. If you trespass and are caught, you will be

---

45  Wall, 1998.
46  See for example, Kohl, 2004.
47  Johnson and Post, 1996; Wall, 1998.
48  Johnson and Post in Lessig, 1999: 24, but see Kohl, 2004.
49  Lessig, 1999: 6. Note that Lessig does not use the term 'code' in the legal, but in the electronic sense, referring to the hardware and software that constitute cyberspace. Still, useful analogies can be drawn.
50  Ibid. 25 fn 1.
51  Ibid. 89–90 (original emphasis).
52  Ibid. 89, 286.

brought within the machinery of the law, and the relevant sanction will be levied against you. The law aims to have a prohibitive effect by the backing of a sanction: you know that if you break it you may be punished. In this way the law requires our subjective knowledge of it to have a prohibitive effect, and requires the police, prosecutors and court systems to execute it. But by that stage it is too late, as the law has already been broken. Code, however, works differently, which can be illustrated by considering the same example of trespass in cyberspace. Software electronically blocks your entry whether you know (or care) that entry into a virtual site is prohibited or not, and is not as easily circumvented as a physical barrier. The timing of the restraint comes prior to the prohibited action – you are prevented from even entering the virtual space, and no supporting forces are required to bring the prohibition into effect; the software works automatically to prevent your access without police, lawyers or judges. Lessig thus concludes that 'the constraints of architecture [in cyberspace] are self-executing in a way that the constraints of law, norms and markets are not.'[53] Some architectures of cyberspace are more amenable to the code's regulation than others, and not all regulation is absolute; but for Lessig, in spite of this, code remains king: 'if code is law, then...."code is power". How the code regulates, who controls the code writers – these are questions that any practice of justice must focus on in the age of cyberspace.'[54]

## Architecture (3): constructing justice?

Lessig's vision of code as a relatively effortless, effective and self-executing law seems, on the surface at least, to be most appealing. Unlike common and statute law, the future of code is potentially more open, unmired by centuries of restrictive precedent and tradition.[55] Lessig is keen to point out that although commerce is increasingly influential in how the regulation of cyberspace emerges, this is not inevitable, and that with code we can actively choose the net we want to build and the style of regulation that goes with it.[56] Thinking from a feminist perspective, such qualities might be uniquely empowering, in that code could literally place the writing and enforcement of law in the hands of the individual, in a way that traditional law does not allow for.[57] Code also promises to separate law from its traditional institutions of enforcement, which have tended

---

53  Lessig, 1999: 238.
54  Ibid. 60 quoting Mitchell.
55  This leaves aside, of course, the question of whether protocol has any influence. I thank the editor for discussion on this point.
56  Ibid. 6, 61.
57  I should point out that I am using the term 'feminism' to indicate or suggest a prioritised focus on women's concerns, but that this does not suggest that there is a singular or unified 'feminist' agenda. There are, however, some common themes running through feminist work which I shall explore further in the following sections.

to be spheres of masculine prerogative. To borrow an architectural metaphor from the feminist writer Audre Lourde, one question regarding feminist action has been whether the master's tools will ever dismantle the master's house.[58] With code as law, this question becomes rephrased, in that there is the possibility that a new and better house will be constructed, on terms perhaps more favourable to women. Code offers women, in theory at least, the possibility of being architects of a new space, which is attentive to their wants and needs.[59] The 'we' of Lessig's vision might be women, feminist architects of new spaces, building (as Virginia Woolf had hoped for) rooms of our own.[60] As feminist commentators on architecture have forcefully observed, the design of urban spaces in particular follows patriarchal values, and architecture as a discourse has a clear influence in constructing gendered and sexualised selves.[61] It is clear to see that space, particularly in cities, is both gendered and sexualised, and thus the (re)appropriation of spaces through design and architecture, is thus a profoundly political act. If law is understood as a force that constrains or enables behaviour, then architecture, in real or virtual space, serves to act as law, in that buildings enable or constrain our movement, and influence in the most profound ways how we live.

Grosz has argued that 'space is the ongoing possibility of a different inhabitation';[62] 'different inhabitations' is what code, and through its construction, cyberspace, might afford: a reconfiguration of the current gendered and sexualised relationship between bodies, architecture and law. Law as code is built into digital spaces – a hyperarchitecture of law constraining and enabling our movements in similar ways to law in real space. In this respect, Lessig's argument that architecture of cyberspace is law, is not that far from the role that architecture plays in real space – the difference being that in cyberspace, who gets to be an architect is (on his reading) a more open question than in real space. Yet how might the architecture of cyberspace work to ensure justice for its communities in practice; and is it as neutral as it appears? In the final section of this chapter, I wish to draw the threads of my discussion together, and seek to consider how code might work as an instrument of regulation and protection. In order to do this, I take the example of the virtual red light district, a community where cyber city, law and sexuality meet.[63]

58  Lourde in Rendell et al., 2000.
59  I do not wish to suggest here that technology is universally accessible to all women, and acknowledge that there remains a digital divide which reflects the traditional hierarchies of oppression. Having said this, I think that it is important to explore any possibility for empowerment. I am not arguing that code will empower all women, but simply that it might be one place to start.
60  Woolf in Rendell et al., 2000. Woolf was originally commenting in the context of women and writing, however, her demand being the importance of having women's space.
61  Rendell et al., 2000.
62  Grosz, 2001: 9.
63  For a wider exploration of this argument see Chatterjee, 2005.

As I have argued earlier, urban architecture helps to construct sexuality and gender. The design of spaces in cities serves to heighten our awareness, as women, of our bodies and their gendered, sexualised constructions. This can easily be seen, for example, in the strategic use of certain architectural choices, such as using steps rather than ramps, or the arrangement and partitioning of space within urban design and construction, such as poorly lit, inaccessible car parks and public transport terminals. Sex work in particular has traditionally been linked with urban or highly industrialised areas, and can be seen as an example of how space helps to construct sexualised and gendered selves. In most 'real' cities there will be an area or areas where the sex trade is conducted, often euphemistically known as 'red light districts'. Red light districts may be formally or informally bounded, for instance, by urban area management policies creating 'managed "safety" zones',[64] or by custom – but either way, the space serves to construct the self. The nature of space defines those within it,[65] and so, for example, a woman simply standing on the street in a particular area will be constructed both socially and legally in one specific way, while seen completely differently if she stands in another.[66] In the United Kingdom, red light districts come under the intense scrutiny of the law,[67] which is overtly concerned with controlling the movements[68] and identities of sex workers, particularly women.[69] Further to the discourse of architecture, the law also actively helps to create the identity of a prostitute[70] and underscores its connection with public space, something that can clearly be seen from considering the relevant law. As brothels are illegal,[71] sex workers are forced on to the streets, where the law can observe and control their movements.[72] It is public visibility and movement through particular public spaces that helps to mark one out as a prostitute in the eyes of the law.

64  For critique see the International Collective of Prostitutes, who argue that such safety zones (in the Netherlands) become 'dumping grounds' where the majority of sex workers and clients are understandably reluctant to go to (www.allwomencount.net/EWC%20Sex%20Workers/Blunkett PR.htm)

65  I acknowledge that this relationship is not unidirectional, see further Ardener in Rendell *et al.*, 2001.

66  See further the Street Offences Act 1959.

67  This is currently subject to a government overhaul, outlined in the consultation paper 'Paying the Price: A Consultation Paper on Prostitution' 2004. For recent critique see Brooks-Gordon (2005) and the International Collective of Prostitutes' response on their website.

68  The International Collective of Prostitutes were critical of David Blunkett's 2004 suggestions when he was Home Secretary that this regime should include making prostitutes the subject of Anti-Social Behaviour Orders (International Collective Prostitutes Press Release (undated). (www.allwomencount.net/EWC%20Sex%20Workers/BlunkettPR.htm) David Blunkett resigned (for unrelated reasons) during the time I was editing this chapter in early 2005.

69  Although the Sexual Offences Act 2003 §56 now extends 'prostitute' to cover men.

70  As defined in Sexual Offences Act 2003 §51(2), a person whom whether or not coerced offers sexual services on one or more occasions to another.

71  Sexual Offences Act 2003 §55. For critique see the International Collective of Prostitutes, who argue that once on the streets, sex workers are vulnerable to violent attacks (www.allwomencount. net/EWC%20Sex%20Workers/BlunkettPR.htm)

72  Street Offences Act 1959 §1.

The law has frequently been subject to critique for what effectively amounts to the criminalisation of prostitutes, its failure to provide them with security and safety, and to respond in any practical way to the needs of sex workers. For example, in Soho, an area of London long associated with sex work, a recent council campaign has sought to remove sex workers by issuing compulsory purchase orders on their flats.[73] The English Collective of Prostitutes state that the Soho area 'has traditionally been a safe place for women to work. Sex workers are part of a strong protective community ... [y]et Westminster Council continues to issue Compulsory Purchase Orders saying that prostitution is a "blight to the local environment and quality of life for people living, working and visiting in the neighbourhood." '[74] The sex workers have argued that whereas not one of their number has ever been murdered in a Soho flat, the council's policy simply forces them on to the streets, where they are 'at the mercy of traffickers and Jack the Rippers.'[75] In the light of such concerns, it is perhaps unsurprising that increasingly, sex workers are providing their services online, and there has been a huge increase in the number of Internet sites advertising sexual services for both domestic and international clients.[76] As noted in the introduction to this chapter, the spaces of the postmodern city disintegrate and reform, and the spaces for sex work also change, from the public street to the private screen. The gentrification of urban spaces as seen in the attempts to change the usage of space in Soho, London, arguably serves to further marginalise the status of sex workers, but the reformation of the city from a physical space of streets and corridors to an increasingly informational matrix opens up new possibilities for sex work, and new spaces to work in. It is undeniable that the linkage to the concrete is still necessary, as one must physically have a space to work from, but that base no longer needs to be in a defined zone or area such as the red light district, as the spaceless place of cyberspace becomes the 'site' of work.

Similar to 'real' red light districts, virtual red light districts are areas of the Internet used to sell sexual services. Virtual red light districts comprise of websites used as shop fronts for people selling sex, either in the form of real time chat or for the purposes of arranging a 'real life' exchange, bulletin boards and/or websites for posting 'reviews' of prostitutes, and live sites, where customers can view sex shows via a web camera.[77] In the virtual red light district, the architecture of cyberspace might be of use in protecting sex workers, as sex workers might have control of the construction of the space in ways that

73  The Guardian, 2004: 7; www.westminster.gov.uk/news/PR-1983.cfm
74  English Collective of Prostitutes Press Release (allwomencount.net.EWCSexWorkers/Press RelFeb03.htm). Presumably, following the logic of the Council, the conclusion must be that prostitution is not 'work'.
75  Ibid.
76  Altman, 2001; Hughes, 2002; Chatterjee, 2003 and 2005.
77  See for example, Hughes, 2002; Chatterjee, 2005.

they are unlikely to have on the physical street. Whilst not entirely free from risk,[78] virtual sites may in some ways be safer for sex workers, as the distance a virtual medium allows can mean more time to be given to considering whether (and under what circumstances) to meet a particular customer or not, as opposed to a pressurised and hurried street transaction, which sex workers have argued only serves to increase the risk of violence from clients.[79] Webcam sex shows arguably decrease the risk of immediate violence from clients, as they are not conducted face-to-face, and the client may not meet the sex worker in person, as the location of the sex worker is remote from that of the client.[80] Software controls can be written in at the point of access to a website, thus effectively regulating who has access to the site and who does not, unlike the space of the 'real' red light district, which, by the legal definition of a prostitute, must inherently be public space and thus open to anyone. Cyberspace does not (and cannot) afford physical shelter, which will always be needed, but what it does offer is distance, time and the potential of some control through self-executing code. If sex workers are able to construct their own sites, then code potentially gives them the power to exercise a degree of effective protection, the architecture of cyberspace being mobilised to create a space of ordered law whereby code as law will be enforced when it is needed, without prejudice, instantly and on demand, unlike traditional law which, as seen earlier, falls far short of providing the protection that sex workers require of it, and effectively places them in danger by criminalising activities associated with their work, and denying them safer places to work in.[81] Although code does not carry the social and moral sanction of traditional law, the extent to which the law's prohibitive force is actually effective, as discussed earlier, must surely be in question. The hypothesis that code can be effective law presumes a lot, such as the degree of control sex workers have over their websites and transactions. Recalling the words of Lessig, if code is law then code is also power; but who writes the code, and who has the power? Whose values and interests does code embody and reflect?

This would appear to be the point, then, where code has its limits as an architecture of justice. As the city disintegrates, law too appears to lose its materiality, in the sense of losing its context and nuances. Code becomes the utopia but also the dystopia of law, an absolute rule that is enforced regardless of circumstance or context, just as the cyber city becomes, in ways, the dystopia of the city itself. In some instances, this absolutist quality will be desirable, as seen earlier. Code can provide certain basic but valuable functions, such as facilitating a potentially safer working environment, but this will largely depend on who sets the parameters or conditions of entry. It would appear that code is

---

78   See for example, Hughes, 2002; Chatterjee, 2005.
79   See n 72.
80   Chatterjee, 2005.
81   Although cyberspace as a safe space for sex is not without criticism, as argued earlier.

good at protecting the integrity of space, but it is difficult to see how it fully protects the integrity of the person within (or rather behind) that space. One cannot (yet) exist purely within cyberspace – the worker in the live show or in the chat room must physically be located somewhere, and once breached (the possibility of which Lessig is careful to remind us of), code can do little either to protect the body that remains physically vulnerable, or punish any violation.

In the space of the 'real' red light district, the architecture of space has some positive aspects as it enables a community to be created. As the sex workers themselves attest to,[82] the physical arrangements of space in red light districts enables them to look out for each other, a point of resistance against the surveillance/power of the law. Yet in cyberspace, this space is necessarily fragmented. There is no similar physical proximity; one sex worker may not know the physical location (or identity) of the next, and geographically, the spread of the workers may potentially be vast, making protection more difficult. Traditional law may not effectively reach into the liquid architectures of cyberspace to protect its communities, traversing, as they do, the boundaries of sovereign jurisdiction and territory, and it would appear that code can only do so much. Law may be one force that creates the city, but the city itself escapes the law, especially in the fluid architectures of cyberspace. As argued earlier, we have seen that as an instrument of protection, and as a facilitator of justice, the law will have to go much further. But so, it would appear, must code.

## Bibliography

Altman, D (2001) *Global Sex*, Chicago: University of Chicago Press

Ardener, S (2001) 'The Partition of Space', in Rendell, J, Penner, B and Borden, I (eds), *Gender Space Architecture: An Interdisciplinary Introduction*, London: Routledge

Arnheim, R (1977) *The Dynamics of Architectural Form*, Berkley, CA: University of California Press

Bell, D and Valentine, G (1995) *Mapping Desire: Geographies of sexualities*, London: Routledge

Blomley, N, Delaney, D and Ford, R T (eds) (2001) *The Legal Geographies Reader*, Oxford: Blackwell

Boyer, M C (1996) *CyberCities: Visual Perception in the Age of Electronic Communication*, New York: Princeton Architectural Press

Brooks-Gordon, B (2005) 'Clients and Commercial Sex: Reflections on Paying the Price: A Consultation Paper on Prostitution', June, *Criminal Law Review* 425–443

Calvino, I (1997) *Invisible Cities*, London: Vintage

Cavallaro, D (2000) *Cyberpunk and Cyberculture*, London: Athlone

Chatterjee, B (2003) 'Screwing with Technology: Cyberpornography, Cyberidentities and Law (PhD thesis)', Department of Law, London: Brunel University

82  See n 72.

Chatterjee, B (2005) 'Pixels, Pimps and Prostitutes: Human Rights and the Cyber Sex Trade' in Klang, M and Murray, A (eds), *Human Rights in the Digital Age*, London: Glasshouse

Crang, P, Crang, M and May, J (eds) (1999) *Virtual Geographies*, London: Routledge

Dodge, M and Kitchin, R (eds) (2001) *The Atlas of Cyberspace*, Harlow: Addison-Wesley

Dürsteler, J (2002) 'Digital Cities', 102 Info@Vis!, at www.infovis.net/printFicha.php? rec=revista&num=102&lang=2&palabra=digital%20cities, Published on 30 September 2002 (accessed on 24 November 2006).

Elden, S (2005) 'Missing the Point: Globalization, Deterritorialisation and the Space of the World', 30(1) *Transactions of the Institute of British Geographers* (New series) 8–19

English Collective of Prostitutes, Press release 10 February 2003, 'On the Eve of Public Inquiry: Sex Workers and other Soho Residents Demand Protection not Eviction' (announcement of Press Conference) at www.allwomencount.net/EWC%20Sex% 20Workers/PressRelFeb03.htm (accessed on 24 November 2006).

Foucault, M (1975/1991) *Discipline and Punish: The Birth of the Prison*, London: Penguin

Frug, G (2001) 'A Legal History of Cities', in Blomley, N, Delaney, D and Ford, R T (eds), *The Legal Geographies Reader*, Oxford: Blackwell

Grosz, E (1999) 'Space, Time and Bodies', in Wolmark, J (ed), *Cybersexualities: A Reader on Feminist Theory, Cyborgs and Cyberspace*, Edinburgh: Edinburgh University Press

Grosz, E (2001) *Architecture from the Outside: Essays on Virtual and Real Space*, Cambridge, MA: MIT Press

*Guardian* (2004) 'Heritage group to fight Soho clean up', 10 July, 7

Gutheim, F (ed) (1975) *In the Cause of Architecture – Frank Lloyd Wright*, New York: Architectural Record Books

Heyer, P (ed) (1966) *Architects on Architecture*, New York: Walker and Co

HMSO (2004) 'Paying The Price: A Consultation Paper on Prostitution', London: HMSO

hooks, b (2000) 'Choosing the Margin as a Space of Radical Openness', in Rendell, J, Penner, B and Borden, I (eds), *Gender Space Architecture: An interdisciplinary introduction*, London: Routledge

Hughes, D (2002) 'The Use of New Communications and Information Technologies for Sexual Exploitation of Women and Children', 13(1) *Hastings Women's Law Journal* 129

International Collective of Prostitutes, Press Release July 2004, 'David Blunkett is no Josephine Butler', at www.allwomencount.net/EWC%20Sex%20Workers/BlunkettPR.htm (accessed on 24 November 2006).

Jencks, C J (1978) *The Language of Post-Modern Architecture*, London: Academy Editions

Jencks, C J (1980) *Late-Modern Architecture and other essays*, London: Academy Editions

Jewson, N and MacGregor, S (eds) (1997) *Transforming Cities: Contested Governance and New Spatial Divisions*, London: Routledge

Johnson, D R and Post, D G (1996) 'Law and Borders: The Rise of Law in Cyberspace', 48 *Stanford Law Review* 1367–1402

King, R (2000) 'Labyrinths', in Pile, S and Thrift, N (eds), *City a–z*, London: Routledge

Klotz, H (1988) *The History of Postmodern Architecture*, Cambridge, MA: MIT Press

Kohl, U (2004) 'The Rule of Law, Jurisdiction and the Internet', 12(1) *International Journal of Law and Information Technology* 365–376

Komninos, N (2002) *Intelligent Cities*, London: Spon Press

Kramer, J L (1994) 'Bachelor Farmers and Spinsters: Gay and Lesbian Identities and Communities in Rural North Dakota', in Bell, D and Valentine, G (eds), *Mapping Desire: Geographies of Sexualities*, 200–213, London: Routledge

Leach, N (ed) (1997) *Rethinking Architecture: A Reader in Cultural Theory*, London: Routledge

LeGates, R and Stout, F (eds) (1996) *The City Reader*, London: Routledge

Lessig, L (1999) *Code and Other Laws of Cyberspace*, New York: Basic Books

Light, J (1999) 'From City Space to Cyberspace', in Crang, M, Crang, P and May, J (eds), *Virtual Geographies: Bodies, Space and Relations*, 109–130, London: Routledge

Lourde, A (2000) 'The Master's Tools will Never Dismantle the Master's House', in Rendell, J, Penner, B and Borden, I (eds), *Gender Space Architecture: An Interdisciplinary Introduction*, London: Routledge

McClung, W (2000) *Landscapes of Desire: Anglo Mythologies of Los Angeles*, Berkley, CA: University of California Press

Mori, T (ed.) (2002) *Immaterial/Ultramaterial: Architecture, Design and Materials*, New York: Harvard University and George Braziller

Mumford, L (1937) 'What is a City?' in LeGates, R and Stout, F (eds) (1996), *The City Reader*, London: Routledge

Novak, M (1991) 'Liquid Architectures in Cyberspace', in Benedikt, M (ed), *Cyberspace: First Steps*, Cambridge, MA: MIT Press

Palumbo, M (2000) *New Wombs: Electronic Bodies and Architectural Disorders*, Basel: Birkhauser

Pawley, M (1998) *Terminal Architecture*, London: Reaktion Books

Phillips, R, Watt, D and Shuttleton, D (eds) (2000) *De-Centring Sexualities: Politics and Representations Beyond the Metropolis*, London: Routledge

Pile, S and Thrift, N (eds) (2000) *City a–z*, London: Routledge

Puglisi, L (1999) *Hyperarchitecture: Spaces in the Electronic Age*, Basel: Birkhauser

Rendell, J, Penner, B and Borden, I (eds) (2000) *Gender Space Architecture: An Interdisciplinary Introduction*, London: Routledge

Rommes, E, Oost, E V and Oudshoorn, N (2001) 'Gender in the Design of the Digital City of Amsterdam', in Green, E and Adam, A (eds), *Virtual Gender*, London: Routledge

Sim, S (2001) *The Routledge Companion to Postmodernism*, London: Routledge

Vidler, A (2000) *Warped Space*, Cambridge, MA: MIT Press

Virilio, P (1997) 'The Overexposed City', in Leach, N (ed.), *Rethinking Architecture: A Reader in Cultural Theory*, 380–390, London: Routledge

Wall, D (1998) 'Catching Cybercriminals: Policing The Internet', 12(2) *International Review of Law Computers and Technology* 201

Westwood, S and Williams, J (eds) (1997) *Imagining Cities: Scripts, Signs, Memory*, London: Routledge

Winterson, J (1988) *The Passion*, London: Penguin

Woolf, Virginia (2000) 'A Room of One's Own', in Rendell, J, Penner, B and Borden, I (eds), *Gender Space Architecture: An Interdisciplinary Introduction*, London: Routledge

## Statutes

Street Offences Act 1959
Sexual Offences Act 2003

# Chapter 15

# First we take Manhattan

## Microtopia and grammatology in Gotham

*Peter Goodrich**

Then we take Berlin. Leonard Cohen no less, an important contributor to complaint jurisprudence,[1] and I still remember hearing the song blaring out of an open-top German car on the South Bridge in Edinburgh. It was one of those rare sunny days in the 1980s when convertibles could actually convert in Scotland. Of course BMW sells more convertibles in California than in Germany, more cars in California than in Germany in fact, but that is a tangent from my time in Los Angeles. We are lawyers and the analogy is the thing, we have to pull together both 'ana' and 'logos', gap and speech. What is the spoken gap, the rhyme that plays, between Manhattan and Berlin? And then how do we figure in the inevitable third, Edinburgh, the first city I loved. Just a detail. Maybe a footnote. *Lex* and sex. Lust and the City. It's an allusion to the cartography of the intimate public sphere but then again it is not so clear to me that law is ready yet for the interiority of demography, for the urbane in the *urbs*, or here the affective lineage of the grid.

New York can be thought in terms of Berlin. No question of that. I have even heard a philosopher or two say '*Ich bin ein Brooklyner*' but while that is phonetically similar it takes us out of Manhattan and dangerously close to phenomenology. So stick with the specific gap, the 'ana' in the heart of Manhattan, if you will, and

* Thanks to various colleagues and comrades, and a especial ontological gratitude to David Carlson, Arthur Jacobson, Jeanne Schroeder, Michel Rosenfeld, Richard Sherwin and Chuck Yablon for cartographic and chorographic insight and information. I owe much also to Jerry Bruner, Simon Critchley, the late Carole Feldman, David Garland, Kevin Stack and the maître d' at Gotham Bar and Grill for profound insights into diverse aspects of the city. Minor thanks to Andreas Philippopoulos-Mihalopoulos, Reader in Law, and to David Graebar, anarchist anthropologist, for looking the text over. Thanks, indeed kisses to Linda Mills for directing me towards the anomalies while she was often professionally engaged in striating them.

1 I will borrow a few lyrics and incite, if you will, the musical space of New York, the jazz, the blues, the punk, the rock. Cohen often sang about New York, all the way from 'the music on Clinton Street' (*Songs of Love and Hate*), to the plaintive chords of 'please don't pass me by' (*Live Songs*, subtitled 'a disgrace'); from suicide and sex in a Chelsea Hotel (*New Skin for the Old Ceremony*) to the artists revenge on Manhattan, which can be found on *I'm Your Man*. As for Leonard Cohen's jurisprudence, the themes of law and resistance run throughout his work. The lyrics are from the last mentioned album. The rest will have to await another chapter.

note that Manhattan is a German name, a variant on Mannheim, a Southern Palatine city. The word, however, is Ashkenazic, at root Jewish rather than German. It means homestead. Take the root further and it is based on the Yiddish *man* meaning manna and the reference, as I recollect it, is to the Biblical story of manna or food appearing miraculously, *ex nihilo*, in the desert just when the tribes of Israel were about to fire their quartermaster and admit that the cupboard was bare. So Manhattan appears, it springs up, an oasis, an island, the home of the exiled, safe harbour for German Jews during the war, port of entry and place of passage. From Avital to Zacheim, if you got out of Berlin mid-twentieth century, or out of Vienna, or Danzig, Warsaw or Prague, then likely as not you passed through New York in flight from Europe to America. So now, 60 years on, the song suggests the revenge of the periphery, the return of the repressed: first we take Manhattan, then we take Berlin.

Who takes Manhattan? And the answer has to be the poets, the musicians, the outsiders and the Jews. We will come to that. Habermas would demand it. He would want to know how you can put those categories together. But first let me make the point through the *nomos* of New York, the name and its nature. It is most immediately from the Latin *Novum Eboracum* which can be found inscribed in the ensign of the City and on many of its public buildings, on the Surrogate's Court downtown, for example, or at the other extreme on the Department of Sanitation's postmodern false plywood Greek arch in front of the shed that stores the sand that is used to grit the roads and visible from the highway on the West side of the city. And multiple sites elsewhere. Any building in fact that houses bureaucratic activities or legal administrative functions that might someday require the heavy gunned defence of Latin.

The monumental city, the written island, may be in Latin but the root is Old English. The word comes from *Eoforwic* composed of *eofor*, wild boar and *wic*, outlying settlement. The outlier is a distant settlement, an extraneous point of passage, a momentary deconstruction. And then finally, just to make a point, 'the surname [York – old and new] has been adopted by Jews as an Anglicanisation of various like-sounding Jewish surnames'.[2] Which is almost a definition of New York, mid-twentieth century, dropping all the European immigrants onto Ellis Island, giving them new names, welcoming them to the American dream, pushing them through. Spot the *différance* as it were, in Avery for Avital, Zach for Zacheim, or indeed Mills for Meisler, Abel for Ablowitz, Herbert for Haverkamp, Goodrich for Grundnorm, or drop the last one but otherwise and so on. Sounds the same, what difference could it possibly make? As the late Derrida put it, deconstruction is/in America, and we will add that grammatology begins in Manhattan but has its roots in Berlin. Their names started changing when they had to leave. Exile, flight, not shibboleth but *nom de guerre* for those few who made it to the new world, to New York. The name, an indelible mark of the great escape.

---

2  Thus in Hanks, P and Hodges, F (1998) *A Dictionary of Surnames*, Oxford: New York.

## Come see the vampires of New York

From Berlin to Manhattan. One has to make the point that Berlin comes first, historically, lexically and as causation. Then move to the common perception of the chaos of New York, a city also known as Gotham – a madhouse, bedlam and in medieval English a place where lunatics were sent: batmen, catwomen, jokers and riddlers.[3] It is also another German name, meaning, of the Goths, a Germanic tribe and latterly a style of architecture, the Gothic, which appropriately enough refers to myriad columns, tall buildings, spires and now skyscrapers, the Empire State building, the World Trade Center as was, and the Freedom tower that is soon to be. Gotham, however, mainly connotes an urban equivalent of the famed incivility of the Gothic tribes. The Romans were constantly at war with the Goths, and eventually it was the Goths and the Visigoths who overran the Roman empire, sacked Rome and left only Constantinople standing as a relic of the former glories of the earlier civilisation and law. Violence and mayhem, savagery and conquest are the nominal marks of Gotham, tokens of an earlier wildness, of the bestial body now resident in Manhattan, making up perhaps the novelty of New York.

Gotham conquers. And first-off, that conquest is of an island. The Goths take Manhattan, that outlier, that insular rock off the coast of the United States, Berlin in America. Both cities were ironically enough insular spaces at various points in the twentieth century. New York, because it was built as an island and designed so as to preclude any large influx of people at any one time.[4] Berlin, because it became a kind of postwar outlier of the West in the East, a *niemensland* or no man's land, a city shared between capitalism and communism, joined by a wall, a double space, an irreal venture taken back, one might say, in part at least, by the return of the Goths: first we take Manhattan, then we take Berlin.

If Manhattan is the priority, *prima regula*, the starting point, that should not obscure the double nature of our reading of it. We start with Manhattan, even though New York is an island, an outlier, a distant settlement. It has multiple names and whichever we choose, Gotham or go between, the initial description, the surface chorography, is both apparent and easy. Manhattan is mainly a grid. What is shown to the world, the map on my tie, the chart on the back of the driver's bench in every city cab, the subway directions, all show a remarkably well

---

3 Thanks to David Graebar for this piece of esoterica. I do not know the source. Could not find it. But recollect in this respect that the movie *Boiler Room* also puts this sense of the insular as exoteric rather well in a scene where a group of homosexuals in a Manhattan restaurant is told by aggressive sub-yuppy Wall Street types to 'go find an island of your own'. They reply: 'We have. This is it'. In medieval Latin, interestingly, Goth (*Gothi*) came to mean godly in a rather romantic sense. So it takes all sorts, all kinds of connotations.

4 Such is the theory of Jacoby, 1987. Design and escalating property prices – a predictable feature, I guess, of limited space – removed the intellectuals to the disaggregation of the suburbs, sent the bohemians to the West coast, and kept the working class in its place.

ordered city of numbered and lettered streets. The island is visually represented very much as Manhattan, and not at all as Gotham. Believe it or not, Harlem does not really even figure on the map in the cabs, not even to this day. If you enter Harlem (the upper portion of Manhattan island) you rapidly leave both the map and the grid, you are off the map, in no-man's land, in Gotham again and at least by implication amongst the Goths. That gives us a hint of the loves and fears of the administration of New York or at least of the Taxi and Limousine Commissioners. It provides us with a sign, not so much a dog that did not bark, as a face that did not appear in the mirror. But we must start with the mirror, the grid, and then move to what it does not show, to what lies beneath.

The obvious law in Manhattan is to be found, chorographically at least, in the ease and simplicity, the speed and accessibility of the grid. I have pointed out that it does not cover the whole city but it comes pretty close, it makes its point even if it fans out irregularly into Harlem to the North and the financial district to the South. My guess is that no one could be bothered to plan Harlem, no lawyers were going to have to look at it, and that the financial district preceded the grid, economy determines consciousness and not the other way around. Or the Southern tip of the island, a triangle, precludes the grid except that, with beautiful symbolism, Broadway, standing sure enough for law's competitor – the theatre, runs all the way through. But suspend that thought, it is time to interpret the grid.

The visible city is a paean to order and to the possibility of imposing the matrix on an irregular space. It is exemplarily legal, the *mos gallicus* or adapted form of Roman law one might say, applied to the new world. Nothing could be more obviously juridical than the grid, the *regulae iuris* of partition, grouping and demarcating a world of quite irregular and frequently anarchic buildings, the architecture of the Goths, according to a Euclidean precision of geometric patterning. We have read our Littleton, we know the name of the law, and so we can acknowledge that the division of land, what the Greeks termed *nomos* meaning visible appropriation, is the initial law, the first order. *Nomos* constitutes the grid, it is the matrix, the first norm. On this theory, the grid marks and striates. The straight lines of the avenues are the modernist equivalent of the furrows of the plough. Who marks the land owns the land, *urbs*, 'city', from *urbare*, 'to plough'. Now, however, *nomos* does not come from the plough but from the matrix, the various modes of modern grid that map flight paths, other transports, communications, the Web and so on. Still, the grid is like the plough, the mark of design over nature. It is the quintessential sign of appropriation over environmentalism. Nature is by and large all curves.

Manhattan then is as nomic as a city on an ovoid island can be. It is all straight lines, and built for lawyers. It will eat you up if you cannot find somewhere off the grid to hide. Put it like this, using the latest statistics: there are close to 100,000 lawyers registered in Manhattan. The population of Manhattan is 1.5 million. That gives us one attorney for every 15 people in the city. One in 15, and by some counts rather more. By whatever measure, that is a lot of lawyers.

New York suits them and I will suggest that superficially, according to the surface, which is all matrix, straight lines, that makes considerable sense. A city that is all *nomos*, that visibly appropriates and regularises by the admixture of the gothic and the grid, both expresses law and expresses the need for lawyers.

More than that, or perhaps a little esoterically, the presence of so many lawyers also suggests a connection between the outlier, the grid and the law. Manhattan is a species of juridical heterotopia, an other space of law, a symbol of jurisdiction. I think of it as follows, and here you will have to forgive a further set of statistics. The American Society of Ophthalmology conducted a survey some years back of congenital eye deficiency amongst different professions. The highest incidence of people born with defective eyes was in the legal profession. Roughly 70 per cent of lawyers had congenital eye conditions. In the nature of things, and granted that corrective procedures for the eyes will not generally be imposed until the child is 5 or 6, this means that during their formative years these lawyers-to-be could not see the world properly. Their personality was formed before their vision was corrected and hence the world they constructed likely depended and depends upon rules rather than experience, norms rather than perceptions. If you cannot see, or you see indistinctly, then the best map is a grid, straight lines, right angles, predictability and foreseeability.

So there is something quite Roman about New York, something of a cult of lawyers within a classical grid. Yet even at the level of law, this superficial observation deserves a double reading. The courts, grouped appropriately enough on Center Street, are classical in style and lavishly ornate. All of the juridical heroes, from Justinian to Blackstone, are painted on the dome in the lobby of the central courthouse. There are the usual Latin inscriptions, figures and façades. It is all quite old-world, *mos gallicus* as I said, and replete with Dickensian offices of records, archives and other invocations of God. Lawyers abound and legality is visible everywhere. That said, the courts are in Gotham, and are famously lawless or at least peculiarly subject to the *arbitrium* of the judge and the whim of the jury. The law is everywhere and yet it is a very dangerous thing to tangle with the system in Gotham. There is no knowing how it will come out, what the local alliances or judicial subscriptions are going to be. You will need a lawyer for that. A very good one. One who is up to all the necessary tricks. That is the reputation, the word on the streets, but rather than casting aspersions or proffering hegemonies I will simply make a brief remark about affect and retention.

The law firms in Gotham grind their associates down. No question of that, and so much is this the case that there is a remarkable attrition rate. Over five years 50 per cent leave. The throughput, like the grid, is kind of fast. In the big firms there is a department of retention that is of equal status and size of budget as that of recruitment. Once recruited, the associates do not stay. They cannot take the 19-hour days, the sightless work on endless invisible transactions, the lack of contact with case and world and so on. To state the obvious, the vampires of New York are not in central park, they are on Wall street, downtown and midtown, carrying out Leonard Cohen's prediction: 'They sentenced me to twenty years of boredom / for trying to change the system from within.' So one could say. There, in the belly of the corporate enterprise, enlisted in the projects of the juggernaut, the spirit can die. It is all law, and as Grant Gilmore remarked long ago, hell is all law whereas heaven is extra-legal, beyond judgment, done with rules. 'I am coming now, I am coming to reward them: first we take Manhattan, then we take Berlin.'

## Remember me, I used to live for music

The lawyers live in their world. We live in ours. I admit that there is a certain dis-identification in that statement, but existentially, in memory and self-perception, the scholar, the theorist, the academic anarchist resides closer to chance than to prediction, closer to thought than to law. Easily said, of course, and much harder to evoke in any comprehensible form. So start with Manhattan the island, the outlier, port of entry, place of escape, its architecture all memory, its grid bordered by small spaces of reprise, islets of autonomy, uncertain and mobile identities formed and dispersed day by day. It is a city in which confusionists thrive, contraries compete, and 'microtopias' form and dissipate in the blink of an historical eye. I will give some examples, and if I had time I would start with the secret life of law professors. They are all close to hand. Go figure. Or read Anne Bottomley's risky, edgy essay on 'shock to thought' and the process of theory.[5]

'Microtopia' is a term taken from relational aesthetics, and it refers in a rather Parisian manner to the incursion of essentially private symbolic spaces, intimate projects, in the public sphere.[6] The image or artwork or performance is a species of ontological anarchism, a mode of sudden symbolic engagement that steps out of the confined spaces of conventional images – the wall, the screen, cinema, theatre, television – and interacts. It is street theatre but without the prescription. A site of encounter. The occasion of the minor event. The capture of public space by the rendering of an interior, the acting out of an intimate vision, an inner world.[7] The image steps down, as it were, and draws the passer-by, the viewer, the auditor into relation.[8] Micro because minor and immediate. Here. This face. These eyes. These words: '... the role of artworks is no longer to form imaginary and utopian realities, but to actually be ways of living and models of action within the existing real, whatever the scale chosen by the artist.'[9]

In a political vein, one could describe this space of engagement in terms of a sudden animation of the public persona, and as a challenge, a self-consciously aesthetic confrontation with the passage of performing subjects as they subconsciously pass by, unnoticed and eyes sideways in their urban shuffle. The

---

5  Bottomley, 2004.
6  Bourriaud, 2002.
7  Berlant, 1998.
8  Bishop, 2004.
9  Bourriaud, 2002: 13.

instantaneous is an input of energy, an enactment, the putting of a face into the movement of the social. But it is not grandiose. It is microtopic because it is immediate and functions as an encounter or what Badiou terms an event.[10] It stages a fidelity, a desire, a connection. And so observe that in Gotham, par excellence, in the hidden spaces of New York, a myriad of different lives are being led. Open up the façade of the apartment block opposite and you will look, as if in a Chantal Ackerman movie, upon 1,100 discrete spaces, separate and distinct lives. That is interesting, those are multiple minor spaces but they are private. The microtopia references the act by which the private collides with the social, the intimate becomes public and symbolic, the affect takes to the streets, or the office, the sports arena or the conference. As the pavement artists of New York for a while put it: 'if in doubt, go nomad'. Which means leave the apartment or at least open the blind and perform in the arc of the gaze. Invite the outside in. And do the inside outside.

The relational aesthetic of New York turns Gotham into the archetype of the city as event, as an expression of love, of fused groups as Sartre described them and as Graebar has more recently elaborated.[11] Here, the ontological reverses the priority of the epistemological, private acts take on political significance, there are glimmers of freedom, whispers of escape from the grid, shocks to thought in public encounters. One might describe the relational aesthetic as a species of aesthetic bricolage in which a local event, or indeed a political convention or declaration of war is suddenly constructed as an image, and then turned into an encounter. The momentary audience is taken out of the grid and engaged in an intimate activity, the performance of the event in the public sphere, wherever there is room to congregate. What is significant is that the artist, activist or academic engages the auditor or viewer, elicits an affective participation, interrupts the quotidian burble and so marginally shifts the frame or takes us out of the matrices of routine, the merely numerical patterns of repetition and into the *interstices* of the social. A temporary autonomous zone is created, an essentially anarchic being comes to presence as the grid disappears. Anything can happen, or that at least is the theory. Usually of course the space is closed down, the police appear, nets are produced to entrap protesters, that kind of thing, but ideally such reaction just incites additional staging, continuations by other means, future encounters. *Nil illegitimi carborundum* – do not let them grind you down.

The double reading of Manhattan, of Gotham in New York, is directed best, indeed because I say so and I am not making this up – how could I? – at the interstices of the urban relation, at the intimacies that are hidden from view and that erupt when the intimate goes public, when zones are crossed and connections made. Take a fairly immediate or at least familiar example, a little homage as it were for the recently departed Kellis Parker. He was the first African-American professor given tenure at the prestigious Ivy league law school at Columbia

---

10 Badiou, 2001.
11 Graebar, 2002.

University in New York. A local guy. He came from the South, he was a cousin I seem to remember – definitely a relative – of Charlie Parker the jazz musician, and he played the trombone. In fact the first thing you noticed on meeting him was his rhythm, the deep modulated voice, the warmth of affect, the intensity of interest, and here's the point, the multiplicity of his microtopic projects. Any moment you felt he might start to play, he might sing, or blow a riff, and the alternative encounter would up and get started.

Professor K, and I use the letter with literary reason, had a horrible time professionally, and I suspect that the trauma of getting tenure sucked him dry. But one does not talk about that, not in memoriam, not about the Ivy League, so all those negative encounters with the grid, the moments of imposition of the mainframe tend to get swept aside: 'he hadn't published that much', 'he wasn't getting on with his colleagues', 'she doesn't really seem to want tenure', 'her work doesn't excite me' and so on. In any event, he made it past the vampires of New York, the tenured law professors, and he had a life in the academy, a bit to the side of print, more rhythm and blues, jazz and law. I am thinking of a story that Kendall Thomas tells in his tribute to Kellis.[12] And Kendall incidentally also gives public concerts, the orator moves, one could say, from the oratory to the oratorio. Anyway, he says that Kellis kept a trombone in his law school office and when frazzled students, or earnest tutees came by, he would pull it out and play them a melody or two. I am smiling already at the encounter. Hard for the colleague next door or down the corridor not to hear, and Columbia Law School is housed in a concrete and glass brutalist building, or it was back then. Then or now, I doubt that the walls are very soundproof. Not for lack of money, mind you, but lack of planning: I am sure the Faculty architectural committee voted that reason is everywhere quiet, logic is tuneless, and that even those bothersome analogies slip silently by across the pages of a book. So the trombone would undoubtedly cause a stir, offer a few post-tenure insights and if it got played once or twice at Faculty meetings, I am sure the minutes would not show it.

The event of the trombone, the 'inaesthetic' or non-law of musical performance in the interstices of law, a remarkable encounter.[13] Funky stuff, and he was a remarkable person, a great talker, and if my limited conversations with him are anything to go by, he must have told the students a lot about music, the secret chord that pleased the lord and about jazz law. Not jazz and law, but jazz law. The beat. About playing and especially, as lawyers, listening. Listening to the sound, the tone, the fourth, the fifth, the minor fall, the major lift, 'but you don't really like music, do you?'[14] There is the thing. Like it or not, there are others who do. It is in the streets, and for a moment there it was in the office and demanding to be heard. Was anybody listening? Gave the students something different, a differently concordant

---

12  Thomas, 2001.
13  Badiou, 2005.
14  The line is from Leonard Cohen, 'Hallelujah', on *I'm Your Man*.

image, a little life in the interstices of law. And maybe some of them heard, listened, listened to something different. A little of Harlem in the Ivy League, a touch of rhythm in the corridor, music in the Faculty, but most of all Kellis picked up the trombone and played, and it is that which I think constitutes the active in the passive, the encounter with jazz law, the legal equivalent of the inaesthetic, the event.

Put it like this, the microtopia refers to an open secret, an encounter that takes the image off the wall or out of the book and at the same time draws the audience into the interaction. They have to play a part, and suddenly there is a coming to consciousness of the elaborately staged nature of all of these everyday routines. The microtopic is a fleshy moment, a mode of 'taking to' the classroom, the corridor, the office or the streets. And that, after all, is probably what it means to be free. Or more precisely it refers us to the roots of freedom, to a before law, an ontology of being prior to law, free association, friendship, the conditions of possibility of law.

## Please don't pass me by

First we take Manhattan, then we take Berlin. Why does Manhattan come first? Perhaps because it is closer to Canada. But that is far too contingent a hypothesis. So maybe it is because Manhattan is more of an archetype, a space of tribes, of Goths, of travellers, of passing by and passing through. The grid and the Goths who subvert it, law and music, art and activism, make up the temporary autonomous zones, the anomalies, the anagrammatics of Manhattan. It is a nodal space, Europe in America, deconstruction in the United States. And it can also maybe remind us that the word 'tribe', from the Latin *tribus*, has its root, at least possibly so according to the aptly named Onions who edited the *Oxford Dictionary of English Etymology*, in the word *tri* or three. Gotham is the space of the third, the zone of the triangulating observer, the artist who looks and listens, the relational aesthete, the poet in the grid, the nomad philosopher who spells out the *différance*.

If we return to this meaning of Manhattan, this site of passage, of exile and renaming, of flight and temporary home constitutes a space of deconstruction in its best connotations. For Derrida, New York, the exemplary space of the United States, was somewhere that one passed through. That was why deconstruction is America, and grammatology is in Gotham, in the musical senses of difference and attentiveness. And does not that attention to difference, that lingering over indefinition, infuriate the conventional philosophers of law? The jurists tend to fear the ear, it takes time and indefinition to listen. Repetition, not as legal precedent but as becoming, as attention to melody and form. And that is really annoying if your project is juridical, if it is that of placing the tune in the grid. If lawyers do not like listening, they also resent the eye and its inspection of surfaces, its apprehension of idiosyncrasies, its promise of uniqueness and its hold upon the face. And then admit as well that they also dislike the playing with signs, the reading of the palm, the rhetorical evaluation or 'chironomia' of the learned hand of the law. All these deconstructive delays, these forms of scholarship, challenge the comfort and commercial commitment of corporate law. Deconstruction involves far too much thought, an excess of imagination, an overflowing of details, an exorbitant delay in the interpretation of words. These are just so many forms of infidelity, so much questioning of authority. And implicit in that, forgive the wordplay, the anagrammatics if you will, is the justice of fidelity to what is said, the challenge of the relational interior – visceral, textual, phonic or visual.

Mainly, the law ignores the detail. Its beauty is abstraction. The matrix, the grid: 'Sir I didn't see nothing, I was just getting home late.'[15] But of course there are exceptions, there is New York, for instance, or the duty of care, which is at one level, though this is not frequently acknowledged, a form of *caritas*, of fidelity to the words or faith in the text. It was Augustine, wily old choreographer that he was, who spelled out that protocol of doctrine, that we walk by faith through the text: we walk unseeing – as jurists – but it also means that we feel, that an affect or love undergirds our willingness to close our eyes to what is near at hand. Just to be a little esoteric, for Augustine the text and the spirit, soul and letter, were joined in speaking the text, in the *sermo humilis*, in talking the talk while walking the walk. But the legal profession tended to forget the substrate of desire, the hermeneutics of love. They need the relational aesthetes, the hermenauts of the interior spaces, to spring into their public lives, to animate their words, to give an inside to the grid.

So begin with that. The lawyer is faithful despite himself and more recently herself. There is an unconscious, an unspoken yet subsisting interior to the tradition. It may be numbed with alcohol, it may be repressed though workaholism, it may be all tied up with the strictest of thongs, the *vinculae iuris*, but it is there. Just look and note our lawyer, our ideal formal rational type, that 'she' occupies from time to time, juridically speaking, a space of proximity, a zone of care, of friendship, of the priority of amity to *lex*, of *caritas* to law. It is there that the trombone comes out, that the art gets down, that a listening occurs. My final hypothesis, taken precisely from the metaphor of music in the corridors of law, from the actuality of the arm and the hand – whatever lonely things these hands have done – and from the relational aesthetic that makes art present in the political, is that, long though this sentence be, New York inscribes a non-law interior to legality. A Gothic law if you will, a postmodern scholasticism, a conjunction of the disparate, a proximity of the different, going up and getting down, norm and resistance in the same zone, temporarily cohabiting.

New York is an ideal epistemic space. I mean that literally. Nothing really sticks. Manhattan is an island. It is an outlier. A third space or zone of triangulation from which to look at Europe or America, where we were or where we went, from whence we came to where we ended up. Which we? The legal one, the we who

---

15  From 'A singer must die', on Leonard Cohen, *New Skin for the Old Ceremony*.

did not see nothing, who just got home late – which is already nicely ambiguous, a double negative, self-deconstructing indeed – or the we who listened to the screams, remembered the bodies, who begged for the mercy that you love to decline? The legists or the anomalists? The point is that in Manhattan the grid is constantly being subverted, the matrix crashes into anomalies and you can not practice law without encountering music. That is just how it is, because of the proximity of differences, the immense singularity of the island, the necessary visibility of the outré, the fact that those who escape to New York cannot escape New York – its idiosyncrasy, its permeability – and, to complete the auditory annotation, they cannot but hear the music on Clinton street all through the evening.

And ontologically too there are distinctions and exposures that seem somehow to conjure an image of Manhattan as a zone not only of temporary autonomy but also of quintessential throwness, of movement and encounter. Get personal for a moment. At my desk at home I look out onto a building comprising 1,100 residential units. About 30 units are visible at a glance through my curtainless window. I look into the interior of some 20 apartments. Intimate lives. There is the corporate let with innumerable business types passing through. They watch late night television, pornography quite often, and they drink, order in massages, that kind of thing. There is the gay couple, and I often see them coming out of the shower; the heterosexual couple who like to eat breakfast together naked; the single parent who often holds her neonate at the window looking wonderingly and wistfully out. I can see the aesthetic choices, the colours, the artwork, the books, the product preferences, the appliances and sometimes see them being used. There is a violinist even, but I have not heard any trombones. And all this about 30 feet away and without any directed attention on my part. On a street where a plane engine killed a pedestrian on 11 September 2001; where Mohammed Atta's passport was found; in a building that for two years after the September attacks had a large metal chunk of fuselage on the roof. There is a restaurant, a comedy club, an alternative medicine centre and a coffee shop on our ground floor. There is a strip joint down the street, a club, several bars. There are people outside 24 hours. A lot of worlds in which to play, and indeed in which to play the law.

On the latter theme, at my office at the Law School I look out onto Fifth Avenue. There is the Forbes Building and the countless comings and goings of grey suits and smart stocking executives. And beside it is the Parson's School of Design. They hold life drawing classes on the fourth floor and from time to time I will see groups of artists drawing a posing, if not necessarily imposing, nude. And they hold fashion displays in the ground floor gallery. There is a bearded man who for a while would dance in a ballroom gown on a pedestal in the window. And in the summer there is a catwalk that extends out onto the street and the students model their fashions. And finally the street artists. The bagpipe player, the dancer, the singer and the elderly African-American who would for years sit on an office chair at the corner of Fifth and Twelfth and bless you while asking for contributions. Art, commerce and law. Separate and joined, distinct yet necessarily colliding. It gives you a sense of the urban proximity of divergent styles, the institutionalised, the veridical, the consecrated and the heretical, the analogous and the anomalous.

It leads to a final point. Manhattan is a city of workaholics and I am far from suggesting that the inevitability of disjunctive encounters necessarily implies attention to difference. Lawyers often cannot correct a certain emotional myopia or a type of blindness to the immediacy of metropolitan and cosmopolitan interruptions. Many are tone deaf. Those who like music often are not that happy with legalism. Head down, and I did not see nothing. Did not hear a thing. But I am digressing again. There is non-law, anomaly, music or panic attack just out of the door. You may not be open to it, but there is a sense in which you cannot help but let it in. Place matters. Chorography is important. You might not care for deconstruction but it was here and passed on through. Non-law in law is how I put it. I think that holds. Nice guy. See him everywhere. And in a more formal vein that is what is reflected, more or less, in the Law School. Ebb and flow, flux and change, and mainly people passing through, because this is New York, this is Manhattan, a place you travel through. The obvious example is that Derrida was on the Faculty for a long time and it is hardly necessary to point out that he was not a lawyer. Even if his initials are J D, *juris doctor* by acronym if not profession. And he would have liked that little joke, that accident of meaning, that other name.[16] The psychoanalytic theorist Zizek, S Z, degree zero, to those in the know, was a fellow and visitor several times; the Lacanian Renata Salecl, R S – V P – keeps coming back; and the seminar room is as likely to host a visiting speaker on poetry or music, philosophy or food, a comedian, a singer, a songwriter, as it is to address, though of course we do, a doctrinalist talking about the dormant commerce clause, or a techno lawyer talking about the economics of bankruptcy legislation.

Recollect the lyric? 'They sentenced me to twenty years of boredom / for trying to change the system from within.' It means doctrine is not enough. And you can not spend a lifetime of obedience in law just because Daddy told you to do it – which is frequently the case if Professor Cownie's conversations with English legal academics is in any way representative.[17] Or if Freud was halfway accurate. Time to live a bit. Time to remember that the law has an arm, and remember that it is a long arm, that it reaches you but it also gives you space. There is an arm, there is a hand, there is a law. There is also the ontology of resistance, the temporary autonomous zones, the microtopia and all the other interstices, the events that we encounter everyday. Put it like this: 'They sentenced me to twenty years of boredom / For trying to change the system from within / I'm coming now I'm coming to reward them / first we take Manhattan, then we take Berlin.'[18]

---

16  Goodrich, 2004.
17  Cownie, 2004.
18  Performed by R.E.M., on I'M YOUR FAN (1991) Warner Music, UK, Ltd.

# Bibliography

Badiou, A (2001) *Ethics. An Essay on the Understanding of Evil*, London: Verso

Badiou, A (2005) *Handbook of Inaesthetics*, Palo Alto, CA: Stanford University Press

Berlant, L (1998) 'Intimacy: A Special Issue', 24(2–3) *Critical Inquiry* 281

Bishop, C (2004) 'Antagonism and Relational Aesthetics', 51(1) *October* 110

Bottomley, A (2004) 'Shock to Thought: An Encounter (of a third kind) with Legal Feminism', 12(1) *Feminist Legal Studies* 29

Bourriaud, N (2002) *Relational Aesthetics*, Paris: Les Presses du Reel

Cownie, F (2004) *Legal Academics. Culture and Identities*, Oxford: Hart

Cusset, F (2003) *French Theory. Foucault, Derrida & Cie et les mutations de la vie intellectuelle aux Etats-Unis*, Paris: Editions La Découverte

Feyerabend, P (1975) *Against Method*, London: New Left Books

Goodrich, P (2004) 'J.D.', 6(1) *German Law Journal* 15

Graebar, D (2002) 'The New Anarchists', 13(1) *New Left Review* 61

Graebar, D (2004) *Fragments of an Anarchist Anthropology*, Chicago, IL: Prickly Paradigm Press

Hanks, P and Hodges, F (1998) *A Dictionary of Surnames*, Oxford: New York

Jacoby, R (1987) *The Last Intellectuals*, New York: Free Press

Mathy, J-P (1993) *Extrême Occident*, Chicago, IL: Chicago University Press

Sartre, J-P (1976) *Critique of Dialectical Reason*, London: New Left Books

Thomas, K (2001) 'Remarks at Memorial Service for Professor Kellis E. Parker', 101(2) *Columbia Law Review* 699

Vismann, C (1997) 'Starting from Scratch: Concepts of Order in No Man's Land', in Hüppauf, B (ed.), *War, Violence and the Modern Condition*, Berlin: W de Gruyter

# Index